Flora of Puná Isla

Jens E. Madsen, Robert L. Mix, and Henrik Balslev

Flora of Puná Island

Plant resources on a Neotropical Island

Aarhus University Press

Cover design: Flemming Nørgaard
Front cover: *Leptochiton quitoensis* (ca. 1802) from Tafalla´s *Flora Huayaquilensis* (with permission from Real Járdin Botánico, Madrid, © CSIC).
Printed in Denmark at Scanprint, Aarhus
ISBN 87 7288 854 7

Aarhus University Press
Langelandsgade 177
DK–8200 Aarhus N
Denmark
Fax (+45) 89 42 53 80
www.unipress.dk

73 Lime Walk
Headington, Oxford OX3 7AD
U.K.
Fax (+44) 1865 750 079

Box 511
Oakville, CT 06779
U.S.A.
Fax (+1) 860 945 9468

Published with financial support from the Anthropology Museum of the Central Bank of Ecuador in Guayaquil and Danida (grants Nos. 104. DAN. 8/383 and 104. DAN.8L/201).

Preface

This study combines botanical, ethnographic, and historical lines of investigation to describe the use and administration of plant resources on Puná Island in the Gulf of Guayaquil in Ecuador. Puná Island was inhabited as early as 5000 BC and since that time has played an important role in the cultural history of the continent. In this book we describe the island and its vegetation. We then review existing evidence of plant use from pre-Columbian times up through history to the present. Finally we present a flora of the island which contains keys and descriptions to the known native and naturalized plant species, as well as keys to the principal cultivated plants.

The study was undertaken thanks to the initiative of Dr. Olaf Holm (1915–1996), former director and co-founder of the Anthropology Museum of the Central Bank of Ecuador in Guayaquil, and a long-time friend of the Department of Systematic Botany in Aarhus (Denmark). Towards the end of the 1980's the museum in Guayaquil carried out archaeological excavations and anthropological surveys on Puná Island. Olaf Holm suggested that a study should be undertaken to complement on-going efforts with baseline information concerning the flora and vegetation of the dry forest and surrounding mangrove environment. This study should provide insight into the past and present-day uses of plant resources on the island and contribute to an improved understanding of the conditions that existed when early civilizations developed agriculture on Puná Island and the west coast of South America.

Systematic data collecting began in 1985, when R. Mix recorded plant names and gathered information on the uses of the plants on the island. The collection of ethnobotanical information was continued throughout 1986 and 1987 during repeated visits to most parts of the island. The collecting of plant specimens was carried out by J. E. Madsen during nine months of residence from April to December in 1987, setting up laboratory facilities at the Hotel Rosita in the parochial capital of Puná Nueva. A quantitative analysis of a plot of dry forest vegetation was carried out during the first two weeks of November 1988 and was followed by re-sampling in 1995. The authors have visited the island on several occasions during the last decade and have been able to observe many changes in infrastructure and in the socioeconomic situation of the islanders that have significantly altered local environmental conditions. Preliminary results of the study (Balslev *et al.* 1988) were published in Spanish and distributed among the islanders in acknowledgment of their generous hospitality and cooperation.

The authors extend their gratitude above all to Don Emilio Montero Chávez of Puná Nueva, who accompanied them on all of their field trips to every part of the island. We are also indebted to our local informants and field assistants. Further thanks go to Dr. Peter M. Jørgensen and Lic. Jaime Jaramillo in Quito (QCA) and Dr. María Flor de Valverde B. in Guayaquil (GUAY), for their help with the preliminary identification of the specimens back in 1988 and to Eva Bjerrum Madsen for field assistance in 1989. Dr. Renato Valencia (QCA) and Dr. Carmen Bonifaz de Elao and Xavier Conejo (GUAY) gave valuable advice on several botanical inquiries and provided practical support. The transcription of the recorded material from the ethnobotanic interviews was undertaken by Alicia Rosales; Margarita Hidalgo classified the uses indicated by the local guides. Flemming Nørgaard helped with the technical aspects of the production of this book. A special thank goes to Benjamin Øllgaard and Elvira Cotton who read the manuscript and suggested several improvements. Simon Laegaard provided extensive help with the grass section.

Several colleagues helped identifying our collections or commented on our taxonomic interpretation. We are most grateful to all of them (A. Gentry, MO; A. Lourteig, P; B. Eriksen, GB; B. B. Klitgaard, K; B. Øllgaard, AAU; B. Ståhl, GB; C. C. Berg, BG; C. Gustavson, AAU; C. H. Dodson, MO; C. Josse, QCA; C. M. Taylor, MO; C. Ott, MJG; C. Reynel, MO; D. F. Austin, FAU; D. Hunt, K; D. Neill, MO; D. Wasshausen, US; E. Bjerrum Madsen, AAU; E. Landolt, ZT; E. Zardini, MO; G. Harling, GB; G. P. Lewis, K; H. Christensen, AAU; H. Iltis, WIS; H. Robinson, US; J. A. Lombardi, BHCB; J. F. Morales, INB; J. Kuijt, LEA; J. E. Lawesson, AAU; J. M. Cardiel, MA; J. M. Leeuwenberg, WAG; J. Pruski, NY; K. Camelbeke, GENT; L. Andersson, GB; L. J. Dorr, US; L. B. Holm-Nielsen, AAU; L. R. Landrum, ASU; M. Blasco, AAU; M. J. Huft, MO; M. Nee, NY; P. Fryxell, TAES; P. Goetghebeur, GENT; P. Hiepko, B; P. J. M. Maas, U; P. Lozano, LOJA; P. M. Jørgensen, MO; R. Barneby, NY; R. C. Moran, AAU; R. Callejas, HUA; R. Haynes, UNA; R. Liesner, MO; S. Knapp, BM; S. Lægaard, AAU; U. Eliasson, GB; U. Molau, GB; W. D. Stevens, MO; W. R. Anderson, MICH.).

The study was carried out under the auspices of the Anthropology Museum of the Central Bank of Ecuador in Guayaquil. The Ministry of Agriculture kindly provided collecting permits and the Military Geographical Institute permitted the use of aerial photographs and geographical maps.

Contents

1

Study Area

Puná Island has a unique geographical setting at the mouth of the Gulf of Guayaquil, an interesting cultural history, and a flora rich in near-endemics. The island is situated in the tropical dry forest zone of southwestern Ecuador of which Dodson and Gentry (1991) estimated that less than 1% remains undisturbed. The mangrove surrounding the island is endangered by the shrimp farm industry which threatens the island's ecological integrity.

Until recently, development of infrastructure was slow on Puná Island and the vegetation remained fairly unaltered compared to the highly disturbed formations on the adjacent continental plains. This is evident if the new vegetation map of Ecuador (Sierra *et al.* 1999a) is compared with the map showing vegetation remnants in 1996 (Sierra 1999). The island therefore harbours a well-preserved sample of the original dry coastal vegetation and mangroves and offers a unique setting for a study of the management and use of plant resources in a tropical environment.

Geography

Puná Island is situated at the mouth of the Guayas river, the largest estuary on the Pacific coast of South America (inside front cover). It lies some 61 km from the Ecuadorian port city of Guayaquil between 2°40' to 3°02' south latitude and 79°54' to 80°16' west longitude. It is 56 km long, 26 km wide, and has an area of approximately 855 km². It is separated from the mainland by the three km wide Morro channel to the north-west and by the 22–33 km wide Jambelí channel to the east.

Of the 5459 inhabitants (Anonymous 1980), approximately one half live on the northeastern part of the island near the parochial town of Puná Nueva, also known as Puná Moza (reduced form of 'hermosa', meaning beautiful). The town is reached from Guayaquil in less than three hours by motor boat or four hours by ferry. Other important villages on the island with a hundred or more inhabitants include Agua Piedra, Bellavista, Campo Alegre, Estero de Boca, Puná Vieja, Subida Alta, and Zapote. Settlements are generally located near the littoral zone or along mangrove estuaries because the people depend on water transport. Scarcity of fresh water limits the population of the dry inland parts of the island.

Surrounded by mud flats which are uncovered at low tide, the island offers a generally level topography. Three hills emerge above the rest of the land mass. On the northeast side, overlooking the Jambelí channel, the highest point in the chain of the Mala hills reaches an altitude of 156 m. The Yanzún rises to 102 m roughly in the center of the island. In the south-east, in the vicinity of Puná Vieja, Zambapala reaches 297 m. This is the highest point on the island, and from the summit it is possible to see the Peruvian frontier at Tumbez in the south, the Santa Clara island to the southwest, and the Santa Elena peninsula in the northwest (figure 7).

While there are no rivers on the island, there are numerous springs and wells and one fresh water lake, the Pozo de la Lechuza. This lake lies in the open end of the u-shaped Zambapala hills near Puná Vieja in the southeast. Recently it has been greatly enlarged by diking and it now provides irrigation for the entire valley which, cleared of vegetation and readied for cultivation, stretches from the shore of the lake in the north to the foot of Zambapala in the south.

The soils are poor in organic material and alkaline to neutral in reaction. Although potentially rich for agriculture, lack of water and excess of salinity limit the use of the soils in agriculture (Erwin 1958).

Geology

The geology of southwestern Ecuador is fairly well documented due to the interests of oil companies who mapped the area, including Puná Island, in the early part of the 20th century (Sheppard 1937).

The geological formation of the island is similar to that of the Ecuadorian coastal plain. The island evidently rose from the sea as a result of the upheavals taking place during the formation of the Andes and the rest of the Ecuadorian coastal plain. It consists of loam, sandstone, and clay laid down some 40 million years ago during the Oligocene. The Miocene formations on the northern half of the island consist of sandy sediments, clays, and partly solidified volcanic conglomerates and are occasionally mixed with Oligocene sediments. The hills on the southwest side of the island consist of Pleistocene sediments of sand and clay (Sauer 1971).

An accumulation of lava along the eastern shore, one mile west of Punta Española, was discovered by Wolf (1892). He hypothesized that a submarine volcanic eruption occurred there during the Quaternary, and that this lava emerged — along with the rest of the island and the adjacent coastal plain — near the end of the Quaternary, about one million years ago. It has also been suggested that the island was separated from the rest of the mainland by the narrow Morro channel during this period.

Climate

Weather conditions on Puná Island conform to those of the dry forest region of southwestern Ecuador, albeit with certain local modifications determined by the island's situation at the mouth of the Guayas river. Generally, the climate is pleasant with soft breezes throughout the year. The area is affected by the cold Humboldt current which causes desertification along the southwestern coast of South America. The dry Ecuadorian summer is eight to ten months long. During this period the days are generally overcast, and the only precipitation that occurs is the weak drizzles, known as *garúas*, which fall at night. These *garúas* are much weaker than those of the continental plain, and not comparable to the *garúas* of the Peruvian *lomas* described by Rauh (1985).

During the winter months, the area may be subject to the effects of the sea-surface temperature anomaly known as *El Niño*, which recurs in the equatorial Pacific Ocean at intervals of two to seven years, accompanied by sometimes dramatic perturbations in the climate. During *El Niño* years the sea surface temperature rises 2–7°C above normal along the Pacific coast as far south as the Gulf of Guayaquil (Glantz 1996), causing heavy rains and thunder storms. The 1982–83 *El Niño* anomaly resulted in a nearly fourfold increase in the rainfall in Guayaquil: 3949 mm as compared to an average of 1100 mm (Naranjo 1985). The dramatic difference in precipitation patterns between a normal and an *El Niño* year is illustrated in Figure 1, which highlights the fact that the inter-annual changes in absolute precipitation are most in evidence in the southern parts of coastal Ecuador, where an arid climate normally prevails.

In fact, precipitation varies considerably in Guayas province, ranging from a low of 63 mm per year at Punta Salinas to 2000 mm at the foot of the Andes. Specific meteorological data are not available for Puná Island. The nearest weather station is located within a similar, but by no means identical, bioclimate some 25 km away at Playas. The average annual rainfall recorded there is 390 mm, with March being the wettest month (Cruz 1983).

Within Puná Island there is a rainfall gradient. In the northeastern region of the island in the vicinity of Puná Nueva, where agriculture is most productive, precipitation was estimated at more than 400 mm in 1981, compared to less than 300 mm along the western part of the island (Figure 1). The temperature on the southwestern coastal plain of Ecuador is lowered a few degrees by the thermal effect of the Pacific waters, but on Puná Island this is counteracted by the warm water of the Gulf of Guayaquil. Eggers (1894) gave the following mean daily temperatures: Guayaquil 28°C, Puná Island 24°C, and the Santa Elena peninsula 23°C. The temperature shows only moderate variations during the year with the highest temperature occurring during the rainy season.

Palaeoclimate

It is generally assumed that the climate of southern Peru and Chile has remained stable for extended periods of time and the arid flora of the region is therefore remarkably old. In contrast, the flora of the northern coast of Peru and southwest Ecuador may well have been exposed to dramatic climatic shifts

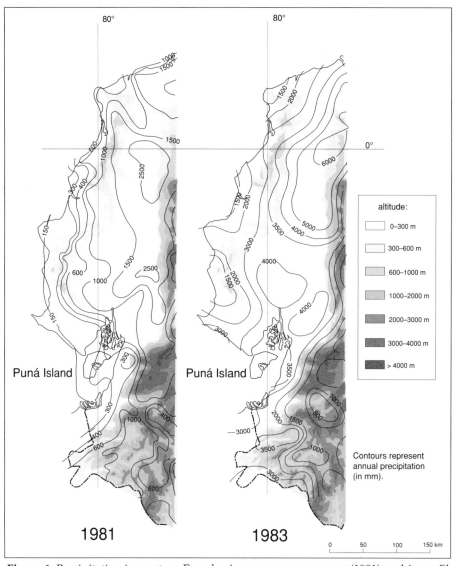

Figure 1. Precipitation in western Ecuador in a near average year (1981) and in an *El Niño* year with increased precipitation (1983). Source: Anonymous (1983, 1986); redrawn from Jørgensen and Ulloa 1994.

during recent glacial epochs (Rundel *et al.* 1991). Evidence of a strong synchronization between the droughts of the Galapagos Islands and glacial advances in the Northern Hemisphere (Colinvaux 1972, 1984, Colinvaux and Schofield 1976b) has been much debated, especially the timing of the climatic fluctuations during the Holocene (Hansen 1995, Heine 1993).

Between 21000 and 14000 BP the climate was particularly cold and dry in the Neotropics (Van der Hammen 1991, Van der Hammen and Absy 1994) and as much as one fourth of the South American continent could well have been desert-like during glacial maximum as compared to less than one tenth today (Clapperton 1993). The cold period was followed by gradually warmer and more humid climates, leading to the conditions reached around 10000 BP. The climate has then remained relatively stable until present times.

Fossil and surface spore assemblages on San Cristóbal in the Galapagos Islands show that, following the drought of the glacial period, approximately a thousand years were required for the establishment of the full fern vegetation of the fern-sedge zone, and that the vegetation has remained stable for the last 9000 years, except for an intervening period (6200–3000 BP) with a slightly drier climate (Colinvaux and Schofield 1976a, Colinvaux 1984). It may be added that a study by Rodbell *et al.* (1999) has proven that the periodicity of the El Niño phenomenon was ≥15 years from 15000–7000 BP and then increased in frequency to the present day situation around 5000 BP.

It is unlikely that the climate on the Galapagos Islands could remain stable while that on the adjacent arid mainland — including Puná Island — underwent noteworthy changes. We therefore assume that the climatic conditions influencing flora and vegetation of Puná Island have remained fairly constant during the time of human inhabitation.

Socioeconomy

The occupations of the islanders include peasant farming, animal husbandry, fishing, retail trade, transportation, and manufacture. Agriculture is gradually becoming less important than fishing because the younger generation is drawn to the more lucrative employment in Guayaquil or to the fishing industry, which is dominated by shrimp farming.

Staple food grown for local consumption include cassava (*Manihot esculenta*), and maize (*Zea mays*). Important cash crops traded on the mainland are papaya (*Carica papaya*), water melon (*Citrullus lanatus*), mango (*Mangifera indica*), and local fruits, such as the hog-plum (*Spondias purpurea*) and sweetsop (*Annona squamosa*). A selection of cultivated plants on the island are listed in Table 19. Though more important in the past there remains a small but economically significant charcoal production. Most families possess only a few hectares of land and rely on simple implements. Peasant farmers have been able to improve dry forest farming techniques without the use of expensive fertilizers, pesticides, and irrigation systems. Several large farms now use modern agricultural techniques.

Animal husbandry is less important and based only on household needs. The most common domestic animals include chickens, cows, pigs, and goats. Cows and goats are bred everywhere on the island and represent an important economic income. Donkeys and horses are used mainly for transportation purposes.

Fishing is the principal occupation of the islanders, above all in relation to the shrimp industry. Collection of larvae for the shrimp farms is the most lucrative. Nevertheless, the destruction of the mangrove environment and over exploitation result in diminishing returns. A small number of islanders are employed as hands at the shrimp farms.

The sale of fruits of the barbasco-tree (*Jacquinia sprucei*) is another minor source of income. Once widely used as a fish poison, it is now used in the shrimp ponds to eliminate fry that are unintentionally pumped into the pools and prey on the larvae.

Small-scale fishing is important for the islanders. It is carried out along the coast using small boats powered by outboard motors. The catch is sold on the mainland, mainly in Guayaquil and Posorja. The islanders are at a disadvantage in relation to the commercial fleets based in Posorja and other ports further up the coast. In addition to the low market prices, a commonly heard complaint is that the yield is steadily decreasing due to over exploitation and pollution.

No industry takes place on the island, but a tannin factory was once operated in Puná Nueva and many islanders also took part in the oil exploration in the 1940's.

Many families are involved in trade and fluvial transportation, along with a limited amount of ship building and carpentry. The bulk of the movement of goods and passengers to and from the mainland is controlled by islanders. Islanders built, own, and operate the two ferries, *Genebra II* and *Genebra III*, which constitute the main source of transportation that connects the island with Guayaquil. The construction of smaller vessels is of some importance.

Infrastructure

Vehicles other than motorcycles and bicycles were unknown on the island until recently. Foot traffic and riding horses and donkeys were the only overland modes of transportation. Indeed, most paths and trails become impassable during the rainy season due to the excessive vegetation and clayey mud and settlements are generally isolated overland from January through April. With the rise of industrialized shrimp farming, a few trucks and small transport vehicles have been brought onto the island, particularly in the Puná Vieja area and along the Morro channel.

The largest human concentration is in Puná Nueva, which maintains daily contact with Guayaquil by means of fluvial transportation. The village is clean and tidy. The entrance halls to the private homes are well-kept and swept daily, and water is sprinkled over the streets to keep down the dust. There is no vehicular traffic to speak of and a short stretch of the main street has recently been paved. Aside from a few motorcycles and bicycles, the islanders move about on foot.

Electric power is supplied by a diesel generator which is in operation from dusk to midnight, or a bit later on Fridays and Saturdays. Small generators are used by a few private individuals. Lighting is provided by flourescent tubes and low wattage light bulbs, candles, kerosene lamps, and battery-powered flashlights. Battery-powered transistor radios are the principal means of mass communication. Television sets are often powered by automobile batteries. Refrigeration is provided by kerosene units and by blocks of ice brought from Guayaquil.

Fresh water for drinking, bathing, and washing comes all year round from two wells, the Pozo de la Virgen and the Pozo de la Patria. The Pozo de la Virgen is located in a gully a short distance inland to the south and the Pozo de la Patria is located on the side of a gully that separates Punta Mandinga from the village. Both wells are lined with stone and concrete and have served the village time out of mind. Until recently, the water was gathered by hand. Plastic or metal pails fixed to long ropes were dropped into the wells, hauled up, and poured into cans. These were carried, two at a time, using a yoke and

Figure 2. Old style architecture seen in 1987 in Puná Nueva. Photo C. Mora.

s-shaped hooks and delivered daily to the houses by water carriers who were paid for the service by the individual home owners.

The houses are one or two story structures (Figure 2). In many cases the family lives on the upper floor and the ground floor functions as retail outlet. These shops offer a well stocked selection of essentials, such as canned goods, batteries, candles, flashlights, and hardware supplies used in the fishing and agricultural pursuits of the villagers, such as machetes, shovels, axes, nylon windbreakers, rope, and so forth. The small grocery stores carry crackers, cheese, eggs, a variety of fruits and vegetables, powdered milk, envelopes and tins of instant coffee and cocoa, candies, salt, sugar, rice, vegetable oil, and cigarettes.

The newer buildings are constructed from concrete and cinder blocks or bricks brought from Guayaquil. The older houses are wooden structures built on mangrove frames, with plank floors, probably from the rain tree (*Pseudosamanea guachapele*) and bamboo lath walls. Roofing is predominantly zinc and asbestos sheets, though a number of the oldest houses have plain red Spanish tiles.

Until the beginning of the 1990s, the largest building in the village was the beautiful wooden church, dating from the end of the 19th century. Erected on a promontory, the park in front of the church commands a panoramic view over the confluence of the Guayas river, the Morro and Jambelí channels, and the estuary that passes through Puná Nueva. Regrettably, the church was renovated into an ungraceful cement structure. Worthy of notice is the new concrete community center, fronted by a large cement courtyard which serves alternatively as an indoor-soccer court, or a plaza where the citizens can listen to political speeches or concerts. The community center also has a telephone station which intermittently permits emergency communication with the mainland. No movie house is available. There are three schools which provide primary level instruction.

Hotel Rosita offers clean and neat accommodations to the visiting scientist, merchant, governmental inspector, journalist, groups of students on their annual outing, occasional pairs of lovers, and tourists. On the ground floor, guests and local inhabitants gather in two large, concrete-floored rooms to watch television, talk, play cards, or shoot pool. A volleyball court, consisting of a net stretched from one side of the main street to the other, directly in front of the hotel also provides occasional entertainment. With one of the two principal *cantinas* — which boasts a powerful jukebox filled with the latest popular tropical music hits, numerous small brightly painted wooden tables and stools, colorful hand painted murals, and plentiful supplies of cold beer, *aguardiente*, and soft drinks — located catercornered from Hotel Rosita, this becomes the cosmopolitan center of the village, particularly on Friday and Saturday nights.

While the more prosperous villagers reside on the eastern side of the estuary,

Table 1. Early naturalists and plant collectors on Puná Island and herbaria where the reference specimens from the island are kept. Source: Acosta-Solís (1968), Holmgren *et al.* (1990), Stafleu and Cowan (1976–1988), Stafleu and Mennega (1992–2000).

	Date of visit	Herbarium
F. W. H. A. von Humboldt (1769–1856)	ca. Feb. 17–20. 1803	no specimens
G. W. Barclay (years unknown)	Sept. 6.–Oct. 4. 1838	London (BM)
A. Sinclair (ca. 1796–1861)	Sept. 6.–Oct. 4. 1838	London (K)
R. B. Hinds (1812–1847)	Sept. 6.–Oct. 4. 1838	London (K)
Linden (years unknown)	Sept. 6.–Oct. 4. 1838	London (BM, K)
N. J. Andersson (1821–1880)	Mar. 25.–Apr. 4. 1852	Stockholm (S)
R. Spruce (1817–1893)	Mar. 17. 1863	no specimens
H. F. A. Baron von Eggers (1844–1903)	Dec. 1891	Berlin, Oslo (B, O)
L. Mille (years unknown)	c. 1900	Washington (US)
F. L. E. Diels (1874–1945)	early 1930's	Berlin (B)
J. F. H. Schimpff (years unknown)	June 1934	Berlin (B)
E. Asplund (1888–1974)	Dec. 1939	Stockholm (S)

Barrio Lindo lays on the western side. Foot traffic is possible between the two by means of a wooden bridge built by a recent mayor of Guayaquil. The dwellings and shops in Barrio Lindo are more modest. This part of the village is built on the sandy beach, and most of the buildings are single storied structures, some of brick and concrete, but usually of wood, many with bamboo lath walls, concrete floors, and zinc roofs. The villagers are mainly fishermen and artisans. The partially finished frames of small boats are in evidence on the beach. Fishing nets are draped over posts and the remaining timbers of the *Ginebra I* lie exposed to the sun and the night mists. Here the streets are sandy and lead out onto a salt marsh toward the trail to Zapote. Recently, a strip of the beach was paved and a large perpendicular pier constructed to accommodate the docking of larger vessels. The evangelists have a small church here, there is a primary school, a number of small grocery stores, the sawmill, the carpentry shop, and the bakery.

History of Botanical Exploration

Because of its geographical situation at the mouth of the Guayas river in the Gulf of Guayaquil, Puná Island was an obligatory stopover for travellers coming to the area. Beginning with the *conquistador*, Francisco Pizarro, in the early 16th century, the island was visited by pirates and buccaneers in the 16th and 17th century, scientific expeditions in the mid 18th century, and many naturalists and botanists who arrived in the early 1800's (Table 1). These expeditions provided valuable insights concerning the status of vegetation cover over time, as well as ethnohistorical information on traditional uses of plant resources.

Table 2. Names of plant taxa described on the basis of specimens collected on Puná Island.

Acalypha subcastrata F. ARESCH. = *Acalypha setosa* A. RICH. [ANDERSSON *s.n.*, S?, 1852]
Alternanthera areschougii R. E. FR. [ANDERSSON 51, S, 1852]
Amaranthus urceolatus BENTH. [SINCLAIR *s.n.*, K, 1838]
Carlowrightia ecuadoriana T. F. DANIEL & WASSH. [MADSEN 63958, AAU, 1987]
Cassia siliquosa F. ARESCH.= *Senna mollissima* (HBK ex WILLD.) H. S. IRWIN & BARNEBY
      [ANDERSSON *s.n.*, S?, 1852]
Chloris angustiflora F. ARESCH.= *Enteropogon mollis* (NEES) CLAYTON[ANDERSSON 23, S?,
      1852]
Cyperus macrocarpus F. ARESCH.= *Cyperus oxylepis* NEES ex STEUD. [ANDERSSON *s.n.*, S,
      1852]
[1]*Cyperus thyrsiflorus* forma *macrior* F. ARESCH. [ANDERSSON *s.n.*, S, 1852]
[1]*Cyperus thyrsiflorus* forma *vegetior* F. ARESCH. [ANDERSSON *s.n.*, S, 1852]
[2]*Diodia incana* F. ARESCH. [ANDERSSON *s.n.*, S, 1852]
Eriochloa pacifica MEZ [EGGERS 14772, US lectotype, 1897]
Eutriana mucronata F. ARESCH.= *Bouteloua disticha* (KUNTH) BENTH. [ANDERSSON *s.n.*, S,
      1852]
Isocarpha divaricata BENTH. = *Isocarpha microcephala* (DC.) S. F. BLAKE [BARCLAY 408,
      BM, 1838]
Mentzelia propinqua F. ARESCH. = *Mentzelia aspera* L. [ANDERSSON *s.n.*, S, 1852]
Piqueria densiflora BENTH. = *Ophryosporus densiflorus* (BENTH.) R. M. KING & H. ROB.
      [HINDS 410; BM, 1838]
Telanthera pulchella F. ARESCH. = *Alternanthera areschougii* R. E. FR. [ANDERSSON 51, S,
      1852]
Thalia anderssonii K. SCHUM. [ANDERSSON *s.n.*, S, 1852] = *Thalia pavonii* KÖRN.
Uralepis anderssonii F. ARESCH.= *Leptochloa uninervia* (J. PRESL) HITCHC. & CHASE
      [ANDERSSON *s.n.*, S, 1852]

[1]Doubtful status; [2]name discussed on p. 238.

Although the 19th and 20th centuries botanical inventories are incomplete, as far as Puná Island is concerned, the collections are of taxonomic interest because a number of taxa have been described on the basis of specimens collected on the island (Table 2).

Buccaneers and Astronomers

Observations recorded by early adventurers are of historical interest but do not offer much information on botanical aspects. In 1587 Cavendish repaired two of his vessels on the island, taking advantage of the materials he found in the dry dock facilities, where two galleons and a pair of galleys happened to be under construction by order of the Lima viceroy (Estrada 1990). In 1684 Dampier gave a detailed description of the construction and use of the typical Puná cargo rafts, and noted the trade and fortifications of Guayaquil (Estrada 1990). In both cases the observations provide little of botanical importance, and it is not until the middle of the 18th century that the beginnings of scientific interest are to be noted.

The inventory of forestry resources carried out by the French botanist Joseph

Jussieu in 1736 as part of the French geodesic expedition directed by C. M. de La Condamine, who was accompanied by the Spaniards Jorge Juan and Antonio de Ulloa, offer considerably more historical information about plants of economic importance. The Gulf of Guayaquil, including Puná Island, was the source of the timber used both in the shipyards and in the building of the city of Lima. In his observations, Jussieu paid particular attention to the woods used in the dry docks (Juan and Ulloa [1748] 1982).

The Spanish engineer Francisco Requena corroborated the importance of the Guayaquil forests in his descriptive report of Guayaquil to the Spanish crown, as did the botanist Luis Nee, who visited Guayaquil as a member of the Malaspina expedition during October of 1790. Upon his return to Madrid, Nee delivered a report which included vernacular names, general properties, and a description of the uses of 55 different trees he had observed in the Guayaquil dry docks (Estrella 1995). However, the first to gather substantial botanical data concerning the dry forest habitat of Guayas province was Juan José Tafalla in February of 1803.

Flora Huayaquilensis

Juan José Tafalla (1755–1811) was a disciple of Ruiz and Pavón, who accompanied by Manzanilla and the artist Rivera, arrived from Callao on May 28, 1799, and remained in Guayaquil until 1803. During the dry summer season between July and December of 1799, they carried out field work in the Daule and Balzar area north of Guayaquil, making descriptions and drawings of numerous species. They were joined the following year by the Quito artist, Xavier Cortés y Alcocer, who had left the Mutis Expedition in Bogotá in July of 1798. In 1800 they explored the Yaguachi and Babahoyo area to the northeast.

Evidently, it was their intention to survey the dry forest along the coast during 1801 and 1802, but Tafalla was seriously injured in a fall while climbing Ayampe hill along the road between Colonche and Jipijapa. Perhaps due to this accident, aside from excursions into the central and western forests, the expedition dedicated its time to laboratory work in Guayaquil, and the investigation of the dry forest was postponed until 1803.

During the rainy winter season, at the end of February of 1803, the Tafalla expedition undertook the botanical inventory of the dry forests of the Santa Elena peninsula and southern Manabí province on the mainland. Their itinerary included El Morro, Chanduy, the Santa Elena peninsula, the Colonche hills, Jipijapa, and Daule. In July they left Guayaquil for Quito, and from there went on to the southern Ecuadorian highlands, where they were to spend the next five years (1804–1808) in the study of the fever-bark tree (*Cinchona officinalis*) in Loja province, a project that had been made impossible on account of the Tupac-Amaruc uprising 20 years earlier in 1782 (Estrella 1995).

Tafalla designated the collection begun in 1799 as *Flora Huayaquilensis* to distinguish it from the work previously carried out in Peru and Chile (*Flora Peruviana et Chilensis*). It was indeed stunning, comprising some 544 reference specimens, along with 310 extraordinary color illustrations (Estrella 1995), many of which portray plants native to Puná Island (see front cover). This extraordinary collection — including reference specimens, plant descriptions, and illustrations — was sent to the *Real Jardín Botánico* in Madrid, where it remained unpublished until 1992, when Dr. Eduardo Estrella brought the work to light as part of the celebration of the Columbus Centenial (Estrella 1989, 1995).

Humboldt and Bonpland

It was the arrival of the great naturalist, Alexander von Humboldt, in Guayaquil in January of 1803 that prevented the silence that engulfed Tafalla's *Flora Huayaquilensis* from being absolute. Accompanied by the botanist Bonpland and Carlos Montúfar, Humboldt remained in Guayaquil until February 17th, when he and Bonpland embarked for Acapulco. Between January 5th and 22nd he edited *Essai sur la Geographie des Plantes*, which he dedicated to the botanist José Celestino Mutis, director since 1783 of the Botanical expedition in New Granada (Estrella 1995, Steele 1982).

With access to the materials assembled in Guayaquil and able to rely on the first-hand knowledge of the region gained since 1799 by Tafalla and Manzanilla, it was possible for Humboldt and Bonpland, notwithstanding the inclemencies of the rainy winter season and the brevity of their stay, to become thoroughly familiar with the local species of economic importance. Thus many of the plants studied by Tafalla became known to science through the publication of *Plantes Equinoxiales* (Humboldt and Bonpland 1808–1809) and *Nova Genera et Species Plantarum* (Humboldt *et al.* 1815–1825), although they remained unpublished in Madrid (Estrella 1995).

Humboldt and Bonpland left Guayaquil on the 17th of February, 1803, and landed in Puná Nueva at the custom-house the same day. Evidently they spent February 18–20th in the vicinity of the village. The interior of the island was no doubt inaccessible because of the season, and as a result, all they managed to observe were some 50 islanders, a few heads of cows, a maize field, and stands of hard woods which Humboldt roughly identified as guachapelí (perhaps *Pseudosamanea guachapele*), madera negra (*Tabebuia billbergii*), and corella (unrecognized). The rest of the island seemed deserted except for a few huts at Punta Salinas which he glimpsed before passing on to spend the 21th and 22nd completing the observations begun a month and a half earlier in the vicinity of Santa Clara island. By nightfall of the 22nd their vessel was off Chanduy and on its way to Acapulco, where they arrived on March 22nd.

Her Majesty's Ship Sulphur

The earliest botanical collections on Puná Island date from the expedition of the English ship *Sulphur* which on its voyage round the world visited the Gulf of Guayaquil in 1838. The visit is described in the travel accounts of the captain, Sir Edward Belscher (Belscher 1843). *H. M. S. Sulphur* anchored at Punta Española on the east coast of Puná Island at 6 am on 6th September. Precise details are not provided concerning the collection of botanical specimens. However, at least four persons are known to have collected plants on the island.

The plant collector formally attached to the expedition was George Barclay (dates unknown), a young botanist from Kew Botanical Gardens in London. According to a personal diary (vide McVaugh 1972), Barclay made plant collecting a full time job whenever he was allowed on land and he was often accompanied in the field by the British physician and plant collector Dr. Andrew Sinclair (ca. 1796–1861). The assistant-surgeon, Mr. Richard Brinsley Hinds (1812–1847) and a certain Mr. Linden (no further data) also collected a few specimens on the island. Barclay's specimens are deposited at the British Museum (BM), while those of Sinclair and Hinds, which were used for the preparation of the taxonomic treatment *Botany of the Voyage of the Sulphur* by Bentham (1844–1846), seem to be kept mainly at Kew (K). In general, the collections lack dates and there are many errors in place names.

The assistant-surgeon Mr. Hinds was a naturalist. He wrote a large section in volume two of Belscher's travel account on the vegetation encountered during the expedition. He edited Bentham's *Botany of the Voyage of the Sulphur* (Bentham 1844–1846) and prepared — albeit this is not explicitly stated — the introduction to the chapter on western tropical America (pages 58–63 in Bentham 1844–1846). In this prologue, Hinds described the abrupt change in vegetation that appears when travelling towards Guayaquil from the south. He was fascinated by what he call the pigmy, *Jacquinia sprucei*, a species collected on Puná Island by Barclay, Hinds, as well as Linden. He described the arid vegetation in the outskirts of Guayaquil with the following words:

"On the whole, the number of species yielding profit or amusement to the botanist will probably fall beneath his estimate; and during the height of the dry season I have traversed these forests without reaping a single specimen, and witnessed such a scene of desolation in the stripped and denuded trees, as I never thought to see within the tropics. The luxuriant vegetation of these latitudes is of short duration, and nearly confined to that period when heat and moisture combine to kindle it. At that time it unquestionably is surprisingly rich" (Hinds in Bentham 1844–1846).

Hinds noticed that the expedition visited the west coast of intertropical America so frequently between the years 1836 and 1839 that they became familiar with its general aspect. However, the expedition seems only to have visited the Gulf of Guayaquil on one occasion according to the itinerary of Belscher (1843), and Hinds's memory may have failed him when he quoted November as the month for the visit to the Santa Elena peninsula and Salango.

The *Sulphur* anchored in front of the summer residence of the English consul, Mr. Cope, on Puná Island on September 6th 1838. After loading stores, the ship was carried to Guayaquil to load coals and complete other necessities on September 25th. The ship stayed in Guayaquil until the 30th of September when it backed through the narrows and reached the old anchorage at Punta Española on the 4th of October. The duration of the second stay at Puná Island is not specified by Belscher, but sufficient time evidently enabled the expedition to collect several varieties of birds, shells, and animals. Captain Belscher personally took part in several of the excursions on the island. According to Jørgensen (1999) the stay may have lasted until about October 12th.

In summary, it seems that the expedition may have remained on Puná Island during the dates September, 6–25th and October, 6–12th, 1838. During this period, Barclay and Sinclair probably made a number of trips on the island but may also have spent time visiting the Santa Elena peninsula and Salango. In spite of the great amount of interesting reading in Belscher's travel accounts remarkably little botanical information is provided. He probably preferred to leave these matters in the hands of Mr. Hinds.

The Frigate Eugenies

The next botanist to visit Puná Island was Nils Johan Andersson (1821–1881), a distinguished young Swedish scientist who became associate professor at Uppsala University in 1846 and continued his honorable career at the universities of Lund and Stockholm (Urban 1906).

In 1851, at 30 years of age, Andersson was assigned botanist by the Royal Swedish Research Academy aboard the frigate *Eugenies* on its circumnavigation during the years 1851–1853. This remarkable journey is thoroughly described by Andersson himself in his letters (Andersson 1853, 1854), which reveal that he was a keen observer with fine narrative skills. His participation in the expedition with *Eugenies* was the fulfillment of a dream from his childhood. Not much botanical information is found in his travel accounts (except in the chapter on the Galapagos Islands) and they may have been written merely for his friends and readers, who like himself, had a strong interest in travellers accounts. Apart from his botanical collections, which are now deposited at Riksmuseet in Stockholm (S), Andersson wrote an important paper on the vegetation of the Galapagos Islands (Andersson 1857) after his return to Sweden.

The frigate *Eugenies* left the harbor Karlskrona (Sweden) on September 30th 1851 with a crew of 400 men. On its travel around the World, the *Eugenies* anchored in front of Puná Nueva in the afternoon of March 25th, 1852 and the large ship remained in this place during the crew's visit to Guayaquil until it continued its journey towards Panama on April 4th. During the stay, which took place towards the end of the rainy season, Puná Island was covered with luxuriant vegetation, and the dense forests surrounding Puná Nueva did not go unnoticed by Andersson. He mentions that the small town comprised approximately 20 houses built directly in the mangrove and borne on massive *Rhizophora mangle* trunks. The houses had usually just a single room surrounded by walls of cane in which entire families were often found resting in their hammocks.

During his visit to the vicinity of Puná Nueva an impressive number of plant collections were gathered and complemented with material collected in the outskirts of Guayaquil. His material, deposited in Stockholm, was studied by Fredric Wilhelm Christian Areschoug (1830–1908) and the results published in 1869 in a paper entitled *Plantae novae sub itinere navis bellicae Eugenieae anno 1852 a N. J. Andersson* (Areschoug 1869). This publication mentions 205 flowering plants most of which are from Puná Island, including nine species and two forms, which where described as new to science.

Botanical Exploration 1892–1940

The last scientist to visit Puná Island during the 19th century was Henrik [Heinrich] Franz Alexander Baron von Eggers (1844–1903), a Danish soldier and botanist with a former career in the Virgin Islands (Jørgensen 1999). It is usually stated that Eggers lived in Ecuador throughout 1891–1897 (Acosta-Solís 1968) and some of his specimens are actually known from 1897. However, Eggers (1894) mentions that he only remained in Ecuador for 18 months (seemingly during 1891–1893). It is possible, nevertheless, that he undertook several travels to Ecuador. His collections from El Recreo (Manabí province), Puná Island (Guayas province), and Balao (El Oro province) are deposited in Berlin-Dahlem (B), with duplicates at K, M, O, and US, and were presumably the first collections originating from Ecuador that were numbered in the field (Jørgensen 1999). Eggers (1894) mentions that he visited Puná Island in the month of May (probably of 1892), but he may have made several trips to the island. His fairly precise observations on the structure of the mangrove and the dry bush forest, as he calls it, as well as remarks on soil and salt marshes show that he had a rather good knowledge at least of the exterior parts of the island.

During the first half of the 20th century, four botanists visited Puná Island and a limited number of specimens from the island are still preserved in herbaria as a result of their investigations. Luis Mille (n.d.), a Belgian with a long career as teacher and plant collector in Ecuador, collected a few specimens from Puná Island around the turn of the century. Ludwig Diels (1874–1945) visited the island in the early 1930's, and Heinrich Schimpff (n.d.) explored the northeast coast of the island in June of 1934. Most of the specimens collected by these two German botanists were destroyed in Berlin during World War II. The Swedish botanist, Erik Asplund (1888–1974), made a trip to Estero de Boca on the west coast of Puná Island between 1939 and 1940, and his materials are deposited in Stockholm. Finally, Henry K. Svenson conducted botanical research in the region. Though he did not explore Puná Island, his critical botanical publications — which compare the arid, coastal regions of southwest Ecuador, northwest Peru, and the Galapagos Islands (Svenson 1946a, 1946b) — are of special interest here.

We have not encountered evidence of botanical exploration of Puná Island in the period after 1940, which illustrates the diminishing role of the island in marine traffic.

2

Vegetation

The vegetation of southwestern Ecuador and adjacent Peru has attracted the attention of travelers and scientists for good reasons. The area constitutes a borderland which separates the arid coastal Peruvian deserts from the Colombian lowland rain forests and the appearance of the vegetation cover and its seasonality reflect the influence of the great inter-annual climatic fluctuations provoked by the *El Niño* phenomenon.

Descriptions of landscape formations of coastal Ecuador are found in the memoirs of the many travelers, such as Belscher (1843) and Enock (1909), who made expeditions along the Pacific coast of South America and visited the Gulf of Guayaquil. Botanical descriptions of the arid zones of southwestern Ecuador and adjacent Peru have been published by Acosta-Solís (1970), Cerón *et al.* (1999), Eggers (1894), Ferreyra (1957), Guppy (1906), Horn (1945), Kessler (1992), Neil (1999), Svenson (1946a, 1946b), Valverde *et al.* (1979, 1991), and Weberbauer (1929, 1945); in addition, Acosta-Solís (1959) and Eggers (1892) have provided insight into the mangrove environment. The vegetation of the area has received attention in large-scale floristic descriptions covering the entire arid Pacific plains of South America, such as the papers by Ferreyra (1983), Koepcke (1961), Rauh (1985), and Rundel *et al.* (1991).

The status of the vegetation remnants of western Ecuador and the need for conservation are highlighted by Bonifaz de Elao (1997), Dodson and Gentry (1991), and the reports edited by Best (1992) and Parker and Carr (1992).

In Walter's classification scheme (1979), Puná Island belongs to the so-called *Zonobiome* II, defined as a region characterized by deciduous dry forest and seasonal tropical rains. This *zonobiome* covers extensive areas south of the Amazonia and is also found in northern Venezuela and on the Pacific side of the Andes from southwestern Ecuador to northwestern Peru. The average precipitation of less than 500 mm per year on Puná Island is considerably lower than that typical of *Zonobiome* II. Only the weak *garúas*, which occur during the dry season, prevent the vegetation from drying up altogether.

In the life zone system of Holdridge *et al.* (1971), Puná Island falls within the category of thorn woodland. In the more detailed life zone map of western Ecuador produced by Cañadas and Estrada (1978) our study area is categorized as tropical thorn scrub (translated from Spanish). A recent large-scale vegetation map of Ecuador (Sierra *et al.* 1999a, 1999b) classified the principal vegetation types of the island as *matorral* (corresponding to our thorn scrub) and deciduous forest (corresponding to our thorn forest).

Plant Communities

Seven principal plant communities are distinguished on Puná Island (inside back cover). The center of the island is covered with wooded plant communities consisting of three main types. The dry plains on the western side are covered with open vegetation dominated by thorn scrub. A thorn forest occupies most of the area inland, while dry forest is restricted to the hilly areas. Anthropogenic savannas are formed in the more densely populated areas in the northeastern parts. A number of fresh water habitats, including seasonal streams, ponds, and marshes, as well as a perennial lake, may also be distinguished. Salt marshes, beaches, and mangroves occur along the coastal zone. Characteristic species from the various plant communities are presented in Table 3.

Mangroves

Mangroves extend in a nearly continuous strip along the west coast of South America from the Caribbean zone to Tumbez, just south of the Ecuadorian border (3°30' S). Puná Island is to a large extent surrounded by mangrove, which is widest in the large delta between Río Hondo and Puná Vieja. The disturbed beach situated south of Puná Nueva may well represent deforested mangrove. Likewise, the mangrove in certain populated areas has often been transformed into salt marshes, with sparse plant cover exposed to intensive grazing by cattle and goats. During the past decades mangroves have been replaced by shrimp farms in many areas. Today, the mangroves reach a height of 10–25 m but they may grow slightly taller in some places.

Rhizophora mangle accounts for about 95% of the vegetation cover in the mangroves. Eggers (1892) and Acosta-Solís (1959) pointed out that *Rhizophora mangle* grows taller and stronger in Ecuador than anywhere else in the World. A second species, *Rhizophora harrisonii*, is mentioned for the Guayas estuary by several authors (Chapman 1976, Terchunian *et al.* 1986, Twilley *et al.* 1997) and is presumably found more frequently in the interior of the delta. Interestingly, Eggers (1892) reported that it is *R. mangle* which grows to huge dimensions in Ecuador and not — as in the Caribbean area — *R. harrisonii*. This observation was later confirmed by Acosta-Solís (1959, 1961) and is in line with our observations from Puná Island, where *R. harrisonii* remains a rare plant.

Table 3. Common or characteristic plant species in the plant communities of Puná Island.

Mangroves

Avicennia germinans	*Laguncularia racemosa*	*Salicornia fruticosa*
Conocarpus erecta	*Rhizophora mangle*	

Salt Marshes

Alternanthera truxillensis	*Heliotropium curassavicum*	*Sesuvium portulacastrum*
Batis maritima	*Maytenus octogona*	*Sporobolus virginicus*
Cryptocarpus pyriformis	*Scutia spicata*	*Trianthema portulacastrum*

Beaches and Dunes

Acacia aroma	*Cyperus ligularis*	*Lycium americanum*
Cocos nucifera	*Ipomoea pes-caprae*	*Scaevola plumieri*

Ponds

Azolla microphylla	*Heteranthera rotundifolia*	*Nymphaea ampla*
Cyperus odoratus	*Heteranthera spicata*	*Pistia stratiotes*
Echinodorus bracteatus	*Lemna aequinoctialis*	*Ruppia maritima*
Egletes viscosa	*Neptunia oleracea*	*Utricularia gibba*

Swamps

Ammannia auriculata	*Croton lobatus*	*Paspalum convexum*
Bergia capensis	*Cyperus haspan*	*Schultesia guianensis*
Caperonia palustris	*Glinus radiatus*	*Thalia pavonii*

Streams

Bacopa monniera	*Bacopa repens*	*Capraria peruviana*

Savannas

Caesalpinia glabrata	*Cochlospermum vitifolium*	*Polygala leptocaulis*
Capparis avicennifolia	*Ipomoea carnea*	*Prosopis juliflora*
Cienfuegosia tripartita	*Pithecellobium excelsum*	*Psittacanthus chanduyensis*

Thorn Scrubs

Armatocereus cartwrightianus	*Croton rivinifolius*	*Ipomoea carnea*
Byttneria parviflora	*Dalechampia scandens*	*Mimosa acantholoba*
Carica parviflora	*Gossypium barbadense*	*Mimosa debilis*
Cordia lutea	*Gronovia scandens*	*Pithecellobium excelsum*

Thorn Forests

Albizia multiflora	*Epidendrum bracteolatum*	*Jacquinia sprucei*
Blechum pyramidatum	*Eriotheca ruizii*	*Macranthisiphon longiflorus*
Browallia americana	*Geoffroea spinosa*	*Tabebuia chrysantha*
Ceiba trichistandra	*Hylocereus polyrhizus*	*Tecoma castanifolia*
Cucumis dipsaceus	*Jacquemontia corymbulosa*	*Tropaeolum harlingii*

Dry Forests

Agonandra excelsa	*Gliricidia brenningii*	*Pisonia floribunda*
Ceiba trichistandra	*Guazuma ulmifolia*	*Sapindus saponaria*
Cordia alliodora	*Ipomoea ophioides*	*Tournefortia bicolor*
Cucurbita ecuadorensis	*Mansoa verrucifera*	*Vitex gigantea*
Eriotheca ruizii	*Pisonia aculeata*	*Ziziphus thyrsiflora*

Disturbed Soils

Achyranthes aspera	*Brickellia diffusa*	*Scoparia dulcis*
Amaranthus spinosus	*Eleusine indica*	*Spigelia anthelmia*
Bidens riparia	*Physalis angulata*	*Synedrella nodiflora*

Other species of mangrove trees include *Avicennia germinans* and *Laguncularia racemosa*. The former establishes itself in disturbed places. The transitional zone between the mangrove and the salt marshes is inhabited by shrubs, such as *Conocarpus erecta* and *Cryptocarpus pyriformis*. *Salicornia fruticosa* seems to be an indicator of disturbance because it rapidly colonizes destroyed mangrove. According to Terchunian *et al.* (1986), *Avicennia* and *Lagungularia* occur behind *Rhizophora* in the Guayas mangrove and this ecological gradient is said to be visible in aerial photographs. Such a gradient is not obvious on Puná Island, perhaps owing to the higher salinity at the mouth of the Gulf of Guayaquil. This might also explain the absence of the mangrove fern, *Acrostichum aureum*, a common species further inland along the Guayas.

Salt Marshes

Extensive salt marshes are flooded during spring tides in the lower parts of the island. These marshes extend for up to several kilometers, with their central parts being almost devoid of plants and covered with white layers of salt crystals. In general, the salt marshes represent disturbed habitats. At present they are exposed to the impact of grazing animals. Formerly, they were also used for extraction of salt (Sheppard 1932).

Toward the end of the rainy season in May and June, the salt marshes become less saline as a consequence of the runoff of the winter rains, and a number of annual grasses and sedges appear. Later the marshes dry up between the spring tides and only halophytic plants, such as *Batis maritima*, *Heliotropium curassavicum*, *Sesuvium portulacastrum*, and *Trianthema portulacastrum*, survive, along with the abundant and patch-forming grass *Sporobolus virginicus* and the prostrate *Alternanthera truxillensis*. Common shrubs found along the margins of the marshes include *Cryptocarpus pyriformis*, *Maytenus octogona*, and *Scutia spicata*. Finally, *Cordia lutea* occurs occasionally as a miniature shrub on the salty flats, as does the columnar cactus, *Armatocereus cartwrightianus*, another xerophytic survivor.

Beaches and Dunes

Beaches cover one third of the coast line. The unbroken beach extending between Punta Gruesa and Punta Salinas on the west side of the island includes broad sandy shores and small dunes and is entirely natural. On the other hand, the origin of the disturbed beach southeast of Puná Nueva is less certain, and it may well have been covered with mangrove during earlier epochs.

The coconut palm, *Cocos nucifera*, is planted or has escaped cultivation everywhere along the beach. The pantropic vine, *Ipomoea pes-caprae*, covers large stretches of sand and *Acacia aroma* forms broad, spiny patches. Sandy dunes are frequently covered with *Cyperus ligularis*. Light rocky and sandy hill sides are the preferred habitat for *Lycium americanum* and *Hibiscus hitchcockii*, as well as the pioneer tree *Muntingia calabura*. The moisture that oozes from springs on the cliffs along the beach in eastern Puná Island permits the presence of a number of ferns, grasses, and sedges not found elsewhere on the island.

The coastline on the west coast was not searched systematically for beach species. It is likely that additional beach plants are to be found in this habitat. Indeed, it is striking that a characteristic beach plant like *Scaevola plumieri* is only recorded once for Puná Island based on one ancient collection.

Ponds, Swamps, and Streams

Seasonal swamps, ponds, and streams are formed in many places during the rainy season. These habitats harbour a flora rich in aquatic and subaquatic plants (6.4% of the species). It is interesting that Svenson (1946a) remarked that the ponds on the nearby Santa Elena peninsula on the mainland were disappointing in the meager numbers of species found at their borders. Much of the species richness in the aquatic flora on Puná Island is due to the existence of many isolated populations of aquatic plants composed by distinctive species, presumably a consequence of long-distance dispersal by foraging birds.

Among the characteristic fresh water plants worth mentioning are *Echinodorus bracteatus*, *Thalia pavonii*, and species of *Eleocharis* and *Heteranthera*. Submerged species include *Najas podostemon*, *Utricularia gibba,* and *Ruppia maritima*, a species adapted to brackish waters. Algae, *Chara*, may also be found. The surfaces of ponds and water holes are frequently covered with one or two species of floaters, such as *Neptunia oleracea*, *Nymphaea ampla*, or *Pistia stratiotes*. The entire water surface is sometimes covered with green colonies of miniature plants like *Azolla microphylla* or *Lemna aequinoctialis*. Species of *Bacopa* are found in small streams with running or standing waters, while *Eichornia crassipes* floats down the Guayas in great quatities during the rainy season and are washed ashore. It can surely be found in ponds on the island as well.

A distinctive flora is found along the margins of fresh water habitats and include *Ammannia auriculata*, *Bergia capensis*, *Caperonia palustris*, *Capraria peruviana*, *Schultesia guianensis*, as well as a multitude of sedges and grasses. *Sesbania emerus* grows on seasonally moist, low-lying terrain. *Egletes viscosa* and *Glinus radiatus* appear when the muddy ground dries up at the onset of the dry season.

Savannas

The vegetation behind the mangrove along the northern edge of the island between Puná Nueva and Agua Piedra is, at least in certain areas, most appropriately designated savanna. This is also the word used by the islanders, and it seems to correspond to the *algarrobal* of Ferreyra (1957). The savanna is clearly anthropogenic and reflects the long-term effects of human activities (fire, logging, grazing, *etc.*) in the original forest. The term savanna has been defined in a variety of ways but may be understood here to refer to a vegetation characterized by a ground layer consisting predominantly of grasses and an emergent layer of loosely spaced shrubs and trees with a canopy cover ranging between 1% and 10% (Werger 1983). The floristic composition of the savannas on Puná Island is fairly different from the climatic and pedological savannas of northern South America described by Beard (1953).

The sparse and widely spaced woody vegetation is mainly made up of the semi-evergreen *Caesalpinia glabrata* and *Prosopis juliflora*, both of which possess broad umbrella-shaped crowns. *Cochlospermum vitifolium*, with its showy flowers, and *Armatocereus cartwrightianus*, an arborescent cactus, are other characteristic elements of the savanna. Xerophytic shrubs form patches or islands rather than providing a homogeneous cover. Those deserving mention are *Capparis avicennifolia*, *Cordia lutea*, *Croton rivinifolius*, and the scandent *Ipomoea carnea*, which is poisonous to the cattle and becomes a pest due to the alacrity with which it propagates. During the rainy season, the ground cover turns into a multicolored carpet and the savanna becomes an almost impenetrable, muddy morass. Common annuals include *Cienfuegosia tripartita*, *Ludwigia erecta*, *Polygala* spp., and various vines. Ephemeral grasses are dominant during the rainy season. *Psittacanthus chanduyensis* is an abundant parasitic mistletoe found on several hosts.

Thorn Scrubs

Along the west coast of the island behind the beach lies a zone of thorn scrub. It is called *matorral* by Cerón *et al.* (1999). The woody vegetation is smaller and more stunted than in the forests further inland and it forms more or less dense, spiny thickets due to the harsher climatic conditions prevailing (drier and windier). The vegetation is probably also influenced by the fairly significant effects of agricultural activities.

Important shrubs include the poisonous *Croton rivinifolius* and *Ipomoea carnea*, along with spinescent species, such as *Byttneria parviflora*, *Mimosa acantholoba*, *Mimosa debilis*, *Pithecellobium excelsum*, *etc.* The thorn scrub is also composed of shrubby species of *Capparis*, *Senna*, and a variety of Malvaceae. The tree, *Loxopterygium huasango*, is essentially restricted to the coastal plains on the extreme west coast, where it is mainly planted. *Coccoloba ruiziana* and *Erythrina velutina* grow in hollows. Various cacti are likewise present, as are vines such as *Dalechampia scandens* and *Gronovia scandens*, which overgrow bushes. There are also numerous herbaceous species of the families Acanthaceae and Asteraceae, which appear during the dry season between May and November.

Thorn Forests

Seasonally dry deciduous thorn forest is the most widespread plant community on the island. It is called deciduous forest by Cerón *et al.* (1999). The thorn forest differs from the savanna in that it has a shrubby, rather than a herbaceous, ground cover. It is uneven in structure and composition owing to the spatial heterogeneity of environmental factors such as soil, topography, wind, humidity, *etc.*

Ceiba trichistandra and *Eriotheca ruizii* are giant trees that in some areas dominate the thorn forest. The former will grow to 35 m in height. They are accompanied by many of the woody plants from the savanna which also grow in the thorn forest where, however, they become much larger. For instance, *Caesalpinia glabrata*, *Geoffroea spinosa*, and *Prosopis juliflora* may reach 15 m in height, and *Cordia lutea*, a shrub in the savanna, grows to a height of eight meters in the thorn forest. *Cochlospermum vitifolium* and the hardwoods *Tabebuia billbergii* and *T. chrysantha* are resplendent with their brilliant yellow flowers on otherwise naked trees. The shrubs are generally armed with spines which makes the forest hard to penetrate off the trails. Common understory shrubs and treelets include *Byttneria parviflora*, *Mimosa* spp., *Jacquinia sprucei*, and *Pithecellobium excelsum*.

The thorn forest becomes spectacular towards the end of the rainy season in April and May with profusely flowering vines such as *Cucumis dipsaceus*, *Jacquemontia corymbulosa*, *Operculina codonantha*, and *Tropaeolum harlingii*. One of the most conspicuous plants during the dry season is the liana *Macranthisiphon longiflorus* with its orange flowers. Only a few epiphytes are seen, but *Hylocereus polyrhizus*, a large shrub with trigonous stems, is common in the crevices formed by the limbs of *Ceiba trichistandra* and the orchid, *Epidendrum bracteolatum*, grows abundantly in *Geoffroea spinosa*. Characteristic herbs include *Blechum pyramidatum* and *Browallia americana*.

Dry Forests

Even small topographic changes in the landscape result in dramatic shifts in local bioclimatic conditions and lead to readily visible differences in the structure, leaf-phenology, and composition of the plant formations. Dry forest occurs in the northeastern part of the island between Puná Nueva and Río Hondo and on the Yanzún hill. It is also found in the southern parts along the chain of hills that include Zambapala and Ramón. The two regions with dry forest on Puná Island are floristically identical but differ in the frequency of the various species involved. The dry forest ranges from 50 m to 300 m above sea level.

The dry forest is characterized by its sub-evergreen understory of shrubs, treelets, and medium-sized trees. The woody plants are facultatively deciduous and become leafless towards the end of the dry season and in years of severe drought. This vegetation is called semi-deciduous forest by Cerón *et al.* (1999).

Ceiba trichistandra and *Eriotheca ruizii* are late deciduous canopy trees. Subevergreen trees, some of which reach a height of 20 m, include *Agonandra excelsa*, *Albizia multiflora*, *Cordia alliodora*, *Guazuma ulmifolia*, *Pisonia* spp., *Sapindus saponaria*, and *Ziziphus thyrsiflora*. The pioneer tree, *Muntingia calabura*, occurs in disturbed places. Important shrubs forming the ground cover include *Adenaria floribunda*, *Lippia americana*, and *Tournefortia bicolor*. The herbaceous flora is particularly rich and numerous vines from the Convolvulaceae, Cucurbitaceae, Fabaceae and Vitaceae families completely overgrow the shrub story towards the end of the rainy season. *Cucurbita ecuadorensis* climbs as high as 10 m with its huge fruits hanging like balls on a string and the prostrate vine *Ipomoea ophioides* is common in shaded places. Several lianas possess showy flowers, such as *Macranthisiphon longiflorus* and the malodorous *Mansoa verrucifera*.

The dry forests on the summit of the Zambapala hills contain many species which are not seen elsewhere on the island, such as the columnar cacti *Pilosocereus tweedyanus* or epiphytic lichens, such as *Ramalina anceps* and *Roccella babingtonii*.

Structure, Composition, and Dynamics of the Thorn Forest

To complement the descriptive section with quantitative data related to the principal vegetation type on the island, a permanent one hectare study plot was established in the thorn forest (Figure 3).

The study plot was placed at three hours walking distance from Puná Vieja, along the cattle trail towards Campo Alegre (80°10'W; 2°53'S) (see inside back cover). Though it is far from the nearest settlements, narrow cattle tracks and numerous stumps reveal a significant impact of man and his livestock on the environment. The plot is situated on a low hill 50 meters above sea level. The topography is undulating with a maximum of nine meters height difference between the highest and lowest points. A seasonal stream-bed runs through the low parts of the area. The soils are sandy and poor in organic material, but probably rich in nutrients.

The vegetation consists of two woody layers and a sparse herbaceous ground layer. The broken canopy attains a maximum height of 15–20 m and is formed by *Ceiba trichistandra* with impressive 3–4 m tall buttresses and *Eriotheca ruizii*. Beneath the canopy, the main woody layer is a mixture of medium-sized trees and multi-stemmed shrubs. Two arborescent cacti with woody stems and a strangling fig, *Ficus citrifolia*, are notable lifeforms which also inhabit the woody layer. The shrub layer forms a mosaic of patches of dense thickets which are almost impenetrable to man and cattle (Figure 3b). The herbaceous flora of the ground layer is poorly developed and heavily affected by the cattle. It includes typical weeds of pastoral land use systems. A limited number of epiphytes, lianas, and mistletoes are evident all year round, along with a profusion of vines, which appear at the onset of the rainy season.

The study plot (100 x 100 m) was subdivided into one hundred, 100 m² subplots (10 x 10 m) using 1 m sections of PVC tubes and colored strings. The slope of the terrain was measured between each set of PVC tubes to permit the preparation of a topographic map of the plot. All trees with a dbh (diameter at breast height, *i.e.*, 135 cm from the base of the plant) of ≥ 5 cm were marked with a numbered aluminum tag. The exact position of each tree in the hectare plot was determined, and the dbh duly noted. Each trunk of multiple-stemmed trees was measured separately, while the diameter of trees with buttresses was taken just above the buttress. Phenological data were also noted. The often sterile trees were identified by experienced local guides on the basis of vernacular names. Only a limited number of voucher specimens were prepared due to a general lack of foliage. The study plot was established in November of 1989 and the trees were re-measured in August of 1995. Formulas applied in the present study are shown in Table 4.

Results of the analysis are shown in Tables 5–9 and Figures 4–5. Comparable data from other studies in Ecuador was published by Josse and Balslev (1994) and Valencia *et al.* (1998). Unless otherwise stated, the following discussion is based on trees with a dbh ≥ 5 cm in 1989.

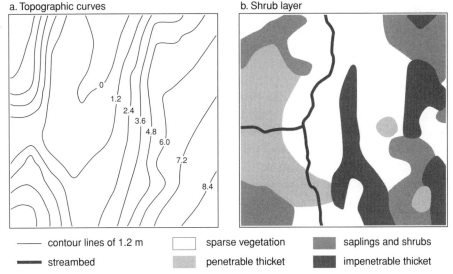

Figure 3. Relief and and main vegetation types of the shrub layer in a 1-ha study plot in the thorn forest on Puná Island.

Table 4. Abbreviations and formulas.

dbh = diameter at breast height measured at 135 cm.

dens. = density = number of individuals per area unit.

rel. dens. = relative density = individuals of a taxon counted as percentage of all individuals in the sample.

dom. = dominance (basal area) = sum of areas formed by cross sections of stems ($\sum \pi r^2$).

rel. dom. = relative dominance = the basal area of a taxon given as percentage of the total basal area in the sample.

freq. = frequency = the number of subplots in which a taxon is represented.

rel. freq. = relative frequency = the frequency of a taxon given as a percentage of the sum of frequencies of all taxa in the sample.

div. = diversity = number of species per family.

IVI = Importance Value Index = rel. dens. + rel. dom. + rel. freq. of a species (Curtis and McIntosh 1951).

FIV = Family Importance Value = rel. dens. + rel. div. + rel. dom. of a family (Mori *et al.* 1983).

ISs = Index of Similarity according to Sørensen = $100 \times \left(\dfrac{2c}{A + B} \right)$ (Sørensen 1948)

Variables: r, radius; A, B = number of species in plot A and B; c = number of species common to plot A and B.

Structure

The study plot contained 420 trees ha[-1] (Table 5). A high proportion of the trees had multiple trunks or trunks that branched near the ground level. The thorn forest plot was therefore characterized by a much higher density of trunks over 5 cm dbh (737) than individual trees (420 trees). It was indeed often difficult to determine whether a tagged tree represented one or several independent individuals. As many as 37% of the trees had at least two trunks and one fourth of all species were represented by individuals with at least four trunks. Small-sized species tended to be multi-stemmed near the ground level and individuals of *Tecoma castanifolia* had for example on the average 2.7 trunks. Nevertheless, other species of almost identical size had mostly simple trunks, for example *Jacquinia sprucei* with an average of 1.2 trunks.

Basal area was measured to 14 m²ha[-1] of which 74% was due to the two canopy trees in the Bombacaceae (*Ceiba trichistandra* and *Eriotheca ruizii*), and 82% was due to the three most dominant species, the third being *Tabebuia chrysantha*. In other words, two species with girths above 1 m dominated the forest community, while the majority of species remained small. An average tree on the study plot had a trunk diameter of 13.1 cm and was 6.3 m tall.

The two canopy species, *Ceiba trichistandra* and *Eriotheca ruizii*, had average heights of 17.8 m and 13.2 m, respectively. The forest has two more or less distinct layers, an upper layer composed by a few canopy trees and an understory composed of numerous, small to medium-sized individuals.

Table 5. Quantitative data for trees with stems over 5 cm from a 1-ha study plot of thorn forest on Puná Island in 1989 and 1995.

	Individuals	Stems	Species	Families	Basal area (m^2ha^{-1})	Mean dbh (cm)	(s.d.)
1989							
dbh ≥ 5 cm	420	737	27	19	14.1	13.0	14.7
dbh ≥ 10 cm	187	341	17	11	12.6	20.5	19.5
dbh ≥ 20 cm	40	60	9	7	9.6	45.2	31.6
1995							
dbh ≥ 5 cm	451	876	29	19	15.6	13.1	14.6
dbh ≥ 10 cm	206	386	22	15	13.7	20.0	19.5
dbh ≥ 20 cm	42	56	10	8	10.1	43.4	34.1

Floristic Composition

The study plot contained 27 tree species ha^{-1} (Table 5). This is the lowest species richness yet recorded for a 1-ha study plot in Ecuador (Valencia *et al.* 1998). At the same time, it also happens to be the driest locality inventoried (<500 mm annual precipitation) in Ecuador. On the other hand, the study plot was as species rich as certain West African savanna plots in protected areas for an annual precipitation of 700–800 mm (Madsen *et al.* 1996).

Approximately 54 tree species are known from Puná Island, many of which are restricted to the dry forest on the hills. The plot was large enough to include the majority of local tree species. Thus, half a hectare included 85% of all species in the plot. Our local field assistants, who are familiar with the woody flora of the island, surveyed the vicinity of the study site for several hours and found only three additional species of trees. In other words, examples of half the tree species of the entire island (919 km²) were found in but 1-ha of forest.

The Importance Value Index (IVI) is a well-known method for ranking the species in a community. The highest scores were recorded for *Jacquinia sprucei* (IVI = 43), *Tabebuia chrysantha* (IVI = 43), and *Ceiba trichistandra* (IVI = 41). The latter species received its importance due to its enormous basal area, while *Jacquinia sprucei* was the most abundant tree (Table 6).

Among the tree families encountered in the study plot, those represented by most individuals were Bignoniaceae (24.7%) and Theophrastaceae (20.1%). The four highest ranked families according to the Family Importance Index were Bombacaceae (FIV = 67), Bignoniaceae (FIV = 51), Mimosaceae (FIV = 32), and Theophrastaceae (FIV = 32). Legumes treated collectively (legumes *s.l.*) would occupy the third position (FIV = 49) (Figure 4).

Table 6. Relative density, dominance, frequency, and Importance Value Index (IVI) for tree species in 1989 and 1995. Based on individuals with trunks over 5 cm dbh in a 1-ha plot of seasonally dry thorn forest on Puná Island.

Scientific name	1989				1995			
	rel. dens.	rel. dom.	rel. freq.	IVI	rel. dens.	rel. dom.	rel. freq.	IVI
Acacia tenuifolia	0.0	0.0	0.0	0.0	0.4	0.0	0.6	1.1
Albizia multiflora	1.2	0.6	1.7	3.5	1.1	0.7	1.6	3.4
Armatocereus cartwrightianus	3.6	0.7	4.8	9.1	3.3	0.9	4.5	8.8
Capparis guayaquilensis	0.7	0.5	1.0	2.3	0.4	0.3	0.6	1.4
Capparis heterophylla	0.7	0.1	1.0	1.8	0.4	0.0	0.6	1.1
Ceiba trichistandra	1.2	38.3	1.7	41.2	1.1	40.0	1.6	42.7
Cereus diffusus	3.3	0.5	2.7	6.5	3.1	0.8	2.6	6.5
Citharexylum sp.	4.3	0.4	4.8	9.5	5.5	0.8	5.8	12.1
Coccoloba ruiziana	1.0	0.5	1.0	2.4	0.9	0.6	1.0	2.4
Cochlospermum vitifolium	0.7	1.6	1.0	3.3	1.1	1.5	1.3	3.9
Cordia alliodora	5.2	1.4	4.4	11.1	6.4	1.9	5.5	13.9
Cordia lutea	1.4	0.6	2.0	4.1	1.1	0.6	1.6	3.3
Eriotheca ruizii	2.6	17.3	3.4	23.4	2.4	14.9	3.2	20.5
Erythroxylum glaucum	1.2	0.1	1.4	2.7	1.8	0.2	2.3	4.3
Ficus citrifolia	0.5	0.1	0.7	1.3	0.7	0.2	1.0	1.8
Geoffroea spinosa	0.5	0.1	0.7	1.3	0.4	0.1	0.6	1.2
Gliricidia brenningii	5.0	3.5	4.8	13.2	4.7	3.6	4.5	12.8
Jacquinia sprucei	20.0	8.2	15.0	43.2	19.3	8.6	14.3	42.2
Leucaena trichodes	1.9	0.3	2.0	4.2	2.2	0.6	2.3	5.0
Malpighia emarginata	3.3	0.7	3.8	7.8	3.1	0.8	3.6	7.5
Pisonia floribunda	1.4	0.9	1.7	4.0	1.3	0.9	1.6	3.8
Pithecellobium excelsum	13.1	4.1	15.0	32.2	12.6	3.9	14.6	31.2
Psidium densicomum	1.7	0.9	2.4	4.9	1.8	0.9	2.3	4.9
Randia sp.	0.7	0.1	1.0	1.8	0.4	0.1	0.6	1.2
Tabebuia chrysantha	14.0	14.4	13.7	42.1	12.9	12.3	12.7	37.8
Tecoma castanifolia	10.2	4.1	7.5	21.9	10.2	4.9	7.5	22.5
Zanthoxylum rigidum	0.2	0.0	0.3	0.6	0.9	0.1	1.0	1.9
Ziziphus thyrsiflora	0.2	0.0	0.3	0.6	0.2	0.1	0.3	0.6

Although the study plot was originally selected as an example of structurally homogeneous thorn forest, the spatial distribution patterns of most species were characterized by clumping (Figure 5), a consequence of the existence of distinct ecological niches. Only two abundant species, *Pithecellobium excelsum* and *Tabebuia chrysantha*, were not clumped. The other species were found in non-random patterns. For example *Gliricidia brenningii* and *Cordia alliodora*, both typical representatives of the more humid dry forest community, were found crowded along the dried-up stream bed (shown in Figure 3b). Other species with uneven distributions included *Tecoma castanifolia* and *Jacquinia sprucei*. Although it is not possible to generalize on the basis of data from a single study plot, it should be noted that clumped distribution patterns are common in tropical forests (Armesto *et al.* 1986).

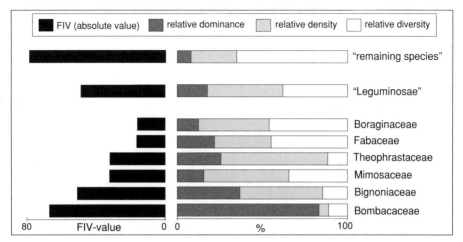

Figure 4. Family Importance Value and relative contribution of dominance, density, and diversity for the dominant plant families on a 1-ha study plot in the thorn forest on Puná Island.

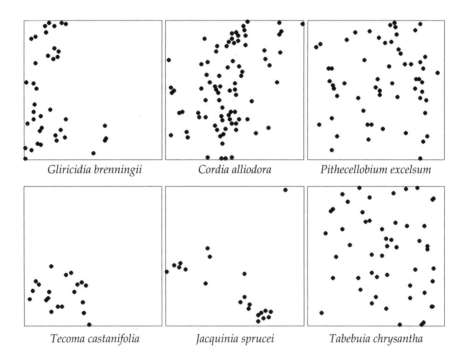

Figure 5. Distribution patterns of selected tree species in a 1-ha study plot in the thorn forest on Puná Island.

Table 7. Dynamics and mortality of trees over 5 cm dbh in a 1-ha plot of thorn forest on Puná Island. Stumps and remains of dead trees recognized in 1989 and status in 1995.

Scientific name	1989			1995	
	Logged	Perished naturally	Sum (all dead)	Died (since 1989)	Recruitment (new trees)
Acacia tenuifolia					2
Caesalpinia glabrata	1	1	2		
Capparis guayaquilensis		1	1	1	
Capparis scabrida		1	1		
Citharexylum sp.		4	4		7
Coccoloba ruiziana		2	2		
Cochlospermum vitifolium		1	1		2
Cordia alliodora	2		2	2	9
Eriotheca ruizii		2	2		
Erythroxylum glaucum					3
Ficus citrifolia					1
Geoffroea spinosa		1	1		
Jacquinia sprucei	2	3	5		3
Leucaena trichodes		4	4		2
Pisonia floribunda		4	4		
Pithecellobium excelsum		4	4	1	5
Psidium densicomum					1
Tabebuia chrysantha	39	23	62		
Tecoma castanifolia		7	7		5
Zanthoxylum rigidum					3
Sum	44	58	102	4	43

Dynamics

When the study plot was established in 1989 a large number of remnants of dead trees were recognized (Table 7). Perished trees with a presumed dbh over 5 cm when alive were identified by our experienced native field assistants.

Approximately 103 dead trees were recognized, of which 44 clearly had been cut by man. These included mostly *Tabebuia chrysantha*, but also a few *Cordia alliodora*. Both species have traditionally been exploited for their valuable wood. The other trees were cut for charcoal. Indeed, the remains of an ancient charcoal stack were still visible on the plot.

The large number of dead trees encountered in 1989 suggested a high turn over rate and significant impact of man on the ecosystem. Six years after the initial inventory, however, we found the area not only essentially untouched, but also showing signs of regeneration. Only four trees had died, and 43 new trees had grown into the size class ≥ 5 cm dbh. These belonged to 12 species and 10 families, and included one individual belonging to a species not encountered in 1989. The basal area had increased by 11% during the six years to 15.6 m²ha⁻¹. New cohorts of *Citharexylum* and *Cordia alliodora* were observed and a couple of small individuals of the fast growing *Cochlospermum vitifolium*

Table 8. Flowering and fruiting cycles of plant species in seasonally dry environments on Puná Island.

	Month:	J	F	M	A	M	J	J	A	S	O	N	D
Trees	Bursera graveolens	**	**										
	Loxopterygium huasango	**	**	oo									
	Gliricidia brenningii	**	**	**	oo	oo							
	Geoffroea spinosa			**	**	oo	oo	oo	oo	oo	oo	oo	oo
	Cordia alliodora				**	**	oo	oo					
	Ceiba trichistandra					**	*o	oo	oo	oo	oo	oo	oo
	Jacquinia sprucei					**	**	**	oo	oo	oo	oo	oo
	Cochlospermum vitifolium					**	*o	oo					
	Tabebuia billbergii						**	**	*o	*o	*o		
	Capparis scabrida						**	*o	*o	*o			
	Erythrina velutina						**	**	*o	oo			
	Pisonia ssp.								**	**	oo		
	Vitex gigantea									**	*o	oo	
	Muntingia calabura	*o	*o	*o	*o	*o	*o	*o	*o	*o	*o	*o	*o
	Tecoma castanifolia			**	**	*o	*o	*o	*o	oo	oo	oo	oo
	Pithecellobium excelsum				**	*o	*o	*o	*o	*o	*o	*o	*o
	Prosopis juliflora				**	**	oo	oo	oo	oo	oo	oo	oo
	Caesalpinia glabrata				**	**	oo	oo	oo	oo	oo	oo	oo
Vines	Tropaeolum harlingii				**	*o	oo						
Lianas	Arrabidaea corallina	**	**							oo	oo	oo	
	Mansoa hymenaea							**	**	**	*o	oo	oo
	Macranthisiphon longiflorus							**	**	*o	*o	oo	oo	oo
Herbs	Cienfuegosia tripartita				**	*o							
	Blechum pyramidatum							**	*o	*o	*o	*o	*o	*o
Bulbs	Eucrosia stricklandii	oo	oo									**	**
	Leptochiton quitoensis	**	*o	oo									

Legend: Flowering (*); Fruiting (o); Principal rainy season in 'normal' years: ▢

had increased their dbh from around 5 cm to 15 cm. The signs of regeneration in the study area are summarized in Table 7.

The study plot shows few signs of recent human interference in spite of the fact that it is located near one of the principal cattle trails. Possibly this is due to the recent construction of a large farm in the vicinity of Pozo de la Lechuza, which has made the area inaccessible to the islanders who had formerly exploited the area for timber. While anecdotal, this highlights the dynamic nature of the forest under the influence of both natural and man-dominated conditions. It also emphasizes the need for extended study periods if long-term alterations in the composition and structure of a forest community are to be adequately monitored.

Phenology

Phenological observations were gathered during a nine months study period and supplemented with information provided by local informants (Table 8). In general, most trees flower and produce fruit within a limited time period during the dry season, when there is less competition with herbaceous plants for the pollinators. The few exceptions are the essentially evergreen *Prosopis juliflora*, *Caesalpinia glabrata*, and the pioneer tree *Muntingia calabura*, which flower all year long.

The first trees to flower during the year are *Bursera graveolens* and *Loxopterygium huasango* that flower in January and February. They are followed by *Geoffroea spinosa*, which comes into flower in March and soon after bears its fruit. Other trees that flower in the rainy season are the white-flowered *Cordia alliodora* and *Gliricidia brenningii*. These early flowering trees all bear leaves and flowers simultaneously. The first deciduous tree to flower in the dry season is *Cochlospermum vitifolium*, and it is followed by *Tabebuia chrysantha* and later by the orange-red flowered *Erythrina velutina*, each of which has a short, pronounced flowering period. *Vitex gigantea* has a very unusual strategy. In November–December, when the climate turns warmer, but still before the rain comes, the leaves and blue flowers appear, and it even produces fruits before the first rain falls.

The most important tree, *Ceiba trichistandra*, sheds its leaves in May–July, and it flowers soon afterwards. During the following dry months, the large capsules with kapok fibers are produced, a few at a time. In the case of a very wet year, the amount of kapok produced is reduced considerably. Unlike most other trees found in the dry forest, kapok trees tend to vary — up to as much as two months — in their time of flowering.

Many shrubs and treelets flower throughout the dry season, whenever there is adequate moisture. The woody lianas are less predictable. The white-flowered *Arrabidaea corallina* flowers during the rainy season, but most Bignoniaceae flower during the dry period, for example *Macranthisiphon longiflorus* and *Mansoa verrucifera*. Herbs and vines generally have a vegetative phase during the moist period from January to March followed by a peak of flowering in April–May. However, a few drought-tolerant herbs, notably from the families Acanthaceae and Asteraceae, flower continuously throughout the dry season. The epiphytes *Hylocereus polyrhizus* and *Epidendrum bracteolatum* flower just before the onset of the rainy season. The few bulbs encountered flower at the onset, *i.e.*, *Eucrosia bicolor*, or throughout the rainy season, *i.e.*, *Leptochiton quitoensis*.

The forest is in general characterized by species with showy, diurnal flowers which, no doubt, constitute considerable inducements for pollinators. Blue and yellow are the most common colors and the pollinators are many different kinds of insects and hummingbirds. Species with nocturnal, white flowers (Cactaceae, Capparaceae, and some Convolvulaceae) are chiefly insect pollinated.

Table 9. Reproductive and vegetative characteristics of trees with stems over 5 cm in one hectare of seasonally dry thorn forest.

	(% ind.)		(% ind.)
Fertility		**Spinescense**	
Fertile	45.3	Spiny trees	68.1
Flowering	11.5	Spineless trees	29.5
Fruiting	41.0		
Sterile	54.7	**Leaf size class**	
		Nanophylls (0.25–2.25 cm^2)	15.2
Sexual system		Microphylls (2.25–20.25 cm^2)	48.1
Polygamous	97.6	Notophylls (20.25–45 cm^2)	36.7
Dioecious	2.4		
		Leaf-ramification	
Leaf persistence		Compound	68.1
Deciduous	68.1	Pinnately compound	29.5
Facultatively deciduous	29.5	Palmately compound	38.6
Perfectly deciduous	38.6	Simple	31.9
Evergreen	31.9		

Ceiba trichistandra and *Pilosocereus tweedyanus*, an arborescent cactus, with fleshy, campanulate flowers, are pollinated by bats. Many tall growing trees and climbers have lanate or winged seeds and are easily dispersed by wind, while edible, fleshy fruits and pods prevail among the small-sized species.

Quantitative phenological data gathered on the 1-ha study plot during the first half of November 1989, two months before the onset of the rainy season, provide a more reliable picture of the phenological strategies of the tree species in the thorn forest. Results are summarized in Table 9. Approximately one half of the individual trees were fertile with 41% in fruit. Flowers were most frequently observed in small trees and often limited to a few flowers per tree. *Gliricidia brenningii* had already flowered well in advance of the rainy season and *Pisonia floribunda* was in bud. The percentage of fertile trees was significantly greater than recorded in an Ecuadorian rainforest (Balslev *et al.* 1987), and the species of the thorn forest exhibited much greater predictability in their phenological patterns. It was for example noticed that many species flowered or fruited synchronously, and more than 90% of the individuals of some species were either in flower or fruit. This is in line with Opler *et al.* (1980) who mentioned a high degree of synchronous phenology for a dry forest in Costa Rica. *Coccoloba ruiziana* and *Pisonia floribunda* were the only true dioecious species recorded. They were represented by ten individuals only.

Defoliation strategies in the forest were also studied by classifying each tree species according to its general year-round behavior and foliation state in November of 1988 according to the following categories: 1) perfectly deciduous species with a definite leaf fall; 2) facultatively deciduous species without an abrupt leaf fall; and 3) evergreen species. This delimitation caused few problems. Tall growing species were consequently deciduous, whereas the few evergreen species tended to be relatively small-sized (*Albizia multiflora*, *Capparis guayaquilensis*, and *Jacquinia sprucei*).

The leaf size class (Raunkiær 1934, modified by Webb 1959) was established for all species based on measurement of herbarium material collected on the island. The forest was dominated by trees with notophyllous and microphyllous leaves, while few trees had nanophyllous leaves (Table 9). Leaf ramification patterns are often given little attention in ecological literature because a leaflet traditionally has been considered functionally analogous to the simple leaf (Raunkiær 1934). Givnish (1978) discussed, however, the adaptive value of compound leaves in xeric environments. In this study, an impressive 68% of the individuals had compound leaves and palmately compound leaves were particularly frequent among the tall growing trees. Finally, many shrubs and treelets were found to posses spiny branches, leaves, and trunks.

3

Flora

The flora of Puná Island forms part of a distinctive arid flora of southwestern Ecuador and adjacent northwestern Peru that occupies a narrow stretch of land extending for at least some 500 km from Manta in Ecuador to northern Peru (Figure 7). Toward its southern end it grades into the Andes and it also shows floristic similarities with the Galapagos Islands. This unique area is here called the *Guayas centre of arid plant endemism*. As a curiosity, the Guayas centre overlaps or fringes other biogeographical areas rich in endemic species of birds (the Tumbesian centre of avian endemism, Best 1992) and algae and invertebrates (the Panamic Maritime province, Norse 1993).

The native and naturalized flora of Puná Island comprises approximately 428 species of vascular plants, including six ferns. The flora is richer in species than the floras of the small Ecuadorian islands located just in front of the continent (Cerón and Montalvo 1998). The flora contains almost as many species as are reported for the dry forests of Capeira with 804 mm annual precipitation (Gentry and Dodson 1987). Floristic inventories carried out in the Guayas centre of arid plant endemism and the Galapagos Islands are summarised in Table 10.

Important plant families and lifeforms on Puná Island ranked according to species richness are shown in Table 11. Species rich families include Fabaceae (9%), Poaceae (8%), and Asteraceae (6%). Legumes *s.l.* (Fabaceae, Mimosaceae,

Table 10. Numbers of species reported for the floras of islands and reserves in the Guayas centre of arid plant endemism and the Galapagos Islands. The situation of the localities are shown in Figures 6–7.

Localities	Area (km^2)	Eleva-tion (m a.s.l.)	Precipi-tation (mm year^{-1})	No. Species	Source
Puná Island	855	0–297	300–400	428	this study
Galapagos Islands	8010	0–1689		700	Wiggins and Porter (1971)
Capeira			804	463	Gentry and Dodson (1987)
SW Ecuador–NW Peru				328	Svenson (1946b)
La Plata Island		0–167	125–250	100	Cerón and Montalvo (1998)
Salango Island		0–120	125–250	59	Cerón and Montalvo (1998)

Table 11. Numbers of native species per plant family and growth form on Puná Island.

	Herbs	Shrubs	Trees	Vines	Lianas	Total	%
Fabaceae	13	3	5	12	1	34	7.9
Poaceae	34					34	7.9
Asteraceae	18	5			1	24	5.6
Convolvulaceae	2	1		20		23	5.4
Malvaceae	8	13				21	4.9
Cyperaceae	20					20	4.7
Mimosaceae		6	8	1	1	16	3.7
Euphorbiaceae	10	3		1		14	3.3
Amaranthaceae	12					12	2.8
Verbenaceae	2	7	2			11	2.6
Boraginaceae	4	5	1			10	2.3
Caesalpiniaceae	1	7	2			10	2.3
Solanaceae	6	3				9	2.1
Bignoniaceae			4		5	9	2.1
Acanthaceae	8					8	1.9
Nyctaginaceae	5	1	2			8	1.9
Scrophulariaceae	7					7	1.6
Ferns	6			1		7	1.6
Rubiaceae	5		2			7	1.6
Sterculiaceae	2	4	1			7	1.6
Capparaceae		2	4			6	1.4
Cucurbitaceae				6		6	1.4
Lamiaceae	4	1				5	1.2
Lythraceae	3	2				5	1.2
Cactaceae		3	2			5	1.2
4 families with 4 species	8	1	3	1	3	16	3.7
8 families with 3 species	10	4	4	4	2	24	5.6
17 families with 2 species	22	5	4	3		34	7.9
36 families with 1 species	17	3	13	2	1	36	8.4
Total	227	79	57	51	14	428	
(%)	53.0	18.5	13.3	11.9	3.3		100

Caesalpiniaceae) represent 14% of all species, while grasses and sedges make up 13% of the flora. Herbs constitute 53% of all species followed by shrubs (19%), trees (13%), vines (12%) and lianas (3%). The flora is poor in geophytes (0.5%), parasites (1%), and epiphytes (2%), but is rich in aquatics and subaquatics (6% altogether). The lack of epiphytes is probably a result of the weak *garúas* that prevail on the island.

Sixteen species on the island are included in the recently published *Libro Rojo de las Plantas Endémicas del Ecuador 2000* (Valencia *et al.* 2000). Two of the species (*Carlowrightia ecuadoriana* and *Encyclia angustiloba*) are categorized as critically endangered and a further five species are included under the category endangered.

Table 12. Puná Island taxa that are endemic to the Guayas centre of arid plant endemism. Species marked * are occasionally found elsewhere in Ecuador and Peru. Species marked [G] are also known from the Galapagos Islands.

Endemic Genera

Leptochiton   *Macranthisiphon*

Endemic Species

Abutilon reflexum	*Coccoloba ruiziana*	*Macranthisiphon longiflorus*
Acanthospermum microcarpum[G]	*Commicarpus tuberosus*[*][G]	*Ophryosporus densiflorus*
Acmella leucantha	*Cordia lutea*[G]	*Passiflora tenella*
*Adiantum alarconianum**	*Croton rivinifolius*	*Peperomia glanduligera**
*Adiantum subvolubile**	*Cryptocarpus pyriformis*[*][G]	*Phyllanthus graveolens*
Aeschynomene pluriarticulata	*Cucurbita ecuadorensis*	*Pilosocereus tweedyanus*
Aeschynomene tumbezensis	*Cuscuta acuta*[G]	*Pithecellobium excelsum*
Alternanthera areschougii	*Cuscuta prismatica*	*Prestonia mollis**
*Alternanthera truxillensis**	*Gliricidia brenningii*	*Psittacanthus chanduyensis*
Amaranthus urceolatus	*Dicliptera peruviana*[G]	*Pseudogynoxys scabra*
Armatocereus cartwrightianus	*Dyschoriste quitensis*	*Randia* sp.
Byttneria parviflora	*Encyclia angustiloba*	*Ruellia floribunda*[G]
Bunchosia plowmanii	*Epidendrum bracteolatum*	*Scutia spicata*[G]
Caesalpinia glabrata	*Eriotheca ruizii*	*Solanum lycopersicum*
Capparis avicennifolia	*Erythroxylum glaucum*	*Stylosanthes sympodialis*[G]
Capparis crotonoides	*Eucrosia stricklandii*	*Tecoma castanifolia**
Capparis heterophylla	*Gossypium barbadense*[G]	*Thalia pavonii*
*Capparis scabrida**	*Hibiscus escobariae**	*Tillandsia disticha*
Carica parviflora	*Isocarpha microcephala*[G]	*Tropaeolum harlingii*
Carlowrightia ecuadoriana	*Jacquemontia corymbulosa*	*Vitex gigantea**
Ceiba trichistandra	*Jacquinia sprucei*	*Waltheria ovata*[*][G]
*Cereus diffusus**	*Lantana svensonii**	*Wedelia grandiflora**
*Chromolaena roseorum**	*Leptochiton quitoensis*	*Wissadula divergens*
Cienfuegosia hitchcockii	*Loxopterygium huasango*	*Ziziphus thyrsiflora**
Cienfuegosia tripartita	*Machaerium millei*	

Endemic Subspecies and Varieties

Coursetia caribaea var. *ochroleuca*	*Senna mollissima* var. *mollissima*
Echinodorus bracteatus subsp. *efenestratus*	*Senna pistaciifolia* var. *picta*[G]
Eucrosia stricklandii var. *stricklandii*	*Tabebuia billbergii* subsp. *ampla*
Mimosa debilis var. *aequatoriana*[G]	

Distribution Patterns

Two genera found on Puná Island, the monotypic liana *Macranthisiphon* and the geophytic *Leptochiton*, are endemic to the Guayas centre of arid plant endemism.

Among the native and naturalized plant species on Puná Island, 15% are endemic to the Guayas centre of arid plant endemism, whereas only 4% are endemic to Ecuador. If subspecies and varieties are also considered the percentage of taxa endemic to the Guayas centre of arid plant endemism is 17%. In comparison, Dodson and Gentry (1991) reported 19% endemic species for western Ecuador in the dry forests of Capeira. It must be kept in mind, however, that the Capeira forest lacks littoral species, which in general are more widely distributed.

The overall rate of endemism for western Ecuador below 900 m above sea level (80000 km^2) has been variously estimated at 13% (Balslev 1988), 20% (Dodson and Gentry 1991), and 7% (Borchsenius 1997); the latter study is not directly comparable, however, because it also included premontane forests elements above 900 m a.s.l. In a few cases species, which in general are widely distributed, are represented by endemic infra-specific taxa (*i.e.*, *Echinodorus bracteatus* var. *efenestratus*, *Tabebuia billbergii* subsp. *ampla*, etc.). Taxa endemic to the Guayas centre of arid plant endemism are show in Table 12.

Due to proximity to the Ecuadorian mainland, Puná Island lacks taxa endemic to the island itself. Many rare and poorly known species are nevertheless found. *Carlowrightia ecuadoriana* was for example described recently and the type was chosen from our material. Only two other collections of this species are known from the mainland. The species represents also the first record of the genus in South America. Other species of which only few specimens exist include *Cienfuegosia hitchcockii*, *Marsdenia ecuadorensis*, and *Ophryosporus densiflorus*. Another interesting plant is *Cucurbita ecuadorensis*, which apparently represents the sole truly wild species of *Cucurbita* in all of South America (Cuttler and Whittaker 1969). A number of taxa are interesting mainly for taxonomic reasons, having been described from collections originating from Puná Island (Table 2).

Besides the plants restricted to the Guayas centre of arid plant endemism, the remaining species found on the island are either native to the New World (48%) or of pantropic distribution (29%). While the latter group mainly consists of a variety of mostly introduced anthropophytes (weeds, ruderates, *etc.*) and numerous grasses and sedges, it also includes a group of pantropic species which may well be native to the area. Examples include species which originate from the littoral and aquatic environments and are capable of long-distance dispersal, such as *Ipomoea pes-caprae*, *Rhizophora mangle*, *etc.* There are also a few taxa with disjunct distribution patterns (*Eichhornia paniculata*, *Ipomoea ophioides*, *Tabebuia chrysantha* subsp. *chrysantha*, *etc.*), which emphasizes the dynamic nature of plant dispersal over time. Many of the endemic taxa in the Guayas centre of arid plant endemism may well represent relict populations that were more widely distributed during the droughts of earlier ice-ages, as evidenced, for example, by the present distribution of certain Cactaceae.

Affinities to the Galapagos Islands

Already Andersson (1857 [1910]) observed that the flora of the Galapagos Islands shows a strong affinity to the flora of the Guayas basin and this finding was later confirmed by Svenson (1946a). Roughly 29% of the species on Puná

Table 13. Names of 124 species occuring on both Puná Island and the Galapagos Islands.

Acacia macracantha	Eleusine indica	Physalis angulata
Acanthospermum microcarpum	Elytraria imbricata	Pisonia floribunda
Amaranthus dubius	Enydra sessilifolia	Pityrogramma calomelanos
Amaranthus spinosus	Eragrostis ciliaris	Plumbago scandens
Anthephora hermaphrodita	Eriochloa pacifica	Porophyllum ruderale
Avicennia germinans	Erythrina velutina	Portulaca oleracea
Batis maritima	Evolvulus convolvuloides	Priva lappulacea
Bidens cynapiifolia	Fimbristylis annua	Prosopis juliflora
Bidens riparia	Galactia striata	Rhizophora mangle
Blechum pyramidatum	Geoffroea spinosa	Rhynchosia minima
Boerhavia coccinea	Gossypium barbadense	Ruellia floribunda
Boerhavia erecta	Heliotropium angiospermum	Ruppia maritima
Bouteloua disticha	Heliotropium curassavicum	Salicornia fruticosa
Brickellia diffusa	Heliotropium indicum	Salvia occidentalis
Browallia americana	Herissantia crispa	Sapindus saponaria
Bursera graveolens	Ipomoea nil	Scaevola plumieri
Canavalia rosea	Ipomoea pes-caprae	Scoparia dulcis
Capraria peruviana	Ipomoea triloba	Scutia spicata
Cardiospermum corindum	Iresine angustifolia	Senna obtusifolia
Chamaesyce ophthalmica	Laguncularia racemosa	Senna occidentalis
Chloris radiata	Laportea aestuans	Senna pistaciifolia
Cissampelos pareira	Leptochloa mucronata	Sesuvium portulacastrum
Cissus verticillata	Ludwigia erecta	Sida acuta
Clerodendrum molle	Ludwigia leptocarpa	Sida repens
Commicarpus tuberosus	Macroptilium lathyroides	Sida rhombifolia
Conocarpus erecta	Malachra alceifolia	Sida spinosa
Corchorus orinocensis	Malvastrum coromandelianum	Sidastrum paniculatum
Cordia alliodora	Maytenus octogona	Spermacoce confusa
Cordia lutea	Mentzelia aspera	Sporobolus pyramidatus
Cryptocarpus pyriformis	Merremia aegyptia	Sporobolus virginicus
Cuscuta acuta	Mimosa acantholoba	Stylosanthes sympodialis
Cyperus compressus	Mimosa debilis	Synedrella nodiflora
Cyperus esculentus	Mimosa pigra	Talinum paniculatum
Cyperus ligularis	Nicandra physalodes	Tephrosia cinerea
Dactyloctenium aegyptium	Ochroma pyramidale	Tetramerium nervosum
Dicliptera peruviana	Oxalis dombeyi	Tournefortia psilostachya
Desmanthus virgatus	Paspalidium geminatum	Trema micrantha
Desmodium glabrum	Paspalum conjugatum	Trianthema portulacastrum
Desmodium procumbens	Paspalum vaginatum	Vallesia glabra
Digitaria horizontalis	Passiflora foetida	Vigna luteola
Echinochloa colona	Phyla strigulosa	Waltheria ovata
Eclipta prostrata		

Island are shared with the Galapagos Islands, which yields an Index of Similarity according to Sørensen (1948) of ISs = 22.1 (Formula in Table 4). A number of considerations suggest that the floristic similarity between the two regions may be greater than this figure indicates. In the first place, the two floras comprise 124 shared native species, of which some are endemic (Tables 12–13). Secondly, the degree of floristic similarity is greater if only the arid flora of the Galapagos Islands is considered. Thirdly, the majority of the near-relatives

Table 14. Selected taxa occurring on Puná Island but not on the Galapagos Islands. A few have been introduced recently but are probably not naturalised.

Abutilon reflexum	*Cochlospermum vitifolium*	*Machaerium millei*
Achatocarpus pubescens	*Croton rivinifolius*	Malpighiaceae
Adenaria floribunda	*Cucurbita ecuadorensis*	*Muntingia calabura*
Aeschynomene tumbezensis	*Dalechampia scandens*	*Passiflora tenella*
Agonandra excelsa	*Diospyros inconstans*	*Pisonia aculeata*
Albizia multiflora	*Eriotheca ruizii*	*Pithecellobium excelsum*
Armatocereus cartwrightianus	*Erythroxylum glaucum*	*Prestonia mollis*
Bauhinia aculeata	*Ficus citrifolia*	*Psittacanthus chanduyensis*
Bignoniaceae	*Gliricidia brenningii*	*Schultesia guianensis*
Byttneria parviflora	*Gronovia scandens*	*Senna mollissima*
Caesalpinia glabrata	*Hibiscus escobariae*	*Solanum lycopersicum*
Capparaceae	*Hydrolea elatior*	*Thalia pavonii*
Carica parviflora	*Jacquinia sprucei*	*Tropaeolum harlingii*
Casearia mariquitensis	*Leptochiton quitoensis*	*Vitex gigantea*
Ceiba trichistandra	*Leucaena trichodes*	*Wedelia grandiflora*
Cienfuegosia hitchcockii	*Lippia americana*	*Wissadula spp.*
Cissus microcarpa	*Lonchocarpus atropurpureus*	*Zanthoxylum rigidum*
Coccoloba ruiziana	*Loxopterygium huasango*	*Ziziphus thyrsiflora*

of the endemic flora of the Galapagos Islands are found on the adjoining continental plains; an estimated 52% of the progenitors of the endemics of the Galapagos Islands came originally from western South America (Porter 1984).

Much effort has been given to explain how the plant species on the Galapagos Islands reached the archipelago more than 800 kilometers west of the Ecuadorian mainland. Porter (1983) proposed that the flora was originally introduced by means of birds (40%), man (32%), wind (22%), and oceanic drift (6%). Less interest has been directed to understand why many mainland species perfectly suited to the ecological conditions prevailing on the Galapagos Islands are absent (Table 14).

Among the characteristic plant families found in the dry forests on Puná Island, but lacking on the Galapagos Islands, Capparaceae and Bignoniaceae are worth mentioning. Their absence may be due to dispersal strategies. The former depend on the intervention of mammals feeding on their fruits, the latter on heavy airborne seeds. Many of the most characteristic trees on Puná Island are entirely absent or have only recently been introduced to the Galapagos Islands by man. In this regard, *Ceiba trichistandra, Cordia alliodora, Eriotheca ruizii,* and *Guazuma ulmifolia*, are worthy of mention; several of these species have actually been brought to the Galapagos Islands by man very recently (Lawesson 1990).

The flora of the Galapagos Islands is usually assumed to be fairly rich in endemics. Porter (1984) reported 34% endemic species for the native flora. However, if the 195 species recently introduced to the Galapagos Island are taken into consideration as well, the rate of endemism is 23%, which is not much higher than figures here provided for the Guayas centre of arid plant

Table 15. Selection of exotic plants presumably introduced to Puná Island by man. Most of the plant species are pantropical weeds. Some are native to America but the exact origin of these species remains often obscure.

Achyranthes aspera	*Eclipta prostrata*	*Pectis elongata*
Aeschynomene americana	*Eleusine indica*	*Phyllanthus amarus*
Alternanthera pungens	*Eragrostis amabilis*	*Physalis angulata*
Amaranthus dubius	*Eragrostis ciliaris*	*Plumbago scandens*
Amaranthus spinosus	*Heliotropium angiospermum*	*Porophyllum ruderale*
Aristida adscensionis	*Heliotropium indicum*	*Portulaca oleracea*
Bidens riparia	*Herissantia crispa*	*Priva lappulacea*
Boerhavia diffusa	*Hyptis suaveolens*	*Rhynchosia minima*
Celosia virgata	*Ipomoea nil*	*Richardia scabra*
Chamaecrista absus	*Ipomoea quamoclit*	*Scoparia dulcis*
Chamaesyce thymifolia	*Kallstroemia pubescens*	*Senna alata*
Commelina erecta	*Lantana camara*	*Senna obtusifolia*
Corchorus aestuans	*Laportea aestuans*	*Senna occidentalis*
Cucumis dipsaceus	*Mimosa pigra*	*Sida rhombifolia*
Cyperus difformis	*Mirabilis jalapa*	*Sida spinosa*
Dactyloctenium aegyptium	*Mollugo verticillata*	*Sola num americanum*
Datura inoxia	*Momordica charantia*	*Spermacoce tenuior*
Desmodium procumbens	*Muntingia calabura*	*Spigelia anthelmia*
Digitaria horizontalis	*Nicandra physalodes*	*Synedrella nodiflora*
Echinochloa colona	*Oldenlandia corymbosa*	*Talinum paniculatum*

endemism. Indeed, already Svenson (1946b) estimated that the flora of the Guayas centre of arid plant endemism was about as rich in endemics as the flora of the Galapagos Island. It should be kept in mind that the mainland flora contains a higher ratio of exotic species due to the much longer and intenser impact of man; on the other hand island speciation gives rise to many weakly distinct, yet morphologically invariable taxa.

Human Impact

The impact of man on the flora of Puná Island is considerable. Exotic species have been introduced and have become established in disturbed habitats. Selective cutting of timber and fuel wood has changed the forest composition and the introduced goats and cattle have affected the ground cover so that it is advantageous to exotic grasses, legumes, *etc.* A selection of plants introduced to Puná Island by man is shown in Table 15. The list is not exhaustive as it is difficult to reconstruct the history of species that have co-existed with man for extended periods of time. Indeed, the present distribution of plants reflects former activities of man because humans move species beyond their native range, deliberately or by chance, when they introduce exotic species (Vitousek *et al.* 1997). As a consequence floras are being homogenized (Lodge 1993).

Numerous weeds of worldwide distribution have been introduced to Puná Island and are indicative of agriculture. Dekker (1997) stated that *"the story of agriculture is the story of weed interference"*. Widespread pantropical weeds introduced to Puná Island include *Amaranthus spinosus*, *Heliotropium angiospermum*, *Spigelia anthelmia*, and *Talinum triangulare*. A limited number of endemic species, such as *Amaranthus urceolatus*, *Leptochiton quitoensis*, and *Passiflora foetida*, have become weedy in the sense that they nowadays usually are found on cultivated soils. These 'native' weeds are often superseded in abundance by introduced weeds with a much longer history of co-evolution with agricultural practices.

A few cultivated plants have become semi-naturalised around homesites, such as *Catharanthus roseus* or *Nicotiana tabacum*. Narrow ruderates that are familiar in waste places near human inhabitations include *Alternanthera pungens*, *Datura inoxia*, and species of *Sida*. When man brought domestic animals to Puná Island it led to the introduction of a number of plants. Livestock browsing contributes, for example, to the dispersal of the mesquite tree (*Prosopis juliflora*) in the savanna. Shrubs such as *Indigofera suffruticosa*, *Senna tora*, and *S. occidentalis* are dispersed by foraging ruminants and chickens feed on the fruits of *Vallesia glabra*. *Achyranthes aspera*, *Pisonia* spp., and *Plumbago scandens* are examples of species that have adhesive fruits, which are dispersed pasively along trails by man and his domesticated animals.

A number of tree species native to southwestern Ecuador are mainly found planted on the island, *i.e.*, *Loxopterygium huasango*, *Pachira* sp., and *Pseudobombax millei*. Giant legumes, such as *Pseudosamanea guachapele*, *Samanea tubulosa*, and *Samanea saman* are found cultivated. It is possible that one or several of these species are truly native to Puná Island but have become rare due to overexploitation of wood for ship-building and house construction. A species like *Crescentia cujete* has been semi-cultivated in ancient times and is now found naturalised in agricultural areas. Likewise, *Muntingia calabura* and *Ochroma pyramidale* are weedy trees that rapidly establishes on disturbed grounds.

4

Plant Use

Puná Island has the longest record of continuous human settlement of any Ecuadorian insular territory. Evidence of sustained human settlements on the island date back more than 5000 years to the Early Formative Period and is intricately linked to the development of the earliest pre-Columbian agrarian and maritime civilizations in western South America. After European contact in the 15th century, the island played a key role during the Colonial Period, serving as an important ship-building and trade facility. For this reason, a wealth of endangered indigenous traditional oral knowledge on plant use and naming is of considerable interest for the ethnobotanist and the historian.

In this chapter we recapitulate the history of plant use on Puná Island from its early inhabitation and up to the present time. The position of place names mentioned is shown on the maps (Figure 6–7, inside front cover).

Pre-Columbian epoch

Given the location of Puná Island at the heart of coastal Ecuador in what has been termed the southwest Ecuador/northwest Peru domestication area (Piperno and Pearsall 1998) it is inconceivable that the Neotropical lowland agricultural revolution initiated by the preceramic forager societies at the onset of the Holocene did not include the island. In all likelihood fishermen who derived their sustenance from the mangrove environment established the first human settlements on Puná Island during Early Las Vegas times (5000 BC).

Archeological evidence attests to the relationship between the island and other pre-Columbian agrarian Valdivia societies developing in southwestern Ecuador during the Early Formative Period (3500–1500 BC). Ceramic evidence indicates that around 2455 BC the islanders were in contact with the Valdivia settlements on the Santa Elena peninsula (Porras and Pedro 1974). With all likelihood, the island was a point from where the Valdivians launched their famous long-distance balsa rafts (Cárdenas and Greiner 1988). Contacts with the mainland included El Oro province by Late Formative times (1000–500 BC), and by AD 500 they extended to the central Ecuadorian coast in Manabí province. At Conquest time (AD 1526) the Manteño-Huancavilca society

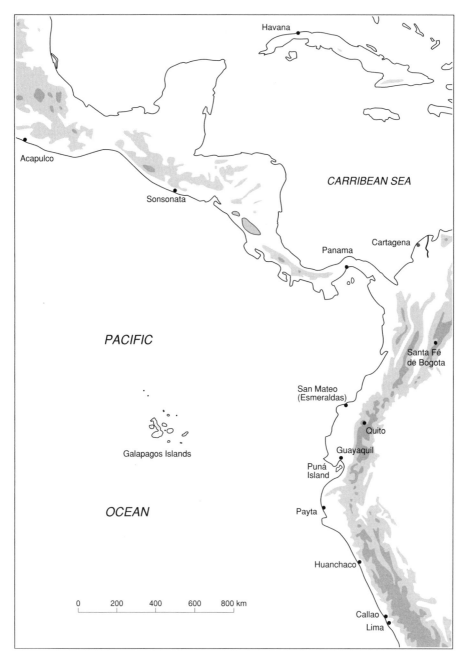

Figure 6. Pacific South America and the Caribbean zone. The indigenous people on Puná Island took part in the Pacific trade between Acapulco and Lima.

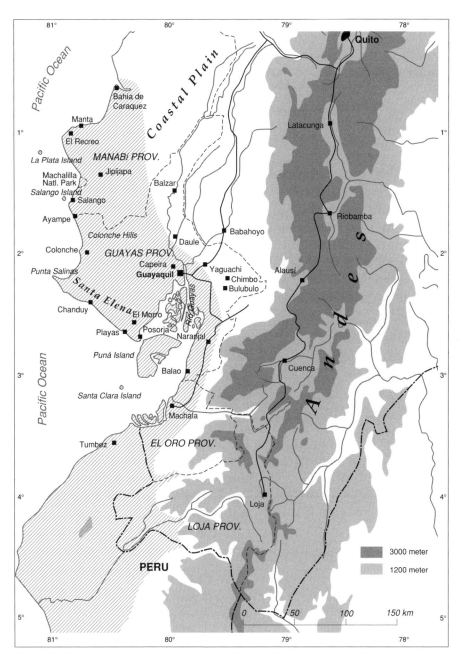

Figure 7. Southern Ecuador and adjacent Peru. The approximate delimitation of the Guayas centre of arid plant endemism is indicated by cross hatching.

Table 16. Early pre-Columbian crops likely to have been in cultivation on Puná Island.

	Scientific name	English	Spanish
Bowls	Lagenaria siceraria[1]	bottle gourd	
Cereals	Zea mays	maize	maíz
Condiments	Capsicum annuum	chili pepper	ají
	Capsicum frutescens	chili pepper	ají de gallinazo
Fruits and vegetables	Cucurbita moschata	pumpkin	zapallo
	Carica papaya	papaya	papaya
Legumes	Arachis hypogaea	peanut	maní
	Canavalia ensiformis	jack bean	
	Canavalia plagiosperma	jack bean	
	Phaseolus lunatus	lima bean	haba (payar)
	Phaseolus vulgaris	common bean	verdura
Textiles	Gossypium barbadense	cotton	algodón de monte
Tubers	Calathea allouia[2]	leren	
	Canna edulis[2]	achira	achira
	Dioscorea trifida	yams	
	Dioscorea trifoliata	yams	
	Ipomoea batatas	sweet potato	camote
	Manihot esculenta	cassava	yuca

[1]The native *Cucurbita ecuadorensis* may have been exploited instead; [2]probably of inferior importance due to the dry climate or only traded.

occupied settlements throughout southwestern Ecuador, both on Puná Island and on the mainland in El Oro, Guayas, and Manabí provinces.

The island lies in an ecozone providing cover for a rich variety of marine fauna (fish, shellfish, crabs), terrestrial animals (peccaries, deer, opossum, and rabbits) and birds, all easily accessible to early foragers. The thorn forest and thorn scrub environment, with well-drained soils and seasonal rainfall just below 500 mm annual precipitation places Puná Island close to those areas in the Americas believed to be home to the wild relatives of the earliest crop plants. These plants are thought to be a key resource for the Neotropical horticulturalists, fisher folk, and foragers who initiated the New World agriculture during the transition between the Late Pleistocene and the onset of the Holocene, some eight to ten thousand years ago.

Early Crops

Many early crops are still present on the island, and it is fair to assume that they have been used during at least the last five thousand years. Crops likely to have been grown on Puná Island are summarized in Table 16.

The principal staples of pre-Columbian America were maize (*Zea mays*) and cassava (*Manihot esculenta*). Both provided starch and they were important sources for fermented beverages to the inhabitants of the New World. Both were under cultivation on Puná Island. Generally believed to have originated in western Mexico, the cultivation of maize in southwestern Ecuador dates to late Las Vegas preceramic times (5000–4700 BC). Similarities in burial patterns have been cited as evidence that maize, along with pumpkin (*Cucurbita moschata*), was introduced through early interactions between the preceramic horticulturalists in parts of Panama, northern Colombia, and the Vegas people on the Santa Elena peninsula (Piperno and Pearsall 1998).

By the early 16th century, a number of varieties of maize had co-evolved as a consequence of human selection, whereby promotion of grains from favored varieties produced cultivars with specific uses. A number of colored varieties were eaten; the white kernelled variety was ground into meal and used to make the famous sponge cakes called *bizcochos* discovered by the Pizarro expedition; there were also popcorn called *canguil*, and the small, very hard kernels that were called *morocho* used in the brewing of the maize beer known as *chicha*.

Of the earliest New World tubers to come under cultivation, only cassava (*Manihot esculenta*) and the sweet potato (*Ipomoea batatas)* are found on Puná Island today. Neither of the yam species believed to be native to northern South America (*Dioscorea trifoliata* and *D. trifida*) and achira (*Canna edulis*) were found during this study. Though the areas of origin of these plants remain undetermined, the open habitats with seasonally dry woody vegetation on Puná Island seem suitable for cultivation of yams. The climate is probably too dry for general cultivation of the evergreen achira (*Canna edulis*), a species found wild at mid-elevations in the Andes. Cooked tubers of achira appear in dry coastal tombs around 2500 BC, which indicate that the roots were so highly appreciated that they were carried all the way to the coast (Anonymous 1989). At any rate the Puná Island evidence is in line with the argument in favor of cassava as the tuber crop of choice in the Neotropical lowlands (Piperno and Pearsall 1998).

Cassava (*Manihot esculenta*) is said to have originated either in Mexico, Central America, or eastern Brazil. Archaeological evidence suggests that cassava was introduced to the Ecuadorian coast from Brazil during the Middle Formative Machalilla Period (1800–1500 BC). There is little doubt that it was under cultivation during the Regional Development Period cultures (500 BC–500 AD), judging by the presence in archaeological sites of cassava graters which have been found on both sides of the Andes.

The earth ridges called *camellones* that were constructed by the Milagro-Quevedo people in the Guayas basin during the Integration Period (500–1500 AD) may well have served for cassava cultivation as they provide the drainage necessary to prevent water logging of the roots. Stones used in the grating of cassava have been found on the Santa Elena peninsula, and the inhabitants of Guayaquil were noted for their fondness for the starchy flour called *cazabe*. Cassava is still consumed in soups and purées, and the leaves are used as a home remedy in treating urinary infections, swellings, and infections in the arms and legs.

A second tuber crop on Puná Island was the sweet potato (*Ipomoea batatas*). Assigned to the southern Central America – northern South America macroregion (Piperno and Pearsall 1998), this species was one of the principal food plants found by the Pizarro expedition in its march along the Ecuadorian coast. Archaeological evidence suggests that sweet potato was under cultivation in coastal Ecuador by 3500 BC (Piperno and Pearsall 1998), and during our fieldwork the Puná islanders noted its use as an ingredient in the preparation of purée, pies, blancmange, and omelettes.

Three of the earliest legumes to be cultivated in the neotropical lowlands are found on Puná Island. The peanut (*Arachis hypogaea*), reportedly once of greater importance, is now only ocassionally grown. The common bean (*Phaseolus vulgaris*) is widely grown and used for salads, vegetable soups, or combined with rice dishes. The lima bean (*Phaseolus lunatus*) may also be found but the extent of its present cultivation on the island is unclear, and we did not find neither of the jack bean species (*Canavalia ensiformis* and *Canavalia plagiosperma*). Whereas *C. ensiformis* is native to Central America and the Caribbean, *C. plagiosperma* is native to South America, and there is macro botanical archaeological evidence suggesting that the Early Formative Valdivia people of western Ecuador utilized this species between 3500 and 1500 BC (Piperno and Pearsall 1998).

Cucurbits are among the first fruits and vegetables to have become established in agriculture in America (Anonymous, 1989). The pumpkin (*Cucurbita moschata*) was probably an important vegetable under cultivation on Puná Island. Its domestication is associated with central Pacific Panama and northern Colombia. During our fieldwork we noted a number of uses for *C. moschata*, including its use in soups, cakes, jams, and candy, as well as the seeds being used against intestinal worms. Another species of the genus, *C. ecuadorensis*, is native to southwestern Ecuador and adjacent Peru. In contrast to the pumpkin, no uses were attributed to the local *C. ecuadorensis*. It can not be excluded, however, that its solid fruit shell has found application as plate or bowl. Indeed, some archaeological evidence for the bottle gourd, (*Lagenaria siceraria*) in seasonal dry forest habitats of southwestern Ecuador from Early Formative times could well refer to our native species (*i.e., C. ecuadorensis*).

Papaya (*Carica papaya*), a native of Central America, was reported from the coast, the temperate Andean valleys, and the eastern Amazonian regions during the early 17th century. It is esteemed for its flavor, and the fruit is used to make candy and jams. The seeds of the papaya are a common household remedy used to eliminate intestinal parasites.

Two species of lowland chili peppers (*Capsicum* spp.) were probably in early cultivation on Puná Island, and *C. annuum* and *C. frutescens* are grown for domestic use in garden plots around house sites to this day. South central Bolivia and the mountains of southern Brazil have been proposed as the center of evolution for chili peppers (Piperno and Pearsall 1998). In Ecuador they were widespread, and their cultivation dates to the Early Formative Valdivia Period (3500–1500 BC).

Puná Island is located in the center of the domestication area of cotton (*Gossypium barbadense*) according to Piperno and Pearsall (1998). The abundance of spindle whorls described by González-Suárez (1904) and Saville (1907–1910) led Emilio Estrada (1957) to the conclusion that by 1500 AD at contact time when Pizarro arrived, a large prehispanic cotton textile industry was in full bloom on Puná Island. The cultivation, spinning, and weaving of cotton had become generalized along the Ecuadorian coast by 2700 BC according to the Ecuadorian archaeologist A. Marcos. The earliest ethno historical documentation concerning Puná Island corroborates the archaeological evidence and suggests the existence of a widespread indigenous cotton textile industry.

During the Colonial Period (1532–1820), manufactured articles included sails, fine cotton garments embellished with designs in rich colors of carmine, yellow, and blue, and purple thread. Marcos has also suggested that this thread — colored with a dye obtained from certain marine gastropod species (*Murex*) gathered from the roots of the red mangrove tree (*Rhizophora mangle*) along the Pacific coast from the Santa Elena peninsula and Puná Island to Guatemala — was highly esteemed during colonial times and was employed in sashes, lace, and other fine textiles.

A good number of domestic articles were also woven from spun cotton and used by the Puná islanders. Many of these items have remained in use up to the present, *i.e.*, saddle bags, tablecloth, tote bags, braids, hammocks, sheets, bedspreads, napkins, towels, mariner's ponchos, belts, cords, and harness straps. It is even likely that many of the native woody plants still associated with cotton textile production on Puná Island (*cf.* Table 23) also were used for making looms and the other paraphernalia needed in cotton textile manufacture during pre-Columbian times.

Early Tree Crops

Many tree crops that Piperno and Pearsall (1998) mention as important and occurring in the archaeological record of the early Holocene are still present on Puná Island. A selection of native trees many of which hold multiple uses and which are supposed to have been of particular importance prior to the arrival of the Europeans are summarized in Table 17.

Among the most important tree crops encountered by the Pizarro expedition from Esmeraldas province to Puná Island were two species of *Spondias*. The expedition probably did not pay attention to the fact that two species were involved. It is therefore unclear to what extent the historical name ciruela refers to *S. mombin* or *S. purpurea*. The former has a fruit of inferior quality and is distributed on both sides of the Andes (Macía and Barfod 2000). The latter, the

Table 17. Important tree species for the Puná islanders in pre-Columbian times.

		English	Vernacular name
Early tree crops	*Annona muricata*	soursop	guanábana
	Annona squamosa	sweetsop	chirimoya
	Crescentia cujete	tree gourd	mate
	Malpighia emarginata	West Indian cherry	cereza
	Pouteria caimito	lucuma	caimito
	Pouteria sapota	mamey sapote	mamey colorado
	Psidium guajava	guava	guayaba
	Spondias purpurea	hog-plum	ciruela, jobo
Native useful trees	*Ceiba trichistandra*	kapok-tree	ceiba
	Cordia alliodora		laurel
	Jacquinia sprucei	tree-barbasco	barbasco
	Ochroma pyramidale	balsa	balsa
	Prosopis juliflora	mesquite	algarrobo
	Pseudosamanea	guachapeli	guachapelí prieto
	Rhizophora mangle	red mangrove	mangle
	Tabebuia chrysantha		guayacán

hog-plum (*Spondias purpurea*), is abundantly cultivated on Puná Island up to the present day. It is probably native to Central America and Mexico. During the early 17th century the province of Guayas was one of the principal centers of cultivation of the hog-plum (and perhaps also *Spondias mombin*). During the 18th century it was used to prepare a fermented beverage. It was also used medicinally: a decoction was made from the bark and applied to wounds. The roots were reputed an important source of water for travelers in arid regions.

Two species of Annonaceae found at present on the island may also belong to the early tree crops. Soursop (*Annona muricata*) is thought to have originated in the Caribbean, northern South America, or Brazil, whereas the sweetsop (*Annona squamosa*) is said to be from Central America or the Caribbean. The soursop is used in beverages and the sweet sop is eaten fresh.

The tree gourd (*Crescentia cujete*) is common along trails in closed forest on Puná Island. Its dry hollow fruit shell is used as a bowl for drinking water or as a cup. The pulp may cure head ache, and the wood is used to make handles for chisels, saws, hammers, and gunstocks.

The West Indian cherry (*Malpighia emarginata*) is common and presumably indigenous to Puná Island. Its fruits are eaten and its wood is used to make charcoal.

Remains of guava (*Psidium guajava*) have been found in pre-Columbian tombs on the Peruvian coast, and the Pizarro expedition found this species from San Mateo Bay in Esmeraldas province to Puná Island. During the 18th century the species was under cultivation in the inter-Andean valleys from Imbabura to Loja, and the seeds were used as a remedy for diarrhea. On Puná Island, guava is cultivated around home sites. A second species, a wild relative of guava (*Psidium densicomum*) occurs as an uncommon understory treelet.

Another native tree species, the barbasco-tree (*Jacquinia sprucei*), probably found application as a fish poison in ancient times on Puná Island. Béarez (1998) identified remains of small rock fish in an archaeological site on the nearby coast of Ecuador dated 1000 BC (Engoroy Culture). It was suggested that the fruits of the barbasco-tree may have been used to kill small fishes used in soups, since larger fishes existed in abundance. Today, the fruits of the barbasco-tree are still collected on the island and used to eliminate fry in the shrimp farms.

Post-Columbian epoch

After the European invasion and subsequent colonization, some native plants preserved their pre-Columbian status while others took on economic importance for the first time. Food plants included maize (*Zea mays*), cassava (*Manihot esculenta*), and chili peppers (*Capsicum* spp.). The Europeans readily adopted medicinal species such as *Smilax aspera* (zarzaparrilla) — a species presumably traded and in use on Puná Island but probably not in cultivation — and sources of fiber such as cotton (*Gossypium barbadense*) and kapok (*Ceiba trichistandra*). They also quickly assimilated the indigenous uses of species such as balsa (*Ochroma pyramidale*) used in building the famous long-range Puná

Figure 8. Home on a balsa raft on the Daule River (upper part of the Guayas River). Photo from Wolf (1892).

merchant rafts (Figure 8). The rise of the shipbuilding industry and the introduction of European-style architecture in the settlement and erection of Lima created a demand for hard woods which brought trees from the mangrove, notably the red mangrove tree (*Rhizophora mangle*) and other species found in abundance on Puná Island, into prominence for the first time. European agricultural practices tended to alter the exploitation patterns of the native botanical resources, and also to introduce a number of species, both from the Old World and from other parts of America.

The Early Colonial Period (1550–1600)

The impact of the European invasion produced dramatic changes in the political, economic, and social structures. The Spanish king incorporated Puná Island as property of the crown, sparing the inhabitants of the island many of the abuses inherent in the *encomendero* system in which the colonist was given a tract of land and its native inhabitants. Puná Island continued to play an active role in regional commerce and industry with the establishment of the royal dry docks on the island, the development of the timber industry, and the increase in maritime traffic between Panama and the Lima vice royalty. These innovations were accompanied by a shift in the pattern of exploitation of the forestry resources of the island and also affected the lives of the inhabitants of Puná Island.

The local chief of the island, Diego Tomalá, was granted a coat of arms by the king and came to be one of the most influential members of the colonial society in Guayaquil. He maneuvered effectively in obtaining rights for the islanders and himself and pursued interests in the most lucrative lines of business of the day: cattle raising, salt extraction, ship building, shipping, and timber exportation to Lima. By the end of the 16th century, Tomalá was far from being a humble minor local chief. His son was enrolled in the school for nobles in Quito, and he was one of the most influential men in the province, native or Spaniard. Though he relinquished his traditional rights to the salt flats on the island and his monopoly over river transport, he considerably extended his influence onto the mainland. He held pasture rights for his herds of cattle in El Oro province and exercised jurisdiction over the richest stands of *Calophyllum brasiliense* (palo maría) and *Pseudosamanea guachapele* (guachapelí) in Yaguachi, both highly prized in the ship building industry.

It was at this time that the earliest exchange of botanical knowledge took place between the two cultural worlds. A number of Old World plant species were introduced of which, for example, lime (*Citrus aurantifolia*), melon (*Cucumis melo*), sugar cane (*Saccharum officinarum*), and thyme (*Thymus vulgaris*) may have come into cultivation on Puná Island (Table 18). Other species such as figs (*Ficus carica*), lemons (*Citrus limon*), oranges (*Citrus sinensis*), and pome-

Table 18. Selected useful species from the Old World introduced to Puná Island during the post-Columbian epoch. Those marked with an asterix (*) were probably only traded. Source: Morton (1987).

	English	Vernacular name	Time of introduction to the New World
Cajanus cajan	pigeon pea	fréjol de palo	
Citrullus lanatus	water melon	sandía	
Citrus aurantifolia	lime tree	limón	16th century
*Citrus limon**	lemon	limón real	1493
*Citrus sinensis**	orange	naranja	16th century
Coffea arabica	coffee	café	
Cucumis melo	melon	melón	
Cymbopogon citratus	lemon grass	hierba luisa	
*Ficus carica**	fig	higo	1560
Mangifera indica	mango	mango	18th century
Panicum maximum	Guinea grass	paja de cebolla	late 20th century
*Punica granatum**	pomegranates	granada	17th century
Ricinus communis	castor-oil plant	higuerilla	
Saccharum officinarum	sugar cane	caña de azúcar	
Sesamum orientale	sesame	ajonjolí	
Tamarindus indica	tamarind	tamarindo	probably 16th century
Terminalia catappa	India almond	almendra	
Thymus vulgaris	thyme	tomillo	

granates *(Punica granatum)* were not grown but presumably traded on the island. At the same time, a number of local species became everyday items in the lives of the colonists. Some of the new plants were revered as miraculous, due to their medicinal properties; others were promptly incorporated into the colonists' diet; and yet others were esteemed for their application in construction of both ships and dwellings. Outstanding examples of plants that came to be important in the shipbuilding industry are balsa *(Ochroma pyramidale)*, the coconut palm *(Cocos nucifera)*, trees of the red mangrove tree *(Rhizophora mangle)*, and *Calophyllum brasiliense* (palo maría).

Balsa *(Ochroma pyramidale)* light, easy to work, durable, and solid, was fundamental to pre-Columbian maritime trade, as has already been mentioned. The native long-range balsa rafts were admired by the Spanish naval engineers and sailors and became indispensable in a number of ways. While they were slower than the Spanish ships on the high seas, they were much more stable, secure, and maneuverable. At the close of the 16th century, it was a common practice for native merchants to convey cargos of up to 70 tons consisting of wine, oil, flour, sugar, Quito cloth, soap, and dressed goat skins to Panama, taking advantage of the favorable winds. There the crew would abandon the raft to return with a merchant ship that was sailing south.

The rafts were especially useful on the rivers because of their shallow draft. They were used in the transportation of heavier timbers, cattle, and merchandise, as well as in the loading and unloading of the European vessels

plying the Pacific trade between Panama and Lima. It soon became an
established practice for the Spanish ships to anchor at Puná Island and unload
merchandise for later transportation upriver via rafts. The rafts were also of
some importance strategically; they could be propelled by manipulation of the
rudders under the water, and in this way could be used in surprise attacks on
moonless nights. With time the native merchant rafts were replaced by the
Spanish shipping. Nevertheless, during the 16th century, they continued to
carry goods to Payta, Lima, and Panama (Clayton 1978, Dampier [1697] 1927,
Juan and Ulloa [1748] 1982, Requena [1774] in Laviana 1984, Velasco [1789]
1981).

The coconut palm (*Cocos nucifera*) was another multifaceted plant resource
that was appreciated for a number of reasons. Its fruit and milk were consumed
of course, and the shells were used to manufacture cups and bowls. The fronds
were used in roofing. The bast was found to be superior to hemp (*Cannabis
sativa*) — a species not in cultivation on Puná Island — for caulking below the
water line because the fibers does not rot in salt water and tend to swell when
immersed. Curiously, while the use of *Cocos nucifera* for this purpose was an
established practice in the Guayaquil and Puná Island dry docks in the middle
of the 18th century, it was unheard of in Havana. The recommendation was
made that coconut bast be shipped back to Spain for this purpose (Clayton
1978, Juan and Ulloa [1748] 1982, Velasco [1789] 1981).

Puná Island was surrounded by thick and virgin stands of mangrove. The
different mangrove species exhibited varying virtues, but all were useful due to
their density, strength, durability, and resistance to seawater. A species known
by the Spaniards as manoa (probably *Laguncularia racemosa*) characterized by its
multiple branching and curving trunk, was easy to work and served well in the
manufacture of stakes and tool handles. In contrast, the so-called gateado
(*Rhizophora mangle*) displayed a tall, straight trunk and was immediately
adopted by master carpenters and architects to serve as pilings and beams.
Enormous quantities were exported from Puná Island for this purpose in the
building of Lima and Callao. Naval carpenters found that *Rhizophora* was also
ideal for keels, given its great strength, length, and resistance to salt water.
With this double usefulness, *Rhizophora mangle* became one of the most heavily
exploited species.

Doubtless, the present *Rhizophora* stands are but meager remnants and poor
reflections of the former glory of the formidable mangrove forests explored by
the Spanish conquerors during the early 16th century. In those days, the forests
of these trees were so thick that in many places it was possible to walk through
the contorted and interlacing roots for large distances without stepping on the
ground. Spanish observers were amazed at its mode of propagation, which
consisted in putting off aerial roots that grew out and down to the mud where
they developed roots of their own and sent up a second trunk. It was in this
way entire forests quickly evolved along the shores of islands and the banks of

estuaries. The wood of this tree was heavy and solid and used in the construction of boats. The leaves were similar to those of the pear, and the seeds contained a bitter pulp similar to bone marrow which some of the native inhabitants consumed when no other food was at hand. The roots were tender, and native people used them to cure the sting and bites of venomous animals.

When Dampier visited the Gulf of Guayaquil in the late 17th century, he reported that both sides of the Guayas river were thickly covered with stands of red mangrove (*Rhizophora mangle*). These mangroves extended from the town of Puná Vieja — which he placed on the southern side of the island, a good distance from Punta Arenas — all the way to the mouth of the river and into the city of Guayaquil. In 1786, Puná Island was shipping 6000 guapareiba — *i.e.* the so-called mangle verdadero or mangle negro (*Rhizophora mangle*) — mangrove trees per year to Lima. These exports had begun at least as early as 1560, and probably before. The height of the trees was estimated to average some 20 m or more in some cases. The trunks were said to range from 24–50 cm in diameter. The wood was so heavy and dense that it would sink. (Clayton 1978, Dampier [1697] 1927, Juan and Ulloa [1748] 1982, Requena [1774] in Laviana 1984).

The single most important tree in the Gulf of Guayaquil for the ship building industry, *Calophyllum brasiliense*, was known as palo maría, or simply, maría. It was not found on Puná Island, but in Yaguachi, and particularly in the district of Bulubulu. Palo maría was esteemed because of the unusual straightness, extraordinary strength, and remarkable flexibility of the trunk. No mast made of its wood had ever been known to break. These trees were also unique in being the only species upon which the Spanish king ever attempted to exact a duty. Evidently now close to be extinct due to overexploitation, this species contributed substantially to the wealth of the most influential members of the Guayaquil ruling class throughout the colonial period. The first to profit from palo maría was the local chief Don Diego Tomalá. He was followed by Toribio Castro who controlled the salt, ship building, and river transport industries after the turn of the 17th century. Finally, the *Calophyllum* forests were controlled by Col. Jacinto Bejarano Lavayen, ship builder, cacao exporter, and one of the main ideologues of the Guayaquil ndependence movement at the end of the 18th century (Clayton 1978, Requena [1774] in Laviana 1984).

Eclipse of Puneño Hegemony: 17th Century

The nascent ship building industry on Puná Island was stimulated by the upsurge of trade between the Spanish settlements along the Pacific coast of the New World. At the same time the discovery of the Pacific by Spain's European competitors led to an incr ease in pirate attacks. As a consequence, the need to provide warships for the South Seas Armada, vital for the protection of the new colonies, was the decisive factor in the establishment of the royal shipyards on

Puná Island. However, the control of this industry passed out of the hands of the local chief on Puná Island.

Other industries which underwent rapid expansion were salt exploitation, lumber extraction, and river transport. And, just as in the case of the ship building industry, these were enterprises which the islanders ceded to Spanish control during the first quarter of the 17th century which saw the building of the flag ship of the South Seas Armada on Puná Island and the attack of the Dutch pirates in 1624 (probably illustrated in Figure 9). This last event led to attempts to regulate the construction of merchant vessels at the ship yards, with the view of assuring their adaptability to bellicose purposes.

The sacking of Panama by Morgan in 1670, and the destruction of Guayaquil by a combined French-English expedition in 1687 made it clear that the security of the colonies on the Pacific coast was seriously at stake. While this tended to increase the importance of the ship yards, it also led to moving from the island to the mainland, where the first warship was constructed in the Guayaquil shipyards.

The need for increased security was also related to a growing awareness of the importance of the natural resources of the province of Guayaquil. During the second half of the 17th century, the issue of the depletion of timber resources

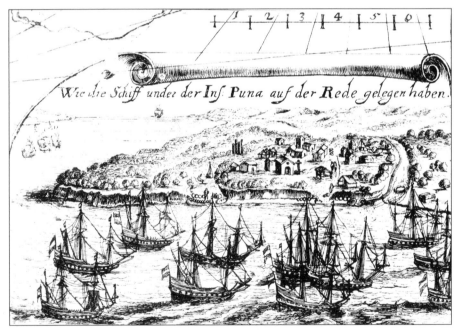

Figure 9. The Dutch squadron *l'Hermite* in front of Puná Island. Drawing by the German cartographer M. Merian (ca. 1630), Nürnberg. This illustration was reproduced in Szaszdi (1988). The version shown here was reproduced by C. Mora from a copy of the original kept at *Archivo Histórico de Guayas*.

led local authorities in Guayaquil to draw up laws intended to control the extraction of the most important species, such as *Calophyllum brasiliense* (palo maría) and palo amarillo (not recognized). The development of local agricultural resources experienced a significant upswing. In addition to the quantities of mangle and other hard woods exported to Lima, cacao (*Theobroma cacao*), which had become popular in Europe, began to take on significance.

Captain Toribio de Castro

The extraction of salt on Puná Island came under the control of captain Toribio de Castro originally in 1577, when, for 40 pesos per year, he rented it from the islanders for the period of six years. On 12th March, 1600, in Quito, Castro obtained a concession of three years for rights over the salt extraction and control of the royal warehouse, located in Babahoyo, through which literally all commerce flowed between Quito and the outside world. This gave Castro an absolute monopoly over the extraction, transportation, and distribution of salt in the audience of Quito. Under this arrangement, the Puná islanders maintained the right to extract salt for their personal uses, without cost. Castro claimed that he had invested more than 30000 pesos in the enterprise.

Castro's presence was also felt in the ship building industry. He sailed as ensign on one of the galleons, *Jesús María* and *La Visitación*, newly built on Puná Island under the supervision of Ordoño de Aguirre, when they were delivered to Callao in 1602.

Toward the end of 1615, the viceroy, Esquilache, took a serious look at the needs of the Armada of the South Seas. As a result, the crown's dock yard on Puná Island received a variety of orders. Between 1617 and 1622, Ordoño de Aguirre was named to oversee a project on Puná Island which included repairs on three large vessels, the *San Felipe*, the *San Pelayo*, and *La Visitación*, the construction of a galleon, *Nuestra Señora de Loreto*, a large tender, the *San Bartolomé*, and at least one galley.

The dry docks run by Aguirre were in operation for the next seven years between 1615 and 1622. It seems that the other ships were built between 1615 and 1617, while the galleon was finished between 1619 and 1622. She became the flagship of the Spanish Armada of the South Seas, carried 44 canons, and had a capacity estimated between four and five hundred tons. The tender was estimated as having a capacity of 100 tons and carried eight canons. Castro was evidently responsible for the provision of the timber needed in these projects.

The growing importance of the dry docks on Puná Island and Guayaquil can be judged by the fact that all galleons of the armada were built on Puná Island or in Guayaquil. The armada served three purposes. It was charged with safe guarding the annual shipments of gold and silver from Lima to Panama, providing transportation of the European goods that helped the colonists survive, and passage to the Spanish administrators, instrumental in maintaining the unity and profitability of the Spanish Empire.

Besides crown contracts, there was a rapidly growing number of merchant ships carrying goods between Acapulco, Panama, Cartagena, Quito, Peru, and Chile. In fact it is the right to free trade between the colonial administrative centers that is invoked in justification of the independence movement that gives rise to the Republican Era during the first half of the next century.

It is estimated that two or three large vessels were launched from the dry docks of Puná Island and Guayaquil per year by the end of the 17th century and that the number of ships in active South Sea service fluctuated between 40 and 60, at any one time. And taking 20 years as an average life time of a vessel operating in the Southern Seas, it is estimated that some 40 vessels were built in these dry docks every 20 years, which would amount to roughly 200 vessels during the course of a century. It seems clear that the majority of the vessels deployed in the South Sea, both naval and merchant, were built in Guayaquil and on Puná Island.

In fact, upon the undertaking of the Ordoño de Aguirre projects on Puná Island, Guayaquil gained the reputation of being the principal ship yard in the viceroyalty of Lima. Two factors made this possible: on the one hand, the ready supply of raw material offered by the exuberant forests densely populated by species uniquely suited to the ship yards made Guayaquil incomparable in the dominions of the Spanish crown; and on the other, a qualified local work force, formed on the basis of those who had been employed in the projects between 1610 and 1614, made it possible to satisfy the demand for carpenters and helpers. It was necessary to bring but few artisans, free or slave, from Lima.

By September of 1617, captain Toribio Castro had thoroughly monopolized the salt trade through his control over the salt flats, and the royal warehouse in Babahoyo. As a result, transportation prices between Puná Island and Babahoyo had more than trebled, and serious accusations of robbery were leveled at the slaves employed by Castro on his vessels. They were said to drink the wine and fill the skins with river water, open bundles, taking what they pleased. Drastically raising the price of all European goods in Quito.

This led to allegations by the colonial administrators in the capital of the audience of Quito, and a number of suggestions were made in reports sent back to the king. Among these proposals was that of Miguel Alonso in 1619 who favored the opening of a road between Bahía de Caraquez and Quito, so as to avoid the necessity of bringing goods through Guayaquil. In 1620, the new president of the audience, Antonio de Morga, recently transferred from the Philipines, suggested that all ships contracted for the Armada of the South Seas be built in Manila.

That Castro was overly concerned by such testimony seems unlikely, for on 9th August, 1623, in Lima, the viceroy decided that instead of making a special appointment of a functionary to oversee the projects requested in name of the viceroyalty, as had been the case with Ordoño de Aguirre, it would be possible to contract well-known local ship builders. By coincidence, Joseph Castro happened to be in Lima, and presented a bid which, after the obligatory three days publication, was accepted by the viceroy, Don Diego Fernández de Córdova, Marqués de Guadalcazar, as being both the best and only available.

The events of the following year highlighted the strategic importance of the ship building facilities under Castro's management. Fernández de Córdova had been transferred from Mexico to Peru in 1622. In 1623 he awarded the Castro contract, and in 1624, forewarned by the Spanish secret service, was urgently preparing for the attack of the Dutch pirate, Jacob Heremite Clerk, who, with 11 ships and 1600 men, was to blockade Lima for five months in 1624.

The viceroy's greatest concern was to protect the valuable cargo of gold, silver, and documents, which included the king's annual tribute, as well as private resources, estimated at over nine million pesos. The shipment was readied, and since no word of the enemy had reached Lima, Fernández de Córdova gave the order for the armada to set sail from Callao for Panama on the 3rd of May. In relation to the value of its cargo, the Lima Armada was relatively modest, consisting of but five vessels which included the flagship, a galleon, the *San José*, or the *Carmen*, accompanied by an admiralship which was an armed tender, and three private vessels carrying merchandise and passengers.

In contrast, Clerk's fleet, belonging to Count Mauricio, was armed to the teeth. In eleven ships with 1600 men, he had sailed from Amsterdam on the 29th of April of 1623, loaded with enough supplies and munitions to last three years, with a duplicate order of arms to be supplied to native and black inhabitants of the Spanish colonies upon their enlistment in the Dutch invasion. After passing the Straits of Magellan in February of 1624, Clerk laid over in the Juan Fernández islands for two months before he fell in full force, with all of his ships, on the kingdom of Peru at Malas, a good distance above Lima on May 7th, missing the Panama shipment by four days. From there the Dutch sent an expedition against Guayaquil which managed to wreck much havoc, but which was ultimately unsuccessful.

In his report the next year, 1625, the president of the audience of Quito, Antonio de Morga, based on interrogation of prisoners, related that the Dutch had made two attempts to take Guayaquil and had left Puná Island for Callao on September 12th. He informed the king that, except for 30000 pesos for the Holy Crusade, the 250000 pesos that were to have been sent on the *San Antonio* had been used to indemnify the citizens for their losses and to pay for the expenses incurred in the defense of the city, including pay for the soldiers, and, as a consequence, no other contributions were to be expected for that year. He recommended that two forts be built, one in Guayaquil, and another on Puná Island, in order to prevent such invasions in the future and sent Dr. Matías de Peralta, the oldest judge in Quito to Latacunga with the mission of setting up a gun powder factory.

It is likely that the most inconvenienced citizen in Guayaquil, and possibly in the audience of Quito, was the magistrate. In the contract between Castro and the Viceroy, the galleon, the *San Diego*, which was under construction in the dry docks on Puná Island, on the Barrio Lindo side of the estuary, was valued at 76000 pesos. If the large galleon, the *San Antonio*, stolen on Puná Island was of equal value, Castro may have lost around 150000 pesos in these two vessels alone. To this loss should be added the *San Ambrosio* and her cargo, as well as at least another lumber transport on Puná Island, as well as his portion of the stacked lumber awaiting transport, which the pirates had burned on the beach. And besides these actual losses, he naturally suffered by the general interruption of trade. Therefore, it seems plausible to suppose that he felt entitled to the lion's share of the unremitted 220000 pesos.

But despite these losses, Castro's position was strengthened. With the threat of foreign invasions, the Armada of the South Seas could only contract more vessels. Around 1630 the viceroy Chinchón ordered that the plans of all merchant vessels privately built on Puná Island, Guayaquil, or any other part of the province, be approved in Lima. This measure was intended to insure that no merchant vessel would be built which could not be readily converted to a war ship capable of carrying at least 20 canons. But the enforcement of this order was difficult, for more than three or four private vessels were being launched every year at the time on Puná Island and Guayaquil. And, as the ship building industry expanded, costs were on a steady rise.

In 1640, the viceroy Mancera commissioned the magistrate of Guayaquil, Martín de Valenzétegui to build two large galleons, the *Santiago* and the *Limpia Concepción*, on Puná Island. These vessels were estimated at 1000 tons, and carried 60 canons, breaking an edict that no vessel should be over 600 tons. At least 257750 pesos were invested in the building of these two vessels, and some estimates run as high as 300000 pesos for the *Limpia Concepción* alone. If this last estimate is accurate, it means that costs had more than tripled during the 16 years between 1624 and 1640.

Security and Conservation of Resources

Some 15 years later, the viceroy in Lima, Luis Henríquez de Guzmán, Count of Alba de Liste, commissioned Cristóbal de Mello, admiral-general of the Armada of the South Seas, to build two new galleons on Puná Island in 1656. Mello had served for many years as one of the captains of the Atlantic fleet, as well as in the Barlovento armada, and he had collaborated in the fortification of Acapulco before taking on the command of the Armada of the South Seas. In this latest commission Mello was made acting governor and superintendent of the crown's shipyard on Puná Island.

The importance of the ship building industry is reflected in the number of citizens it involved, all the way from the magistrate to the slave, and when the work was being done on Puná Island it was not unusual for the town council to suspend all of its business because its members were fulfilling their duties to the crown's shipyard. And it seems, that at times, ship building eclipsed even the ecclesiastical concerns, for it is recorded that on 21st September, 1656, the reception of the Archangel San Miguel, as the patron saint of the city, had to be suspended because all of the members of the town council were on Puná Island at the crown's shipyard, owing to the construction of the two galleons under Mello's supervision.

A number of factors combined to drive up costs. In the first place, there was the perceptible thinning of the resources. As early as 1650, the magistrate, Francisco Vásquez de Silva, and the Guayaquil city council, prohibited the use of *Pseudosamanea guachapele* (guachapelí) and *Calophyllum brasiliense* (palo maría) for any use other than naval construction. Ten years later, in 1660, on 15th September, the town council denounced the rapid disappearance of *Calophyllum brasiliense* (palo maría) stands in the Bulubulu forests of Yaguachi and announced an ordinance whereby the trees could be cut only by special license. At the same time, the expansion of commerce kept the demand for resources on the rise. Maritime commerce, ship construction, and logging underwent continual expansion for the next 100 years. This affected forestry resources and likewise involved important agricultural exports such as cacao (*Theobroma cacao*), tobacco (*Nicotiana tabacum*), and textiles made of cotton (*Gossypium barbadense*).

In 1657 a Frenchman advertised the first chocolate house in London and when María Teresa de Austria, daugther of the Spanish king Felipe IV, married Louis the XIV in 1660, she and her retainers carried their 'Spanish' customs, including the drinking of chocolate, to Paris.

The year of 1681 saw the first warship constructed in the shipyards of Guayaquil. The vessel was built at the request of a Guayaquil magistrate who wished to exchange the ship for the right to assume the magistery of Otavalo for three years. In 1682, the citizens of Guayaquil raised 4000 pesos for the construction of the *Planchada* fort in the 'Old Town' at the base of the Santa Ana hill. Between 1684 and 1689, the acts of the Guayaquil town council included an increasing number of denunciations of unauthorized extractions of timber for ship building purposes. Though there can be little doubt that leading citizens were involved, punishment was, however, meted out only to blacks, mulattos, and mestizos, for the most part.

The weakness of the Spanish defenses was demonstrated in 1670 when Henry Morgan, the English pirate, sacked Panama. Such attacks became more common during the late 17th century, as the South Seas became infested with pirates. In April of 1687, a motley crew of English and French adventurers commanded by Jorge D. Hout, Picard, and Grogniet leveled Guayaquil and left the city in ashes, having made their entrance overland guided by a dissatisfied mulatto. They were the first invaders to successfully sack Guayaquil. As the number of attacks increased, the colonial administrators felt a growing concern for the security of the shipyards on Puná Island and at Guayaquil, along with the forest resources of the province. Local authorities made inventory of the abundant forests of fine woods. In addition to *Pseudosamanea guachapele* (guachapelí), *Calophyllum brasiliense* (palo maría), and the palo amarillo (unidentified), already the objects of special ordinances in 1650 and 1660, other valuable woods were roble (unidentified), canelo (unidentified), red mangrove (*Rhizophora mangle*), *Lonchocarpus atropurpureus* (bálsamo), *Cordia alliodora* (laurel), *Vitex gigantea* (pechiche), *Guadua* sp. (cañafístola), and *Ochroma pyramidale* (balsa). It was also during this period that coconut husk was recognized as an important resource in the industry on Puná Island and in Guayaquil.

Commerce and Industry: 18th Century

At the turn of the 18th century, the relationship between Spain and her American colonies was changing rapidly, owing to the depletion of the most easily accessible reserves of gold and silver. The Spanish crown responded to the reduction in the profitability of her colonies by stressing administrative reorganization and the sponsorship of scientific expeditions. In this way, the king hoped to arrive at a realistic assessment of his possessions, discover new sources of revenue and, at the same time, enhance the efficiency of the exploitation of established resources. Nevertheless, the situation was precarious, owing to a number of factors. The attacks perpetrated by English pirates on Spanish shipping were increasingly successful. Furthermore, the intensification of trade between the colonies gave rise to a growing sense of economic self-sufficiency among the socially prominent creoles, who became ever more determined to assume the economic control of what they perceived as their own destinies. This was reflected in the proliferation of contraband trade that far outstripped the commerce defined as legitimate by the Spanish authorities.

Two examples of administrative reorganization designed to improve the government of the provinces of Peru occurred in the first quarter of the 18th century. In 1705, Guayaquil was promoted to the status of *gobernación*, and Felipe V created the viceroyalty of Santa Fé de Bogotá, to which Guayaquil was annexed in 1718. In 1735, Dionisio de Alsedo y Herrera became president of the audience of Quito. His compilation of the vital economic data related to the province of Guayaquil was crucial in the determination of the amount of revenue due to the crown. While he reported the impressive commercial activity through the port of Puná Island in the Gulf of Guayaquil and provided the first itemized description of the shipbuilding industry established in Guayaquil, he also revealed serious administrative deficiencies and the loss of significant sums for the crown due mainly to the extensive contraband trade.

A second source of information concerning the province of Guayaquil and its port at Puná Island in the early part of the 18th century is provided by the scientific expedition outfitted in 1736 by the Academy of Science of Paris in collaboration with the Spanish court. The purpose of the expedition was to measure the arc of the meridian at the equator and it was headed by the French astronomers Godin, Bouguer, and La Condamine, who were accompanied by the Spanish engineers Jorge Juan de Santacilia and Antonio de Ulloa. The latter were assigned the secret mission of keeping an eye on the French scientists while ascertaining the true political situation of Venezuela, Colombia, Ecuador, and Peru and evaluating the defensive capabilities and requirements of the colonial possessions.

By the beginning of the 18th century, the influx of trade into the province of Guayaquil from abroad was substantial. The articles of trade originated both from other parts of the New World, Spain, and China. From Peru and Chile came items such as wine, oil, olives, raisins, almonds, copper, and rigging. From Guatemala and Nicaragua came snuff, dyes, indigo, pitch, tar, and pharmaceuticals. Through Panama arrived the products and Spanish merchandise referred to as *de Castilla*, such as, low quality cloth, baize, cotton linen, flour, dried vegetables, hams, cheese, sugar, and fruit preserves. Other products that arrived by sea from the intermediate ports of Huanchaco, Cherrepe, and Payta included flour, sweets, soap, tallow, and Spanish leather.

This is also about the time when the Puná islanders may have begun to cultivate important exotic fruits such as mango (*Mangifera indica*) and water melon (*Citrullus lanatus*), along with coffee (*Coffea arabica*) for household consumption.

All of these products flowed through Guayaquil and Puná Island, making the province an emporium that provided the inland provinces of the audience of Quito with many of the necessities and luxuries of life. At the same time, an even greater volume of exports left the province of Guayaquil. The principal exports were cacao (*Theobroma cacao*), timber, salt, dried fish, and livestock. But other products were equally important. By 1719 substantial exports of cacao were being shipped to Panama, Sonsonata, el Realejo, and other ports along the coast of Mexico. Cacao was also exported, though in smaller quantities, to Peru. An indication of the growing importance of cacao is the suggestion as early as 1719 that a tax of half a real be placed on every 80 lbs. of cacao exported to raise money for the construction of fortification for Guayaquil.

It was estimated that some 1500 loads of cacao were harvested in the Machala district alone and that brought Puná Island some 7500 pesos per year. It was in Machala and Naranjal where the best cacao was grown, with that from the former held to be the best grown anywhere in the province of Guayaquil. Timber was the major export to Callao and the intervening ports. Handsome profits were made in the lumber trade, since the only costs involved were occasioned by its cutting, trimming, and transport. The logs were carried to the nearest estuary or river and floated down to Guayaquil, or directly to Puná Island, where they were loaded for export. Generally, the larger merchant vessels that needed careening or repairs would be serviced at Puná Island and then loaded with this timber. Such a procedure more than covered the cost of the repairs and resulted in a profit. The construction costs of brand new vessels were recovered almost entirely with the sale of their first shipment of timber.

It was impossible for either the scientists or the administrator to determine exactly the quantity of lumber sent yearly for the construction of houses in Lima, Callao, and the intermediate ports. The total was estimated at some 24000 pesos per year on the average. However, there were some years when extraordinary amounts of timber were shipped to these ports for the purpose of careening and repairs of His Majesty's ships. For instance, in 1735 the total income for timber amounted to 32800 pesos, when 8000 pesos of timber were destined for the repair of three vessels belonging to the royal navy, the *Capitana*, the *Almirante*, and the *Patache* of the Southern Fleet (Alsedo y Herrera [1741] 1987).

The principal source of income generated for the lieutenant of Puná Island and the inhabitants of the three small villages consisted of the export of mangrove trees for the factories in Lima, Callao, and the intermediate ports. Along the beaches of both Machala and Puná Island, great stands of red mangrove (*Rhizophora mangle*) were to be found. This species deeply impressed Juan and Ulloa, who went into prolix detail concerning its superior qualities (Juan and Ulloa [1748] 1982). The red mangrove tree had multiple applications, and besides its use in house construction, it found important application in walls of fortifications, and was preferred for the keels of vessels due to its incorruptibility in salt water and because of the great length of its trunks, which reached more than 30 meters. It was estimated that 6000 trees were harvested on Puná Island each year with a value of 3000 pesos.

Salt was another equally valuable and important trade article. But whereas cacao was principally destined for markets in the provinces to the north, and timber exported to those to the south, salt was sold mainly in the interior in the highland settlements in the audience of Quito. Along with salt, cotton, rice, and salted fish constituted the third principal class of merchandise. The cotton and the rice were sold both in the Andes and along the coast, while the other items were destined principally for the interior. Puná Island earned 10900 pesos annually from the sale of timber, cacao, and salted fish.

Other sources of income are less easily estimated. For instance, the provision of fruits, meat, and water for the crews of the ships that laid over in the port of Puná Island without entering the river to anchor in Guayaquil provided the islanders with significant income. Another source of income came from careening, caulking, and other repairs on the larger vessels unable to enter the river due to the shoals and shallows. Finally, of course there were the incalculable sums resulting from contraband trade.

The fourth important category of merchandise originating in the province of Guayaquil was livestock, including cows, young bulls, mules, and horses for the Andes. Like the salt and cotton, the livestock was generally destined for the hinterland provinces and settlements mentioned above.

Other important items that brought in significant, though smaller, sums were tobacco, peanuts, wax, chili peppers, and kapok, the last three of which were abundant on Puná Island. And, there were yet other products, which, though unimportant by themselves, altogether were as important as any of the first four categories mentioned, such as rice, cotton, sesame seeds, honey, and coconuts, all of which, except for rice, were also plentiful on the island. During eight months of the year, these products were taken to Quito, Cuenca, Riobamba, Chimbo, and Alausí (Juan and Ulloa [1748] 1982).

Natural Resources

Although the province of Guayaquil contained no mineral resources in sufficiently sizable concentrations to make their exploitation profitable for the Spanish, the diversity, quality and quantity of the plant resources were nothing short of extraordinary. In their description of the Guayaquil dry docks, both Alsedo y Herrera and the Spanish engineers, Juan and Ulloa, gave an extensive inventory of the trees and their uses in the fabrication of the vessels. The most important trees included *Calophyllum brasiliense* (palo maría), *Cordia alliodora* (laurel), *Lonchocarpus atropurpureus* (bálsamo), *Pseudosamanea guachapele* (guachapelí), *Rhizophora mangle* (mangle), as well as canelo and roble amarillo (both unidentified). Each tree species possessed characteristics that made it especially suited for use in different parts of the vessels.

Perhaps the single most valuable tree to be found in the province of Guayaquil was *Calophyllum brasiliense* (palo maría) that was used for masts and yards. The palo maría from Guayaquil was much lighter and more flexible than that of the same name found in Havana, along the coast of Cartagena, and other parts of the coast to the north. And though it was not quite as flexible as the European pine, it was much stronger, such that the Spanish engineers reported that cases of demasting were virtually unheard of.

The esteem in which palo maría was held by local industrialists is indicated by the fact that it was the only wood produced in the mountains around Guayaquil that came to be considered the exclusive property of certain privileged residents of Guayaquil, who paid a small amount to the royal treasury in return for the exclusive right to extract *Calophyllum brasiliense* trees to be used in the construction of the masts and yards of the crown's navy.

The stands of palo maría were located on the brow of Mount Bulubulu in the Yaguachi district. In addition to their use in ship building, it seems that the palo maría trees also were the source of a resin or 'balsam of life', which was especially effective in the curing of inflammations caused by blows and wounds. The value of this balsam is incalculable, but, evidently, considerable.

A second species, also found in abundance in the Bulubulu area, was *Pseudosamanea guachapele* (guachapelí). It was greatly admired due to its solidity, few knots, the ease with which it could be worked, and its extraordinary durability, such that even after 60 or more years it maintained its resin as though it had been cut but the day before. Its only defect consisted of certain whitish spots subject to rotting, but these could be cut away and thereby the durability of the wood assured.

For both large and small vessels, ordinarily *Pseudosamanea guachapele* (guachapelí) was preferred for the trusses because of its resistance to the effects of sea water and shipworms. The trunk was used for the keel, the roots for deck and frame timbers, and the branches for the base of the cutwater, the sternpost, knees, top-timbers, and futtock. *Pseudosamanea guachapele* (guachapelí) was also used in blocks and pulleys, and the best trees were those whose wood was a grayish color, called guachapelí mulato.

Guachapelí was also used for house construction and *Pseudosamanea guachapele* is still cultivated on Puná Island where it is known for its usefulness in the building of houses, furniture, and small boats. The pods of the tree are used as fodder for domestic animals.

A third highly appreciated tree found in abundance in the Bulubulu mountain area of the Yaguachi district was the roble of Guayaquil (unidentified). It was not as sturdy as the Spanish roble (oak), but at the same time it was less subject to splitting and easily worked. It was commonly used in planking, and, like guachapelí, it was resistant to shipworms, long lasting, and also used in houses. Though uncommon along the coasts of Chile and Peru, it was found in abundance in the province of Guayaquil and from Panama to Mexico.

Other important trees also found in the hills of Bulubulu were amarillo and colorado (both unidentified). The colors are indicated by their names. The former had very compact and strong wood of great duration, and was used in beams, crosstrees, shelfpieces, and keelsons. Along with colorado, it was next in importance and preference after guachapelí and roble (unidentified).

A sixth tree of great importance and of extremely widespread application was the red mangrove (*Rhizophora mangle*). It was the single most important timber found in the province, above all for house construction and in the building of fortifications. As noted above, it was the principal source of income for the lieutenant and inhabitants of the three small villages on Puná Island. Shipped to the factories in Lima, Callao, and the intermediate ports, it was estimated that 6000 trees were sent each year with a value of 3000 pesos.

Coconut palms were especially productive in the district, growing to the height of 12 or 15 meters. The leaves were similar to those of the date palms of the Barbary Coast. The coconuts were said to obey the phases of the moon, and each month approximately 16 coconuts were produced. The tow taken from the husks was also used to fill the cracks between the boards of the walls of the houses, and the medulla in the form of candied fruit was the basis of the famous *cocada* of the Indies.

Other useful trees mentioned included the kapok-tree (*Ceiba trichistandra*) and the cedro which probabably is identical to *Cedrela odorata*. These were useful in the making of canoes. The former was valuable in that it produced kapok used for mattress ticking, and grew in abundance on Puná Island. Oars were made from *Cordia alliodora* (laurel), which was heavy but not flexible. Canelo (unrecognised) was a very hard, heavy wood which was used in the keels and other pieces requiring strength. *Lonchocarpus atropurpureus* (bálsamo) was another firm, solid, heavy wood that was used in pumps.

Another forest product that played a key role in the economic activities of the Gulf of Guayaquil during the 18th century was balsa (*Ochroma pyramidale*) an essential wood used in the great cargo rafts that carried the produce to the port on Puná Island. These rafts had been the backbone of the great merchant fleets deployed by the league of merchants centered on Puná Island and Salango in pre-Columbian times.

In 1738 Juan and Ulloa described the rafts plying the Guayas river, some of which were as long as 30 meters. Entire families often lived aboard rafts with a 20–25 tons capacity. The Spanish mariners were especially impressed with the ingenious design whereby the rafts possessed sufficient maneuverability to render them perfectly sea worthy, even in the strong currents of the open sea outside the river and the immediate vicinity of Puná Island.

Although rudderless, the rafts were more maneuverable than European vessels, owing to the use of numerous movable keels called *guaras*, which allowed the sailors to take advantage of contrary winds. About 2.5–3.5 m long and about 45 cm wide, the *guaras* were introduced between the balsa logs of the raft, both forward and aft, and depending upon the depth to which they were thrust down into the water and raised out of the water, the raft could be made to take the desired course.

This made for a craft which was very responsive in handling, quite secure when sailing close to the wind, and prompt to negotiate whirlpools in the rivers and breakers in the sea, even when loaded with up to 3500 kg of cargo such as flour, fruit, maize, and crates of preserves.

Mention was also made of a wild cane (*Guadua* sp.) that grew to a height of up to 15 m in the Yaguachi district. This cane was employed in the construction of the floor boards and walls of many of the houses in the countryside, and was also used on the balsa rafts as decks.

Another sort of cane was also to be found in this district. The nodes of this cane were as much as a geometrical foot apart, and these canes contained fresh water which during the periods when the moon was waxing could be taken by travellers by drilling a hole in the node and letting the fresh cold water pour into a glass or cup. This water was also considered a valuable medicinal draught for the ill. Finally, *Prosopis juliflora* (algarrobo) was mentioned as a tree which was abundant in the nearby mountains and also on the island. It was used for kitchen fires.

With the transfer of the ship building industry from Puná Island to Guayaquil, and the establishment of the royal customs house in Naranjal during the 18th century, the island lost much of its importance as an administrative center. Also, the steady growth in the importance of the cacao and cattle production in the mainland settlements encouraged migration off the island, and, in 1784, eventually resulted in the separation of Machala from the jurisdiction of the island. These trends led to a drastic depopulation of Puná Island, as the skilled ship's carpenters no doubt took up residence in Guayaquil, and the farmers and cattle hands left for the more productive and profitable plots and haciendas across the Jambelí channel in Machala and Naranjal.

Alsedo y Herrera estimated that of the 12–20000 original native inhabitants only 96 remained in 1734. And when the members of the La Condamine expedition went ashore at Puná Island on 24th March, 1736, they found a scant number of houses made of loose canes with thatched roofs, none of which was adequate for the setting up of their equipment. Juan and Ulloa noted that only a few inhabitants — principally mestizos, a few Spaniards, and but a scant number of native inhabitants — were to be found in the small village located in the northeastern part of the island near the port.

Though estimates vary, it seems that there was only a small stable population in the village on the northeastern end of the island during the latter half of the 18th century, with between 60 and 114 inhabitants living in some 60 houses, the tiny church being the only building having a tile roof. No troops were posted on the island, and there was a single much neglected cannon, to be fired by the sentinels in order to warn Guayaquil in the event of a pirate attack. Besides the village of Puná, the only other reported inhabitants were to be found on a small cattle ranch in an area known as La Trinchera in 1774.

But be this as it may, a word of caution is conceivably in order in regard to these figures, which seem in some respects much too low in relation to the activities evidently underway on the island, and it is reasonable to suppose that the actual population was a good deal greater. There is also the fact that a maritime district like Puná Island would support a much larger population widely dispersed over the island.

After all, Puná Island remained the main port of the province, through which the very voluminous commerce generated in the province moved. Also, the exploitation of exportable products included an estimated 6000 logs of the red mangrove (*Rhizophora mangle*) per year in 1786, and 2.5 tons of dried fish. There was also a significant exploitation of the extensive salt flats, and the raising of 1300 heads of cattle.

Besides these labors, the loading and unloading of artillery and cargo onto the big merchant vessels, the piloting of ships up and down the river, the transport of cargo to and from Guayaquil, as well as careening and ship repairs, and the procurement and preparation of dried meat — both venison and beef — for the crews of passing vessels must be taken into account.

And, of course, in addition to all of the above, must be added the work in the domestic plots needed to produce fruit and food needed for local consumption.

One estimate puts the population of the entire Puná district — *i.e.*, Puná Island, Machala, and Naranjal — at 1700 between 1761 and 1764, while the populations of each settlement were said to be 114, 106, and 127 respectively. Machala produced 3000 *cargas* of cacao (at 2 pesos each this meant 6000 pesos per year free of tribute) and 2000 head of cattle, while Naranjal contributed another 1200 head besides commercial quantities of cacao (*Theobroma cacao*), roble (unrecognised) for shipbuilding, rice (*Oryza sativa*), chili peppers (*Capsicum* spp.), cotton (*Gossypium* sp.), and maize (*Zea mays*), along with other products such as plantain (*Musa x paradisiaca*), cassava (*Manihot esculenta*), and a variety of fruit for local consumption.

Demise of Colonial Rule: 19th Century

The 19th century marked the transition from the colonial to the republican era, and bristled with the clash of great personalities. In Europe it was the century of romanticism, Napoleon, and industrialism. In Latin America it was the century of democracy, Bolívar, San Martin, and the rise of imperialism.

For the province of Guayaquil, it marked the end of the sailing ship, the

Figure 10. Street in Puná Nueva near the end of the 19th century. The mangrove estuary is visible in the horizon. Photo from Wolf (1892).

introduction of the steam boat, and the rapid expansion of the already
substantial cacao trade. Interestingly, the province achieved its own liberation
and was the home of two of the leading figures in the South American
independence movements. With the opening of commerce after the
revolutionary struggles, Guayaquil was visited by a number of naturalists who
made the first scientific inventories of its botanical and zoological resources.

For Puná Island, the 19th century meant an increasingly marginal historical
role, though as the principal port of the province it maintained its importance
in the maritime and fluvial traffic moving through the Gulf of Guayaquil, and
continued to provide significant quantities of timber. During the revolutionary
struggles, the island attracted the interest of Chile as a potential naval base,
served as headquarters for the first native-born president of Ecuador, and
became the site of the summer home of the British consul. The principal town,
Puná Nueva, was well kept and a decent place to rest on the naval journey
(Figure 10).

Post Revolutionary Period

During the Revolutionary Period — which may be said to begin with Bolívar's
incorporation of Bogotá into the united provinces and the initiation of the
liberation of Chile by San Martín in 1814 and end with the dissolution of Gran
Colombia in 1830 — the continent of South America was caught up in the
struggle for independence and there was no scientific investigation on Puná
Island or in the province of Guayaquil. Nevertheless, it is evident that
commerce and industry continued, though somewhat abated.

During the revolutionary period, industry, commerce, and science had
languished in the face of the conflicts and hostilities effected by the great armies
of mercenaries and adventurers which marched across the continent. In 1832,
the activity in the Guayaquil ship yards had abated somewhat, and there were
only 242 carpenters, 25 caulkers, 241 shore carpenters, and 9 masons. With the
end of the large scale hostilities, European expeditions again returned to the
Gulf of Guayaquil and naturalists and scientists took up the study of the local
terrain.

Present day

Very little literature concerning plant use of direct relevance to our study area
is available. Valverde (1998) gave a general overview of useful plants of the
Ecuadorian coastal plain. Hernández and Josse (1997) published a small booklet
on edible plants from the semi-arid Machalilla National Park in the Manabí
province. Information on useful plants, notably on economic botany aspects,
may also be found in papers by Acosta-Solís (1959, 1961) and Valverde *et al.*
(1979, 1991).

Table 19. Principal cultivated plants presently grown on Puná Island.

	Vernacular name	Scientific name	English name
Beverages	café	*Coffea arabica*	coffee
	maracuyá	*Passiflora edulis*	passion fruit
	ciruela, jobo	*Spondias purpurea*	hog-plum
	tamarindo	*Tamarindus indica*	tamarind
	almendra	*Terminalia catappa*	India almond
Condiments	ají	*Capsicum annuum*	chili pepper
	caña dulce	*Saccharum officinarum*	sugar cane
Fruits	guanábana	*Annona muricata*	soursop
	chirimoya	*Annona squamosa*	sweetsop
	papaya	*Carica papaya*	papaya
	sandía	*Citrullus lanatus*	water melon
	limón	*Citrus aurantifolia*	lime
	melón	*Cucumis melo*	melon
	mango	*Mangifera indica*	mango
Grains	ajonjolí	*Sesamum orientale*	sesame
	maíz	*Zea mays*	maize
Nuts	maní	*Arachis hypogaea*	ground nut, peanut
	palma de coco	*Cocos nucifera*	coconut palm
Root crops	camote	*Ipomoea batatas*	sweet potato
	yuca	*Manihot esculenta*	cassava
Vegetables	fréjol de palo	*Cajanus cajan*	pigeon pea
	haba payar	*Phaseolus cf. lunatus*	
	zapallo	*Cucurbita moschata*	pumpkin
	verdura	*Phaseolus vulgaris*	bean

The present study provides insight into vernacular knowledge shared by campesino elders and threatened by imminent extinction because it is not being transmitted to the younger generation. In order to gather evidence that would make it possible to estimate the extent to which the Puná islanders exploit their native flora, ethnobotanical information and vernacular plant names were collected during several interviews in 1987. The elders included seven men and one woman. All were over 50, had a lifetime of experience with the vernacular agricultural practices on the island, and hailed from different regions of the island: Bellavista (2), Campo Alegre (1), Río Hondo (1), Puná Nueva (1), Puná Vieja (2), and Zapote (1) (*cf.* inside front cover map).

The interviews were recorded on cassettes and consist of approximately 22 hours of recording. This material is deposited at the Anthropology Museum in Guayaquil. The data were mainly elicited on the basis of a list of vernacular plant names compiled during the botanical fieldwork. When feasible the vernacular names are documented by complementary herbarium specimens with the source (name and residence of informant) written on the specimen label. The uses mentioned by the islanders were classified into nine general categories: food, forage, remedies, woods, textiles, medicines, poisons, magical, and miscellaneous. The results of the interviews are outlined in Tables 19–24.

Table 20. Plants eaten by animals on Puná Island.

	Scientific name	Habit	Birds	Cattle	Deer	Dogs	Donkeys	Goats	Pigs	Rabbits
achocha de monte	*Momordica charantia*	vine	+							
albahaca de monte	Acanthaceae spp.	herb		+			+			
albahaca de vaca	Acanthaceae spp.	herb		+						
albahaca morada	Acanthaceae spp.	herb		+						
algarrobo	*Prosopis juliflora*	tree					+			
aroma	*Acacia aroma*	tree						+		
	Acacia farnesiana	tree						+		
	Acacia tortuosa	tree						+		
barbasco	*Jacquinia sprucei*	tree				+				
bedoca	*Passiflora foetida*	vine	+							
bejuco de playa	*Ipomoea pes-caprae*	vine					+			
bichaya	*Capparis avicennifolia*	shrub	+					+		
bichayita	*Capparis* sp.	shrub	+							
bledo blanco	*Amaranthus urceolatus*	herb		+			+			
bledo colorado	*Amaranthus dubius*	herb		+			+			
	Amaranthus spinosus	herb		+			+			
bledo macho	*Amaranthus* sp.	herb						+		
camote	*Ipomoea batatas*	vine							+	
camotillo	*Ipomoea* spp.	vine		+						
canilla de venado	*Acalypha cuspidata*	shrub			+					
capué	*Erythrina velutina*	tree		+				+		
cardón	*Armatocereus cartwrightianus*	tree						+		
cascol	*Caesalpinia glabrata*	tree		+	+			+		
catarama	*Alternanthera pungens*	herb		+				+		
ceibo	*Ceiba trichistandra*	tree		+			+			
chiquihua	*Byttneria parviflora*	shrub						+	+	
chirigoyo	*Eriotheca ruizii*	tree		+	+					
chupaflor	*Abutilon reflexum*	shrub		+						
compoño	*Albizia multiflora*	tree		+						
cucuñique	*Clerodendrum molle*	shrub		+						
ébano	*Ziziphus thyrsiflora*	tree		+	+		+	+		
escoba	*Sida* spp.	herb	+							
escoba de montaña	*Sida* spp.	herb	+							
espino colorado	*Bauhinia aculeata*	tree						+		
flor de abejón	*Senna mollissima*	shrub		+			+	+		
	Senna pistaciifolia	shrub		+			+	+		
flor de verano	*Bougainvillea spectabilis*	liana		+						
frejolillo de monte	*Senna obtusifolia*	shrub						+		
fruta de gallina silvestre	*Citharexylum* sp.	shrub	+	+				+		
fruta de paloma	*Tournefortia bicolor*	shrub	+							
fruta de pan	*Artocarpus altilis*	tree							+	
guasmo	*Guazuma ulmifolia*	tree		+						
guayaba de monte	*Psidium densicomum*	tree		+		+				
guayacán	*Tabebuia chrysantha*	tree		+						
haba de montaña	Fabaceae spp. (vines)	vine		+						
hierba de pajarito	*Psittacanthus chanduyensis*	shrub	+	+				+		
hierba luisa	*Cymbopogon citratus*	herb		+			+			
jobo	*Spondias purpurea*	tree		+						
jaboncillo	*Sapindus saponaria*	tree					+			
jazmín de cruz	*Randia* sp.	tree						+		

Table 20 (continued). Plants eaten by animals on Puná Island.

	Scientific name	Habit	Birds	Cattle	Deer	Dogs	Donkeys	Goats	Pigs	Rabbits
jazmín de montaña	*Randia* sp.	tree		+						
jeneiro	*Eriochloa* sp.	herb		+						
jiso	*Cereus diffusus*	shrub		+						
lentejilla	*Senna robinifloia*	shrub		+						
licuanco	*Coccoloba ruiziana*	shrub	+							
limoncillo de monte	*Agonandra excelsa*	tree		+	+					
madera negra	*Tabebuia billbergii*	tree					+			
maíz	*Zea mays*	herb	+							
maíz colorado	*Zea mays*	herb	+						+	
maíz sesenta días	*Zea mays*	herb	+						+	
mangle salado	*Avicennia germinans*	tree						+		
manglillo salado	*Cryptocarpus pyriformis*	shrub		+						
manoa	*Laguncularia racemosa*	tree						+		
manzanilla de vaca	*Isocarpha microcephala,*	herb		+						
	Ruellia floribunda	herb		+						
maravilla	*Nymphaea ampla*	herb		+						
matapalo	*Ficus citrifolia*	tree						+		
mate chino	*Cucurbita ecuadorensis*	vine					+			
mostaza de monte	*Sesbania emerus*	herb						+		
mostacilla	Fabaceae spp. (herbs)	herb						+		
muyuyo hembra	*Cordia lutea*	shrub		+				+		
niguito	*Muntingia calabura*	tree	+							
paja de cebolla	*Panicum maximum*	herb					+			
paja de la virgen	Poaceae sp.	herb								+
paja de sabana	Poaceae spp.	herb	+							
palo prieto	*Capparis heterophylla*	shrub		+		+				
palo salado	*Cryptocarpus pyriformis*	shrub		+						
papaya de monte	*Carica parviflora*	herb					+			
patacón	*Maytenus octogona*	shrub						+		
pegajoso	*Boerhavia erecta*	herb					+			
	Plumbago scandens	herb				+				
perlilla	*Vallesia glabra*	shrub	+							
picamano	*Cissus microcarpa*	vine	+							
pitajaya	*Hylocereus polyrhizus*	shrub					+			
platanillo silvestre	*Thalia pavonii*	herb		+						
quiriquinche	*Pithecellobium excelsum*	tree	+							
rabo de gallo	*Amaranthus spinosus,*	herb	+							
	Heliotropium indicum	herb	+							
salsafrán	*Zanthoxylum rigidum*	shrub						+		
samán	*Samanea saman*	tree					+			
sapán de paloma	*Trema micrantha*	tree	+							
sebastián	*Capparis lanceolata*	shrub						+		
seca	*Geoffroea spinosa*	tree		+				+		
tapatapa	*Mimosa debilis*	shrub						+		
tomatillo	*Solanum lycopersicum*	herb	+							
verdolaga	*Sesuvium portulacastrum,*	herb	+					+		
	Portulaca oleracea	herb	+					+		
vidrillo	*Batis maritima*	herb						+		
vidrillo salado	*Salicornia fruticosa*	herb						+		
zapote de perro	*Capparis scabrida*	tree	+			+				

Inasmuch as the present study is based on local vernacular plant names these are usually cited in the running text.

The Puná islanders are apparently aware of the possible uses of many plants on the island. Herbal medicine was once of much greater importance, but knowledge concerning this area is disappearing with the present generation of elders. We know little about the preparation of the remedies employed by the midwives in the past. This is also the case with many of the uses of various woods mentioned during the interviews. To correct this deficit, it would be necessary to conduct interviews with islanders with specialized knowledge. There is a good likelihood that additional magical associations will become known on the basis of such interviews as well.

Edible Plants

The majority of the food plants consist of fruits, condiments, and vegetables. Their use was mentioned in connection with the preparation of a wide variety of dishes and beverages, many of which are less in evidence today than they were 30 years ago. Some 30 different fruits were mentioned, while there were 11 condiments, and seven vegetables. A selection of important crops is illustrated in Table 19.

Other categories of food plants are not recognized by the islanders as such, but are mentioned in the preparation of dishes and beverages and may be classified as remedies. These include the grains and roots. Cassava (*Manihot esculenta*) is used for example in soups, purées, cakes, and omelettes. Another source of flour is maize (*Zea mays*), which is also employed in fermented beverages, soft drinks, and popcorn. The sesame (*Sesamum orientale*) is an ingredient in fermented beverages; it is also added as seasoning to bread and crackers, besides being roasted and eaten alone or mixed with brown sugar and prepared as candy. The Puná islanders considered peanuts (*Arachis hypogaea*) a condiment because they are frequently used to make a sauce for the seasoning of soups, fish, and meat dishes.

Plants mentioned by the islanders as serving as forage for domestic animals (cattle, goats, donkeys, pigs, and dogs), and sustenance for the wild fauna (birds, deer and rabbits) are numerous and varied. All together some 86 names were mentioned (Table 20). Many of the names are collective terms used for several or many species. Species of Acanthaceae are for example known as albahaca. Trees and shrubs represented 55% of the sample although they make up only 31% of the flora. Domestic animals and birds consume nearly all of the species mentioned; deer and rabbits account for the remainder. Numbers of plants names mentioned for each animal were in the order of: birds (24), cattle (40), deer (9), dogs (1), donkeys (24), goats (23), pigs (5), and rabbits (1). Interestingly, no plants were mentioned as being eaten by horses although the herders surely keep this kind of knowledge as well. The informants are evidently experienced herders with a good general understanding of complex plant-animal interactions. This is a branch of knowledge that they have accumulated through a lifetime of observations.

Healing and Poisonous Plants

Information provided during the interviews may give a reliable picture on the status of knowledge of possible uses of plants for medicinal purposes among ordinary peasant farmers. It does not, however, go into such interesting details as the importance of herbal medicines in practical life or the preparation of the remedies themselves. Nor does it represent the totality of the vernacular medical knowledge and belief possessed by the islanders. A large part of this knowledge, especially that branch concerned with childbirth, resides in the memories of the elderly midwives who still live on the island; however, the islanders who participated in the congresses were men, with one exception. It is clear that the islanders are aware of the possible use of a great number of native and domesticated plants for medicinal purposes. Herbal medicine, once of greater importance, is nowadays largely replaced by modern medicine.

The medicinal and magical uses of plants are related to a broad range of complaints that include common diseases, aches and pains, inflammations, wounds, broken bones, pimples, and baldness. Some of these plants were associated with specific organs, and there were also remedies for menstruation and birth pangs. There were also a number of plants that were the basis for remedies that could be used to rid domestic animals of fleas or to cure bat bites. The list of vernacular medicinal plants and their scientific equivalents is shown in Table 21.

Two magical complaints were mentioned: the evil eye and spells. Five different plants were associated with cures for the evil eye, all of which were either cultivated or ruderates. These included *Ocimum basilicum* (albahaca de comer), the flower of *Mirabilis jalapa* (buenas tardes), *Datura inoxia* (campanita de castilla), *Menta piperita* (hierba buena), and *Solanum lycopersicum* (tomatillo). *Aloe vera* (sábila), which is still found in many homes today just for good luck, was mentioned as an effective cure for warding off evil spells.

The common diseases mentioned included colds, hepatitis, malaria, and intestinal worms. Five plants were recommended in the treatment of colds: albahaca morada (*Blechum pyramidatum* or *Dicliptera peruviana*), *Citrus aurantifolia* (limón), *Psittacanthus chanduyensis* (hierba de pajarito), *Malachra alceifolia* (malva), and *Cryptocarpus pyriformis* (manglillo salado). Three plants were used to cure intestinal parasites such as worms: *Cocos nucifera* (palma de coco), *Cucurbita moschata* (zapallo), and *Carica papaya* (papaya blanca). *Tamarindus indica* (tamarindo) was mentioned as a purgative, and *Malachra alceifolia* (malva) was used for cleaning out the stomach. *Centaurium quitense* (canchalagua) was once administered as a cure for malaria and *Petiveria alliacea*

Table 21. Medicinal, magical, and poisonous plants on Puná Island. Domesticated plants are marked with an asterix (*).

	Vernacular name	Scientific Name
Medicines used for / to treat		
Aches or pains	matapalo	*Ficus citrifolia*
	reseda	*Lawsonia inermis*
	manglillo salado	*Cryptocarpus pyriformis*
Acne and blackheads	hierba mora	*Solanum americanum*
	suelda con suelda	*Epidendrum bracteolatum*
	tiatina	*Scoparia dulcis*
	resina de varita	*Wedelia grandiflora*
	palo santo	*Bursera graveolens*
Alleviate birth pangs	capué	*Erythrina velutina*
	opio*	*Papaver somniferum*
Baldness	balsa	*Ochroma pyramidale*
	grama	Poaceae sp.
Bloody vomiting	rabo de gallo	probably *Amaranthus* sp.
Bone aches	mastranto*	*Lippia alba*
	malva	*Malachra alceifolia*
	palo santo	*Bursera graveolens*
Cleaning the stomach	malva	*Malachra alceifolia*
Colds	limón*	*Citrus aurantifolia*
	malva	*Malachra alceifolia*
	manglillo salado	*Cryptocarpus pyriformis*
	suelda con suelda	*Epidendrum bracteolatum*
	albahaca morada	*Blechum brownei*
		Dicliptera peruviana
Coughs	bejuco de hilar corral	*Macranthisiphon longiflorus*
	palo santo	*Bursera graveolens*
	reseda	*Lawsonia inermis*
Cramps and colics	mastranto*	*Lippia alba*
Detach the umbilical cord	matapalo	*Ficus citrifolia*
Ear aches	mastuerzo	*Tropaeolum harlingii*
Fungus infections	muyuyo hembra	*Cordia lutea*
Head aches	mate	*Crescentia cujete*
Heal wounds	hierba mora	*Solanum americanum*
	limón*	*Citrus aurantifolia*
	resina de varita	*Wedelia grandiflora*
	sanalotodo	*Prestonia mollis*
	suelda con suelda	*Epidendrum bracteolatum*
	tiatina	*Scoparia dulcis*
Intestinal parasites	palma de coco	*Cocos nucifera*
	papaya blanca*	*Carica papaya*
	zapallo*	*Cucurbita moschata*
Jaundice and hepatitis	zorrila	*Peteveria alliacea*
Kidneys and colons	ceibo	*Ceiba trichistandra*
	palma de coco	*Cocos nucifera*
	sábila*	*Aloe vera*
	matapalo	*Ficus citrifolia*
	hierba mora	*Solanum americanum*
Malaria	canchalagua	*Centaurium quitense*
Purgatives	tamarindo*	*Tamarindus indica*
Remove thorns	hierba mora	*Solanum americanum*
	resina de varita	*Wedelia grandiflora*
	suelda con suelda	*Epidendrum bracteolatum*

Table 21 (continued). Medicinal, magical, and poisonous plants on Puná Island. Domesticated plants are marked with an asterix (*).

	Vernacular name	Scientific Name
Medicines used for / to treat		
Remove thorns	tiatina	*Scoparia dulcis*
Ringworm infections	muyuyo hembra	*Cordia lutea*
	palo santo	*Bursera graveolens*
Stomach pains	mastranto*	*Lippia alba*
Swellings	hierba mora	*Solanum americanum*
	mastuerzo	*Tropaeolum harlingii*
	palo santo	*Bursera graveolens*
	resina de varita	*Wedelia grandiflora*
	suelda con suelda	*Epidendrum bracteolatum*
	tiatina	*Scoparia dulcis*
Tooth aches	chala	*Croton rivinifolius*
	florón	*Ipomoea carnea*
	manglillo salado	*Cryptocarpus pyriformis*
Magical complaints	albahaca de comer*	*Ocimum basilicum*
	buenas tardes*	*Mirabilis jalapa*
	campanita de castilla*	*Datura inoxia**
	hierba buena*	*Menta piperita*
	sábila*	*Aloe vera*
	tomatillo	*Solanum lycopersicum*
Poisons		
Cure bat bites on animals	barbasco	*Jacquinia pubescens*
Fish poison	barbasco	*Jacquinia pubescens*
Flea repellent	bichaya	*Capparis avicennifolia*
	palo santo	*Bursera graveolens*
Poisonous to the cattle	chala	*Croton rivinifolius*
	florón	*Ipomoea carnea*
Rat poison	yuca de ratón	*Gliricidia brenningii*

(zorrila) was used for jaundice or hepatitis.

Aches and pains and inflammations of various kinds also had their remedies. Inflammations and swellings had the greatest number of cures. Ten different plants were said to be effective in case of swelling, and two more plants were recommended for inflammations in particular. Colic, spasms, and stomach pains had at least five different remedies, whereas coughs, tooth aches, bone aches, and general body pains could each be cured with preparations derived from four different plants. Finally, *Tropaeolum harlingii* (mastuerzo) was recommended for ear aches, while rabo de gallo (in this connection probably a species of *Amaranthus*) was used to cure bloody vomiting.

Six plants were associated with particular organs. The kidneys and the colon are treated with preparations made from *Aloe vera* (sábila), *Cocos nucifera* (palma de coco), *Ficus citrifolia* (matapalo), and *Solanum americanum* (hierba mora). Though no mention was made during the recordings of the interviews, one informant recommended the water drained from the roots of the kapok-tree (*Ceiba trichistandra*) as beneficial for the kidneys.

Other medicinal uses were indicated for a miscellany of ailments. Five different plants were named as sources for remedies intended to aid the removal of thorns, the curing of pimples, and the healing of wounds of all sorts. Plants of particular interest to women included those utilized in preparations destined to aid menstruation and to alleviate birth pangs. These included *Erythrina velutina* (capué) and *Papaver somniferum* (opio). *Ficus citrifolia* (matapalo) is used to detach the umbilical cord of newborn infants.

Cuts, wounds, and fractures called for *Citrus aurantifolia* (limón), *Epidendrum bracteolatum* (suelda con suelda), or *Prestonia mollis* (sanalotodo). Ringworm is cured with *Cordia lutea* (muyuyo hembra) and *Bursera graveolens* (palo santo), baldness with *Ochroma pyramidale* (balsa) and Poaceae sp. (grama). Finally, *Jacquinia sprucei* (barbasco) is rubbed into the wounds caused in domestic animals by bat bites, and *Capparis avicennifolia* (bichaya) is a flea repellent for the chickens.

Few poisons were mentioned in the congresses. In particular, the well-known fish poison, *Jacquinia sprucei* (barbasco), went unmentioned. Its use was prohibited by law because of the effect it exercises on all the fry and small fishes inhabiting the estuaries. At present it is taking on a certain degree of economic significance in relation to the shrimp farming industry where it is being used to eliminate predator fish inadvertently pumped into the ponds. *Bursera graveolens* (palo santo) was used to repel mosquitoes and bats. *Gliricidia brenningii* (yuca de ratón) was considered effective as rat poison. Other poisons were considered to be a threat to cattle and man. *Bauhinia aculeata* (picapica) and Mimosaceae spp. (uña de gato) caused rashes, and *Ipomoea carnea* (florón) and *Croton rivinifolius* (palosangre) were believed to constitute a threat to the cattle, above all in the dry season when the animals can find no other forage.

Useful Woods

Puná Island is known for its hard woods. The interviews give testimony to a long tradition of craftsmanship in carpentry. It is important to remember that the islanders were not entirely within the domain of their own greatest expertise in describing the uses of the woods in question. Certainly, they were perfectly familiar with the woods used in agricultural work, and there can be little doubt that they possessed much more than a mere passing knowledge of the other uses related to the construction of houses and the manufacture of household items, furniture and tools. But all the same, there are many reasons to believe that naval carpenters are bound to possess much more knowledge concerning the woods used in ship building, and, similarly, that the cabinet makers will know a great deal more about the making of furniture. It is important to remember such limitations when considering this evidence, not only in regard to the woods used in carpentry, but also insofar as the plants employed in the manufacture of textiles is concerned.

A large number of local woods were used by carpenters, both in the construction of boats of various types and canoes, and in the building of houses, and the manufacture of furniture and other household items. Many woody plants served agricultural purposes, yet others as fuel, and still others had applications in the making of tools, firearms, and statues. Tree species of importance in construction are summarized in Table 22.

Naval carpenters used *Muntingia calabura* (niguito) and *Vitex gigantea* (pechiche) for deck strakes. Shores and stanchions were made of bálsamo (perhaps *Lonchocarpus atropurpureus*), *Tecoma castanifolia* (muyuyo macho), *Muntingia calabura* (niguito), and *Vitex gigantea* (pechiche). *Rhizophora mangle* (mangle colorado and mangle blanco), *Laguncularia racemosa* (manoa), and *Leucaena trichodes* (aguia) were used for ribs. Frame timbers were made of *Psidium densicomum* (guayaba de monte) and *Muntingia calabura* (niguito). Other woods that were also used in the construction of boats, rafts, and canoes included *Prosopis juliflora* (algarrobo), *Ochroma pyramidale* (balsa), *Caesalpinia glabrata* (cascol), *Eriotheca ruizii* (chirigoyo), *Samanea tubulosa* (guachapelí blanco), *Pseudosamanea guachapele* (guachapelí prieto), *Loxopterygium huasango* (guasango), *Tabebuia chrysantha* (guayacán), *Conocarpus erecta* (jelí), *Cordia alliodora* (laurel and laurel de montaña), *Tabebuia billbergii* (madera negra), *Cordia lutea* (muyuyo hembra), and *Geoffroea spinosa* (seca).

Many of these fine woods also found household applications, both in the building of houses and in the manufacture of furniture. However, in addition to the woods already mentioned, there were a number of woods mentioned only in connection with uses on shore. *Acacia tortuosa* (aroma), which served as fuel, both as fire wood and as a source of charcoal, seems to have found occasional use in house construction. *Machaerium milleii* (cabo de hacha), as its name implies, was used to make hatchet handles, charcoal, and floor boards. Another wood which was used to make charcoal, and was employed in furniture, was *Erythroxylum glaucum* (coquito). The same is true of *Ziziphus thyrsiflora* (ébano), *Bauhinia aculeata* (espino colorado), *Loxopterygium huasango* (guasango) — which also served as wedges — and *Capparis lanceolata* (sebastián).

In the fields, water troughs were made of *Capparis scabrida* (zapote de perro), which also provided the raw material for washtubs, wheels, and basins. Other woods with applications in the fields were pegapega (in this connection probably identical to *Pisonia aculeata*), which served for corral gates, *Loxopterygium huasango* (guasango), which served as fence posts and also, because of its resistance to water, as restraining walls in wells. It was also used in barrels and tubs.

Many, if not most, of the above mentioned woods which served the naval carpenters, the shore carpenters, the cabinet makers, and the agricultural field hands, were also used in the making of charcoal for fuel. Nevertheless, there was

Table 22. Woods used on Puná Island (excl. textile manufacture).

	Scientific Name	Specific uses
Naval woods		
algarrobo	*Prosopis juliflora*	
balsa	*Ochroma pyramidale*	boards, rafts, floats (no longer used)
bálsamo	*Lonchocarpus atropurpureus*	
cascol	*Caesalpinia glabrata*	
chirigoyo	*Eriotheca ruizii*	
guachapelí blanco	*Samanea tubulosa*	
guachapelí prieto	*Pseudosamanea guachapele*	
guasango	*Loxopterygium huasango*	
guayaba de monte	*Psidium densicomum*	
guayacán	*Tabebuia chrysantha*	
jelí	*Conocarpus erecta*	
laurel	*Cordia alliodora*	
madera negra	*Tabebuia billbergii*	
mangle blanco	*Rhizophora mangle*	ribs of ships frames
manoa	*Laguncularia racemosa*	conoes, ribs of ships frames
muyuyo hembra	*Cordia lutea*	
muyuyo macho	*Tecoma castanifolia*	
niguito	*Muntingia calabura*	
palo salado	*Avicennia germinans*	canoes
patacón	*Maytenus octogona*	
pechiche	*Vitex gigantea*	
pelacaballo	*Leucaena trichodes*	ribs of ships frames
seca	*Geoffroea spinosa*	
House construction, often also for furniture		
algarrobo	*Prosopis juliflora*	
aroma	*Acacia farnesiana*	
aroma	*Acacia tortuosa*	
bálsamo	*Lonchocarpus atropurpureus*	boards, floors, shores, stanchions
cabo de hacha	*Machaerium millei*	floor boards
cascol	*Caesalpinia glabrata*	rigging posts
chirigoyo	*Eriotheca ruizii*	boards
coquito	*Erythroxylum glaucum*	
ébano	*Ziziphus thyrsiflora*	boards
guachapelí blanco	*Samanea tubulosa*	boards
guachapelí prieto	*Pseudosamanea guachapele*	boards
guarango	*Acacia macracantha*	
guasango	*Loxopterygium huasango*	restrain walls in wells
guasmo	*Guazuma ulmifolia*	boards
guayaba de monte	*Psidium densicomum*	frames, lashing posts for ridging
guayacán	*Tabebuia chrysantha*	posts
laurel	*Cordia alliodora*	boards
limoncillo de monte	*Agonandra excelsa*	
madera negra	*Tabebuia billbergii*	boards
mangle blanco	*Rhizophora mangle*	boards
manoa	*Laguncularia racemosa*	
muyuyo macho	*Tecoma castanifolia*	shores and stanchions
niguito	*Muntingia calabura*	deck strakes, frames, shores, stanchions
pechiche	*Vitex gigantea*	boards, deck strakes, shores, stanchions
pelacaballo	*Leucaena trichodes*	field huts
sapán	*Trema micrantha*	

Table 22 (continued). Woods used on Puná Island (excl. textile manufacture).

	Scientific Name	Specific uses
House Construction, often also for furniture		
sebastián	*Capparis lanceolata*	
seca	*Geoffroea spinosa*	boards
tamarindo	*Tamarindus indica*	boards
zapote de perro	*Capparis scabrida*	boards
Furniture		
bálsamo	*Lonchocarpus atropurpureus*	
chirigoyo	*Eriotheca ruizii*	
coquito	*Erythroxylum glaucum*	
ébano	*Ziziphus thyrsiflora*	
guachapelí blanco	*Samanea tubulosa*	
guachapelí prieto	*Pseudosamanea guachapele*	
guayacán	*Tabebuia chrysanthai*	
laurel	*Cordia alliodora*	
madera negra	*Tabebuia billbergii*	
palo santo	*Bursera graveolens*	statues of saints
Tools		
balsa	*Ochroma pyramidale*	boxes (no longer made)
barbasco	*Jacquinia sprucei*	make nets
cabo de hacha	*Machaerium millei*	handles, hatchets
cascol	*Caesalpinia glabrata*	wedges
guarango	*Acacia macracantha*	wedges
guasango	*Loxopterygium huasango*	barrels, tubs, wedges
guayacán	*Tabebuia chrysantha*	wedges
licuanco	*Coccoloba ruiziana*	charcoal ovens, net frames, neddles, shovels, wooden pins
mate	*Crescentia cujete*	gunstocks and handles
muyuyo macho	*Tecoma castanifolia*	shovels
patacón	*Maytenus octogona*	fishing nets
pechiche	*Vitex gigantea*	barrels, tubs
pelacaballo	*Leucaena trichodes*	props for trees and vines
zapote de perro	*Capparis scabrida*	anvils, troughts, tubs, washtubs, wheels
Enclosures and stakes in the field		
algarrobo	*Prosopis juliflora*	stakes
bálsamo	*Lonchocarpus atropurpureus*	stakes
coquito	*Erythroxylum glaucum*	stakes
ébano	*Ziziphus thyrsiflora*	stakes
flor de abejón	*Senna obtusifolia*	stakes
guarango	*Acacia macracantha*	stakes
guasango	*Loxopterygium huasango*	fence posts, stakes
guayacán	*Tabebuia chrysantha*	fences, stakes
licuanco	*Coccoloba ruiziana*	stakes
madera negra	*Tabebuia billbergii*	fences
manoa	*Laguncularia racemosa*	fences
muyuyo hembra	*Cordia lutea*	fences, stakes
muyuyo macho	*Tecoma castanifolia*	fences, stakes
palo de rana	*Capparis heterophylla*	stakes
pegapega	*Pisonia aculeata*	corral gates
pelacaballo	*Leucaena trichodes*	fences, stakes
quiriquinche	*Pithecellobium excelsum*	stakes

a good number of other woods that served strictly as fuel, either as fire wood, or in the form of charcoal. These included *Malpighia emarginata* (cereza), *Albizia multiflora* (compoño), *Randia* sp. (crucita), Mimosaceae spp. (espina de sabana), *Psidium guajava* (guayaba de comer), *Sapindus saponaria* (jaboncillo), *Capparis guayaquilensis* (margarita), *Capparis heterophylla* (rana), *Lawsonia inermis* (reseda), *Zanthoxylum rigidum* (salsafrán), and Mimosaceae spp. (uña de gato).

Handles for tools such as chisels, hammers and saws were frequently made of *Crescentia cujete* (mate), which also was used in gun stocks. Another important tool was the needle for weaving fishing nets. This needle was made of *Coccoloba ruiziana* (licuanco). Shovels were made from *Tecoma castanifolia* (muyuyo macho). Finally, statues of saints were carved from *Bursera graveolens* (palo santo), no doubt due to its relative uncorruptibility owing to its resinous properties.

Textiles

The manufacture of textiles represents one further branch of vernacular knowledge which lays outside the ken of the male participants in the interviews. It is of interest, consequently, to compare the extent of the combined knowledge of the men regarding the weaving of cotton with that exhibited by the most accomplished weaver still living on the island. This will give some idea of the sorts of limitations that must be taken into account when considering data provided by the islanders in relation to a field that lies beyond their own experience. Plants used in the production of textiles are shown in Table 23.

The seven male informants mentioned but three woven articles: saddle bags, table clothes, and ponchos. The female weaver, on the other hand, speaks of 15 different articles. Besides the three articles mentioned by the male islanders, she remembers tote bags, braids, hammocks, sheets, bed spreads, napkins, mariner's ponchos, belts, large tote bags, shirt fronts, *guruperas*, cords, and harness straps for animals.

Regarding the plants involved in the weaving of cotton, the seven men mention the following plants as sources of fiber: brown cotton (probably *Gossypium hirsutum*), cocre cotton (probably *Gossypium hirsutum*), criollo cotton (probably *Gossypium hirsutum*), kapok-tree (*Ceiba trichistandra*), *Cochlospermum vitifolium* (bototillo), *Pachira* sp. (capó), *Pseudobombax millei* (beldaco), and an unidentified species (albaricoque). The master weaver insists that the fiber taken from the kapok-tree (*Ceiba trichistandra*) cannot be used to spin. She also mentions eight kinds of cotton. In addition to the three cottons mentioned by the islanders, she adds the following: white cotton (probably *Gossypium hirsutum*), chillado cotton (probably *Gossypium hirsutum*), and wild cotton (*Gossypium barbadense*). She also mentions two kinds of brown cotton, to wit, light brown cotton (probably *Gossypium hirsutum*), and reddish-brown cotton

Table 23. Plants used in the manufacture of textiles or as ticking on Puná Island.

	Vernacular Name	Scientific Name
Fibre Plants		
cotton for textiles	algodón blanco	probably *Gossypium hirsutum*
	algodón cocre	probably *Gossypium hirsutum*
	algodón chillado	probably *Gossypium hirsutum*
	algodón criollo	probably *Gossypium hirsutum*
	algodón pardo	probably *Gossypium hirsutum*
	algodón de monte	*Gossypium barbadense*
ticking	albaricoque	not recognized
	beldaco	*Pseudobombax millei*
	bototillo	*Cochlospermum vitifolium*
	capó	*Pachira* sp.
	ceibo	*Ceiba trichistandra*
Woods used for the loom		
battens	chonta	*Bactris* sp.
	madera negra	*Tabebuia billbergii*
heddles	negrito	*Achatocarpus pubescens*
	muyuyo	*Cordia lutea*
loom bars	guayacán	*Tabebuia chrysantha*
	licuanco	*Coccoloba ruiziana*
	madera negra	*Tabebuia billbergii*
spindles	chonta	*Bactris* sp.
	madera seca	*Geoffroea spinosa*
temple rods	chiquihua	*Byttneria parviflora*
	guasmo	*Guazuma ulmifolia*
	muyuyo	*Cordia lutea*
warping boards	balsa	*Ochroma pyramidale*
	muyuyo	*Cordia lutea*

(probably *Gossypium hirsutum*). It is furthermore stated that the seeds of the two latter land-races have been lost and that there have been a general demise of cotton as a cash crop during the past 30 years.

Insofar as the plants used in the loom are concerned, the islanders mention only *Byttneria parviflora* (chiquihua), which serves as the temple rod; though none of them indicate this. The weaver, on the other hand, mentions loom bars made of *Tabebuia billbergii* (madera negra) or *Tabebuia chrysantha* (guayacán), shed rods made of *Cordia lutea* (muyuyo), *Guazuma ulmifolia* (guasmo), or cane (*Guadua* sp.), battens made of *Tabebuia billbergii* (madera negra) or *Bactris* sp. (chonta), heddles made of what is supposedly *Achatocarpus pubescens* (negrito), or *Cordia lutea* (muyuyo), temple rods that were made either of *Byttneria parviflora* (chiquihua) or a piece of flexible cane (*Guadua* sp.). The islanders did not mention some important auxiliary equipment involved in the spinning process, whereas the weaver recalls *Cordia lutea* (muyuyo) stands, spindles of *Geoffroea spinosa* (madera seca), *Bactris* sp. (chonta), or a strip of cane (*Guadua* sp.), warping boards of *Ochroma pyramidale* (balsa), and warping posts of *Cordia lutea* (muyuyo).

Miscellaneous Uses

Besides the uses mentioned so far, the islanders recalled a number of applications which are best characterized as miscellaneous. Some of the plants were considered ornamentals, either on account of their attractive flowers or due to their agreeable aroma. This is by far the most numerous of the so-called miscellaneous categories, 19 different plants being mentioned as ornamentals, along with two which were remembered for their agreeable perfume (Table 24).

Some 11 different plants were given household applications. Brooms were made of *Sida* spp. (escoba and escoba de castilla). A source of soap for the washing of clothes was *Sapindus saponaria* (jaboncillo). The ashes of the kapok-tree (*Ceiba trichistandra*) were likewise mentioned as having played an important role in the domestic manufacture of soap. Scrubbers for use in the kitchen in washing dishes were provided by *Luffa sepium* (esponjillo). Vessels and cups and bowls were made from coconut shells (*Cocos nucifera*), and from the tree gourd (*Crescentia cujete*). Also, roofing was made possible by taking advantage of the leaves of the coconut palm (*Cocos nucifera*).

Plants which were important in field work included sources of cordage, as well as flexible lianas which were used in the making of saddles for donkeys and horses. Some of the sources of cordage were used for tying up sacks. These included 5 different species: *Arrabidaea corallina* (bejuco blanco), *Ipomoea ophioides* (bejuco pachón), *Agave* sp. or *Furcraea* sp. (cabuya), *Avicennia germinans* (mangle salado), and *Trema micrantha* (sapán de paloma). The cordage used for heavier lashings on rafts and in the making of fences included *Tetrapterys jamesonii* (bejuco canelo), *Mansoa* spp. (bejuco de ajo macho) — which was also used in the saddles —, and *Macranthisiphon longiflorus* (bejuco de hilar corral).

Sources of vegetable dyes, glue, and hair wax were also mentioned. There were evidently at least four sources of dyes. These were *Rhizophora mangle* (mangle blanco and mangle colorado), *Achatocarpus pubescens* (negrita de cerro), *Cocos nucifera* (palma de coco), and *Hylocereus polyrhizus* (pitajaya). *Cordia lutea* (muyuyo hembra) was used in the preparation of hair wax, and *Wedelia grandiflora* (resina de varita) were cited as sources of glue.

A number of plants were used as toys. *Guadua* sp. (caña guadúa) provided the framework for kites. Also, a game like marbles was played using the hard round seeds of *Sapindus saponaria* (jaboncillo). The calyx of *Physalis angulata* (chapuca and chapuca morada) was used by children to play practical jokes on one another; by inflating like a ballon, the practical joker could surprise another, suddenly popping the inflated calyx against the other's forehead.

Finally, *Hylocereus polyrhizus* (pitajaya) was employed as a source of non-permanent dye during the celebration of carnival when it served as a reddish color to water which was custumarily splashed on fellow celebrants.

Wreaths were made from an ornamental which possibly is *Gomphrena globosa* (siempreviva) and left on the graves in the cemetery by mourners.

Table 24. Plants of miscellaneous uses on Puná Island.

	Vernacular name	Scientific name
cordage for rafts, corrals, and fences	bejuco canelo	*Tetrapterys jamesonii*
	bejuco de hilar corral	*Macranthisiphon longiflorus*
	bejuco de ajo macho	*Mansoa hymenaea*
	bejuco de ajo macho	*Mansoa verrucifera*
cordage for sacks	cabuya	*Agave* sp. or *Furcraea* sp.
	bejuco blanco	*Arrabidaea corallina*
	mangle salado	*Avicennia germinans*
	bejuco pachón	*Ipomoea ophioides*
	sapán de paloma	*Trema micrantha*
dyes	negrita de cerro	*Achatocarpus pubescens*
	palma de coco	*Cocos nucifera*
	pitajaya	*Hylocereus polyrhizus*
	mangle blanco	*Rhizophora mangle*
fish poison	barbasco	*Jacquinia sprucei*
glue	muyuyo hembra	*Cordia lutea*
	resina de varita	*Wedelia grandiflora*
hair wax	muyuyo hembra	*Cordia lutea*
household brooms	escoba (de castilla)	*Sida* spp.
nets	barbasco	*Jacquinia sprucei*
ornamentals (selection only)	birondesa	*Caesalpinia pulcherrima*
	buenas tardes	*Mirabilis jalapa*
	chavelita	*Catharanthus roseus*
	laurel de jardín	*Nerium oleander*
	peregrina	*Hibiscus rosa-sinensis*
perfume	reseda	*Lawsonia inermis*
	cananga	not recognised
roofing	palma de coco	*Cocus nucifera*
saddles	bejuco de ajo macho	*Mansoa hymenaea*
	bejuco de ajo macho	*Mansoa verrucifera*
soap for washing of clothes	jaboncillo	*Sapindus saponaria*
soap for washing (previously used)	ceiba	*Ceiba trichistandra*
tabaco for cigarettes	tabaco	*Nicotiana tabacum*
toys for children – games	pitajaya	*Hylocereus polyrhizus*
	chapuca	*Physalis angulata*
toys for children - kites	caña guadúa	*Guadua angustifolia*
vessels and cups	palma de coco	*Cocus nucifera*
	mate	*Crescentia cujete*
	bejuco canelo	*Tetrapterys jamesonii*
washing dishes	esponjillo	*Luffa sepium*
wreaths for the cementary	siempreviva	*Gomphrena globosa?*

Ethnolinguistic Observations

The vernacular plant names recorded in the interviews provide evidence of both diachronic and synchronic significance. Diachronically, there is evidence of possible relationship between the pre-Columbian language spoken on the island, *Puneño*, *Cha'palaachi* (Cayapa), *Tsafiqui* (Colorado), and *Quechua*. Synchronically, there is evidence of dialectal variation.

Traces of the pre-Columbian nominal classification system shared by

Cha'palaachi and *Tsafiqui* (F. Avilés, pers. comm.) are to be found in the following vernacular plant names: chichihua (*Psittacanthus chanduyensis),* chiquihua (*Byttneria parviflora),* and chapuca (*Physalis angulata*). This system distinguished between the long, extended and flexible and the compact, unified, and dense. The forms in *Cha'palaachi* which mark this distinction are 'chuhua' and 'puca'.

Psittacanthus chanduyensis (chichihua) has oblong leaves. *Byttneria parviflora* (chiquihua) produces a fruit which bears spine-like tubercles and its long thin branches stripped of their thorns serve as the temple rod in the loom. It should be noted in regard to the last, that it is both the name of the part of the loom and the vernacular name of the plant itself. Furthermore, it was the only part of the loom mentioned by the participants in the congresses. Finally, *Physalis angulata* (chapuca) produces an edible, berry-like seed which served island children in their games of marbles. In *Tsafiqui* 'eyeball' is kaka.

Another relation with Tsafiqui is suggested by the term 'chayo' which was mentioned as a use for *Coccoloba ruiziana* (licuanco). In *Tsafiqui* the 'chayo' is a kind of basket to carry firewood (Juan Aguavil, pers. comm.). However, this could well be a Spanish loan word which has entered *Tsafiqui*, since in Chile the same term is used to denominate a sieve (Presley Norton, pers. comm.). A Quechua suffix, '-yuyu', is found in the vernacular name for *Cordia lutea* (muyuyo hembra) (Olaf Holm, pers. comm.). Other forms such as Jambelí (the name of the channel which separates the island from the mainland on the southeastern side) and *Conocarpus erecta* (jelí) reveal a pre-Columbian suffix which may be identified as '-eli' (Olaf Holm, pers. comm.).

Certain indigenous, pre-Columbian names for mangrove species have come down to us. It is likely that these names were in use on Puná Island before the arrival of the Europeans. The species known to Spanish speakers as mangle blanco 'white mangrove' (*Avicennia germinans*) was said to be called cereiba in the native tongue. It was compared to the willow due to its whitish flowers and leaves covered with white salt crystals. A second species (*Laguncularia racemosa*) characterized by beautiful shinny round green leaves and bitter seeds as thick as walnuts was called cereibuna in the indigenous vernacular. A third species was said to be much bigger than the two former trees. It was known in Spanish as mangle negro 'black mangrove' (*Rhizophora mangle*) and as guapareiba in the vernacular.

Dialect Areas

There was generel agreement amongst the native speakers concerning the vernacular plant names on the island except for 13 names (Table 25). These 13 names may be taken as diagnostic lexical items which suggest dialect areas on Puná Island. The distribution of the variation in vernacular names for these plants suggests the existence of two dialect areas separated by an intermediate

Table 25. Plants species with more than one vernacular name on Puná Island.

	Puná Nueva	Zapote	Río Hondo	Bellavista	Campo Alegre	Puná Vieja
Achatocarpus pubescens						
negrita de cerro				+		
negrito				+		
palo de cruz						+?
Avicennia germinans						
mangle salado	+					
palo salado				+		
Bauhinia aculeata						
espino colorado	+	+	+		+	
pica, picapica						+
Byttneria parviflora						
barbaimanta	+	+	+			
chiquihua				+	+	+
Capparis heterophylla						
palo de rana, rana						+
palo prieto			+			
Croton rivinifolius						
chala				+		+
palosangre	+	+				
Erythrina velutina						
capué				+	+	+
porotillo	+	+				
Leucaena trichodes						
aguia					+	+
pelacaballo	+	+	+	+		
Mimosa debilis						
tapatapa	+	+	+	+		+
uña de gato					+	
Psittacanthus chanduyensis						
chichihua		+		+	+	
hierba de pajarito	+	+	+			+
Randia sp.						
crucita						+
jazmín de cruz					+	
Rhizophora mangle						
gateado				+		
mangle blanco	+	+	+	+	+	+
mangle colorado	+	+	+	+	+	+
Senna tora						
fréjol de monte			+		+	
cafetillo		+				+
Spondias purpurea						
ciruela	+	+	+	+	+	+
jobo	+	+	+	+	+	+
Wedelia grandiflora						
miracielo					+	
trementina						+
resina de varita	+	+	+	+		

Table 26. Differences in vernacular plant naming on Puná Island and the Santa Elena peninsula. Source for the Santa Elena peninsula: Quimi and Stothert (1994).

	Puná Island	Santa Elena peninsula
Achatocarpus pubescens	negrita de cerro, palo de cruz	sebastián
Crescentia cujete	mate	mate longollo
Ipomoea carnea	florón	mata cabra
Maytenus octogona	patacón	arallan
Muntingia calabura	niguito	frutilla, niguito
Psittacanthus chanduyensis	chichihua, hierba de pajarito	caguachivo
Scutia spicata	pechiche (silvestre)	capay
Vallesia glabra	perlilla	monteverde

zone. Puná Nueva, Zapote, and Río Hondo constitute the northern dialect area, while the southern area is represented by Puná Vieja. Bellavista and Campo Alegre fall in an intermediate position, in some cases coincides with the northern zone, in others with the southern.

In Campo Alegre, *Bauhinia aculeata* is known as espino colorado, just as it is in the north, and in the distinction with Puná Vieja, where it is called pica or picapica. But on the other hand, *Erythrina velutina* and *Leucaena trichodes* are denominated as capué and aguia respectively, in accord with the terms employed in Puná Vieja and in contrast with Puná Nueva and Zapote, where these species are called porotillo and pelacaballo. A similar ambivalence can be observed in the vernacular names used in Bellavista for this plants. Nevertheless, there is a generel tendency for both Bellavista and Campo Alegre to be more closely in agreement with the southern dialect area than with the northern. Note in addition to the above mentioned distinctions, the distributions of the terms chiquihua and chala (*Byttneria parviflora* and *Croton rivinifolius*) in opposition to the northern zone's barbaimanta and palosangre.

The contrast between the island and the mainland is manifested in a number of vernacular plant names, as indicated by an informant in his remarks concerning *Mimosa debilis* (tapatapa), which he noted was called cariño de suegra in Vinces and Chone. Another plant that highlights this distinction is *Rhizophora mangle*, which is known on the mainland as mangle rojo, mangle verdadero, or less frequently mangle blanco and mangle colorado. On Puná Island this species is generally known as mangle blanco, and gateado and mangle colorado are used only occasionally to distinguish woods with specific, and in part inferior, qualities. Some notable differences in the vernacular plant naming between the island and the adjoining Santa Elena peninsula are highlighted in Table 26.

The few documented mainland data availiable to us further suggest that the variation in vernacular names is much less pronounced if the island is compared with the Guayas province instead of the neighboring provinces of El Oro and Manabí. *Cochlospermum vitifolium* is known as bototillo in Guayas, but

Plate 1. *Top*: Rocks visited by sea birds in the Morro channel west of Puná Island. In previous centuries naval traffic to Guayaquil avoided this dangerous passage and went east of Puná Island through the Jambelí channel (see inside front cover). *Bottom*: View of anchorage in Puná Nueva the principal town of Puná Island.

Plate 2. *Top*: Salt marsh with halophytic succulents and shrubs along the edges. The central part lacks vegetation due to the high salt concentration. *Bottom*: Cleared mangrove invaded by *Salicornia*.

Plate 3. *Top*: Mangrove vegetation with stands of red mangrove, *Rhizophora mangle*, along estuary at low tide. *Bottom*: The aerial roots of the red mangrove reach several meters lenght.

Plate 4. *Top*: Seasonal pond with floathing *Pistia stratiotes* bordered by exuberant vegetation in April near the end of the rainy season. *Bottom*: Close-up showing aquatic vegetation dominated by *Nymphaea ampla, Neptunia oleracea* and sedges.

Plate 5. *Top*: The thorn scrub is overgrown by twining vines in April near the end of the rainy season. *Bottom*: Savanna vegetation with a typical broad-crowned tree and browsing goats

Plate 6. *Top*: Thorn forests dominated by the kapok-tree *Ceiba trichistandra*, a species endemic to southwest Ecuador and adjacent Peru. Photo taken during rainy season with dense undergrowth. *Bottom*: Fruiting kapok-tree during the dry season (photo from nearby Manta on the continental plain).

Plate 7. *Top*: View of the dry forest from Ramón hill with Pozo de la Lechuza in the horizon. *Bottom*: Close-up showing dense stands of dry forest.

Plate 8. *Top*: When the vegetation is cleared for agricultural purposes, the wood is often used as firewood. *Bottom*: Trunks of red mangrove, *Rhizophora mangle*, is used for timber and charcoal.

Plate 9. *Top*: Small-scale shrimp farm built by Puná islanders along an estuary near Bellavista. *Bottom*: Construction site for a new large-scale shrimp farm near Puná Nueva in 1998.

Plate 10. *Top left*: Fruit of the soursop, *Annona muricata*. *Top right*: Fruit of the sweetsop, *Annona squamosa*, another widely cultivated species of the Annonaceae found on Puná Island. *Bottom*: Flower of the passion fruit, *Passiflora edulis*.

Plate 11. Orchard with hog-plum, *Spondias purpurea*. Close-up showing inflorescence and unripe fruit.

Plate 12. *Top*: Indigenous cotton, *Gossypium barbadense*, was of major importance in the early agriculture on Puná Island. *Bottom*: Locally produced textiles based on traditional design.

Plate 13. *Top left*: The barbasco-tree, *Jacquinia sprucei,* has poisonous fruits that are collected and used to eliminate fry in the shrimp farms. *Top right*: The cactus, cardón, *Armatocereus cartwrightianus,* has edible fruits. The stout spines were once used by weavers as needles. *Bottom*: Trunk of fallen kapok-tree, *Ceiba trichistandra*. The kapok is still collected by a few islanders and used for ticking.

Plate 14. *Top left*: The tree gourd, *Crescentia cujete*, is a tree with multiple uses that occurs semi-cultivated on the island. *Top right*: The vine *Cucurbita ecuadorensis* is probably the only wild species of *Cuburbita* in America. The fruit of this species may have been used as a bowl or a cup since ancient times. *Bottom left and right*: Habit and close-up showing *Leptochiton quitoensis*, a bulbose species often found in deep soils in the fields.

Plate 15. *Top*: *Byttneria parviflora* is known as 'barbaimanta' and 'chiquihua' on Puná Island. The latter name may have roots in the indigenous language once spoken on the island. *Bottom*: *Croton rivinifolius* is known by the Puná islanders as 'chala' and 'palos-angre' and is an example showing the existence of separate dialect areas on the island. Both species are endemic to southwest Ecuador and adjacent Peru.

Plate 16. School children mounting plant specimens in a high school in Puná Nueva. Vernacular knowledge on plants and their uses is a branch of wisdom threatened by extinction on Puná Island because the knowledge is only shared by the elders and no longer transmitted to the younger generation. As part of the present project a small herbarium was set up in collaboration with a local school on Puná Island.

Table 27. Vernacular plant names used for more than one species on Puná Island.

escoba	pechiche	trementina
Sida rhombifolia	*Scutia spicata*	*Bidens rubifolia*
Sida spinosa	*Tournefortia bicolor*	*Wedelia grandiflora*
esponjillo	*Vitex gigantea*	uña de gato
Cucumis anguria	pegajoso	*Acacia tenuifolia*
Cucumis dipsaceus	*Boerhavia diffusa*	*Mimosa acantholoba*
Luffa sepium	*Boerhavia erecta*	*Mimosa debilis*
flor de abejón	*Plumbago scandens*	*Piptadenia flava*
Senna mollissima	pegapega	verdolaga
Senna pistaciifolia	*Mentzelia aspera*	*Bacopa monniera*
palito blanco	*Pisonia aculeata*	*Portulaca oleracea*
Casearia mariquitensis	*Pisonia floribunda*	*Sesuvium portulacastrum*
Cordia macrosephala	*Plumbago scandens*	vidrillo
Lippia americana	rabo de gallo	*Batis maritima*
palo salado	*Amaranthus spinosus*	*Salicornia fruticosa*
Avicennia germinans	*Heliotropium indicum*	
Cryptocarpus pyriformis	*Tournefortia bicolor*	

is called polopolo in El Oro. Likewise chirigoyo is used for *Eriotheca ruizii* in the Guayas province, but is called jaile in the Manabí province. It will be impossible to draw any but the most tentative conclusions about the vernacular linguistic context of the island before the necessary study materials become available.

The diachronic evidence may be interpreted by assuming that *Puneño* was genetically related to *Cha'palaachi* and *Tsafiqui*, and that due to borrowing, linguistic loan words from Quechua were also incorporated. *Puneño* would probably have been related to the languages used by other nations in the League of Merchants, and to the pre-incan languages spoken on the northern Peruvian coast. However, inasmuch as these languages are now extinct, such considerations may very well never go beyond being purely speculative and unprovable.

Finally, it may be added that a number of vernacular names are used collectively for a large number of species with identical characteristics or appearance (Table 27). Escoba is for example used for all species of *Sida* which are useful for making a broom. Esponjillo is used for a multitude of vines in the Cucurbitaceae although only one of the species is actually used for washing. Pegajoso and pegapega are used for all kind of herbs, shrubs, or trees that have adhering or clinging fruits, while uña de gato are spinescent plants in the Mimosaceae family causing rashes.

5

Keys and Plant Descriptions

The Flora of Puná Island provides brief descriptions and keys to identification of native and naturalised species on Puná Island in the Gulf of Guayaquil. Common cultivated species are also included in the keys but not described.

We have attempted to include all known native and important cultivated species but the coverage is nevertheless incomplete for certain groups, such as grasses and sedges, beach plants, weeds and species of highly seasonal nature (aquatics, annual vines, *etc.*). In addition to its use on Puná Island it is expected that the Flora can also be used to identify many plant species found in the semi-arid littoral zone of Ecuador and adjacent Peru.

A number of floras covering small areas of western Ecuador have appeared during the past decades and often proven particularly useful for plant identification. They include the illustrated floras of the Río Palenque Science Center (Dodson and Gentry 1978) and Jauneche (Dodson *et al.* 1985), as well as floristic works on the Santa Elena peninsula (Valverde *et al.* 1979) and the Cordillera Chongon-Colonche (Valverde *et al.* 1991), notwithstanding the prime flora of the Galapagos Islands by Wiggins and Porter (1971).

The plant descriptions in this Flora are based on the specimens cited and information from the literature. We have attempted to make the Flora detailed enough to allow identifications without illustrations. The principal literature consulted includes the *Flora of Ecuador* (Harling and Sparre, eds. 1973–1986, Harling and Andersson, eds. 1986–1999), the *Flora of Peru*, the *Flora de Venezuela* and, of course, the *Flora of the Galapagos Islands* (Wiggins and Porter 1971). Another valuable source has been the catalogues of the higher plants of Ecuador (Jørgensen and León-Yánez 1999) and Peru (Brako and Zarucchi 1993), and the W^3Tropicos-database of the Missouri Botanical Garden.

The plant specimens used for the present flora were gathered by J. E. Madsen during April–December, 1987, and a few later visits. The herbarium material comprises approximately 1100 specimens. The first three sets are deposited at the herbaria of the University of Aarhus (AAU), the Pontificia Universidad Católica del Ecuador (QCA), and the Museo Nacional de Ciencias Naturales in Quito (QCNE). Some additional specimens are deposited at Universidad Estatal de Guayaquil (GUAY). Acronyms according to Holmgren *et al.* 1990. Only a few species were included without reference specimens. The majority of the specimens were identified by specialists. Family delimitation follows Cronquist (1981) for the dicotyledons and Dahlgren *et al.* (1985) for the monocotyledons, while author abbreviations follow Brummitt and Powell (1992).

   The flora is organized alphabetically by families, genera, and species. Ferns (Filicopsida) are treated separately. Keys to the families and species are based on fertile material, notably flowers in case of herbaceous plants and fruits and seeds for the woody plants. The species are numbered consecutively within each family and cultivated species (crops, ornamentals, planted trees, *etc.*) are marked with [cult.] after the name. Specimens cited as five or six digit numbers refer to specimens collected by Madsen *et al.* Specimens by other collectors are cited, when known, but have not been consulted. The area of distribution (origin of cultivated plants) is also indicated and it is mentioned if a species occurs on the Galapagos Islands according to Wiggins and Porter (1971) and Lawesson *et al.* (1987).

Key to Major Groups

1a. Plants without flowers, reproducing by microscopic spores, either terrestrial or
    epiphytic with the spores variously inserted on the underside of the leaves, or
    aquatic and less than 2 cm long with alternating leaves (ferns)   p. 115
1b. Plants with flowers (seed plants)
    2b. Plants wild
        3a. Aquatic and mangrove plants; emerging, floating or submersed   I, p. 102
        3b. Terrestrial (includes swamp plants)
            4a. Epiphytes, lianas, parasites (on other plants) or vines   II, p. 104
            4b. Herbs, shrubs or trees
                5a. Trees and shrubs (includes palm trees)   III, p. 106
                5b. Herbs and subshrubs   IV, p. 109
    2b. Plants cultivated   V, p. 113

I. Aquatic and Mangrove Plants

1a. Woody plants
    2a. Fruits longer than 15 cm   **Rhizophoraceae**
    2b. Fruits (or infructescence) to 3 cm long
        3a. Leaves opposite; flowers in distal clusters; pneumatophores (aerial root
            organs) numerous   (*Avicennia*) **Verbenaceae**
        3b. Leaves opposite or alternate, if opposite then flowers on elongated spikes;
            pneumatophores wanting   **Combretaceae**
1b. Herbaceous plants
    4a. Plants only a few mm long, forming floating colonies   **Lemnaceae**
    4b. Plants longer than 2 cm
        5a. Stems succulent, jointed; leaves lacking or rudimentary
                        (*Salicornia*) **Chenopodiaceae**
        5b. Stems not succulent; leaves present or lacking
            6a. Plants grass-like; leaves usually linear; flowers variously reduced, rarely
                colored
                7a. Inflorescence a stout, dimorphic cylinder, 20–50 cm long, with pistillate
                    flowers in lower half; flowers unisexual   **Typhaceae**
                7b. Inflorescence not as above; flowers bisexual or rarely unisexual
                    8a. Stem usually solid; nodes wanting; sheaths closed
                                Cyperaceae
                    8b. Stem usually terete, hollow; nodes often conspicuously swollen;
                      sheaths open or at least partially so   **Poaceae**
            6b. Plants not grass-like; leaves variable, if linear then less than 2 mm wide;
                flowers variable, often colored
                9a. Leaves to 2 mm wide, linear or filiform (Note: stoneworths, *Chara*, an
                    algae with filiform green thallus is also found on Puná Island)
                    10a. Stems bearing numerous 1–1.5 mm long bladders **Lentibulariaceae**
                    10b. Stems without bladders
                          11a. Spathe-like sheaths absent   **Najadaceae**
                        11b. Spathe-like sheaths present   **Potamogetonaceae**
            9b. Leaves broader than 3 mm
                12a. Leaves very thick, swollen or spongy; plants floating
                    13a. Leaves sessile, obovate-spathulate   **Araceae**
                    13b. Leaves petiolate, elliptic   **Hydrocharitaceae**
             12b. Leaves not very thick, neither swollen nor spongy; plants floating,
                immersed or emerging
                14a. Leaves compound
                    15a. Floating; inflorescence head-like   (*Neptunia*) **Mimosaceae**
                    15b. Rooted; inflorescence racemose   **Fabaceae**
                14b. Leaves simple
                  16a. Flowers 3-merous
                    17a. Leaves parallel-veined; flowers yellow   **Limnocharitaceae**
                    17b. Leaves digitately to pinnately veined;
                      flowers white or blue
                      18a. Flowers not exceeding the spathe; leaf-base rounded

                                                                   Marantaceae

18b. Flowers exceeding the spathe, if only slightly so then
    with cordate leaf-base; leaf-base variable
        19a. Flowers inserted in whorls of 4–10   **Alismataceae**
        19b. Flowers inserted in spikes or panicles, not in
            separate whorls   **Pontederiaceae**
16b. Flowers 4–5(–many)-merous
    20a. Flowers 10 cm wide   **Nymphaeaceae**
    20b. Flowers less than 2 cm wide   **Scrophulariaceae**

II. Epiphytes, Lianas, Parasites, and Vines

1a. Plants parasitic on other plants, with or without chlorophyll
    2a. Leaves and sometimes also the stems wanting when in flower   **Cuscutaceae**
    2b. Leaves and stems present   **Loranthaceae**
1b. Plants not parasitic
    3a. Epiphytes
        4a. Stems trigonous, succulent, spiny   (*Hylocereus*) **Cactaceae**
        4b. Stems not as above
            5a. Leaves linear
                6a. Leaves grey-white; pseudobulb absent   **Bromeliaceae**
                6b. Leaves green; pseudobulb present   **Orchidaceae**
            5b. Leaves broad   **Piperaceae**
    3b. Lianas or vines
        7a. Leaves compound
            8a. Stems spiny   **Mimosaceae**
            8b. Stems spineless
                9a. Leaves opposite
                    10a. Flowering heads with tubular disc flowers and ligulate ray flowers;
                        fruit an achene   (*Pseudogynoxys*) **Asteraceae**
                    10b. Flowers tubular funnel-formed; fruit a capsule   **Bignoniaceae**
                9b. Leaves alternate
                    11a. Flowers papilionaceous; fruit a pod   **Fabaceae**
                    11b. Flowers not papilionaceous; fruit a berry or a capsule
                        12a. Tendrils present
                            13a. Fruit 3-winged or bladder-like   **Sapindaceae**
                            13b. Fruit a berry   **Vitaceae**
                      12b. Tendrils absent
                          14a. Leaves 4–7-foliolate   **Convolvulaceae**
                        14b. Leaves 3-foliolate   (*Allophylus*) **Sapindaceae**
        7b. Leaves simple, often deeply lobed
            15a. Leaves opposite
                16a. Fruits shorter than 3 cm; petals clawed   **Malpighiaceae**
                16b. Fruits longer than 8 cm; petals not clawed
                    17a. Flowers rotate; seeds wooly   **Asclepiadaceae**
                    17b. Flowers tubular funnel-formed; seeds winged   **Bignoniaceae**
            15b. Leaves alternate
                18a. Tendrils present
                  19a. Fruits less than 1 cm long; inflorescence opposed to a leaf   **Vitaceae**
                  19b. Fruits longer than 1 cm; inflorescence usually not leaf-opposed
                    20a. Bracts wanting; flowers uni-sexual, without annular corona of
                      filaments   **Cucurbitaceae**
                    20b. Bracts present; flowers bi-sexual, with conspicuous annular
                      corona of filaments between the corolla and the androecium
                        Passifloraceae
              18b. Tendrils absent
                21a. Leaves peltate

22a. Flowers white, minute; fruit a drupe **Menispermaceae**
22b. Flowers orange red, 5 cm long; fruit a schizocarp **Tropaeolaceae**
21b. Leaves not peltate, the petiole joined at base of leaf-blade
    23a. Inflorescence enclosed by two conspicuous foliose bracts
                              (*Dalechampia*) **Euphorbiaceae**
    23b. Inflorescence not enclosed by two conspicuous bracts
        24a. Fruits 3-winged; flowers minute, white **Rhamnaceae**
        24b. Fruits not winged; flowers variable
            25a. Flowers sessile, yellow **Loasaceae**
            25b. Flowers pedicellate, of various colors **Convolvulaceae**

III. Shrubs and Trees

1a. Stems succulent; leaves absent   **Cactaceae**
1b. Stems not succulent; leaves present
  2a. Leaves compound
    3a. Leaves palmately compound
      4a. Seeds embedded in white wool; fruit a capsule   **Bombacaceae**
      4a. Seeds not embedded in white wool; fruit not a capsule
        5a. Shrub to 3 m high; fruit an achene   (*Bidens*) **Asteraceae**
        5b. Tree to 10 m high; fruit a drupe   (*Vitex*) **Verbenaceae**
    3b. Leaves pinnately compound
      6a. Plants a palm tree; fruit the coconut   **Arecaceae**
      6b. Plants not a palm tree
        7a. Trunks and twigs bearing thorn-like spines, the basis 3–5 mm wide on
          twigs and 1–2 cm wide on trunks; fruit splitting into two valves,
          exposing the black seeds   **Rutaceae**
        7b. Trunks and twigs with or without spines, if spiny then spines not as
          above; fruit not as above
          8a. Fruit dry
            9a. Fruit a pod, 2–to many-seeded
              10a. Flowers in densely crowded heads or fascicles; stamens
                long-exserted, conspicuous   **Mimosaceae**
              10b. Flowers usually in racemose inflorescences; stamens less
                conspicuous than the perianth
                11a. Flowers subactinomorphic; petals nearly equal
                        Caesalpiniaceae
                11b. Flowers papilionaceous; petals distinctly heteromorphic,
                  the upper forms the standard, the two lateral the wings,
                  and the lower two the keel   **Fabaceae**
            9b. Fruit drupaceous or samaroid, 1-seeded
              12a. Leaflets entire   (*Geoffroea* or *Machaerium*) **Fabaceae**
              12b. Leaflets serrate   (*Loxopterygium*) **Anacardiaceae**
          8b. Fruit fleshy
            13a. Fruit 1 cm long; leaflets crenate   **Burseraceae**
            13b. Fruit 2–3 cm long, sticky; leaflets entire   **Sapindaceae**
  2b. Leaves simple
    14a. Fruit 1–1.5 cm long, bearing 5–10 longitudinal rows of black trichomes;
      flowers unisexual; staminate ones campanulate, pistillate ones tubular
                  (*Pisonia*) **Nyctaginaceae**
    14b. Fruit and flowers not as above
      15a. Fruit an achene, often with pappus; inflorescence a compound head on a
        receptacle, superficially resembling a 'flower'   **Asteraceae**
      15b. Fruit not an achene; inflorescence not as above
        16a. Leaves opposite
          17a. Interpetiolar stipules broadly ovate, caducous or persistent, if
            caducous then short-shoots bearing clusters of 3–4 spines **Rubiaceae**
          17b. Interpetioaler stipules wanting or inconspicuous

18a. Petiole 0–5 mm long and stem 4-angled; fruit a capsule;
    stamens 8–12   **Lythraceae**

18b. Petiole 2–30 mm long, if less than 5 mm long then stem terete;
    fruit not a capsule; stamens 2 or 4   **Verbenaceae**

16b. Leaves alternate or fasciculate

  19a. Stems spiny, the spines sometimes caducous

    20a. Leaves bilobed   (*Bauhinia*) **Caesalpiniaceae**

    20b. Leaves not bilobed

      21a. Fruits smooth, at least somewhat fleshy   **Rhamnaceae**

      21b. Fruits echinate (spinescent), dry   (*Byttneria*) **Sterculiaceae**

  19b. Stems spineless

    22a. Gynophore present, fruits superior to a distinctive node on stalk
                                                      Capparaceae

    22b. Gynophore absent

      23a. Filaments numerous, fused into a tube surrounding the style;
        fruit a capsule or a schizocarp; stellate hairs usually present
                                                     Malvaceae

      23b. Filaments few or numerous but, not inserted as above; fruits
        variable, sometimes as above; stellate hairs absent or present

        24a. Flowers in a subglobose head, 0.5 cm long; infructescence
          1–1.5 cm long, cone-like; halophytic shrubs
                              (*Conocarpus*) **Combretaceae**

        24b. Inflorescence and infructescence not as above

          25a. Petiole of most leaves longer than 1 cm

            26a. Seeds embedded in wool; fruit a capsule

              27a. Trees, taller than 5 m

                28a. Fruits less than 10 cm long; leaves deeply lobed
                                        Bixaceae

                28b. Fruits longer than 15 cm; leaves shallowly
                  lobed   **Bombacaceae**

              27b. Shrubs, mostly 1–2 m tall
                            (*Ipomoea carnea*) **Convolvulaceae**

            26b. Seeds not embedded in wool; fruit variable

              29a. Inflorescence spicate with uni-sexual flowers;
                fruits 3-parted   **Euphorbiaceae**

              29b. Inflorescence and fruits not as above

                30a. Trees, mostly 5–10 m tall

                  31a. Leaves serrate, pubescent
                            (*Muntingia*) **Flacourtiaceae**

                  31b. Leaves entire, glabrous   **Moraceae**

                30b. Shrubs, less than 5 m tall

                  32a. Fruit a berry, 8–10 mm wide; stamens
                    inserted on the corolla tube   **Solanaceae**

                32b. Fruit and stamens not as above

                  33a. Leaves covered with stellate hairs; fruit
                    at least 3 mm long

                    34a. Fruit spineless (*Waltheria*) **Sterculiaceae**

                    34b. Fruit spiny   (*Triumfetta*) **Tiliaceae**

33b. Leaves with simple hairs; fruit 1 mm
wide   (*Cryptocarpus*) **Nyctaginaceae**
25b. Petiole of most leaves indistinct or shorter than 1 cm
34a. Stamens numerous, long-exserted; fruits 2–4 cm
wide yellowish, edible   **Myrtaceae**
34b. Stamens to ca. 10; fruits variable, not as above
35a. Leaves serrate
36a. Flowers and fruits longer than 4 mm
(*Casearia*) **Flacourtiaceae**
36b. Flowers and fruits to 3 mm long   **Ulmaceae**
35b. Leaves subentire
37a. Fruits longer than 2 cm
38a. Fruit 2–5 cm long
39a. Fruit elongated, winged (a samara)
(*Securidaca*) **Polygalaceae**
39b. Fruit globose, not winged
40a. Largest leaves more than 2 cm wide,
not mucronate   **Ebenaceae**
40b. Largest leaves less than 2 cm wide,
mucronate   **Theophrastaceae**
38b. Fruit 10–20 cm wide
(*Crescentia*) **Bignoniaceae**
37b. Fruit 0.4–2 cm long
41a. Fruit a berry, 8–10 mm wide; stamens
inserted on the corolla tube   **Solanaceae**
41b. Fruit and stamens not as above
42a. Leaves generally less than 2.5 cm wide
43a. Fruits 3–4-parted
44a. Fruit dehiscent by four valves
Celastraceae
44b. Fruit 3-merous
(*Phyllanthus*) **Euphorbiaceae**
43b. Fruits not 3–4-parted
45a. Fruits elliptic, 1 cm long
Erythroxylaceae
45b. Fruits globose, 1–2 cm long
Malpighiaceae
42b. Larger leaves more than 2.5 cm wide
46a. Trees, to 8 m tall
47a. Plants pubescent in distal parts;
fruits ellipsoid   **Achaetocarpaceae**
47b. Plants essentially glabrous; fruits
globose   **Opiliaceae**
46b. Shrubs, 0.5–6 m tall
48a. Leaves decurrent at base
Goodeniaceae
48b. Leaves shallowly cordate at base
Polygonaceae

IV. Herbs and Subshrubs

1a. Inflorescence a compound head on a receptacle, superficially resembling a flower; flowers appear in centripetal sequence, variously divided into disc flowers and petaloid ray flowers; fruit an achene, often with pappus, or conspicuously prickled and 1 cm wide (in *Acanthospermum*) **Asteraceae**

1b. Inflorescence and flowers not as above; fruit only rarely an achene

  2a. Geophyte with subterranean bulb **Amaryllidaceae**

  2b. Not a geophyte

    3a. Stem-succulents without leaves or the leaves subulate

      4a. Stems armed with spines **Cactaceae**

      4b. Stems without spines **Chenopodiaceae**

    3b. Stem-succulents with leaves or not stem-succulent

      5a. Leaves alternate

        6a. Filaments numerous, fused into a tube surrounding the style; fruit a capsule or schizocarp; stellate hairs usually present **Malvaceae**

        6b. Filaments few or numerous, not inserted as above; fruit variable, sometimes as above; stellate hairs absent or present

          7a. Inflorescence usually appearing on a leaf-less stem, conspicuous with numerous pink flowers; leaves palmately 3–7-lobate **Caricaceae**

          7b. Inflorescence and leaves not as above

            8a. Leaves parellel-veined, usually linear and with a sheath at base; plants not grasslike or grasslike

              9a. Flowers perfect, white or blue; plants not grasslike **Commelinaceae**

              9b. Flowers various reduced, usually colorless; plants grasslike

                10a. Inflorescence a stout, dimorphic cylinder, 20–50 cm long, the pistillate flowers in lower half; flowers unisexual **Typhaceae**

                10b. Inflorescence not as above; flowers bisexual or rarely unisexual

                  11a. Stem usually trigonous, solid; nodes wanting; sheaths closed **Cyperaceae**

                  11b. Stem usually terete, hollow; nodes often conspicuously swollen; sheaths open or at least partially so **Poaceae**

            8b. Leaves not as above; plants not grasslike

              12a. Leaves compound

                13a. Leaves 3-foliolate; fruits a capsule **Oxalidaceae**

                13b. Leaves 2–many-foliolate; if 2–3-foliolate then fruits a pod

                  14a. Fruits a berry; flowers actinomorphic with 5 stamens **Solanaceae**

                14b. Fruits a pod; flowers more or less zygomorhic with 10 or fewer stamens

                  15a. Petals nearly equal **Caesalpiniaceae**

                  15b. Petals distinctly heteromorphic, the upper forms the standard, the two lateral the wings, and the lower two the keel **Fabaceae**

12b. Leaves simple
  16a. Fruit 3-lobed or 3-valvate
    17a. Flowers perfect, bisexual, orange   **Turneraceae**
    17b. Flowers variously reduced, unisexual, not orange
                                  Euphorbiaceae
  16b. Fruit not 3-parted
    18a. Inflorescenced a fleshy spikes, 0.5–2 mm wide; flowers
      barely discernible; leaves palmately 3–5-nerved
                                  Piperaceae
    18b. Inflorescence, flowers, and leaves not as above
      19a. Flowers unisexual with 1–2 mm long tepals or
        bisexual with 5 mm long tepals; inflorescence
        composed of axillary and terminal, compact or
        elongate spikes or the flowers in axillary clusters
                                Amaranthaceae
      19b. Flowers and fruits not as above
        20a. Flowers more or less zygomorphic
          21a. Flowers solitary   (*Lindernia*) **Scrophulariaceae**
          21b. Flowers in many-flowered inflorescences
            22a. Leaves crowded distally; inflorescence
              bracteate   (*Elytraria*) **Acanthaceae**
            22b. Leaves distributed along the stem;
              inflorescence not bracteate   **Polygalaceae**
        20b. Flowers actinomorphic
          23a. Inflorescence spicate
            24a. Calyx bearing stipitate glands
                            Plumbaginaceae
            24b. Calyx without stipitate glands
              25a. Fruit 2–3 mm long; inflorescence
                uncurling as the flowers opens
                              Boraginaceae
             25b. Fruit 6–10 mm long; inflorescence
                otherwise different   **Phytolaccaceae**
          23b. Inflorescence highly variable, but not spicate
            26a. Flowers unisexual, 1–2 mm wide, white;
              stems glandular hirsute   **Urticaceae**
            26b. Flowers and stems not as above
              27a. Stamens inserted on the corolla tube;
                fruit a berry or a capsule   **Solanaceae**
              27a. Stamens not as above; fruit not a berry
                28a. Leaves serrate; stellate hairs often
                  present
                  29a. Fruit to 1 cm long; flowers white
                    or violet, sometimes with yellow
                    center   **Sterculiaceae**
                  29b. Fruit 2–6 cm long; flowers yellow
                              Tiliaceae
                28b. Leaves entire; stellate hairs rarely
                present

29a. Capsule to 6 mm long
    30a. Flowers blue
        31a. Leaves more than 4 cm long
            Hydrophyllaceae
        31b. Leaves less than 4 cm long
            Convolvulaceae
    30b. Flowers white, pink, or yellow
        Portulacaceae
29b. Capsule longer than 8 mm
    32a. Stem bearing glochidiate hairs;
        leaves more or less 3-lobed
            Loasaceae
    32b. Stem without glochidiate hairs;
        leaves not 3-lobed   **Onagraceae**
5b. Leaves opposite
  33a. Leaves compound   **Zygophyllaceae**
  33b. Leaves simple, sometimes deeply lobed
    34a. Flowers solitary, concealed within the petiolar sheet   **Aizoaceae**
    34b. Flowers 1–numerous, not concealed within the petiolar sheet
      35a. Plants creeping to prostrate with succulent leaves
        36a. Leaves semi-amplexicaul at base; monoecious
            (*Blutaparon*) **Amaranthaceae**
        36b. Leaves sessile; dioecious   **Bataceae**
      35b. Plants of various habits, if creeping or prostrate then leaves not
        succulent
        37a. Leaves in whorls of 3–6 per node, leaf-margin entire
            Molluginaceae
        37b. Leaves paired, sometimes in a distal cluster of decussate
          pairs, or in whorls of 3–4 with leaf-margin distinctly serrate
          38a. Fruit 3-lobed   **Euphorbiaceae**
          38b. Fruit not 3-lobed
            39a. Inflorescence large and lax; flowers and fruit embedded
              in silvery white hairs   (*Iresine*) **Amaranthaceae**
            39b. Inflorescence, flowers, and fruit not as above
              40a. Inflorescence headlike
                41a. Flower-heads paired in each node
                  (*Phyla*) **Verbenaceae**
                41b. Flower-heads single or up to three per node, but
                  not in regular pairs   (*Alternanthera*) **Amaranthaceae**
              40b. Inflorescence variable, not head-like
                42a. Inflorescence composed of spikes or racemes
                  43a. Leaves entire
                    44a. Flowers green; fruit a downwards pointed
                      utricle   (*Achyranthes*) **Amaranthaceae**
                    44b. Flowers white; fruit a muricate capsule
                      Loganiaceae
                  43b. Leaves serrate   (*Priva*) **Verbenaceae**
              42b. Inflorescence not as above
                45a. Interpetiolar stipules present, sometimes

caducous or inconspicuous
46a. Interpetiolar sheaths without hyaline teeths; stems glabrous **Elatinaceae**
46b. Interpetiolar sheaths bearing hyaline teeths; stem pubescent or glabrous **Rubiaceae**
45b. Interpetiolar stipules lacking
47a. Flowers supported by bracts
48a. Flowers actinomorphic; stamens numerous, exserted; fruit indehiscent (*Mirabilis*) **Nyctaginaceae**
48b. Flowers zygomorphic; stamens 2–4 , not exserted; fruit a dehiscent capsule **Acanthaceae**
47b. Flowers not supported by bracts
49a. Fruit composed of 4 nutlets; flowers more or less bilabiate with 2 or 4 stamens **Lamiaceae**
49b. Fruit and flowers not as above
50a. Fruit a capsule
51a. Flowers 4-merous with 8 stamens **Lythraceae**
51b. Flowers 4–5-merous with 4–5 stamens
52a. Inflorescence dichotomously branched; flowers twisted in bud, actinomorphic **Gentianaceae**
52b. Inflorescence spiciform or the flowers solitary; flowers not twisted in bud, more or less zygomorphic **Scrophulariaceae**
50b. Fruit an achene (anthocarp) **Nyctaginaceae**

V. Cultivated Plants

1a. Plants with subterranean, edible fruits or roots
  2a. Roots fleshy and edible (root fruits); fruit a capsule
    3a. Plant a vine   (*Ipomoea batatas*) **Convolvulaceae**
    3b. Plant a shrub   (*Manihot*) **Euphorbiaceae**
  2b. Roots not fleshy and edible; fruit a nut (the groundnut)   (*Arachis*) **Fabaceae**
1b. Plants not with subterranean, edible roots or fruits
  4a. Plant a vine, producing edible vegetables or fruits
    5a. Bracts absent; flowers uni-sexual, without annular corona of filaments
      Cucurbitaceae
    5b. Bracts present; flowers bi-sexual, with conspicuous annular corona of
      filaments between the corolla and the androecium   **Passifloraceae**
  4b. Plant not a vine
    6a. Fruits a pod (legumes)
      7a. Flowers in densely crowded heads or fascicles; stamens long-exserted,
        conspicuous   **Mimosaceae**
      7b. Flowers usually in racemose inflorescences; stamens less conspicuous
        than the perianth
        8a. Flowers subactinomorphic; petals nearly equal   **Caesalpiniaceae**
        8b. Flowers papilionaceous; petals distinctly heteromorphic, the upper
          forms the standard, the two lateral the wings, and the lower two the
          keel   **Fabaceae**
    6b. Fruits variable, not a pod
      9a. Seeds surrounded by white wooly fibers
        10a. Trees, more than 5 m high   **Bombacaceae**
        10b. Shrubs, to 4 m high   (*Gossypium*) **Malvaceae**
      9b. Seeds not surrounded by white wooly fibers
        11a. Plants grass-like (grain crops)   **Poaceae**
        11b. Plants not grass-like
          12a. Plants grown for their edible fruits, medicine or wood
            13a. Plants a palm tree; fruit the coconut   (*Cocos*) **Arecaceae**
            13b. Plants not a palm tree
              14a. Herbs
                15a. Fruits 15–50 cm long; plants 2–8 m high   **Caricaceae**
                15b. Fruits generally 2–10 cm long; plants to 2 m high
                  16a. Leaves opposite; stamens 4   **Pedaliaceae**
                  16b. Leaves alternate; stamens 5   **Solanaceae**
              14b. Shrubs or trees
                17a. Inflorescence head-like   (*Lippia*) **Verbenaceae**
                17b. Inflorescense variable, not head-like
                  18a. Flesh of fruit consumed; fruit a berry or drupe
                    19a. Fruit 1 cm long   (*Coffea*) **Rubiaceae**
                    19b. Fruit longer than 2 cm
                      20a. Leaves alternate
                        21a. Leaves compound   **Anacardiaceae**
                        21b. Leaves simple

22a. Plants spiny (*Citrus*) **Rutaceae**
22b. Plants without spines
    23a. Seeds numerous per fruit, flesh of fruit
        white **Annonaceae**
    23b. Seeds 1–few per fruit, flesh of fruit
        not white **Sapotaceae**
20b. Leaves opposite
    24a. Ovary superior **Clusiaceae**
    24b. Ovary inferior **Myrtaceae**
18b. Flesh of fruit not used; fruit dry or somewhat fleshy, if fleshy
    then only the seed consumed
    25a. Leaves simple
        26a. Fruit a spiny capsule (*Bixa*) **Bixaceae**
        26b. Fruit not spiny (seed edible) (*Terminalia*) **Combretaceae**
    25b. Leaves compound, planted or wild
        (*Loxopterygium*) **Anacardiaceae**
12b. Plants grown as ornamentals in gardens and parks
    27a. Stems spiny
        28a. Shrubs; stems succulent (*Euphorbia*) **Euphorbiaceae**
        28b. Lianas; stems not succulent
        (*Bougainvillea*) **Nyctaginaceae**
    27b. Stems without spines
        29a. Flowers subtended by bracts; herbs with rhizome **Cannaceae**
        29b. Flowers not subtended by bracts; shrubs or herbs without
        rhizome
            30a. Filaments not fused into a tube surrounding the bud; fruits
            in pairs **Apocynaceae**
            30b. Filaments fused into a tube surrounding the style; fruit
            many-carpelled **Malvaceae**

Ferns

FILICOPSIDA (FERNS)

Herbs or vines, often epiphytic, rarely aquatic (*Azolla*); usually rhizomatous. Leaves usually large (minute in *Azolla*), variously divided or entire, uncurling apically in opening. Flowers wanting; instead spore producing sporangia spread on the leaf-underside or on distinct fertile leaves. A cosmopolitan group of plants with about 8550 species. Specialist knowledge is needed to separate the various fern families. The names of the families are therefore indicated in brackets only.

Key to the Species

1a. Plants aquatic   3. *Azolla microphylla*
1b. Plants terrestrial or epiphytic
   2a. Leaves compound
      3a. Plants creeping, vine-like   4. *Lygodium venustum*
      3b. Plants suberect herbs
         4a. Ultimate segments cuneate-flabellate, less than twice as long as broad
                             2. *Adiantum subvolubile*
         4a. Ultimate segments elongated, more than twice as long as broad
            5a. Sori on upper side of segments   1. *Adiantum alarconianum*
            5b. Sori on under side of segments
               6a. Leaves silvery-white beneath; sori throughout
                          6. *Pityrogramma calomelanos*
               6b. Leaves green beneath; sori in two rows   7. *Thelypteris tetragona*
   2b. Leaves simple   5. *Niphidium crassifolium*

1. *Adiantum alarconianum* GAUDICH. (Pteridaceae)

Suberect herb, to 50 cm high; rhizome short and creeping. Leaves 1–2-pinnate; blade to 50 cm long; leaf-segments oblong-falcate to triangular, alternate, oblique at base, subsessile. Sori marginal, borne on upper side of segments. Collection: 63455.

Common fern. — Endemic to the area near Guayaquil and adjacent Peru.

2. *Adiantum subvolubile* METT. ex KUHN (Pteridaceae)
Suberect to leaning herb, to 30 cm high, slender; rhizome creeping. Leaves 2–3-pinnate; blade to 50 cm long, narrowly ovate; ultimate segments cuneate-flabellate. Sori few, crescent-shaped in outline. Collections: 63452, 64045.
Common along streams. — Ecuador and Peru.

3. *Azolla microphylla* KAULF. (Salviniaceae)
Floating, to 2 cm long, forming large colonies; roots present. Stem horizontal, freely and pinnately branched. Leaves sessile, ca. 1 mm long, 2-lobed, alternating in two rows; upper lobe photosynthetic, aerial; lower lobe floating. Collections: 63307, 63609.
In ponds together with *Lemna*. — Widespread in warm America.

4. *Lygodium venustum* SW. (Schizaeaceae)
Creeping and twining vine, to several meters long. Leaves 2–3-pinnate; leaflets dichotomously arranged along rachis, petiolate; pinnae alternate, irregular, gradually diminishing in size towards apex. Sporangia form a single row at lacerate margin of leaflets. Collections: 63454, 64043.
Occasional. — Widespread in tropical America.

5. *Niphidium crassifolium* (L.) LELLINGER (Polypodiaceae)
Epiphytic herb, to 60 cm high. Leaves numerous, simple, petiolate; blade 30–70 cm long, oblong-lanceolate, entire. Sori large, borne along lateral nerves. Collection: 64133.
Rare epiphyte near the summit of Zambapala. — Widespread in South America.

6. *Pityrogramma calomelanos* (L.) LINK (Pteridaceae)
Herb, to 40 cm high; rhizome short, suberect, brown-scaly. Leaves numerous, bi-pinnate; blade to 50 cm long, ovate; leaflets lacerate to dentate, characteristically silvery-white beneath. Sori throughout the underside of the segments. Collections: 63451, 63464, 64026, 64042.
Common, terrestrial along stream banks. — Widespred in America, including the Galapagos Islands, and naturalized in Africa.

7. *Thelypteris tetragona* (SW.) SMALL (Thelypteridaceae)
Herb, to 1 m high; rhizome short-creeping. Leaves 2-pinnate; blade to 50 cm long; pinnae subopposite, 12–20, deeply incised. Sori in two rows centrally on underside of leaves.
Known from only a single collection from Puná Island. — Widespread in America
Collection: BARCLAY *s.n.* (BM, mentioned in Fl. Ec.).

Seed Plants

ACANTHACEAE (ACANTHUS FAMILY)
Herbs, shrubs, or vines. Leaves opposite or alternate, simple; stipules absent. Flowers usually subtended by prominent, colored bracts, bisexual, more or less zygomorphic; corolla 5-lobed or 2-lipped; stamens 4 or 2. Fruit a few seeded capsule with conspicuous thorn-like ejaculators. A family of 2500 species, mainly in the tropics and subtropics. Many species are late flowering during the dry season.

Key to the Species

1a. Leaves alternate — 5. *Elytraria imbricata*
1b. Leaves opposite
  2a. Inflorescence congested and subspicate
    3a. Bracts spatulate; capsule 15 mm long — 6. *Justicia carthaginensis*
    3b. Bracts narrowly ovate to lanceolate or ovate; capsule 5–6 mm long
      4a. Bracts narrowly ovate to lanceolate, long-mucronate; inflorescence forming spike-like thyrses — 3. *Dicliptera peruviana*
      4b. Bracts ovate, short-mucronate or not mucronate; inflorescense a compact four-sided spike
        5a. Flowers blue or white, 5-lobed — 1. *Blechum pyramidatum*
        5b. Flowers white with a purple spot, distinctly 2-lipped, lower lip 3-lobed at apex — 8. *Tetramerium nervosum*
  2b. Inflorescence paniculate or axillary clustered
    6a. Inflorescence of numerous flowers
      7a. Leaves subsessile; flowers 1 cm long — 2. *Carlowrightia ecuadoriana*
      7b. Leaves petiolate; flowers 2 cm long — 7. *Ruellia floribunda*
    6b. Inflorescence 1–few-flowered — 4. *Dyschoriste quitensis*

1. *Blechum pyramidatum* (LAM.) URB.
Herb, to 1 m high. Stem 4-angled, pilose. Leaves opposite; blade 3–7 cm long, ovate, acute or obtuse, ciliate, rounded to narrowed at base; petiole 2–10 mm long. Inflorescence a compact 4-sided spike, to 6 cm long; bracts 1–2 cm long, ovate, ciliate. Flowers blue or white, 2 cm long, 5-lobed. Capsule 6 mm long. Collections: 63476, 63777, 63984.
Common in open places of the thorn forest. — Mexico to northern South

America and the Galapagos Islands.
Uses: To prepare a tea to cure colds.
Vernacular names: albahaca morada, albahaca de vaca.

2. *Carlowrightia ecuadoriana* T. F. DANIEL & WASSH.
Herb, to 0.5 m high. Stem puberulous. Leaves opposite, subsessile; blade 2–5 cm long, lanceolate, acuminate, acute at base. Inflorescence composed of dichotomously branched panicles of spikes, each spike 2–17 cm long. Flowers sessile, 1–2 together per node; bracts narrow; corolla violet, 1 cm long. Capsule 1 cm long, clavate. Seeds 2.5 mm long, tuberculate. Collection: 63958 (type).
Rare along trails. — Endemic to southwestern Ecuador. Described by Daniel and Wasshausen (1993) and known only from three specimens. Categorized as critically endangered by Valencia *et al.* (2000).

3. *Dicliptera peruviana* (LAM.) JUSS.
Slender herb, to 2 m high. Stem striate, hirtellous. Leaves opposite; blade 5–9 cm long, ovate, acute to mucronate, rounded to cuneate at base; petiole 1–2 cm long. Inflorescence axillary and terminal, forming spike-like thyrses; bracts to 1 cm long, narrowly ovate to lanceolate, long-mucronate. Flowers purple, 3 cm long, 2-lipped, lower lip 3-lobed at apex. Capsule 5 mm long. Collections: 63477, 63815, 64000.
Common in sunny places. — Ecuador, including the Galapagos Islands, and Peru.
Uses: To prepare a tea to cure colds.
Vernacular names: albahaca morada, albahaca de vaca.

4. *Dyschoriste quitensis* (KUNTH) KUNTZE
Herb, to 80 cm high. Stem slightly angled. Leaves opposite; blade 2–6 cm long, ovate, acute, ciliate, narrowed at base; petiole 5–10 mm long. Inflorescence axillary, forming 1–few-flowered clusters. Flowers blue, 2–3 cm long, 5-lobed, subtended by foliaceous bracts; calyx-lobes subulate, setaceous. Collections: 63042, 63079, 63118, 63222, 63478, 63628.
Very common in moist places towards the end of the rainy season. — Endemic to semi-arid Ecuador and Peru, including the highlands.
Vernacular name: albahaca.

5. *Elytraria imbricata* (VAHL) PERS.
Herb, to 50 cm high. Stem unbranched, subglabrous. Leaves alternate, crowded distally; blade 5–15 cm long, narrowly ovate to obovate, subacute, decurrent at base to a winged petiole. Inflorescence to 25 cm long, spicate, simple or branched; scapes several, axillary; bracts to 6 mm long, narrow, slightly appressed. Flowers blue, 5–8 mm long, sessile. Capsule 3 mm long. Collection: 63387.

Occasional weed in waste places. — United States to Brazil and Ecuador, including the Galapagos Islands.

6. *Justicia carthaginensis* JACQ.
Herb, to 1 m high. Stem obscurely tetrangular, sparsely pilose. Leaves opposite; blade 6–12 cm long, ovate, acuminate, decurrent at base; petiole 1–2.5 cm long. Inflorescence a compact spike, to 8 cm long; bracts 1–1.5 cm long, spatulate. Flowers blue or purple, 3 cm long; calyx-lobes 5, narrowly lanceolate; lower lip 3-lobed; upper lip erect. Capsule 15 mm long; seeds 4. Collections: 63025, 63113, 63178, ANDERSSON *s.n.* (S, cited in Areschoug 1869).
Common in wet places. — Mexico to Peru.

7. *Ruellia floribunda* HOOK.
Herb, to 1.5 m high. Stem terete, glandular-pilose. Leaves opposite; blade 3–9 cm long, ovate, subacute, more or less decurrent at base; petiole 1–3 cm long. Inflorescence dichotomously branched, large and lax; bracts 2–6 mm long, ovate. Flowers purple to pink, 2 cm long, 6–8 mm wide at apex. Capsule to 1 cm long, clavate. Collections: 63638, 63785, 63999.
Locally abundant in sunny places. — Endemic to arid Ecuador and adjacent Peru, including the Galapagos Islands.
Note: It is eaten by cattle.
Vernacular name: veranero, mazanilla, mazanilla de vaca.

8. *Tetramerium nervosum* NEES
Herb, to 60 cm high. Stem terete, slender. Leaves opposite, sparsely pubescent; blade 2–4 cm long, ovate, acute or acuminate, obtuse or truncate at base; petiole 0.5–2 cm long. Inflorescence spicate, 2–6 cm long 4-sided; bracts imbricate, 7 mm long, ovate, hispid-ciliate, mucronate. Flowers white, the upper lip with a purple spot, the lower lip 3-lobed. Capsule 5 mm long, clavate. Collections: 63271, 63711, 63747, 63985.
Common in sunny places. — Lowlands of Central America and northern South America and the Galapagos Islands.
Vernacular name: barrerhorno.

ACHATOCARPACEAE (ACHATOCARPUS FAMILY)
Dioecious shrubs or trees. Leaves alternate, simple, entire; stipules wanting. Flowers unisexual, 4–5-merous; petals wanting; stamens 10–20. Fruit a berry. A small family with six species in America.

1. *Achatocarpus pubescens* C. H. WRIGHT
Dioecious shrub or tree, to 8 m high. Twigs sometimes bearing 1 cm long spines, pubescent when young. Leaves alternate; blade 3–11 cm long, ovate to

obovate, obtuse and submucronate, cuneate at base; petiole 1–5 mm long, poorly defined. Inflorescence 2–6 cm long, 5–10-flowered. Perianth segments 2–3 mm long; pedicels 5 mm long. Fruit a drupaceous berry, whitish when juvenile, later black, 10–13 mm long, ellipsoid; stalk 0.5 cm long. Collections: 63784, 63931, 75481, 85305, 85334, 85346, 85355, 85366.

Occasional in the dry forests on the southern hills. — Widespread in the Andes. Uses: Previously used to make heddles for looms in the cotton textile manufacture.

Vernacular names: negrita de cerro, negrito, palo de cruz.

AIZOACEAE (FIG-MARIGOLD FAMILY)

Herbs or shrubs, often succulent. Leaves usually opposite, simple; stipules mostly absent. Flowers usually bisexual and actinomorphic; corolla 4–many-parted; stamens 4 to numerous. Fruit usually a capsule. A family with over 2000 species in tropical and subtropical regions, rich in halophytes and succulents.

Key to the Species

1a. Leaves sessile, linear to spatulate, usually of equal size   1. *Sesuvium portulacastrum*
1b. Leaves petiolate, obovate to orbicular, of strikingly unequal size
                                                                2. *Trianthema portulacastrum*

1. *Sesuvium portulacastrum* (L.) L.

Succulent, creeping herb, rooting at nodes. Stem glabrous. Leaves opposite, usually of equal size, sessile; blade 1.5–6 cm long, linear to spatulate, subacute, gradually tapering and clasping at base. Flowers solitary, concealed within the petiolar sheet; tepals 4–6, purple or pink; pedicels 3–10 mm long. Capsule 6 mm long, ovoid. Collections: 63241, 63296, 63885, 63982, ANDERSSON 130 (S, cited in Fl. Ec.), SCHIMPFF 1187 (G, MO, US; cited in Fl. Ec.).

Common on salt flats. — Widely distributed in the tropics, including the Galapagos Islands.

Note: It is eaten by donkeys and birds.

Vernacular name: verdolaga.

2. *Trianthema portulacastrum* L.

Creeping herb. Leaves opposite, of strikingly unequal size, glabrous except along the nerves; blade 1.5–4 cm long, obovate to orbicular, rounded and mucronate, obtuse to cuneate at base; petiole 0.5–2 cm long, connate into a sheath surrounding the stem. Flowers solitary, violet, pink, or white, concealed within the petiolar sheet; tepals 1.5 mm long. Capsule, 5 mm long, turbinate. Collections: 63292, 63616, 85863.

Occasional in saline environments. — Pantropical, also the Galapagos Islands.

ALISMATACEAE (WATER-PLANTAIN FAMILY)
Semiaquatic herbs. Leaves usually in a basal rosette, with sheath, parallel-veined. Inflorescence mostly large and much branched; flowers 3-parted; stamens 6 or more; carpels many. Fruit an achene. A nearly cosmopolitan family with close to 100 species.

Key to the Species

1a. Pedicels longer than 10 mm; fruits 10 mm long   1. *Echinodorus berteroi*
1b. Pedicels to 5 mm long; fruits 2 mm long   2. *Echinodorus bracteatus*

1. *Echinodorus berteroi* (SPRENG.) FASSETT
Rhizomatous herb, 0.5–1 m high, erect, glabrous. Leaves inserted at base of plant; blade with pellucid lines, 7–9 cm long, ovate, subacute, cordate at base, to 6–8-nerved; petiole to 40 cm long, sheating. Inflorescence barely branched, the flowers in whorls of 6–10. Flowers white, 1 cm wide; pedicels 2–3 cm long. Fruit 1 cm long, ovoid, echinate. Collection: 63654.
Pond on the east coast. — Disjunct in California to West Indies and Ecuador to Argentina. Our collection from Puná Island is the second record of this species for Ecuador.

2. *Echinodorus bracteatus* MICHELI subsp. *efenestratus* (FASSETT) R. R. HAYNES & HOLM-NIELS.
Rhizomatous herb, to 1.5 m high, erect, glabrous. Leaves inserted at base of plant; blade glabrous without pellucid dots (characteristic of the subspecies), typically 20–40 cm long, cordate-ovate, at least 9–11-nerved; petiole to 1 m long, sheathing. Inflorescence to 1.5 m long, paniculate, the flowers in whorls of 10–15. Flowers, white, 2 cm wide; pedicels to 5 mm long. Fruit 2 mm long, oblanceolate. Collections: 63069, 63153, 63216.
Very common marsh plant in shallow waters. — Distributed from the Caribbean area to Ecuador. The subspecies *efenestratus* is endemic to the Guayas river drainage and vicinity.
Vernacular name: biguagiyo.

AMARANTHACEAE (AMARANTH FAMILY)
Herbs or shrubs. Leaves opposite or alternate, simple; stipules absent. Flowers uni- or bisexual, usually individually inconspicuous but gathered in more or less showy inflorescences; tepals 3–5; stamens as many as tepals and opposite these. Fruit usually a nutlet. A cosmopolitan family with 900 species, many of which are weedy. The center of diversity lies in semi-arid regions of America.

Key to the Species

1a. Leaves opposite
    2a. Leaves succulent, clasping at base   10. *Blutaparon vermiculare*
    2b. Leaves not as above
        3a. Inflorescence headlike
            4a. Inflorescence sessile
                5a. Flower heads stiff, the tepals pungent   5. *Alternanthera pungens*
                5b. Flower heads soft, the tepals flexible   6. *Alternanthera truxillensis*
            4b. Inflorescence pedunculate
                6a. Flower heads 3–4 mm wide   2. *Alternanthera areschougii*
                6b. Flower heads 8–15 mm wide
                    7a. Flower heads terminal, solitary; flowers pedicellate
                               3. *Alternanthera brasiliana*
                    7b. Flower heads axillary, several per node; flowers subsessile
                               4. *Alternanthera pubiflora*
        3b. Inflorescence elongate
            8a. Inflorescence composed of axillary and terminal spikes; tepals 5–8 mm
                long   1. *Achyranthes aspera*
            8a. Inflorescence much branched, lax, the flowers in few-flowered glomerate
                heads; tepals 1–1.5 mm long   12. *Iresine angustifolia*
1b. Leaves alternate
    9a. Stem spineless
        10a. Tepals 5 mm long; flowers bisexual; fruit many-seeded   11. *Celosia virgata*
        10b. Tepals 1–2.5 mm long; flowers unisexual or both uni- and bisexual;
            fruit 1-seeded
            11a. Leaf-blades to 4 cm long; inflorescences axillary, clustered along the
                entire stem; flowers urceolate   9. *Amaranthus urceolatus*
            11b. Leaf-blades of largest leaves longer than 4 cm; inflorescences terminal
                and axillary; flowers not urceolate   7. *Amaranthus dubius*
    9b. Stem spiny   8. *Amaranthus spinosus*

1. *Achyranthes aspera* L.

Herb, to 1 m high. Stem obtusely 4-angled, pubescent. Leaves opposite; blade 4–16 cm long, elliptic, acuminate, tapering at base; petiole 0.5–3 cm long. Inflorescence to 30 cm long, composed of terminal and axillary spikes; uppermost flowers more densely congested. Flowers bisexual; tepals 5–8 mm long. Fruit and persistent floral remnants pointed downwards and appressed to rachis; utricle proper 1–2 mm long. Collections: 63487, 63510, SCHIMPFF 1173 (G, GH, MO, NY; cited in Fl. Ec.).

Common on disturbed soils, especially along cattle tracks. — A nearly cosmopolitan species; its fruits adher easily to animals and humans.

Note: Causes rashes.

Vernacular name: picha de gato.

2. *Alternanthera areschougii* R. E. FR.

Erect herb, to 60 cm high. Stem subglabrous to villous. Leaves opposite; blade

3–8 cm long, lanceolate to ovate, acuminate to cuspidate, tapering at base; petiole 5–15 mm long, more or less distinct. Inflorescence axillary; heads 3–4 mm wide; peduncle to 7 cm long, filiform. Collection: ANDERSSON 51 (S type, cited in Fl. Ec.).

Known from a single record. — Probably endemic to coastal Ecuador.

3. *Alternanthera brasiliana* (L.) KUNTZE var. *villosa* (MOQ.) KUNTZE
Herbaceous vine, to 0.5 m high (lianescent shrub and mostly 1.5–2.5 m high according to Fl. Ec.). Stem pilose. Leaves opposite; blade 4–8 cm long, ovate to lanceolate, subacute, rounded-cuneate at base; petiole to 1 cm long. Inflorescence terminal, solitary; heads 1.5 cm wide; peduncle 5–15 cm long. Flowers pedicellate. Collections: 63020, 63107, 63162, 63756 (species); 63259, 63361 (variety); ANDERSSON 53 (S, cited in Fl. Ec.).

Very common along trails. — Tropical America, especially common in eastern South America.

4. *Alternanthera pubiflora* (BENTH.) KUNTZE
Herb or half-shrub, 1–3 m high. Stem appresed-pubescent. Leaves opposite; blade 5–15 cm long, ovate-elliptic, subacute, cuneate at base; petiole 5–10 mm long. Inflorescence terminal and axillary; heads 1–3 per node, 1 cm wide; peduncles 0–5 cm long. Flowers subsessile. Collections: 63530, 63561, 63642, 63707, 63712, 63752, 63804, ANDERSSON 52 (S, cited in Fl. Ec.), EGGERS 14771 (A, cited in Fl. Ec.).

Very common on sandy beaches and open places. — Central America to Chile.

5. *Alternanthera pungens* KUNTH
Prostrate herb, 30 cm wide, richly branched with taproot. Stem villose. Leaves opposite, often unequal; blade 1.5–3 cm long, ovate to almost orbicular, mucronate, cuneate at base; petiole 2–10 mm long, indistinct. Inflorescence axillary, sessile; heads mostly solitary, stiff due to pungent bracteoles and tepals. Collections: 63776, ANDERSSON 50 (S, cited in Fl. Ec.).

Uncommon on trampled soils around homesites. — A pantropical weed.

Note: The plant is eaten by cattle and goats.

Vernacular name: catarama.

6. *Alternanthera truxillensis* KUNTH
Prostrate to ascending herb, often rooting at nodes. Stem densely puberulent when young. Leaves opposite; blade 1–4.5 cm long, mostly obovate, rounded and mucronulate, tapering at base; petiole short, indistinct. Inflorescence axillary, sessile; heads solitary or several per node, 5 mm wide, soft. Collections: 63472, 63501, 63905.

Common on salt flats and sandy beaches. — Ecuador and Peru.

7. *Amaranthus dubius* MART. ex THELL.
Erect herb, 0.3–1.5 m high. Stem glabrous, spineless. Leaves alternate; blade 4–9 cm long, rhombic-ovate, subacuminate to obtuse and mucronulate, more or less cuneate at base; petiole to 8 cm long. Inflorescence terminal, and axillary, much branched, formed by clusters of spicate cymes. Flowers unisexual; tepals 2 mm long. Collections: 63074, 63521, ANDERSSON 54 (S, cited in Fl. Ec.).
Common weed in dried-up places. — Subcosmopolitan, less common in temperate regions. Known from the Galapagos Islands.
Note: It is eaten by cattle and donkeys.
Vernacular name: bledo colorado.

8. *Amaranthus spinosus* L.
Erect herb, to 1.5 m high. Stem glabrous, bearing 0.5–1.5 cm long spines. Leaves alternate; blade 3–10 cm long, rhombic-ovate, obtuse and mucronulate, attenuate or cuneate at base; petiole to 7 cm long. Inflorescence formed by clusters of terminal spikes and axillary heads. Flowers unisexual; tepals 2 mm long. Collections: 63032, 63315, 63520, 63890, ANDERSSSON 95 (S, cited in Fl. Ec.), BARCLAY 424 (BM, cited in Fl. Ec.).
Common in disturbed places. — Subcosmopolitan, less common in temperate regions. Also on the Galapagos Islands.
Uses: It is used to cure bloody vomiting. The plant is eaten by cattle, donkeys, and birds.
Vernacular names: bledo colorado, rabo de gallo.

9. *Amaranthus urceolatus* BENTH.
Erect herb, to 1 m high. Stem glabrous, spineless. Leaves alternate, progressively smaller towards apex of plant; blade to 4 cm long, ovate, rounded or emarginate and minutely notched, tapering into a winged petiole at base. Inflorescence axillary, clustered along the stem. Flowers urceolate, mostly unisexual; tepals 1 mm long. Collections: 63511, 63557, SINCLAIR *s.n.* (K type, cited in Fl. Ec.).
Occasional weed in cultivated fields. — Endemic to arid southwestern Ecuador and adjacent Peru, mainly in the lowlands.
Note: It is eaten by cattle and donkeys.
Common name: bledo blanco.

10. *Blutaparon vermiculare* (L.) MEARS
Prostrate herb. Stem glabrous. Leaves opposite, succulent; blade 1–4 cm long, linear to oblanceolate, obtuse to acute, narrowed into a semi-amplexicaul base; midnerve prominent. Inflorescence terminal, mostly solitary, 0.5–3 cm long, rounded to cylindrical. Bracts 1.5–2 mm long, exceeded in length by bracteoles and tepals. Collection: SCHIMPFF 1186 (F, G, S; cited in Fl. Ec.).
A single record on the east coast. – Widespread in America and Africa.

11. *Celosia virgata* JACQ.

Herb, to 1 m high. Stem glabrous. Leaves alternate, progressively smaller towards apex of plant; blade 5–14 cm long, ovate, acuminate, attenuate at base; petiole to 3 cm long. Inflorescence of terminal and axillary compact or elongated spikes. Flowers bisexual, green; tepals 5 mm long. Capsule 2 mm long, many-seeded. Collections: 63251, 63323, BARCLAY 370 (BM, cited in Fl. Ec.).

Common along trails. — Mexico and the West Indies to Peru.

12. *Iresine angustifolia* EUPHRASÉN

Herb or half-shrub, to 3 m high. Stem subglabrous. Leaves opposite; blade 4–10(–14) cm long, narrowly ovate, acute or acuminate, cuneate at base. Inflorescence to 50 cm long, much branched, the flowers minute and in few-flowered glomerate heads. Flowers and fruits embedded in silvery white hairs; tepals 1–1.5 mm long. Collections: 63086, 63706, 63909, BARCLAY 467 (BM, cited in Fl. Ec.).

Common in open places. — Mexico to Ecuador and Brazil. Also known from the Galapagos Islands.

AMARYLLIDACEAE (DAFFODIL FAMILY)

Bulbous herbs. Leaves narrow. Inflorescence umbellate, subtended by a involucre. Flowers 3-parted, showy; stamens 6; ovary inferior. Fruit usually a capsule. A nearly cosmopolitan family with 860 species.

Key to the Species

1a. Flowers red; leaves elliptic, petiolate   1. *Eucrosia stricklandii*
1b. Flowers white; leaves linear, non-petiolate   2. *Leptochiton quitoensis*

1. *Eucrosia stricklandii* (BAKER) MEEROW var. *stricklandii*

Herb, to 40 cm high; bulb 2–3 cm wide. Leaves 1–2, deciduous; blade 21–23 cm long, elliptic, short-acuminate, petiolate. Inflorescence 3–7-flowered; scape 30–45 cm long. Flowers red, 3–4 cm long, narrowly funnelform; pedicels 1–5 cm long. Capsule 2–3 cm wide. Collection: 64142.

Common in dry scrub. — Endemic to Ecuador, the variety being limited to the lowlands.

Phenology: Flowering in December.

Vernacular name: varita de San José.

2. *Leptochiton quitoensis* (HERB.) SEALY (Plate 14)

Herb, 30–60 cm high; bulb 3–5 cm wide. Leaves 5–7, deciduous; blade 30–60 cm long, linear; petiole indistinct. Inflorescence 1-flowered, appearing after the leaves; scape to 35 cm long. Flowers white, 13–18 cm wide; tube much

elongated, 5 mm wide. Capsule 2 cm wide. Collections: no specimens.
Common, often on cultivated soils. — Endemic to south western Ecuador and adjacent Peru.
Phenology: Flowering in January and February. Observed in abundance on a field in November of 1998 during a strong *El Niño*.
Vernacular name: amancay.

ANACARDIACEAE (SUMAC FAMILY)

Tree or shrubs, with allergenic resins in bark and leaves; stipules absent or caducous. Leaves alternate, compound or simple. Flowers small, bi- or unisexual, mostly actinomorphic, 4–5-parted. Fruit drupaceous. A family with 600 species in the tropics and subtropics.

Key to the Species

1a. Leaves pinnately compound
    2a. Leaflets 7–9 per leaf; flowers green; native or in small plantations
                                    1. *Loxopterygium huasango*
    2b. Leaflets 13–31 per leaf; flowers red; cultivated   3. *Spondias purpurea*
1b. Leaves simple   2. *Mangifera indica*

1. *Loxopterygium huasango* SPRUCE ex ENGL. [cult.]
Dioecious tree, to 10 m high. Branchlets pilose when young. Leaves deciduous, imparipinnately compound, 30–40 cm long; leaflets 7–9 per leaf, subsessile, 5–15 cm long, ovate, serrate. Inflorescence to 15 cm long. Flowers green, 3 mm wide, 5-merous. Fruit a 1.5 cm long samara. Collections: 63876, 64016, 85360.
Planted on dry hills along western Puná Island, otherwise rare due to overexploitation. — Endemic to southwestern Ecuador and northern Peru.
Phenology: Flowers appear in December and January.
Uses: Produces valuable wood used for lining wells, to make barrels and tubs, for fence posts in the field, in the construction of houses and boats, and to make wedges.
Vernacular name: guasango.

2. *Mangifera indica* L. [cult.]
A great variety of mangos (Collection: 63840) are cultivated. — It is supposedly native to the Indo-Burma region and still growing wild in India. It was introduced to the New World by the Portuguese and reached Brazil as late as the beginning of the 18th century.
Uses: The fruits are edible and vary in size and taste.
Vernacular names: mango, mango alcanfora, mango bocado, mango colorado, mango de chupar, mango lechoso, mango peruviano.

3. *Spondias purpurea* L. [cult.] (Plate 11)

The hog-plum (Collections: 63428, 63845, 63853A) is widely cultivated as a living fence. — It is known from Mexico to Brazil and Peru but the true origin remains uncertain.

Phenology: The flowers appear when the leaves are shed in August. The fruits ripen in enormous quantities around October and November. New leaves are produced before the onset of the rainy season.

Uses: The juicy fruit is eaten raw or used in beverages and jams. It is eaten by cattle.

Vernacular names: ciruela, jobo.

ANNONACEAE (CUSTARD-APPLE FAMILY)

Trees. Leaves alternate, simple, entire; stipules lacking. Flowers rather large, bisexual; sepals 3; petals usually 6; stamens numerous, spirally arranged. Fruit composed of more or less fused carpels. A pantropic family with about 850 species.

Key to the Species

1a. Fruits 15–40 cm long	1. *Annona muricata*
1b. Fruits 7–12 cm long	2. *Annona squamosa*

1. *Annona muricata* L. [cult.] (Plate 10)

The soursop (Collection:63772) is a fruit tree. — It is widely cultivated in South America since ancient time and originated in the Caribbean, northern South America, or Brazil.

Uses: The fruit is excellent for beverages.

Vernacular name: guanábana. Another fruit tree known as 'anona' (Collection: 63580) may also belong here or represent another fruit species of the genus *Annona*.

2. *Annona squamosa* L. [cult.] (Plate 10)

The sweetsop (Collections: 63560, 63851) is among the principal economic crops on Puná Island. — It is native to the Caribbean region and Central America.

Phenology: The fruits ripen from April to June.

Uses: The granular pulp surrounding the seeds is delicious in fruit desserts or just fresh.

Vernacular name: chirimoya.

APOCYNACEAE (DOGBANE FAMILY)

Trees, shrubs or herbs, often with milky sap. Leaves opposite or alternate, simple, entire; stipules mostly minute or lacking. Flowers bisexual,

actinomorphic, 5-merous; petals convolute in bud; stamens 5. Fruit a pair of
follicles, drupes, or berries. A cosmopolitan family with 1300 species.

Key to the Species

1a. Herbs, shrubs or small trees
    2a. Flowers shorter than 1 cm; plants wild
        3a. Leaves in whorls of four   4. *Rauvolfia tetraphylla*
        3b. Leaves alternate   6. *Vallesia glabra*
    2b. Flowers longer than 2 cm; plants cultivated
        4a. Flowers yellow; fruit drupaceous   5. *Thevetia peruviana*
        4b. Flowers red or white; fruit a pair of follicles
            5a. Leaves shorter than 6 cm; flowers in pairs   1. *Catharanthus roseus*
            5b. Leaves longer than 6 cm; flowers many together   2. *Nerium oleander*
1b. Lianas or vines   3. *Prestonia mollis*

1. *Catharanthus roseus* (L.) G. DON [cult.]
The Madagascar periwinkle (Collection: 64137) is cultivated around homesites
and occasionally found escaped on sandy dunes. — It is native to Madagascar.
Uses: Grown as ornamental.
Vernacular name: chavelita.

2. *Nerium oleander* L. [cult.]
The oleander (Collection: 63568) is cultivated for its showy flowers. — It is
native to the Mediterranean.
Uses: Grown as ornamental in gardens.
Vernacular names: laurel, laurel de jardín.

3. *Prestonia mollis* KUNTH
Twining vine, to 3 m long. Leaves opposite, subglabrous above, puberulent
beneath; blade to 13 cm long, ovate to oblong, acuminate or obtuse, cordate to
subtruncate at base; petiole to 3 cm long. Inflorescense a dense many-flowered
corymb. Flowers pale yellow, 5 cm wide, salver-shaped; pedicels 1 cm long.
Follicles 20–30 cm long, narrow. Seeds 1 cm long. Collections: 63398, 63645,
64151.
Common in dry thickets and disturbed places. — Endemic to Ecuador and
adjacent Peru.
Phenology: It flowers throughout the dry season.
Uses: Medicinal plant used to heal wounds.
Vernacular names: bejuco sanalotodo, sanalotodo.

4. *Rauvolfia tetraphylla* L.
Shrub, 0.8–2 m high, with milky sap. Stem glabrescent. Leaves in whorls of
four, unequal in size, glabrous except along nerves; larger blades 4–9 cm long,
elliptic or oblanceolate, attenuate, cuneate at base. Inflorescence of ca. 10

flowers, dichotomously branching; peduncle 1–2 cm long. Flowers white, 5 mm long; pedicels 1–2 mm long. Drupe 6 mm wide, black to reddish brown; stones 2. Collections: 63245, 63406, 63926, 85861.

Common in fences and disturbed sites. — Mexico to Peru.

5. *Thevetia peruviana* (PERS.) K. SCHUM. [cult.]
The yellow oleander (Collection: 85361) is occasionally grown for its beautiful flowers. — Perhaps native to Mexico, becoming pantropic.
Vernacular name: suchede de cerro.

6. *Vallesia glabra* (CAV.) LINK
Shrub, to 3 m high. Stem glabrous. Leaves alternate; blade 4–9 cm long, lanceolate, acute, rounded at base; petiole 3–8 mm long. Inflorescence cymose, 10–20-flowered; peduncle 1–3 cm long. Flowers white, 7 mm long; pedicels 2–5 mm long. Fruit translucent-white, 1 cm long, fleshy. Collections: 63637, 63861, 63863.
Disturbed places around homesites and slopes bordering the beach. — Florida and Mexico to northern South America. Also the Galapagos Islands.
Uses: The stems are cut for charcoal and forked props for trees and vines. It is eaten by birds.
Vernacular name: perlilla.

ARACEAE (ARUM FAMILY)
Herbs of various habits. Leaves alternate, simple or compound, usually sheathed. Inflorescence subtended by a single bract (spathe), and composed of minute flowers crowded on a central column. Fruit usually a berry. A family with 2000 species, mainly in the tropics and subtropics. The aquatic species here treated is atypical.

1. *Pistia stratiotes* L.
Floating herb, forming lettuce-like, 10–30 cm wide rosettes and emitting stolons with new plants; roots fibrous. Leaves simple, thick and spongy; blade 5–12 cm long, obovate-spatulate, truncate and emarginate, cuneately narrowed to a broad base. Inflorescence reduced; female flowers below; male flowers above; spathe green. Berry small, irregularly dehiscent. Collection: 63721.
Dense colonies, one observation only. — Pantropical aquatic weed.

ARECACEAE (PALM FAMILY)
Palm trees. Leaves clustered distally, sheathed, petiolate, simple or compound, very large. Flowers in variable inflorescences, usually small and unisexual,

actinomorphic; perianth with 6 segments; stamens 6 to numerous. Fruit a berry or a drupe with large seeds. A tropical family with 2700 species.

1. *Cocos nucifera* L. [cult.]
The coconut palm (no specimen) is commonly planted and semi-naturalised on sandy beaches. — Widespread along tropical shores. The origin of this palm tree remains uncertain, but it is usually assumed that it may have originated in Melanesia.
Uses: The coconut palm is known for its many uses and its value in nourishment and as snack or refreshments. Medicinally it is used in the treatment of the kidneys and to cure for intestinal worms. The hollow endocarp is used as a vessel, cup or bowl. Leaves are used as thatch. Fibers from the husk are used in dyes for textiles and, due to its resistance to sea water, in the caulking of ships.
Vernacular name: palma de coco.

ASCLEPIADACEAE (MILKWEED FAMILY)
Mostly woody plants, often with milky sap. Leaves opposite or whorled, simple, entire; stipules wanting or minute. Flowers bisexual, 5-merous; corolla fused, convolute in bud; stamens 5. Fruit a pair of follicles. Seeds wooly. A tropical family with about 2000 species.
A species of *Sarcostemma*, perhaps *S. clausum* (JACQ.) SCHULT., is expected to occur on Puná Island based on Andersson *s.n.* (S, cited in Areschoug 1869).

1. *Marsdenia* cf. *ecuadorensis* MORILLO & SPELLMAN
Twining liana, to 2 m long. Stem glabrescent to sparsely pubescent. Leaves opposite; blade 4–9 cm long, subrotund, rounded to short-acuminate, attenuate at base; petiole 1–2 cm long. Flowers not seen (inflorescence probably a many-flowered, short-pedunculate umbel of white flowers). Follicles 10 cm long, 3 cm wide, woody, dehiscent into two valves. Seeds 8 mm long, ovate, flat, bearing a cluster of 2 cm long wooly hairs. Collection: 75483.
Rare in disturbed site. – Endemic to the Guayas province.
If correctly identified this is the first fruiting specimen of this rare plant, which is otherwise known only from the flowering type specimen.

ASPHODELACEAE JUSS.
Herbs or trees. Leaves alternate, forming a rosette, often succulent. Flowers 3-merous; stamens 6. Fruit a capsule. A tropical family with 750 species mainly in Africa.

1. *Aloe vera* (L.) Burm. f.

The aloe vera (no specimen) is grown in gardens. It is native to Africa.

Uses: It is used as an effective protection against evil spells, and medicinally to treat sickness in the kidneys and the colon.

Vernacular name: sábila.

Asteraceae (Aster Family)

Herbaceous or woody plants. Leaves alternate, whorled, or opposite, simple or compound; stipules lacking. Inflorescence a compound head on a receptacle (superficially resembling a flower). Flowers appear in centripetal sequence, variously divided into disc flowers and petaloid ray flowers. Fruit an achene, often with pappus. A cosmopolitan family with more than 15000 species. Many of the 24 species on Puná Island are weedy.

Key to the Species

1a. Leaves alternate
  2a. Lianas or shrubs
    3a. Leaf-base cordate; heads orange .... 21. *Pseudogynoxys scabra*
    3b. Leaf-base gradually narrowing; heads white .... 3. *Baccharis trinervis*
  2b. Herbs
    4a. Leaf-margin deeply and irregularly incised
      5a. Heads solitary in each leaf-axil .... 11. *Egletes viscosa*
      5b. Heads numerous together in terminal inflorescences
          18. *Parthenium hysterophorus*
    4b. Leaf-margin entire, crenate or serrate
      6a. Plant glabrous; petiole mostly 2–4 cm long .... 20. *Porophyllum ruderale*
      6b. Plant at least distally pubescent or hirtellous; petiole less than 1 cm long
        7a. Heads solitary; involucral bracts 8–12 mm long .... 15. *Lagascea mollis*
        7b. Heads several per inflorescence; involucral bracts 3–4 mm long
          14. *Isocarpha microcephala*
1b. Leaves opposite
  8a. Leaves 3–5-foliolate
    9a. Scrambling shrub .... 6. *Bidens rubifolia*
    9b. Herbs
      10a. Achenes curved when fully ripe; leaves 3(–5)-foliolate; leaflets usually
        serrate .... 4. *Bidens cynapiifolia*
      10b. Achenes straight when fully ripe; leaves (bi-)pinnately divided;
        leaflets more or less toothed .... 5. *Bidens riparia*
  8b. Leaves simple
    11a. Inflorescence 8–many-headed
      12a. Leaves petiolate; ray flowers many per head or wanting, not yellow
        13a. Inflorescence large and diffuse; heads typically 1–3 cm apart
          7. *Brickellia diffusa*
        13b. Inflorescence variable, fairly dense; heads less than 1 cm apart
          14a. Leaf-margin subentire .... 9. *Condylidium iresinoides*

14b. Leaf-margin crenate or serrate
  15a. Leaf-base gradually narrowing; flowers white
                               17. *Ophryosporus densiflorus*
  15b. Leaf-base cordate to subtruncate; flowers violet to pinkish
    16a. Heads 6–12 mm long; involucral bracts caducous,
        awnless   8. *Chromolaena roseorum*
    16b. Heads 5–6 mm long; involucral bracts bearing awns
                           13. *Fleischmannia pratensis*
12b. Leaves subsessile; ray flowers 1 per head, yellow, 3-lobed
                         16. *Milleria quinqueflora*

11b. Inflorescence 1–4-headed
  17a. Heads subsessile
    18a. Leaves petiolate   23. *Synedrella nodiflora*
    18b. Leaves subsessile
      19a. Leaves 1–3 cm wide; achenes broad, conspicuously prickled
                 1. *Acanthospermum microcarpum*
      19b. Leaves to 1 cm wide; achenes narrow, not prickled
                   12. *Enydra sessilifolia*
  17b. Heads pedunculate
    20a. Leaves 2–3 mm wide   19. *Pectis elongata*
    20b. Leaves generally wider than 5 mm
      21a. Herbs
        22a. Heads yellow, in compound inflorescences
                 22. *Schizoptera peduncularis*
        22b. Heads white; solitary or a few separate ones per axil
          23a. Leaves ovate to broadly ovate; peduncles 8–15 cm long
                 2. *Acmella leucantha*
          23b. Leaves lanceolate; peduncles 1–4 cm long
                 10. *Eclipta prostrata*
      21b. Shrubs   24. *Wedelia grandiflora*

1. *Acanthospermum microcarpum* B. L. ROB.
Much branched herb, to 50 cm high. Stem hirsute. Leaves opposite, subsessile; blade 2–6 cm long, rhombic to obovate, more or less serrate, obtuse, gradually tapering into a narrow base. Flowers yellow. Fruiting heads 1 cm wide, sessile; achenes conspicuously prickled. Collections: 63002, 63096, 63319, 63648.
Common weed and on sandy beaches. — Endemic to coastal Ecuador and adjacent Peru, including the Galapagos Islands.
Vernacular name: roseta.

2. *Acmella leucantha* (KUNTH) R. K. JANSEN
Herb, to 1 m high. Stem sparsely pilose. Leaves opposite; blade 3–6 cm long, ovate to broadly ovate, subentire, acuminate, slightly oblique and attenuate at base; petiole to 2 cm long. Heads solitary, to 1 cm long; disc flowers white; peduncle 8–15 cm long. Achenes 2 mm long; pappus wanting. Collections: 63137, 63196, 63288.
Weedy plant along trails. — Endemic to Ecuador.

3. *Baccharis trinervis* PERS.
Shrub, to 3 m high. Twigs pubescent. Leaves alternate, glossy green; blade 4–8 cm long, elliptic to narrowly elliptic, entire, subacuminate, cuneate at base; petiole to 5 mm long. Inflorescence terminal, composed of dense panicles; heads numerous, 5 mm wide, subsessile; flowers white. Achenes 1 mm long; pappus 3 mm long. Collections: 64001, 64041.
Occasional understory shrub of the dry forest. — Tropical South America.

4. *Bidens cynapiifolia* KUNTH
Herb, 50–80 cm high. Stem subglabrous. Leaves opposite, petiolate; blade to 12 cm long, (bi-)pinnately 3–5 foliolate; leaflets more or less toothed-dentate, acuminate. Inflorescence long-pedunculate; heads 1 cm wide; outer involucral bracts almost linear; ray flowers yellow, caducous. Achenes 1 cm long, narrow, curved when fully ripe, a few outer ones hirsute; awns 4, erect, retrorsely barbed. Collections: 63249, 63351, ANDERSSON *s.n.* (S, cited in Areschoug 1869).
Common in disturbed places. — Pantropic weed, also known from the Galapagos Islands. This and the following species are closely related and difficult to separate.

5. *Bidens riparia* KUNTH
Herb, to 1 m high. Stem subglabrous to sparsely hirsute. Leaves opposite, petiolate; blade to 12 cm long, pinnately 3–5-foliolate; leaflets serrate or toothed-serrate, acuminate. Inflorescence long-pedunculate; heads to 1 cm wide; outer involucral bracts almost linear; ray flowers white (our specimens) or yellow, caducous. Achenes narrow, straight, a few outer ones hirsute; awns 3–4, divergent, retrorsely barbed. Collections: 63052, 63114, 63218.
Common weed along trails and waste places. — Tropical America, including the Galapagos Islands.
Vernacular name: canutillo.

6. *Bidens rubifolia* KUNTH
Scrambling shrub, to 3 m high. Stem sparsely hirsute. Leaves opposite, petiolate; blade to 16 cm long, 3-foliolate; leaflets ovate, serrate, acute. Inflorescence a terminal panicle of 5–15 heads; heads 5 cm wide, pedunculate; ray flowers yellow, 2 cm long; disc flowers with 5 mm long tube. Achenes armed with awns. Collections: 63888, 64038, 64040.
Uncommon understory shrub in dry forest. – Andes from Venezuela to Peru.
Vernacular name: trementina.

7. *Brickellia diffusa* (VAHL) A. GRAY
Herb, to 1 m high. Stem puberulent. Leaves opposite; blade to 5 cm long, broadly ovate, crenate, subtruncate at base, 3-nerved from base. Inflorescence large and diffuse; heads very numerous, 8 mm long, elongate; peduncle almost

filiform; disc flowers green. Achenes 2 mm long; pappus 4 mm long. Collection: 63841.

Occasional weed on disturbed soils. — Tropical America, also on the Galapagos Islands.

8. *Chromolaena roseorum* (B. L. ROB.) R. M. KING & H. ROB.

Shrub or herb, to 2 m high. Leaves opposite; blade 3–7 cm long, ovate-cordate, cordate or truncate at base, serrate, 3-nerved from base, white-pubescent beneath. Inflorescence a terminal panicle; heads numerous, light blue, 8 mm long, narrow. Achenes with pappus. Collections: 63780, 63829.

Common in open places. — Endemic to western Ecuador and the southern highlands.

9. *Condylidium iresinoides* (KUNTH) R. M. KING & H. ROB.

Herb, to 1 m high. Stem hirsute. Leaves opposite; blade 3–9 cm long, ovate, subentire, acute, abruptly tapering at base; petiole 5–15 mm long. Inflorescence foliaceous, branched; branchlets bearing 5–15 congested heads; heads subsessile, 5–7 mm long, narrow; disc flowers white, short-pedicellate. Achenes 2 mm long; pappus 3 mm long. Collection: 63894.

Occasional at lake shore. — Central America to Bolivia.

10. *Eclipta prostrata* (L.) L.

Herb, to 40 cm high. Stem sparsely pubescent. Leaves opposite, more or less scabrous, subsessile or short-petiolate; blade 2–7 cm long, lanceolate, slightly serrate, narrowed at base. Heads solitary, 8 mm wide; peduncle 1–4 cm long; flowers white. Achenes without pappus. Collections: 63101, 63129, 63334.

Common weed in moist places. — Native to the New World, including the Galapagos Islands.

11. *Egletes viscosa* (L.) LESS.

Herb, to 20 cm high. Stem pubescent. Leaves alternate; blade 3–9 cm long, spatulate, deeply and irregularly incised, auriculate at base; petiole indistinct. Heads solitary and axillary, 8 mm wide; peduncle 1–2 cm long; ray flowers white; disc flowers yellow. Collections: 63883, 63978.

Occasional at dried-up ponds. — Mexico to Brazil.

12. *Enydra sessilifolia* (RUIZ & PAV.) CABRERA

Prostrate fleshy herb, to 20 cm high. Stem pubescent. Leaves opposite, sessile; blade 2–4 cm long, lanceolate, subentire, auriculate at the base. Heads sessile, solitary, 1–1.5 cm wide, globose; disc flowers green, involucral bracts broadly ovate. Achenes without pappus. Collection: 63724.

A single collection on the beach. — Coastal America, also on the Galapagos Islands.

13. *Fleischmannia cf. pratensis* (KLATT) R. M. KING & H. ROB.
Sprawling herb, to 1.5 m high. Stem sparsely hirsute. Leaves alternate, nearly glabrous; blade to 7 cm long, broadly ovate, serrate, acute at apex; petiole to 4 cm long. Inflorescence terminal, corymbose; heads 8 mm long, narrow; disc flowers violet. Collection: 63705.
Common in disturbed, open places. — Mexico to Ecuador.

14. *Isocarpha microcephala* (DC.) S. F. BLAKE
Herb, to 0.5 m high. Stem pubescent. Leaves alternate; blade 2–5 cm long, narrowly elliptic to lanceolate, entire to somewhat serrate, acute, tapering at base; petiole 1–5 mm long. Inflorescence terminal; heads few per branch, 6 mm long, ovoid; disc flowers violet. Achenes 1 mm long; pappus wanting. Collections: 63142, 63471, BARCLAY 408 (BM, US; cited by Keil and Stuessy 1981).
Common along trails and on salty flats. — Endemic to the lowlands of southwestern Ecuador and northwestern Peru, and on the Galapagos Islands.
Note: It is eaten by cattle.
Vernacular name: mazanilla de vaca.

15. *Lagascea mollis* CAV.
Suberect herb, to 60 cm high, hirtellous in distal parts. Leaves alternate; blade 2–5 cm long, ovate, serrate, acuminate, rounded at base; petiole to 1 cm long. Heads solitary, 1.5 cm wide, surrounded by 8–12 mm long foliaceous bracts, long-pedunculate; flowers white. Achenes 3 mm long; with 4 erect, stiff awns. Collection: 63740.
Weedy plant along forest edges. — Pantropical.

16. *Milleria quinqueflora* L.
Herb, to 1.5 m high. Stem slightly scabrous. Leaves opposite; blades at base of plant to 15–30 cm long, broadly ovate to elliptic in upper half, merging with petiole in lower half; leaves distally on plant gradually diminishing in size and becoming monomorphic. Inflorescence terminal, subspicate, the heads widely separated; ray flowers solitary on each head, yellow, 1 cm long, 3-lobed. Achenes 5 mm wide, leatherly, stiff when dry. Collections: 63076, 63314, ANDERSSON s.n. (S, cited in Areschoug 1869).
Common in disturbed sites. — Mexico to Peru.
Vernacular name: carrizo.

17. *Ophryosporus densiflorus* (BENTH.) R. M. KING & H. ROB.
Shrub, 1–2 m high. Stem glabrous. Leaves opposite; blade 4–13 cm long, ovate, acute, tapering at base, coarsely serrate except in lower one third; petiole 0.5–3 cm long. Inflorescence terminal, many-headed, the branchlets corymbose; flowers white. Collections: 63858, 63902; HINDS 410 (BM type of *Piqueria*

densiflora BENTH., K; cited by Robinson in Jørgensen and León-Yánez, 1999).
On hills in the dry forest. — Endemic to southwestern Ecuador.

18. *Parthenium hysterophorus* L.
Herb, 80 cm high. Stem sparsely pubescent, strongly ridged. Leaves alternate,
petiolate; blade to 25 cm long, broadly ovate, very deeply and concavely
incised. Inflorescence large and open, with up to several hundred heads; heads
white, 4 mm wide; pedicels slender. Achenes minute, with scale-like pappus.
Collection: 63983.
Rare weed in moist habitats. — Mexico and northern South America.

19. *Pectis cf. elongata* KUNTH
Erect, annual herb, 20–40 cm high. Stem glabrescent to minutely puberulent.
Leaves opposite, dotted beneath, sessile; blade 1–3 cm long, 2–3 mm wide,
linear, ciliate in the form of 3–6 bristly pairs in lower half. Heads terminal,
solitary or in separate pairs on each branchlet, yellow, 7 mm long, narrow;
involucral bracts 5 mm long; peduncle 1–2 cm long, bracteate. Achenes 3 mm
long, black; pappus 2 mm long. Collections: 63136, 63200, 63379.
Weed on open soils. — Widespread in America.

20. *Porophyllum ruderale* (JACQ.) CASS.
Erect herb, to 1 m high. Stem glabrous. Leaves alternate; blade 1–4 cm long,
broadly elliptic, entire, subobtuse at both ends; petiole 2–4 cm long. Heads 2 cm
long, solitary, long-pedunculate. Achenes 12 mm long, flat; pappus 8 mm long.
Collection: 63381.
Weed on open soils. — America, also on the Galapagos Islands.
Vernacular name: ruda de gallinazo llano.

21. *Pseudogynoxys scabra* (BENTH.) CUATREC.
Lianescent, to many meters long. Leaves alternate, puberulous beneath; blade
5–11 cm long, broadly ovate, entire, acute, cordate at base; petiole to 3 cm long.
Inflorescence on lateral branchlets of ca. 10 heads; heads 2 cm long; involucral
bracts 7 mm long, linear; flowers orange. Achenes 2 mm long; pappus 1 cm
long. Collection: 64046.
Rare in the dry forest. — Endemic to southwestern Ecuador and adjacent Peru.

22. *Schizoptera peduncularis* (BENTH.) S. F. BLAKE
Herb, to 80 cm high. Stem hirsute when young. Leaves opposite; blade 3–9 cm
long, elliptic, attenuate at both ends, serrate; petiole 0.5–2 cm long.
Inflorescence composed of several heads; heads 5 mm wide; peduncle 4–6 cm
long; flowers yellow. Collections: 63009, 63268, 63324.
Common in disturbed places. — Widespread in Mexico and Central America.

23. *Synedrella nodiflora* (L.) GAERTN.

Herb, to 0.5 m high. Stem more or less hirsute. Leaves opposite; blade 4–11 cm long, ovate, serrate, acute, attenuate at base; petiole 1–4 cm long. Heads sessile in leaf axils, to 1 cm long; disc and ray flowers yellow. Achenes 4 mm long; awns 2–3, spreading. Collections: 63057, 63517, ANDERSSON *s.n.* (S, cited in Areschoug 1869).

Common weed in the shadow of trees along trails. — Tropical America, including the Galapagos Islands.

24. *Wedelia grandiflora* BENTH.

Shrub, to 3 m high. Twigs hirsute. Leaves opposite, scabrous; blade 3–14 cm long, narrowly to broadly ovate, slightly to coarsely serrate, attenuate at both ends; petiole to 4 cm long. Heads 4 cm wide, mostly solitary; peduncle 2–10 cm long; flowers yellow. Collections: 63165, 63327, 63540, 63630, 64048.

Very common in open places. — Coastal Ecuador and Peru.

Uses: The sap is used to cure swellings, heal wounds, and remove blackheads and acne. The plant is also used to remove thorns and as glue.

Vernacular names: miracielo, resina de varita, trementina.

BATACEAE (SALTWORT FAMILY)

Succulent, dioecious or monoecious herbs or shrubs. Leaves opposite, entire. Flowers in axillary spikes or solitary. Staminate flowers with perianth and 4 stamens. Pistillate flowers without perianth. A family with only two species in mangroves and salt marshes in the tropics.

1. *Batis maritima* L.

Succulent herb, to 20 cm high, creeping and sprawling, rooting at nodes, dioecious. Stem glabrous. Leaves sessile, 1–3.5 cm long, narrowly oblanceolate. Staminate spikes to 8 mm long, ovoid; flowers subtended by rounded bracts. Pistillate spikes to 2 cm long, cylindrical. Collections: 63475, 63951, 63980.

Common on salt flats. — Widespread from Florida to Brazil, also on the Galapagos Islands.

Note: It is eaten by donkeys.

Vernacular name: vidrillo

BIGNONIACEAE (TRUMPET-CREEPER FAMILY)

Trees or lianas. Leaves mostly opposite, simple or compound, often with tendrils. Inflorescence racemose, paniculate, or reduced. Flowers large and showy, bisexual, zygomorphic; calyx cup-shaped or bilabiate; corolla 5-parted; stamens usually 4. Fruit a capsule with winged seeds or a berry. A family of 800 species in warm parts of the world, richly developed in South America.

Key to the Species

1a. Shrubs or trees
   2a. Leaves simple
      3a. Leaves entire; flowers green   2. *Crescentia cujete*
      3b. Leaves serrate; flowers yellow   9. *Tecoma castanifolia*
   2b. Leaves palmately 5-foliolate
      4a. Calyx 1–1.5 cm long   7. *Tabebuia billbergii*
      4b. Calyx 0.7–1 cm long   8. *Tabebuia chrysantha*
1b. Lianas
   5a. Leaves simple   4. *Macranthisiphon longiflorus*
   5b. Leaves compound
      6a. Leaves 2-foliolate
         7a. Stem not with strong garlic odour; flowers yellow
                                       3. *Macfadyena unguis-cati*
         7b. Stem with strong garlic odour; flowers purple with white throat
                                           5. *Mansoa hymenaea*
      6b. Leaves 3-foliolate
         8a. Flowers white   1. *Arrabidaea corallina*
         8b. Flowers purple or violet with white throat   6. *Mansoa verrucifera*

1. *Arrabidaea corallina* (JACQ.) SANDWITH
Liana, high climbing. Leaves 3-foliolate; leaflets to 19 cm long, elliptic-ovate, subattenuate, rounded at base. Flowers (not seen) white, 3–5 cm long. Capsule 39–60 cm long, 2 cm wide, flat. Seeds 4.5 cm long, flat. Collections: 63946, 63953. Probably common in the dry forest. — Mexico to Argentina.
Phenology: Flowers in January according to local informants.
Uses: The stems are used to tie up sacks.
Vernacular name: bejuco blanco.

2. *Crescentia cujete* L. (Plate 14)
Tree, to 10 m high. Leaves alternate to fascicled, simple, sessile; blade 5–23 cm long, obovate, entire, subobtuse, attenuate at base. Cauliflorous inflorescence composed of one or two stout flowers. Corolla lobes green, to 6 cm long. Fruit yellow-green, to 20 cm wide, globose. Collections: 63582, 64145, 85362.
Common and spontaneous along trails in closed forest. — The native range of the tree gourd is obscure but it is semi-cultivated throughout most of tropical America.
Uses: The dry, hollow fruit shell is used as a bowl for drinking water or as a cup. The pulp is used to cure head aches and the wood is used for tool handles in chisels, saws, hammers, and gun stocks.
Vernacular name: mate.

3. *Macfadyena unguis-cati* (L.) A. H. GENTRY
Liana, trailing and adhering to trees by adventitious roots. Leaves 2-foliolate, petiolate for up to 5 cm; leaflets to 12 cm long, elliptic, entire, attenuate at apex.

Leaflets of juvenile plants 1–2 cm long. Flowers yellow, to 10 cm long. Capsule to 90 cm long, 1 cm wide, linear, flat. Seeds 4 cm long, very flat, winged. Collections: 63954, 64152.

Probably common in closed forest, the juveniles more common than the adults. — Mexico, West Indies to Argentina.

4. *Macranthisiphon longiflorus* (CAV.) K. SCHUM.
Liana, to 10 m long. Leaves simple or 2-foliolate; blade to 13 cm long, elliptic-lanceolate, entire; petiole to 2 cm long. Flowers several together, orange, 10 cm long, slender. Capsule to 30 cm long, 1.5 cm wide, flat. Seeds 4.5 cm long, winged. Collections: 63610, 63787, 63848, 64050, EGGERS 14009 (US, cited in Fl. Ec.).

Very common in thorn forest. — Monotypic genus endemic to coastal Ecuador and adjacent Peru.

Uses: It is used medicinally to cure coughs. The strong, flexible stems were previously used as lashings in the construction of rafts and making of fences and corrals.

Vernacular name: bejuco de hilar corral.

5. *Mansoa hymenaea* (DC.) A. H. GENTRY
Liana, to several meters long. Stem with strong garlic odour. Leaves 2-foliolate, often with a tendril, petiolate; leaflets 5–20 cm long, ovate-elliptic. Inflorescence paniculate. Flowers purple with white throat, 6 cm long. Fruit 25 cm long, 2 cm wide, flat, with prominent midrib. Collections: 63832A, 63921, 64113, 64116.

Common in closed forest. — Mexico to Brazil.

Uses: The stem is used as lashing in rafts, fences, corrals, and saddles.

Vernacular name: bejuco de ajo hacho.

6. *Mansoa verrucifera* (SCHLTDL.) A. H. GENTRY
Liana, high climbing. Leaves 3-foliolate; leaflets 7–18 cm long, attenuate, rounded at base. Inflorescence much elongate, many-flowered. Flowers purple or violet with white throat, 6 cm long. Capsule 22–30 cm long, 2–3 cm wide, rough like sandpaper. Seeds 5 cm long; wings distinctly delimited. Collections: 63832B, 63935, 64047, 64117, 64147, 85364.

Common in closed forest. — Southern Mexico to Guayana and Brazil.

Phenology: Flowers in August.

Uses: The stems are used as lashing in rafts, fences, and corrals.

Vernacular name: bejuco de ajo hacho.

7. *Tabebuia billbergii* (BUREAU & K. SCHUM.) STANDL. subsp. *ampla* A. H. GENTRY
Shrub or tree, 4–10 m high. Leaves palmately 5-foliolate; leaflets 5–10 cm long, entire, below mostly glabrate with simple hairs at axils of nerves. Inflorescence a few-flowered distal cluster. Flowers yellow, 6–8 cm long; calyx 1–1.5 cm long,

sparsely pubescent. Capsule 10–18 cm long, 1 cm wide, hairy. Collections: 64007, 64126.
Common in the thorn forest. — Endemic to western Ecuador and adjacent Peru. Uses: The wood is used as timber for furniture, boats, boards, houses, fences, and charcoal. Previously it was used for battens and loom bars in the cotton textile manufacture. It is eaten by donkeys.
Vernacular name: madera negra.

8. *Tabebuia chrysantha* (JACQ.) G. NICHOLSON subsp. *chrysantha*
Tree, to 20 m high. Leaves palmately 5-foliolate; leaflets to 14 cm long, entire, below with stellate hairs along nerves. Inflorescence a few-flowered distal cluster. Flowers yellow, 6 cm long; calyx 7–10 mm long, densely pubescent. Fruit 8–18 cm long, 1 cm wide, copiously hairy. Collections: 63949, 63950, 63991, 64104, 64135, 85332.
Very common in the thorn forest. — Mexico to Venezuela. Disjunct in Ecuador. Uses: The valuable hard wood of this species is widely used in construction of houses, boats, furnitures, fences, and to make stakes, wedges, posts, and charcoal. Previously it was used to make loom bars in the cotton textile manufacture. It is eaten by cattle.
Vernacular name: guayacán.

9. *Tecoma castanifolia* (D. DON) MELCH.
Shrub or small tree, 5–8 m high. Twigs white-spotted. Leaves simple; blade 8–19 cm long, narrowly ovate, serrate. Inflorescence many-flowered. Flowers yellow, 5 cm long. Capsule 8–20 cm long, 5 mm wide. Collections: 63760, 63859, 85335.
Common in the thorn forest. — Endemic to coastal Ecuador and adjacent Peru. Uses: The wood is used as timber for construction of houses, stakes, fences, shores, stanchions, and shovels.
Vernacular name: muyuyo macho.

BIXACEAE (LIPSTICK-TREE FAMILY)
Trees, shrubs, or herbs, sometimes with red sap. Leaves alternate, simple or compound, entire or palmately lobed; stipules present. Flowers actinomorphic, bisexual, 5-merous; stamens numerous. Fruit a capsule. Seeds often embedded in wool. A small tropical family with 16 species.

Key to the Species

1a. Shrub; leaves entire; cultivated — 1. *Bixa orellana*
1b. Tree; leaves deeply 3–7-lobed; native — 2. *Cochlospermum vitifolium*

1. *Bixa orellana* L. [cult.]

The annatto-tree (Collection: BARCLAY 425; BM, F, US; cited in Fl. Ec.) is a wellknown dye in food. It was already collected on the island by the English botanist Barclay a century ago.

2. *Cochlospermum vitifolium* (WILLD.) SPRENG.

Tree, 10–18 m high. Trunk simple; bark grey, smooth. Leaves deciduous, simple, deeply (3–)5–7-lobed; lobes to 10–15 cm long, ovate-elliptic, serrate. Inflorescence many-flowered, racemose. Flowers yellow, 11 cm wide, rotate. Capsule 6–8 cm long, obovoid, 5-valvate, pendent; seeds 4 mm long, embedded in white wool. Collections: 63794, 63843, 63870, 63880, 64096, 85316.

Very common in savanna and thorn forest. - Mexico to Peru.

Phenology: Flowers from July to September.

Uses: Wool occasionally gathered for ticking.

Vernacular name: bototillo.

BOMBACACEAE (KAPOK-TREE FAMILY)

Large trees, often with armed trunks. Leaves alternate, simple or digitately compound; stipules caducous. Flowers solitary or fascicled, usually large, bisexual, zygomorphic, 5-merous. Stamens 5 or numerous. Fruit a fleshy or dry capsule. Seeds often embedded in wool. A tropical family with 200 species.

Key to the Species

1a. Leaves simple	3. *Ochroma pyramidale*
1b. Leaves palmately compound	
2a. Flowers shorter than 2 cm; fruits shorter than 4 cm	2. *Eriotheca ruizii*
2b. Flowers longer than 3 cm; fruits longer than 10 cm	
3a. Stamens 5; native	1. *Ceiba trichistandra*
3b. Stamens numerous; introduced and planted	
4a. Flowers 5 cm long	4. *Pachira* sp.
4b. Flowers 10 cm long	5. *Pseudobombax millei*

1. *Ceiba trichistandra* (A. GRAY) BAKH. (Plates 6, 13).

Giant tree, to 30 m high. Trunk grey-green, columnar, with 4–6 prominent buttresses; spines usually present, 1.5 cm wide, broad-based. Leaves deciduous, palmately 5–9-foliolate; leaflets 5–15 cm long, oblanceolate, entire. Inflorescence 1–3-flowered. Flowers appear after defoliation; calyx purple, 2–3 cm long; petals white, 5 cm long, tomentose; stamens 5. Capsule 15–20 cm long, woody, dehiscent. Seeds 7 mm long, embedded in white wool. Collections: 63631, 63808, 63816, 64105, 85338.

The kapok-tree is common and widespread in the thorn forest and abundant locally in mature dry forest. — Endemic to southwestern Ecuador and adjacent Peru.

Phenology: Flowering in June and July on leafless trees. The capsules ripen during the following months, few at a time.

Uses: Gathering of kapok for ticking is still a source of income for a few islanders. The wood is burnt to ash for soap. Water drained from the roots is used to treat kidney problems. It is eaten by cattle and donkeys.

Vernacular name: ceibo.

2. *Eriotheca ruizii* (K. SCHUM.) A. ROBYNS

Broad-crowned tree, 10–25 m high; subterranean root tubers 10–15 cm wide, globose. Trunk usually unbranched; bark grey, more or less sculptured and with a smooth surface. Leaves deciduous, palmately lobed; leaflets 7–15 cm long, elliptic or obovate, serrulate. Inflorescence many-flowered, much branched. Flowers creamy white; petals 1 cm long; pedicels 2–5 mm long. Capsule 2–3 cm long, dehiscent by five valves. Seeds embedded in creamy wool. Collections: 63805, 63941, 64011, 64109, 85314.

Characteristic tree in the dry forest but also common in the thorn forest. — Endemic to southwestern Ecuador and adjacent Peru.

Phenology: Flowers from July to November.

Uses: The wood is used for boards, boats, houses, furnitures, and charcoal. It is eaten by cattle and deer.

Vernacular name: chirigoyo.

3. *Ochroma pyramidale* (CAV. EX LAM.) URB.

Tree, to 10 m high. Trunk unbranched; wood very light. Leaves persistent, simple; blade 20–30 cm wide, broadly ovate or orbiculate, more or less 3-lobed, 7-nerved, rounded or subacute, cordate at base. Flowers white, 15 cm long, fleshy. Capsule 12–20 cm long, 2.5 cm wide, fusiform. Seeds embedded in wool. Collection: 63834.

Spontaneous, but rare, on disturbed soils. — Widespread from Mexico to Bolivia, including the Galapagos Islands.

This species was often named *Ochroma lagopus* in older literature. In western Ecuador, the balsa has its natural area of distribution in the evergreen rain forest at the foot of the Andes. It occurs as a pioneer tree in gaps in virgin vegetation and becomes dominant in disturbed places. The species never grows tall on Puná Island due to the poor ecological conditions. The balsa tree has never been worth exploiting commercially on the island. In ancient times, balsa logs were, no doubt, extracted further upstream along the Guayas river and rafted downwards for final belabouring.

Uses: The balsa tree was once used to treat baldness. The light wood is usefull for rafts, floats, boards, and boxes. Previously also used to make warping boards in the cotton textile manufacture. The native islanders still remember all these uses of the tree, although they are no longer practiced.

Vernacular name: balsa.

4. *Pachira* sp. [cult.]
A few stands of this large tree (Collection: 75486) are planted on Puná Island.
Uses: Kapok for ticking, but barely exploited any longer.
Vernacular names: capó, ceibo capó.

5. *Pseudobombax millei* (STANDL.) A. ROBYNS [cult.]
Occasionally cultivated (Collection: 75485) but probably not found in a wild
state. More common in cultivation in erlier times. — Endemic to coastal
Ecuador.
Uses: Kapok for ticking, but barely exploited any longer.
Vernacular name: beldaco.

BORAGINACEAE (BORAGE FAMILY)
Herbs, shrubs, or trees. Leaves alternate, simple; stipules lacking. Inflorescence
cymose, globose, or spicate and uncurling as the flowers open. Flowers small to
medium-sized, bisexual, 5-merous; stamens 5. Fruit a 4-parted schizocarp or a
drupe. A family with 2000 species of worldwide distribution.

Key to the Species

1a. Shrubs or trees
  2a. Inflorescence broad, cymose
    3a. Flowers white, 1 cm long; leaves short-acuminate   1. *Cordia alliodora*
    3b. Flowers yellow, 3 cm long; leaves obtuse   2. *Cordia lutea*
  2b. Inflorescence narrow, composed of spikes or the flowers crowded distally
    4a. Flowers orange; corona-lobes filiform   10. *Tournefortia psilostachya*
    4b. Flowers white; corona-lobes not filiform
      5a. Flowers crowded in a distal head   3. *Cordia macrocephala*
      5b. Flowers on spicate inflorescences
        6a. Leaves serrate; stems stiff hairy   4. *Cordia*
        6b. Leaves entire; stems nearly glabrous   9. *Tournefortia bicolor*
1b. Herbs
  7a. Flowers blue or violet   7. *Heliotropium indicum*
  7b. Flowers white
    8a. Leaves subsessile, succulent   6. *Heliotropium curassavicum*
    8b. Leaves petiolate, not succulent
      9a. Plants sparsely pubescent, erect   5. *Heliotropium angiospermum*
      9b. Plants densely pilose throughout, prostrate   8. *Heliotropium procumbens*

1. *Cordia alliodora* (RUIZ & PAV.) OKEN
Tree, to 20 m high. Stem stellately pubescent; nodes inhabited by ants. Leaves
deciduous; blade 8–20 cm long, elliptic, entire, short-acuminate at apex, oblique
at base; petiole 1.5–3 cm long. Inflorescence cymose, with over 100 flowers.
Flowers 1 cm long, subsessile; corolla white; calyx 5–7 mm long, ribbed,
persistent. Fruit cylindrical, not drupaceous, one-seeded. Collections: 63426,

63563A, 85331.

Common in the dry forest. — Tropical America, also on the Galapagos Islands. A related species, *Cordia macrantha* CHODAT, is mentioned for Puná Island by Valverde (1998) (no specimen cited). It is endemic to the Guayas province and is known as 'laurel fino' and 'laurel de Puná'. The latter name is also widely applied to *Cordia alliodora* elsewhere on the coastal plain of Ecuador.

Phenology: Flowers from May through June.

Uses: The wood is excellent and used for furniture, beds, boards, boats, and houses.

Vernacular name: laurel, laurel de montaña.

2. *Cordia lutea* LAM.

Shrub or occasionally a tree, 0.5–8 m high. Stem pubescent. Leaves scabrous above; blade 5–11(–25) cm long, ovate, obscurely crenulate, obtuse, rounded at base; petiole 1–2.5 cm long. Inflorescence cymose, many-flowered. Flower sessile; corolla 3–4 cm wide, pale yellow; calyx 1 cm long, ribbed. Drupe white, 2 cm long, fleshy, 1-celled. Collections: 63004, 63413, 63429, 63874, 85317.

This is perhaps the most common woody plant on Puná Island. A dwarf shrub in the salt marsh, a bush or treelet in the thorn scrub, and an occasional medium sized tree in the dry forest. — Endemic to the dry lowlands of Ecuador, including the Galapagos Islands, and northwestern Peru.

Phenology: Flowers appear throughout the dry season and the fruits ripen before the onset of the rainy season.

Uses: Used medicinally to treat dermal fungus infections and to cure attacks of ringworm. Wood used for boats, stakes, fences, and charcoal. The sticky flesh of the fruit is used to paste paper and as hair wax. Previously it was used to make heddles, rods, and warping posts for looms in the cotton textile manufacture. It is eaten by cattle and goats.

Vernacular names: muyuyo, muyuyo hembra.

3. *Cordia macrocephala* (DESV.) KUNTH

Shrub, 1–4 m high. Stem stellately puberulent. Leaves slightly scabrous above; blade 6–16 cm long, ovate, serrate-crenate, more or less decurrent at base; petiole 1–2 cm long. Inflorescence terminal, the flowers crowded in a distal head; penduncle 3–6 cm long. Flowers white, 1 cm wide. Collections: 63187, 63438, 63786, 63934.

Occasional understory shrub. — The Caribbean area and northern South America.

Phenology: Flowers throughout the dry season.

Vernacular names: palo negro, palito blanco.

4. *Cordia* sp.

Shrub, to 3 m high. Stem with stiff hairs. Leaves scabrous above, pubescent below; blade 6–18 cm long, narrowly ovate to lanceolate, acute, coarsely serrate distally, narrowed at base; petiole 5–15 mm long. Inflorescence a terminal or axillary spike, to 12 cm long, 10–30 flowered; flowers crowded in distal half, white, 0.5 cm long; calyx 2–3 mm long, persistent. Drupe red. Collections: 63513, 63855, 86012.

Uncommon in the dry forest.

Phenology: Flowering begins in June.

5. *Heliotropium angiospermum* MURRAY

Herb, 20–80 cm high, sometimes woody at base. Stem sparsely pubescent. Leaf-blade 5–9 cm long, elliptic, acute to short-acuminate, narrowed at base; petiole 4–8 mm long. Inflorescence pedunculate; spikes 1–2, 5–10 cm long. Flowers white, 2 mm long. Fruit 2 mm long, 2-carpelled. Collections: 63061, 63066, 63257, 63345, 63359.

Common weed. — Widespread from Florida to Argentina. Also on the Galapagos Islands.

6. *Heliotropium curassavicum* L.

Prostrate herb, forming dense mats. Leaves succulent, subsessile; blade 2–4 cm long, oblanceolate, subacute, gradually narrowing at base. Inflorescence pedunculate; spikes 2, to 4 cm long. Flowers white, 2 mm long. Fruit 2 mm long, globose. Collection: 63903.

Occasional on salt flats. — Tropical coasts of both hemispheres, including the Galapagos Islands.

7. *Heliotropium indicum* L.

Herb, 30–60 cm high, with a well developed taproot. Stem densely pilose on young parts. Leaf-blade 7–12 cm long, ovate, acute, subcuneate at base; petiole 1–5 cm long, more or less merging with blade. Inflorescence to 20 cm long, spicate. Flowers blue or violet, 4 mm long, sessile. Fruit 2–3 mm long, deeply 4-lobed. Collections: 63093, 63295, 63458, 63620.

Common on sandy beaches and in clearings. — Pantropical weed. Known from the Galapagos Islands.

Uses: It is eaten by birds.

Vernacular name: rabo de gallo.

8. *Heliotropium procumbens* MILL.

Prostrate herb. Stem densely pilose. Leaf-blade 1.5–3 cm long, ovate-elliptic, mucronulate, cuneate at base; petiole 4–8 mm long. Inflorescence short-pedunculate; spikes 2–3, 2–5 cm long. Flowers white, 1 mm long. Fruit 4-lobed. Collection: 63778.

Uncommon at dried-up water holes. — Widespread in warm parts of the New World.

9. *Tournefortia bicolor* Sw.
Shrub, to 2 m high. Stem nearly glabrous. Leaf-blade 6–11 cm long, elliptic, acute-acuminate, entire, cuneate at base; petiole 3–7 mm long. Inflorescence cymose; spikes to 5 cm long, curled. Flowers white, 5 mm long. Fruit 5 mm wide, globose, white, pulpy. Collections: 63514, 63710, 63817, 63911.
Common understory shrub in the dry forest. — The Caribbean and tropical America.
Phenology: Flowering in June.
Note: It is eaten by birds.
Vernacular names: fruta de paloma, pechiche, rabo de gallo.

10. *Tournefortia psilostachya* KUNTH
Shrub or scrambler, to 3 m high, often strigose in young parts. Leaf-blade 4–9 cm long, narrowly ovate, acuminate, obtuse at base; petiole 5–10 mm long. Inflorescence much branched; spikes 4–7 cm long. Flowers 7 mm long, orange; corolla-lobes filiform. Fruit 5 mm long, pulpy. Collections: 63937, 64002, 64037.
Uncommon understory shrub in the dry forest. — Northwestern South America and the Galapagos Islands.
Phenology: Flowers from September to November.

BROMELIACEAE (BROMELIAD FAMILY)
Mostly epiphytic plants. Leaves in a basal rosette, linear. Inflorescence terminal; bracts often strongly colored. Flowers 3-parted; sepals green; petals colored. Fruits a capsule or a berry. A family with 1700 species in the New World.

Key to the Species

1a. Leaves longer than 5 cm
    2a. Inflorescence once branched; leaves to 15 cm long   1. *Tillandsia disticha*
    2b. Inflorescence twice branched; leaves to 50 cm long   2. *Tillandsia latifolia*
1b. Leaves to 5 cm long   3. *Tillandsia recurvata*

1. *Tillandsia disticha* KUNTH
Epiphyte, 25 cm high. Leaves to 15 cm long, with white scales; sheaths broadly ovate, slightly fleshy. Inflorescence once branched with the branches originating from one point; spikes 3–8, to 5 cm long; bracts 1 cm long. Flowers yellow. Capsule 4–5 cm long, linear. Seeds including the woolly thread to 5 cm long. Collections: 63809, 85344.
Common locally in the forest. — Endemic to western Ecuador and adjacent Peru.

2. *Tillandsia latifolia* MEYEN

Erect epiphyte, to 80 cm high. Leaves to 50 cm long, narrow, filiform-acuminate at apex, silvery white-scaly; sheaths indistinct. Inflorescence orange-red, twice branched; lateral spikes 3–8 cm long; bracts 1.5 cm long. Flowers violet or pink. Capsule 3 cm long. Seeds including the woolly thread 2 cm long. Collections: 63792, 63988, 64034, 64124, 85345.

Common epiphyte in the thorn and dry forest. — Peru to Colombia.

3. *Tillandsia recurvata* (L.) L.

Epiphyte, forming dense clumps, typically 10 cm wide. Leaves distichous, to 5 cm long, very narrow, white-scaly; sheaths completely concealing the stem. Inflorescence simple to occasionally 5-flowered; peduncle to 8 cm long. Flowers erect. Capsule 1.5–3 cm long. Seeds including the woolly thread 1 cm long. Collections: 64006, 64125, 85343.

Common locally in the forest. — Widespread from southern United States to Chile and Argentina.

BURSERACEAE (FRANKINCENSE FAMILY)

Trees or shrubs with aromatic oils in the bark. Leaves alternate, pinnately compound; stipules absent. Flowers small, uni- or bisexual; sepals and petals 3–5; stamens 6–10. Fruit drupaceous with 1–5 stones. A pantropical family with 600 species.

1. *Bursera graveolens* (KUNTH) TRIANA & PLANCH.

Tree, to 8 m high. Stem subglabrous, ferrugineous, emiting a strong scent when broken. Leaves to 20 cm long, borne in distal clusters; leaflets 7–9, 4–7 cm long, ovate, coarsely crenate, acuminate, cuneate at base; rachis winged. Inflorescence 10 cm long. Flowers (not seen) 3 mm long, 4-parted. Fruit 1 cm long, fleshy. Collections: 63802, 85342.

Occasional in thorn forest. — The Caribbean to Ecuador, including the Galapagos Islands and adjacent Peru.

Uses: Broken branches are used as repellant against plages of insects. The species is also used to cure coughs, swellings, bone aches, ringworm, and to remove blackheads and acne. The wood is used to make statuettes of saints and for charcoal.

Vernacular name: palo santo.

CACTACEAE (CACTUS FAMILY)

Stem-succulents of variable habit, sometimes epiphytic. Spines usually present, borne in woolly clusters. Leaves absent or reduced. Flowers usually large and showy, naked or with spines or hairs; sepals and petals numerous, in gradual transition; stamens numerous. Fruit a berry. A family with nearly 2000 species, mostly in arid parts of America.

Key to the Species

1a. Stem-segments longer than 20 cm
  2a. Stems 4–10-ribbed; plants terrestrial
    3a. Flowers and fruits spiny   1. *Armatocereus cartwrightianus*
    3b. Flowers and fruits spineless
      4a. Floral tube and fruit purple; flowering stems
        covered by a conspicuous, hairy beard   5. *Pilosocereus tweedyanus*
      4b. Floral tube and fruits green; flowering stems hairless   2. *Cereus diffusus*
  2b. Stems trigonous; plant epiphytic or epilithic   3. *Hylocereus polyrhizus*
1b. Stem-segments shorter than 10 cm   4. *Opuntia pubescens*

1. *Armatocereus cartwrightianus* (BRITTON & ROSE) BACKEB. ex A. W. HILL (Plate 13)
Arborescent, to 10 m high. Stem 7–9-ribbed, segmented. Spines many per areole, those on the trunk sometimes to 20 cm long. Flowers 7–10 cm long, bearing woolly areoles and bristly spines; petals white. Fruit 6–10 cm long, first green and spiny, later red and smooth. Collections: 63154, 63238, 63404, 85341, 85357, 85358.
Abundant in the savanna and thorn scrub, less common on salt flats. — Endemic to semi-arid regions of western Ecuador and northern Peru.
Phenology: Flowers principally in April and May and the fruits ripen from September to December.
Uses: The fruit is eaten by children. The stout spines are used by weavers as needles or are inserted in the ends of the *piquigua* to keep the threads apart. The plant is only eaten by goats.
Vernacular name: cardón.

2. *Cereus diffusus* (BRITTON & ROSE) WERDERM.
Shrubby, mostly 2–5 m tall, with elongated, arching to suberect branches. Stem 6–9-ribbed. Spines many per areole, stout. Flowers 7–9 cm long; tube green, spineless, bearing small bracts; petals white. Fruit 4–7 cm long, green. Collections: 63170, 64087, 85340.
Common in thorn scrub. — Ecuador and northern Peru.
Phenology: Flowers chiefly in November and December.
Note: The fruit is edible, but not appreciated. It is eaten by cattle.
Vernacular name: jiso.

3. *Hylocereus polyrhizus* (F. A. C. WEBER) BRITTON & ROSE
Epiphytic or epilithic shrub, 2–4 m wide. Stem trigonous, with aerial roots. Spines few per areole, short, and broad-based. Flowers 30 cm long, bearing foliaceous bracts; petals white. Fruit 8–10 cm long, red, tubercled. Collections:

64089, 85354.

Common epiphyte on *Ceiba trichistandra* and on large boulders on the beach. — Northern Peru to Panama.

Uses: The flesh of the edible fruit makes a red coloring in a watery solution, which is used during carnival games to paint the victims red. It is also used as a dye for textiles. It is eaten by donkeys.

Vernacular name: pitajaya.

4. *Opuntia pubescens* J. C. WENDL. ex PFEIFF.

Prostrate, to 20 cm high, much branched. Stem segmented; joints typically 5 cm long, terete to slightly flattened, readily detaching. Spines many per areole, acicular, straight. Flowers yellow, 4 cm long, spiny. Collection: EGGERS *s.n.* (B, cited in Fl. Ec.).

Known only from one ancient collection on Puná Island from El Limbo and generally rare in the Ecuadorian lowlands. — Widespread from Mexico to Argentina.

5. *Pilosocereus tweedyanus* (BRITTON & ROSE) BYLES & G. D. ROWLEY

Arborescent, 5–7 m high. Stem 6–9-ribbed, bluish. Spines many per areole, stout. Flowering stems producing a copious, hairy beard. Flowers 7 cm long, stout; tube purple, spineless, with minute bracts; petals white. Fruit purple, 2 cm long, depresssed globose. Collection: 64027.

A few plants grow near the summit of Zambapala hill and others along Estero de Boca. — Endemic to arid Ecuador and adjacent Peru, to at least 1000 m above sea level.

CAESALPINIACEAE (CAESALPINIA FAMILY)

Trees, shrubs, or herbs. Leaves usually alternate and pinnately compound, occasionally bilobed; stipules common. Inflorescence racemose. Flowers usually zygomorphic, 5-merous; stamens 1–10. Fruit a pod. A family with about 2500 species in warm regions of the world. Several of the 12 species here described are not native.

Key to the Species

1a. Leaves simple, shallowly bilobed   1. *Bauhinia aculeata*
1b. Leaves compound
  2a. Leaves pinnate
    3a. Flowers brown; cultivated and escaped   12. *Tamarindus indica*
    3b. Flowers yellow, except for brown venation
      4a. Herbs, woody at base; leaflets 13–18 pairs   5. *Chamaecrista nictitans*
      4b. Shrubs or trees; leaflets 2–14 pairs
        5a. Leaflets 3–14 pairs, if 3 pairs then leaflets longer than 5 cm
          6a. Pods longer than 30 cm   7. *Senna mollissima*

6b. Pods shorter than 20 cm
    7a. Pods alate from the middle   6. *Senna alata*
    7b. Pods not alate
        8a. Pods papery and transversally ridged   10. *Senna pistaciifolia*
        8b. Pods not papery and transversally ridged
            9a. Leaflets 4–5 pairs, 4–7 cm long   9. *Senna occidentalis*
            9b. Leaflets 6–9 pairs, 2–4 cm long   11. *Senna robiniifolia*
   5b. Leaflets 2–3 pairs, to 5 cm long
       10a. Stems hirsute; pods 5 cm long   4. *Chamaecrista absus*
       10b. Stems glabrous; pods 8–20 cm long   8. *Senna obtusifolia*
2b. Leaves bipinnate
   11a. Pinnae 3–5 cm long; native   2. *Caesalpinia glabrata*
   11b. Pinnae 10–20 cm long; cultivated   3. *Caesalpinia pulcherrima*

1. *Bauhinia aculeata* L.
Shrub, to 4 m high. Twigs puberulent; spinescent stipules paired, 2–5 mm long, recurved. Leaves shallowly bilobed; blade 5–12 cm long, broadly ovate, palmately nerved, cordate at base; petiole 2–3 cm long. Flowers white, 10 cm across; petals 8 cm long. Pods 12–19 cm long, 1.5–2 cm wide, flat. Collections: 63445, 63509, 63853B, 63887, 85321.
Common in open forest. — West Indies to Peru.
Uses: The wood is used for stakes and charcoal. The plant may cause skin rashes. It is eaten by donkeys.
Vernacular names: espino colorado, pica, picapica.

2. *Caesalpinia glabrata* KUNTH
Tree, to 15 m high. Trunk smooth with large, white spots. Twigs unarmed. Leaves bipinnate; pinnae in 5–8 pairs, 3–5 cm long; leaftlets 4–8 pairs, 5–12 mm long, oblong, entire, sessile, obtuse at apex. Inflorescence to 10 cm long, flowers few at a time. Flowers yellow, 1.5 cm long; pedicels 0.5–1 cm long. Pods 4–7 cm long, 1 cm thick, black. Collections: 63237, 63349, 63534, 63945, 85323.
Very common in savanna and thorn forest. — Arid Ecuador and Peru.
Phenology: Flowers throughout the year.
Uses: The wood is used for wedges, rigging posts, houses, and boats and also for firewood and charcoal. It is eaten by cattle, goats, and deer.
Vernacular name: cascol.

3. *Caesalpinia pulcherrima* (L.) Sw. [cult.]
The Pride of Barbados (Collection: 63566) is grown in gardens and parks. — Well known pantropical ornamental of uncertain origin.
Vernacular name: birondesa.

4. *Chamaecrista absus* (L.) H. S. IRWIN & BARNEBY
Slender shrub, to 1 m high. Stem stiff hairy. Leaves pinnate, petiolate for 3 cm; leaflets 2 pairs, 2–4.5 cm long, obliquely elliptic; petiolules 2 mm long.

Inflorescence terminal, racemose. Flowers yellow, 5–7 mm long, short-pedicellate. Pods 5 cm long, 7 mm wide, flat, slightly hairy. Collection: 63579. Rare in waste places. — Pantropical.

5. *Chamaecrista nictitans* (L.) MOENCH
Herb, 0.5–1 m high, woody at base. Leaves pinnate, 6–8 cm long; leaflets 13–18 pairs, 1–1.5 cm long, linear, subsessile. Inflorescence axillary, few-flowered. Flowers yellow. Pod to 5 cm long, 3–5 mm wide, flat, hirsute. Collections: 63109, 63215, 63435.
Common in open places. — Widely distributed in the Americas.

6. *Senna alata* (L.) ROXB.
Shrub, 1.5 m high. Leaves pinnate; leaflets 6–14 pairs, 5–17 cm long, oblong-obovate, rounded and mucronulate, obliquely inequilateral at base; petiolules 1–2 mm long; rachis angled. Inflorescence much elongated, spike-like, many-flowered, with caducous bracts at apex. Flowers yellow, showy. Pods 13–15 cm long, 1.5 cm wide, longitudinally alate from the middle of each valve. Collection: 63388.
Occasional around homesites. — Warm regions of America, Africa, and Asia.

7. *Senna mollissima* (HUMB. & BONPL. ex WILLD.) H. S. IRWIN & BARNEBY var. *mollissima*
Slender tree, 4–7 m high. Twigs pubescent. Leaves pinnate; leaflets 3–5 pairs, 7–19 cm long, elliptic, attenuate, rounded at base; petiolules to 5 mm long. Inflorescence a panicle of racemes. Flowers yellow with brown venation, 3 cm wide; pedicels to 2 cm long. Pods 30–45 cm long, 1.5 cm wide, flat with conspicuously raised margins. Collections: 63328, 63524, 63923, 85337, ANDERSSON *s.n.* (S, cited in Areschoug 1869).
Common pioneer in clearings. — Mexico to Peru. The variety is endemic to arid coastal Ecuador and Peru.
Uses: The wood is used to make stakes and charcoal. It is eaten by cattle, goats, and donkeys.
Vernacular name: abejón, flor de abejón.

8. *Senna obtusifolia* (L.) H. S. IRWIN & BARNEBY
Shrub, 0.5–1.5 m high. Stem glabrous. Leaves pinnate; leaflets 2–3 pairs, 2.5–4.5 cm long, obovate, rounded and mucronulate; petiolules 2 mm long. Inflorescence axillary, several-flowered, short-pedunculate. Flowers yellow. Pods 8–20 cm long, 3–5 mm wide, narrow, conspicuously curved. Collections: 63003, 63243, 63357, 63617, ANDERSSON *s.n.* (S, cited in Areschoug 1869).
Abundant in disturbed, rural places. — Pantropical weed. Known from the Galapagos Islands. It is eaten by goats.
Vernacular names: cafetillo, fréjol de monte, frejolillo de monte.

9. *Senna occidentalis* (L.) LINK
Shrub, 0.5–1 m high. Leaves pinnate, to 25 cm long, with columnar glands at the base of the petiole; leaflets 4–5 pairs, 4–7 cm long, elliptic, acuminate and mucronulate; petiolules 1–2 mm long. Inflorescence with several flowers at a time, axillary to terminal, shorter than leaves. Flowers yellow, 3 cm wide. Pods 8–10 cm long, 1 cm wide, linear, flat. Collections: 63207, 63356.
Common around homesites. — An almost pantropical weed, also on the Galapagos Islands.
Vernacular name: cafetillo de monte.

10. *Senna pistaciifolia* (KUNTH) H. S. IRWIN & BARNEBY var. *picta* (G. DON) H. S. IRWIN & BARNEBY
Shrub, to 2 m high. Leaves pinnate; leaflets 6–8 pairs, 4–8 cm long, becoming larger distally, narrowly obovate, obtuse and mucronulate; petiolules 1–2 mm long. Inflorescence a many-flowered panicle of racemes. Flowers yellow with brown venation, 4 cm wide. Pods 6–10 cm long, 1.5–2 cm wide, flat, papery, transversely ridged. Collections: 63541, 63575, 63704.
Common in open places. — The variety is endemic to coastal Ecuador, including the Galapagos Islands, and Peru.
Note: It is eaten by cattle, goats, and donkeys.
Vernacular name: flor de abejón.

11. *Senna robiniifolia* (BENTH.) H. S. IRWIN & BARNEBY
Shrub, 1.5–4 m high. Leaves pinnate; leaflets 6–9 pairs, 2–4 cm long, oblong, obtuse-rounded and mucronulate; petiolules 1–2 mm long. Inflorescence as long as the leaves, axillary to terminal, many-flowered; racemes subumbellate. Flowers yellow, 2 cm long. Pods 7–11 cm long, 5–7 mm wide, flat, partially constricted. Collections: 63591, 63844, 64014, 64101, 85351.
Common near homesites on central and southern Puná Island. — Cuba and northern South America.
Note: It is eaten by cattle.
Vernacular name: lentejilla.

12. *Tamarindus indica* L. [cult.]
The tamarind (Collections: 63422, 64139) is semi-cultivated on Puná Island. — It is native to the African savanna and was introduced to India long time ago. It has been introduced more recently to the New World.
Uses: The seed-pulp is used in refreshments. The wood is used for boards and charcoal. Medicinally it is a purgative.
Vernacular name: tamarindo.

CANNACEAE (CANNA FAMILY)

Erect herbs with rhizome. Leaves sheating. Flowers large and showy, irregular, 3-merous, subtended by bracts; stamens 6, some of these petaloid and sterile. Fruit a warty capsule. A family with about 30 species, chiefly in tropical America.

1. *Canna generalis* BAILEY [cult.]

The canna (Collection: 63564) is an ornamental in gardens. – It is a hybrid of American origin.

CAPPARACEAE (CAPER FAMILY)

Herbs, shrubs or trees. Leaves alternate, simple or compound; stipules minute or lacking. Inflorescence mostly racemose. Flowers actinomorphic or zygomorphic, usually bisexual, mostly 4-merous; stamens 4–100 or more; ovary superior on a short to elongate gynophore. Fruit a capsule or a berry. A family with 800 species in warm regions of the world. The family is not native to the Galapagos Islands.

Key to the Species

1a. Leaves stellately pubescent, at least beneath; sepals of equal length
    2a. Leaves broadly ovate-cordate   *2. Capparis crotonoides*
    2b. Leaves oblong to oblong-elliptic
        3a. Leaf-blade 7–16 cm long, bright yellow and varnished above; fruit 6–12 cm
            long   *6. Capparis scabrida*
        3b. Leaf-blade 3–7 cm long, dark green above; fruit 2–3 cm long
                                              1. Capparis avicennifolia
1b. Leaves glabrous or pubescent with short simple hairs; sepals in 2 series of unequal length
    4a. Gynophore in flower and fruit 2–5 mm long; fruit subspherical, 2–3 cm long
                                          4. Capparis heterophylla
    4b. Gynophore in flower and fruit longer than 5 mm; fruit linear-cylindric, more than 3 cm long
        5a. Leaves flexible, puberulous; petiole 5–12 mm long;
            tree with definite trunk at maturity   *3. Capparis guayaquilensis*
        5b. Leaves stiff, subglabrous; petiole 1–2 mm long; shrub   *5. Capparis lanceolata*

1. *Capparis avicennifolia* KUNTH

Shrub or small tree, 0.5–4 m high. Leaves glabrous and glossy above, stellately pubescent beneath; blade 3–6.5 cm long, elliptic, obtuse, cuneate or rounded at base; petiole 5 mm long. Inflorescence few to many flowered. Flowers greenish white, 2 cm wide. Fruit yellow-green, 2–3 cm long, fleshy; spike 1 cm long. Collections: 63826, 63879, 64140.

Very common in the savanna. — Endemic to coastal Ecuador and northern

Peru.

Phenology: Flowers in August and the fruits appear soon after.

Uses: As a flea repellant for chickens. It is eaten by goats and birds.

Vernacular name: bichaya.

2. *Capparis crotonoides* KUNTH (Plate 15)

Shrub, 1–2 m high. Leaves stellately pubescent, more densely so below; blade 4–8 cm long, broadly ovate-cordate, acute, subtruncate at base; petiole 1 cm long. Inflorescence few to many flowered. Flowers yellow. Fruit spherical, 1 cm wide, fleshy. Collections: 63881, 63891, 63981, 75480.

Rather common in the thorn scrub. — Endemic to arid Ecuador and adjacent Peru.

Phenology: Flowers from September.

3. *Capparis guayaquilensis* KUNTH

Tree, 5–8 m high. Leaves flexible, puberulous, more densely so beneath; blade 4–9 cm long, lanceolate; petiole 5–12 mm long. Inflorescence elongate, many-flowered. Flowers white, 3 cm wide; filaments erect. Fruit 10–20 cm long, 1 cm wide, constricted, resembling a legume. Collections: 63963, 64012, 64102, 85324, 85359.

Occasional in the dry forest. — Western America. This name and *Capparis lanceolata* (described below) were treated as synonyms of *Capparis flexuosa* (L.) L. by Jørgensen and León-Yánez (1999). They appear very different in the field and are kept separate here.

Phenology: Flowering begins in October.

Uses: The wood is used for charcoal.

Vernacular name: margarita.

4. *Capparis heterophylla* RUIZ & PAV. ex DC.

Shrub, to 3 m high. Leaves pubescent; blade 4–9 cm long, oblong-elliptic, attenuate, rounded at base; petiole 12 mm long. Inflorescence few to many flowered. Flowers white. Fruit to 3 cm long, ovoid, 1–2-seeded; gynophore 2–5 mm long. Collections: 63892, 63996, 64099, 64119, 64143, 85300, 85308.

Common in thorn forest and dry forest. — Endemic to the arid zone of Ecuador and adjacent Peru.

Phenology: Flowers from November.

Uses: The wood is used for firewood, charcoal, and to make stakes. The plants is eaten by cattle and deer.

Vernacular names: palo de rana, rana, palo prieto.

5. *Capparis lanceolata* RUIZ & PAV. ex DC.

Shrub, 1–3 m high. Leaves rather stiff, nearly glabrous; blade 3–10 cm long, variously lanceolate or narrowly elliptic, acute at apex; petiole 1–2 mm long.

Inflorescence few-flowered. Flowers white; petals reflexed; filaments 7 cm long, long-exserted. Fruit linear-cylindrical. Collections: 63781, 63782, 63942, 64106, 85352, 85367.

Common in thorn forest. — Endemic to coastal Ecuador; belongs to the *Capparis flexuosa* (L.) L. complex (see note under *Capparis guayaquilensis*).

Uses: The wood is used for construction, firewood, and charcoal. The plant is eaten by donkeys.

Vernacular name: sebastián.

6. *Capparis scabrida* KUNTH

Tree, 4–8 m high. Bark brown, rough and thick. Leaves bright yellow, varnished and subglabrous above, stellately pubescent beneath; blade 7–16 cm long, oblong, rounded at both ends; petiole 1 cm long. Inflorescence large and many-flowered. Flowers white. Fruit 7–12 cm long, pyriform, woody. Seeds 1 cm long. Collections: 63987, 64103, 64134A, 85310.

Common in thorn forest. — Probably endemic to southwestern Ecuador and adjacent Peru.

Phenology: Flowers from October.

Uses: The wood is used to make washtubs, troughs in the field, wheels, anvils, boards, tubs, timber for houses, and charcoal. It is eaten by dogs and birds.

Vernacular name: zapote de perro.

CARICACEAE (PAPAYA FAMILY)

Trees or shrubs. Leaves alternate, palmately lobed or compound. Staminate inflorescence large and compound. Pistillate inflorescence smaller and more simple. Flowers 5-merous. Fruit a berry. A family of 45 species in tropical and subtropical America and Africa.

Key to the Species

1a. Flowers cream colored; fruits longer than 10 cm; cultivated	1. *Carica papaya*
1b. Flowers pink; fruits 2–2.5 cm long; native	2. *Carica parviflora*

1. *Carica papaya* L. [cult.]

The papaya (Collection: 63550) is widely cultivated and of major importance in local consumption. — Probably native to southern Mexico and Costa Rica (Purseglove 1968) and naturalized in the tropics of the Old World.

Uses: The fruit is used as a refreshment, a snack, and for jams. The seeds are used medicinally to prevent intestinal worms.

Vernacular names: papaya blanca, papaya colorada, papaya de castilla, papaya hembra (pistillate), papaya de mico, papaya macho (staminate), papaya morada.

2. *Carica parviflora* (A. DC.) SOLMS
Herb, to 2 m high; trunk usually simple, succulent. Leaves palmately 3–7-lobate, deciduous; blade to 30 cm long, broadly ovate to suborbicular. Inflorescence and flowers pink, usually appearing on leafless stems; staminate flowers 2 cm long, subsessile; pistillate flowers 3 cm long; pedicels 4–7 mm long. Fruit reddish orange, 2–2.5 cm long. Seeds 5 mm long. Collections: 63793, 63827.
Common in the thorn scrub and in clearings in the thorn forest. — Endemic to arid Ecuador and adjacent Peru.
Note: It is eaten by donkeys.
Vernacular name: papaya de monte.

CELASTRACEAE (BITTERSWEET FAMILY)
Shrubs, trees or lianas. Leaves opposite or alternate, simple; stipules sometimes present. Flowers small and usually greenish, 4–5-parted; stamens 4–5, borne on a disc. Fruit a capsule, berry, or a drupe. A tropical and subtropical family of both hemispheres with 850 species.

1. *Maytenus octogona* (L'HÉR.) DC.
Shrub or tree, to 3 m high. Twigs glabrous. Leaves alternate, slightly fleshy; blade mostly 2–3.5 cm long, ovate to obovate, entire or dentate, rounded, cuneate or rounded at base; petiole to 5 mm long. Flowers 1–3 together, axillary, green, 3–4 mm wide; pedicels 2–4 mm long. Fruit green, dehiscent by four valves, releasing four seeds embedded in red flesh. Collections: 63293, 63459, 63468, 63976, ANDERSSON *s.n.* (S, cited in Areschoug 1869).
Very common in thorn forest and borders of salt marshes. — Coastal Ecuador, Peru, and Chile. Recorded on the Galapagos Islands.
Uses: The wood is used for boats, fishing nets, firewood, and charcoal. It is eaten by goats.
Vernacular name: patacón.

CHENOPODIACEAE (GOOSEFOOT FAMILY)
Herbs, shrubs, or rarely trees, sometimes succulent. Leaves alternate, simple, sometimes reduced; stipules absent. Flowers small and inconspicuous, uni- or bisexual; perianth persistent. Fruit a nutlet or an utricle. A cosmopolitan family of 1400 species, richly represented in saline habitats.

Key to the Species

1a. Leaves rudimentary; stems segmented   1. *Salicornia fruticosa*
1b. Leaves present, subulate; stems not segmented   2. *Suaeda*

1. *Salicornia fruticosa* (L.) L. (Plate 2)

Erect perennial herb, 0.5–2 m high. Stem green, succulent, segmented continuously, branching in a candelabrum-like fashion; distal segments 1–2 cm long, typically 4 mm thick, forming a sheath apically. Leaves rudimentary. Flowers reduced, perfect or polygamous, sunken in short, terminal joints; flowering areas decussately opposite. Collections: 63333, 63473, 63972.

A pioneer in disturbed mangroves and along margins of salt marshes. — Sea shores throughout the world, also on the Galapagos Islands.

Note: It is eaten by donkeys.

Vernacular name: vidrillo, vidrillo salado.

2. *Suaeda* sp.

Herb, to 30 cm high, forming broad patches. Stem succulent, pubescent, woody at base. Leaves 5–10 mm long, 1–2 mm wide, subulate, inconspicuous. Filaments yellow. Fruit 4 mm wide, 4–5-parted, hemispherical. Collection: 104085.

Rare halophyte found on a construction site for a new shrimp farm. This species is not mentioned in the *Catalogue of the Vascular Plants of Ecuador* (Jørgensen and León-Yánez, 1999).

CLUSIACEAE (MANGOSTEEN FAMILY)

Plants of varible habit (here trees). Leaves opposite or whorled, simple, entire. Flowers uni- or bisexual, often fleshy, mostly 3–6-merous; stamens numerous or variously reduced, often in bundles and opposite to the petals. Fruit a berry or drupe. A tropical family with 1200 species.

The genus *Calophyllum* is not growing wild on Puná Island but the wood, once used in the dry docks on the island, is still widely known among the old generations as 'palo maría'.

1. *Mammea americana* L. [cult.]

The mammee-apple (Collections: none) is a rare fruit tree on Puná Island.

Vernacular name: mamey cartagena.

COMBRETACEAE (INDIAN ALMOND FAMILY)

Trees, shrubs or lianas. Leaves opposite or alternate, simple and entire; stipules lacking. Flowers mostly bisexual, actinomorphic, sessile, 4–5-merous, in panicles or globose heads. Fruit fleshy or dry.

A family with 500 species in the tropics, mainly in Africa.

Key to the Species

1a. Leaves 5–12 cm long; native
    2a. Leaves alternate   1. *Conocarpus erecta*
    2b. Leaves opposite   2. *Laguncularia racemosa*
1b. Leaves longer than 15 cm; cultivated   3. *Terminalia catappa*

1. *Conocarpus erecta* L.
Shrub, 1–4 m high. Bark brown. Twigs slightly winged, tomentose when young. Leaves alternate; blade 5–8 cm long, narrowly elliptic, decurrent at base, with prominent midrib below. Inflorescence subglobose, 0.5 cm wide; peduncle 0.5–1 cm long. Flowers minute. Infructescence 1–1.5 cm long, cone-like. Collections: 63157, 63470, 63977, ANDERSSON *s.n.* (S, cited in Areschoug 1869). Common in salt marshes and margins of mangroves. — Widespread along seashores from Florida to Ecuador, including the Galapagos Islands, and Brazil. Also in western Africa.
Uses: The wood is used for boats and charcoal.
Vernacular name: jelí.

2. *Laguncularia racemosa* (L.) C. F. GAERTN.
Shrub or small tree, to 10 m high. Branches reddish brown, slightly swollen at nodes. Leaves opposite; blade 6–12 cm long, oblong to elliptic, subobtuse, rounded to cuneate at base, with prominent midrib below; petiole 1.5–2 cm long. Inflorescence ramified; branches 3–7 cm long. Flowers white, 6 mm long, sessile. Fruit 1.5–2 cm long, obovoid, dry. Collections: 63973, 64098, 85870. Common mangrove tree. — Tropical shores from Florida to Peru and Brazil. Known from the Galapagos Islands.
Uses: The wood is used for canoes, fences, houses, nets, ribs of timber of ship frames, and charcoal. It is eaten by goats.
Vernacular name: manoa.

3. *Terminalia catappa* L. [cult.]
The India almond (Collection: 64138) is occasionally grown in gardens and parks. — Native to Polynesia and Malaysia.
Uses: Grown for its edible seeds.
Vernacular name: almendra.

COMMELINACEAE (SPIDERWORT FAMILY)
Annual or perennial herbs, often swollen at nodes. Leaves alternate, parallel-veined, with a closed sheath at base. Flowers 3-merous; stamens 3 or 6. Fruit a capsule. A family with 600 species in warm regions of the world.

Key to the Species

1a. Flowers white; inflorescence few–many flowered   1. *Callisia gracilis*
1b. Flowers blue; inflorescence with one flower at a time   2. *Commelina erecta*

1. *Callisia gracilis* (KUNTH) D. R. HUNT

Herb, forming patches. Leaves 2–4 cm long, ovate-lanceolate, acute, rounded at base; sheaths 0.5 cm long. Inflorescence terminal and axillary, few to many flowered; flowers crowded distally, white , 5 mm wide; pedicels to 6 mm long. Capsule to 2 mm wide, globose. Collection: 63708.
Occasional along trails. — Panama to Peru.

2. *Commelina erecta* L.

Creeping to suberect herb, to 60 cm long, rooting at nodes. Leaves 3–8 cm long, ovate-lanceolate, short-acuminate, rounded at base; sheaths 2 cm long. Flowers blue, 1–2 cm long, solitary, pedicels to 1 cm long. Capsule 2–3-seeded; seeds 4 mm long. Collections: 63012, 63064, 63244, 63376, 63889.
Very common in disturbed places. — Cosmopolitan weed.
Vernacular name: chocliyo.

CONVOLVULACEAE (MORNING-GLORY FAMILY)

Erect or twining herbs or vines, without tendrils. Leaves alternate, simple or palmately compound; stipules absent. Flowers large and showy, bisexual, actinomorphic, 5-merous. Fruit a capsule. A family of some 1500 species distributed throughout the world. About 23 species on Puná Island, chiefly vines that flower at the end of the rainy season.

Key to the Species

1a. Herbs
    2a. Leaves wider than 5 mm; flowers 8–10 mm wide   2. *Evolvulus convolvuloides*
    2b. Leaves to 3 mm wide; flowers 4 mm wide   3. *Evolvulus filipes*
1b. Vines, lianas and shrubs
    3a. Leaves deeply pinnatifid   13. *Ipomoea quamoclit*
    3b. Leaves not pinnatifid
        4a. Leaves 5-foliolate
            5a. Sepals 15–20 mm long; flowers 4 cm wide   20. *Merremia aegyptia*
            5b. Sepals 3–7 mm long; flowers 2 cm wide   21. *Merremia quinquefolia*
        4b. Leaves simple
            6a. Flowers yellow   22. *Merremia umbellata*
            6b. Flowers of another color than yellow
                7a. Flowers wider than 6 cm
                    8a. Stem bearing 4–8 mm long fleshy setae   14. *Ipomoea setosa*
                    8b. Stems without fleshy setae

9a. Sepals 3 cm long   23. *Operculina codonantha*
9b. Sepals less than 1.5 cm long
    10a. Shrub or rarely lianescent   6. *Ipomoea carnea*
    10b. Vines
        11a. Stem hirsute; leaves cordate   11. *Ipomoea ophioides*
        11b. Stem glabrous; leaves rounded   12. *Ipomoea pes-caprae*
7b. Flowers less than 6 cm wide
    12a. Flowers red to orange-red; sepals bearing 3–6 mm long arista
                              7. *Ipomoea hederifolia*
    12b. Flowers variously colored; sepals not with 3–6 mm long arista
        13a. Sepals 1.5–4 cm long, hirsute at base
            14a. Sepals linear, 1.5 mm wide; leaves 3-lobed   10. *Ipomoea nil*
            14b. Sepals linear-lanceolate, the larger 2–4 mm wide; leaves
                cordate, not lobed   9. *Ipomoea meyeri*
        13b. Sepals to 1.5 cm long, variously pubescent or glabrous
            15a. Inflorescence 10–30-flowered, congested
                16a. Peduncle to 3 cm long; flowers white
                            1. *Convolvulus nodiflorus*
                16b. Peduncle longer than 5 cm; flowers blue or rarely
                    pinkish white   19. *Jacquemontia corymbulosa*
            15b. Inflorescence few–many-flowered, if many-flowered then
            lax and open
            17a. Flowers 1.5 cm wide
                18a. Sepals 10–14 mm long; leaves shallowly 3–5-lobed
                            8. *Ipomoea leucantha*
                18b. Sepals 4–6 mm long; leaves not lobed
                          18. *Jacquemontia agrestia*
             17b. Flowers 3–4 cm wide
                19a. Sepals 3–5 mm long, glabrous
                        4. *Ipomoea aristolochiifolia*
                19b. Sepals longer than 5 mm, variously pubescent
                  20a. Flowers widely separated in lax inflorescences
                        17. *Ipomoea velardei*
                  20b. Flowers in a distal cluster
                    21a. Leaves, at least some, more or less sagittate
                        15. *Ipomoea trifida*
                    21b. Leaves variable, generally not sagittate
                      22a. Inflorescence 1–3-flowered
                        16. *Ipomoea triloba*
                    22b. Inflorescence mostly 4–10 flowered;
                    native or cultivated   5. *Ipomoea batatas*

1. *Convolvulus nodiflorus* Desr.
Tomentose vine, several meters long. Leaves simple; blade 3–7 cm long, ovate, acute to acuminate, subtruncate at base; petiole 1–2 cm long. Inflorescence 10–30-flowered, cymose, short-pedunculate. Flowers white, 1 cm wide, sepals 2–3 mm long, pedicels 5–8 mm long. Capsule 4 mm long. Collection: 63742. Rare along stream-beds. — Central and South America.

2. *Evolvulus convolvuloides* (WILLD. ex SCHULT.) STEARN

Prostrate herb. Stem pubescent. Leaves subsessile; blade 1–3(–4) cm long, ovate to oblong, rounded to emarginate, subcordate at base. Inflorescence 1–3-flowered. Flowers blue, 8–10 mm wide, subrotate; sepals 3 mm long. Capsule 2–3 mm long. Collections: 63038, 63077, 63163, 63188, 63373, ANDERSSON *s.n.* (S, cited in Fl. Ec.), SINCLAIR *s.n.* (K, cited in Fl. Ec.).

Common along trails and in waste places. — Widespread from United States to Paraguay. Known from the Galapagos Islands.

3. *Evolvulus filipes* MART.

Annual, erect herb, 20–40 cm high. Stem appressed pubescent. Leaves subsessile; blade 1–2 cm long, linear-lanceolate, acute at base and apex. Inflorescence axillary, 1–3 flowered; peduncle to 4 cm long. Flowers light blue, 4 mm wide; sepals 2 mm long. Capsule globose, 3–4 mm wide. Collections: 63122, 63164, 63284.

Common in the savanna. — Widespread in America.

4. *Ipomoea aristolochiifolia* G. DON

Twining vine. Stem glabrous to puberulent. Leaves simple; blade 3–9 cm long, cordate, acuminate; petiole 1–4 cm long. Inflorescence 1–2-flowered; peduncle pass between basal lobes of leaves, to 7 cm long. Flowers 3 cm wide, blue to purple with white throat, outside with white stripes, 4 cm wide; sepals 3–5 mm long, ovate. Capsule 1 cm long. Collections: 63499, 63570, 63754.

Common. — Mexico to Argentina.

5. *Ipomoea batatas* (L.) LAM. [cult. and wild]

Vine; roots fibrous with tubers. Leaves cordate and entire or 5–7-lobed. Inflorescence a few flowered, umbellate cluster, long-pedunculate. Flowers lavender to violet, sepals 8–12 mm long. Collections: 63866 (cultivated), 64032.

The sweet potato is an important root crop and is also found naturalized. — Pantropic, originating in the Americas.

Uses: The starchy tubers are cooked and variously prepared for purée, pies, blancmange, and omelettes. It is eaten by pigs.

Vernacular name: camote.

6. *Ipomoea carnea* JACQ. ssp. *carnea*

Shrubby scrambler, 1–2 m high, rarely lianescent to 6 m long and 8 cm wide at base. Stem puberulent when young. Leaves simple; blade 5–18 cm long, broadly ovate-cordate, acuminate, cordate at base; petiole 2–6 cm long. Inflorescence many-flowered. Flowers purple or rarely white, 10 cm wide; sepals 4–6 mm long, obtuse. Capsule 2 cm long. Seeds embedded in wool. Collections: 63198, 63482, 63878, 85318.

Very common in the savanna and thorn scrub. — Ecuador to Venezuela.

Uses: Used medicinally to treat tooth aches. It is said to be poisonous to the cattle.

Vernacular name: florón.

7. *Ipomoea hederifolia* L.
Slender vine. Stem subglabrous. Leaves simple; blade 8–11 cm long, broadly ovate, subacuminate, deeply cordate at base; petiole 3–7 cm long. Inflorescence 30 cm long, few–10-flowered. Flowers red or orange-red, 4 cm long; sepals 3 mm long, outer ones bearing a 3–6 mm long arista. Collections: 63312, 63441, ANDERSSON 100 (S, cited in Fl. Ec.), SINCLAIR *s.n.* (K, cited in Fl. Ec.), HINDS *s.n.* (K, cited in Fl. Ec.).
Common in open places. — Widespread in America, becoming pantropic.
Vernacular name: mastuerzo.

8. *Ipomoea leucantha* JACQ.
Vine, twining. Stem sparsely hirsute. Leaves simple; blade 6–9 cm long, cordate, shallowly 3–5-lobed; petiole 2–3 cm long. Inflorescence axillary, 1–few-flowered; pedicels to 7 cm long. Flowers white, pink, or purple, 1.5 cm wide; sepals narrow, 10–14 mm long. Collections: 63274, 63434.
Common in disturbed places. — Widespread, also beyond the tropics.

9. *Ipomoea meyeri* (SPRENG.) G. DON
Vine. Stem hirsute. Leaves simple; blade 4–9 cm long, cordate, acuminate at apex; petiole to 3 cm long. Inflorescence short-pedunculate, the flowers crowded. Flowers blue with white throat, outside with white stripes; sepals 1.5–2.5 cm long, linear-lanceolate hairy. Collection: 63753.
In waste places. — Southern Mexico to northern South America.

10. *Ipomoea nil* (L.) ROTH
Vine. Stem hirsute. Leaves simple; blade 6–13 cm long, broadly ovate-cordate, 3-lobed, acuminate at apex; petiole 2–10 cm long. Inflorescence 1–2-flowered, long-pedicellate. Flowers blue, the throat sometimes white, 4 cm; sepals 2–4 cm long, 1.5 mm wide, linear, yellow-brown hirsute at base. Capsule 1 cm long. Collections: 63008, 63629, 63800.
Common in disturbed places. — Pantropical, also on the Galapagos Islands.

11. *Ipomoea ophioides* STANDL. & STEYERM.
Prostrate vine on ground, rooting along nodes. Stem usually conspicously hirsute. Leaves simple; blade 4–10 cm long, cordate, acute at apex; petiole to 7 cm long. Inflorescence 1–3-flowered; peduncle to 15 cm long. Flowers blue, 8 cm wide; sepals 9–12 mm long, narrow. Collections: 63005, 63085, 63613.
Very common in shaded places of mature dry forest. — Guatemala and El Salvador. Disjunct in Ecuador.

Uses: The stem is used to tie up sacks.
Vernacular name: bejuco pachón.

12. *Ipomoea pes-caprae* (L.) R. BR.
Long creeping vine with latex. Stem fleshy, glabrous. Leaves simple, fleshy; blade 6–12 cm long, oblong to suborbicular, emarginate, truncate to cordate at base; petiole to 10 cm long. Flowers solitary, blue or purple, 8 cm wide; sepals 8–10 mm long, obtuse. Collections: 63460, 63655.
Common on sandy beaches. — Pantropical, rarely inland. Reported from the Galapagos Islands.
Note: It is eaten by donkeys.
Vernacular name: bejuco de playa.

13. *Ipomoea quamoclit* L.
Slender vine. Stem glabrous. Leaves 3–7 cm long, deeply pinnatifid; leaflets 12–14 pairs, 1.5–2 cm long, almost filiform. Inflorescence 1–3-flowered; peduncle to 8 cm long. Flowers red, 2 cm wide, salver-shaped; sepals 4–6 mm long. Collections: 63585, SINCLAIR *s.n.* (K, cited in Fl. Ec.).
Rare on cultivated land. — Pantropical.

14. *Ipomoea setosa* KER GAWL.
Stout vine, often longer than 5 m. Stem bearing conspicuous, 4–8 mm long fleshy setae. Leaves simple; blade 10–17 cm long, suborbicular, deeply to shallowly 3–7-lobed; petiole to 8 cm long. Inflorescence 2–5-flowered; peduncle to 20 cm long. Flowers white, 7 cm wide; bracts and sepals 1–2 cm long. Capsule 2 cm long, 1.5–2 cm wide, stout-mucronate. Collections: 63605, 63797.
Common and high climbing in the forests. — Widespread in Mexico and Central and South America.

15. *Ipomoea trifida* (KUNTH) DON
Vine. Stem nearly glabrous. Leaves simple; blade 4–9 cm long, broadly cordate to subsagittate, entire to deeply 3-lobed; petiole 2–7 cm long. Inflorescence in 1–5-flowered umbels; peduncle 5–15 cm long. Flowers pink or violet, 4 cm wide; sepals 10–14 mm long. Collections: 63490, 63741.
Occasional. — Probably restricted to warm America.

16. *Ipomoea triloba* L.
Vine, prostrate on ground or twining. Stem glabrous. Leaves simple; blade 3–8 cm long, broadly ovate-cordate, acuminate; petiole 2–10 cm long. Inflorescence 1–3-flowered; peduncle to 10 cm long. Flowers white with pink or purple striped throat, darker at center, 3 cm wide; sepals 8–10 mm long. Collections: 63116, 63158, 63350, 63481.
Very common in disturbed sites. — Mainly in the West Indies. Also on the

Galapagos Islands.
Vernacular name: camotillo.

17. *Ipomoea velardei* O´DONELL
Vine. Stem adhering when touching, sparsely hirsute. Leaves simple; blade 4–7 cm long, ovate-cordate, variable, long-acuminate; petiole to 3 cm long. Inflorescence to 50 cm long, branched, racemose, many-flowered. Flowers blue, 3–4 cm wide; sepals 7–8 mm long. Collection: 63799.
Probably rare. — Ecuador and Peru.

18. *Jacquemontia agrestia* (MART. ex CHOISY) MEISN.
Pubescent vine. Leaves simple; blade 2–6 cm long, broadly to narrowly ovate, acute to acuminate, cordate to subtruncate at base, petiole short. Inflorescence 1–6-flowered. Flowers blue, 1.5 cm wide, sepals subequal, 4–6 mm long. Capsule 5 mm wide. Collection: ANDERSSON 18 (S, cited in Fl. Ec.).
On Puná Island known only from the above collection. — Widespread in America.

19. *Jacquemontia corymbulosa* BENTH.
Vine, overgrowing bushes. Stem usually glabrous. Leaves simple; blade 5–9 cm long, subrotund to broadly cordate, cuspidate, deeply cordate at base; petiole 1–4 cm long. Inflorescence a 10–30-flowered, umbellate clusters; peduncle 5–20 cm long. Flowers blue or rarely pink, 2 cm wide; sepals narrow, 3–6 mm long. Capsule 8-valvate. Collections: 63194, 63417, 63592, 63812, ANDERSSON 96 (S, cited in Fl. Ec.), SINCLAIR *s.n.* (K, cited in Fl. Ec.).
Very common in thorn forest. — Endemic to southwestern Ecuador and adjacent Peru.

20. *Merremia aegyptia* (L.) URB.
Medium-sized vine. Stem conspicuously hirsute. Leaves 5-foliolate, 6–12 cm long; leaflets sessile, elliptic to rhombic, acuminate; petiole 3–10 cm long. Inflorescence many-flowered, cymose; peduncle to 30 cm long. Flowers white, 4 cm wide; sepals 1.5–2 cm long, yellow-brown hirsute. Capsule subtended by the enlarged calyx. Collections: 63500, 63651, BARCLAY 351 (F, cited in Fl. Ec.), SINCLAIR s. n. (K, cited in Fl. Ec.).
Common in clearings and along the beach. — Almost pantropical. Known from the Galapagos Islands.

21. *Merremia quinquefolia* (L.) HALLIER F.
Vines. Stem glabrous or hirsute. Leaves 5-foliolate; leaflets sessile, serrate. Inflorescence 1–few-flowered simple cymes. Flowers white, 2 cm wide; unequal, 3–7 mm long. Capsule 7–8 mm wide. Collection: SINCLAIR *s.n.* (K, cited in Fl. Ec.).

On Puná Island known only from the cited specimen. — Widespread in the Americas.

22. *Merremia umbellata* (L.) HALLIER F.
Vine on the ground and climbering. Stems glabrous. Leaves simple; blade 4–9 cm long, cordate to narrowly triangular, acute to acuminate, cordate at base; petiole 1–5 cm long. Inflorescence in few to many-flowered, umbels; peduncle to 8 cm long. Flowers yellow, 3 cm wide; sepals 6–7 mm long. Capsule 1 cm wide. Collections: 63825, 63962.
Rare along trails in closed and disturbed forest. — Pantropical.
Phenology: Flowers late in the dry season.

23. *Operculina codonantha* (BENTH.) HALLIER F.
Stout vine, often longer than 5 m. Stem glabrous. Leaves simple; blade 10–25 cm long, cordate or sagitate, acute; petiole 3–14 cm long. Flowers solitary, white, to 10 cm wide; sepals 3 cm long; pedicels to 28 cm long. Capsule 4 cm wide. Seeds 1 cm long, black. Collections: 63007, 63270, 63311, 634050, 63994.
Common throughout the island. — Peru to Panama.

CUCURBITACEAE (CUCURBIT FAMILY)
Tendrillate vines. Leaves alternate, simple, entire to lobed; stipules lacking. Flowers solitary or in few-flowered inflorescences, unisexual, 5-merous; carpels 3. Fruit a berry with or without a hard shell or a capsule. A family with 850 species, chiefly in the tropics and subtropics. Nine species on Puná Island. Several of the cultivated species persist in abandoned fields.

Key to the Species

1a. Leaves pinnately lobed; cultivated   1. *Citrullus lanatus*
1b. Leaves palmately lobed or entire; wild or cultivated
   2a. Fruits more than 8 cm wide
      3a. Flowers campanulate, corolla 6–8 cm long
         4a. Fruit non-bitter; seed-margin dark-colored; wild   5. *Cucurbita ecuadorensis*
         4b. Fruit bitter; seed margin not conspicuously dark-colored; cultivated
                       6. *Cucurbita moschata*
      3b. Flowers rotate, corolla 3 cm wide; cultivated   4. *Cucumis melo*
   2b. Fruits less than 7 cm wide
      5a. Flowers white   7. *Echinopepon racemosus*
      5b. Flowers yellow
         6a. Fruits fleshy
            7a. Fruits orange, irregularly dehiscing by three valves
                       9. *Momordica charantia*
            7b. Fruits yellow, not dehiscing by three valves
               8a. Fruits sparsely prickly, not spiny; flowers campanulate
                       2. *Cucumis anguria*

8b. Fruits not prickly, spiny; flowers rotate   3. *Cucumis dipsaceus*
6b. Fruits dry
    9a. Fruits operculate; pistillate flowers solitary; wild   8. *Luffa sepium*
    9b. Fruits not operculate; pistillate flowers forming a globose head;
        cultivated   10. *Sechium edule*

1. *Citrullus lanatus* (THUNB.) MATSUM. & NAKAI [cult.]
The water melon (Collections: 63049, 63549) is a common crop and occasionally
escapes. — Native to the Kalahari region in Africa, introduced to the New
World in post-Columbian times.
Uses: The juicy fruit is consumed fresh.
Vernacular name: sandía.

2. *Cucumis anguria* L.
Stiff hairy vine, prostrate. Leaves deeply and palmately 3–5-lobed; blade 7–10
cm long, suborbicular, dentate, cordate at base; petiole 3–6 cm long. Flowers
yellow, perianth 1 cm long; pedicels of staminate flowers 1 cm long, those of
pistillate flowers 4–15 cm long. Berry yellow, 4–7 cm long, ellipsoid, sparsely
prickly. Seeds 4 mm long. Collections: 63138, 63838, 64015.
Common in waste places and on beaches. — Tropics and subtropics of the New
World.
Vernacular names: esponjillo, sandía de ratón.

3. *Cucumis dipsaceus* EHRENB. ex SPACH
Stiff hairy vine, to 2 m long. Leaves simple to shallowly 3-lobed; blade 6–10 cm
long, very broadly ovate to subrotund, cordate, dentate; petiole 4–8 cm long.
Flowers yellow, 2 cm wide; pedicellate for 1–1.5 cm long; male flowers in 1–4-
flowered fascicles; female flowers solitary. Berry yellow, 4–7 cm long, ovoid,
densely covered with 5 mm long spines. Seeds 4–5 mm long. Collections: 63091,
63260, 63384, 63505, 63767, 64010.
Very common vine in thickets. — Native to Africa.
Vernacular name: esponjillo.

4. *Cucumis melo* L. [cult.]
The melon (Collection: 63556) is common in cultivation on Puná Island. —
Originated in Africa.
Uses: The fruit is used in jams, snacks, and refreshments.
Vernacular name: melón.

5. *Cucurbita ecuadorensis* H. C. CUTLER & WHITAKER (Plate 14)
Climbing vine, to 10 m long, sparsely stiff-hirsute. Tendrils trifid. Leaves
simple; blade 10–25 cm long, subrotund, shallowly to deeply 5-lobed, serrulate-
denticulate; petiole to 15 cm long. Flowers solitary, yellow; corolla to 8 cm long,
campanulate. Fruit green, 10–20 cm wide, globose, hard-shelled. Seeds 1–1.5 cm

long, with conspicuous dark margin. Collections: 63083, 63523, 63537, 63912.
Very common in the dry forest. — Endemic to southwestern Ecuador and
nearby Peru.
Note: The fruit is eaten by donkeys.
Vernacular name: mate chino.

6. *Cucurbita moschata* (DUCHESNE ex LAM.) DUCHESNE ex POIR. [cult.]
The pumpkin (Collections: 63553, 63559) is common in cultivation. — Native of
Central or South America but not known in a wild state.
Uses: Cooked as a vegetable in soups, pies, jams, and snacks. Medicinally it is
used against intestinal worms.
Vernacular name: zapallo.

7. *Echinopepon racemosus* (STEUD.) C. JEFFREY
Hirsute vine, 2 m long. Leaves shallowly to deeply 5-foliolate; blade 7–15 cm
long, subrotund, slightly dentate, cordate at base, lobes mucronate; petiole 4–9
cm long. Staminate inflorescence composed of 10 flowers; flowers white, 1 cm
wide; peduncle 10–20 cm long. Pistillate flowers subsessile, in axils of staminate
inflorescences. Fruit 5–7 cm long, ellipsoid, dry, hirsute, bearing 1.5 cm long
spines. Collections: 63365, 64013.
Occasional in thorn scrub on the west coast. — Mexico to Argentina.
Vernacular name: iflojo.

8. *Luffa sepium* (G. MEY.) C. JEFFREY
Scabrous vine, scrambling over bushes. Stem grooved. Leaves palmately 5-
lobate; blade 9–14 cm long, subrotund with rounded incisions, deeply cordate,
remotely dentate; petiole 4–9 cm long. Flowers yellow, 3 cm wide; staminate
flowers in long-pedunculate racemes; pistillate flowers solitary, pedunculate
for only 1–2 cm. Fruit 7–10 cm long, ellipsoid, ribbed, dry, echinate, dehiscent
by a terminal operculum; pulp fibrous. Collections: 63011, 63536, 63573, 63775.
Very common on waste grounds. — The Caribbean to Peru, also on the
Galapagos Islands.
Uses: The pulp is used as scrubber for washing dishes.
Vernacular name: esponjillo.

9. *Momordica charantia* L.
Sparsely hirsute vine. Leaves palmately 5–7-lobate; blade 3–7 cm long,
subrotund, dentate, cordate at base; petiole 3–6 cm long. Flowers solitary,
yellow, 3–4 cm wide; peduncle 3–10 cm long, below with a foliaceous bract.
Fruit orange, 4–7 cm long, fusiform, tuberculate, irregularly dehiscent by three
valves; flesh bright red. Seeds 8–10 mm long. Collections: 63247, 63344, 63399,
63773.
Very common in disturbed sites. — Pantropical. Also on the Galapagos Islands.

Note: It is eaten by birds.
Vernacular names: achocha, achocha de monte.

10. *Sechium edule* (JACQ.) SW. [cult.]
The chayote is sometimes found cultivated on the island. — Widely distributed crop in the Neotropics.
Uses: As a vegetable in soups.
Vernacular name: achocha.

CUSCUTACEAE (DODDER FAMILY)
Parasitic plants without chlorophyll. Stem slender and twining, often wanting when in flower. Flowers crowded in globose or spicate inflorescences, small, 4–5-merous. Fruit a capsule or a berry. A family of 170 species in tropical and temperate regions.

Key to the Species

1a. Flowers shorter than 4 mm
  2a. Flowers pedicellate; calyx campanulate, the lobes acute to acuminate; fruit not
      circumscissile   1. *Cuscuta acuta*
  2b. Flowers subsessile; calyx tubular, the lobes obtuse; fruit circumscissile
                                                             2. *Cuscuta americana*
1b. Flowers longer than 4 mm   3. *Cuscuta prismatica*

1. *Cuscuta acuta* ENGELM.
Stem often wanting when in flower. Inflorescence composed of umbellate clusters, to 2 cm wide. Flowers white at first, straw yellow when dry, 2–3 mm long, pedicellate; calyx campanulate, the lobes acute to acuminate. Capsule not circumscissile. Collections: 63850, 63936.
Occasional. — Endemic to the dry zone of coastal Ecuador, including the Galapagos Islands.

2. *Cuscuta americana* L.
Stem vine-like. Inflorescence composed of compact many-flowered clusters. Flowers green-white, 3 mm long, subsessile; calyx tubular, the lobes obtuse. Capsule circumscissile. Collections: 63444, 63601.
Common parasite. — United States, West Indies, and South America.

3. *Cuscuta prismatica* PAV. ex CHOISY
Stem often wanting when in flower. Inflorescence composed of many-flowered clusters. Flowers straw yellow, 8 mm long, subsessile; calyx tubular, the lobes acute. Fruit a capsule. Collections: 63790, 63940.
Occasional on woody plants. — Endemic to the Guayas province.

CYPERACEAE (SEDGE FAMILY)

Annual or perennial, grasslike plants. Stem usually 3-angled, solid. Leaves in basal tuft, linear and narrow, with a closed sheath. Inflorescence variously congested, subtended by leafy bracts. Flowers minute. Fruit a small nutlet. A family with about 3700 species throughout the world. — Nineteen species, mostly well known and widely distributed species, are included here, but the actual number of sedges on Puná Island is surely higher. Sedges are difficult to key-out and to identify correctly without a comparison with authentically named specimens (Standley and Steyermark 1958). Our material was studied by Camelbeke (1993).

Key to the Species

1a. Stems bearing a single terminal spikelet
  2a. Stems to 1 mm wide; spikelets to 6 mm long   12. *Eleocharis geniculata*
  2b. Stems wider than 3 mm; spikelets longer than 8 mm
    3a. Sheath truncate, reddish brown   11. *Eleocharis elegans*
    3b. Sheath pointed, membranous   13. *Eleocharis interstincta*
1b. Stems bearing more than a single spikelet
    4a. Spikelets 1–1.5 mm long, in lax inflorescences; pedicels 1–15 mm long
             19. *Rhyncospora contracta*
    4b. Spikelets either longer than 2 mm and borne in congested inflorescences or subsessile
      5a. Spikelets ovoid to cylindical, usually pedicellate
        6a. Spikelets 8–10 mm long   16. *Fimbristylis spadicea*
        6b. Spikelets less than 7 mm long
          7a. Spikelets 3–6 mm long; stem and leaves barely 2 mm wide
               14. *Fimbristylis annua*
          7b. Spikelets mostly 2–3 mm long; largest leaves 2–4 mm wide
               15. *Fimbristylis miliacea*
      5b. Spikelets flattened, sessile or pedicellate (branchlets composed of numerous spikelets may be cylindrical)
        8a. Stems conspicuously septate, terete; leaves absent
             1. *Cyperus articulatus*
        8b. Stems not septate, trigonous; leaves present
          9a. Achenes white, 3 mm long; spikelets relatively few per inflorescence; flowers unisexual   20. *Scleria reticularis*
          9b. Achenes not white and not readily visible; spikelets numerous per inflorescence; flowers bisexual
            10a. Spikelets forming globose or elongated heads, the spikelets to 5 mm long
              11a. Heads of spikelets all subsessile   7. *Cyperus ligularis*
              11b. Heads of spikelets variously pedunculate for 0–3 cm
                12a. Heads of spikelets subglobose, fairly loose; leaves to 5 mm wide   3. *Cyperus difformis*
                12b. Heads of spikelets more or less elongated, broadest at base, densely congested; leaves to 10 mm wide
                   8. *Cyperus luzulae*

10b. Spikelets loosely arranged
   13a. Inflorescence of spikelets loosely scattered along branches
                                                    6. *Cyperus iria*
   13b. Inflorescence of spikelets in rather dense cylindrical to
      subglobose heads
      14a. Spikelets barely 1 mm wide, hardly flattened; leaves
         4–10 mm wide   9. *Cyperus odoratus*
      14b. Spikelets wider than 1 mm; leaves of variable width
         (if the spikelets are only 1–1.5 mm wide then leaves
         consequently less than 4 mm wide)
         15a. Spikelets inserted over a zone 0–5 mm long
            16a. Spikelets 1–1.5 mm wide   5. *Cyperus haspan*
            16b. Spikelets 2–3 mm wide
               17a. Plants 30–60 cm tall; spikelets golden brown
                                 10. *Cyperus oxylepis*
               17b. Plants 5–25 cm tall; spikelets silvery green
                              2. *Cyperus compressus*
         15b. Spikelets inserted over a zone 1–2 cm long
            18a. Leaves 4–8 mm wide; spikelets 2 mm wide
                             4. *Cyperus esculentus*
            18b. Leaves to 5 mm wide; spikelets 1–1.5 mm
              wide
              19a. Plants usually 30–50 cm high
                           17. *Pycreus macrostachyos*
              19b. Plants usually 10–30 cm high
                           18. *Pycreus pelophilus*

1. *Cyperus articulatus* L.
Stout, 1–2 m high. Stems terete, spongy, conspicuously transverse-septate. Leaves reduced to a few sheaths. Inflorescence digitate; spikelets to 20 per spike, 2–5 cm long, 1 mm wide. Collections: 63895, 85865.
Common in shallow waters. — Pantropical.

2. *Cyperus compressus* L.
Fairly loose tufts, 5–25 cm high. Leaves 1–3 mm wide. Inflorescence commonly 5 cm long; involucral leaves exceeding inflorescence; spikes few, sessile or pedunculate for up to 5 cm; spikelets subsessile, in clusters of 3–20, 1–2 cm long, 2–3 mm wide, silvery green. Collections: 63041, 63094, ANDERSSON *s.n.* (S, cited in Areschoug 1869).
Occasional on sandy beaches. — Pantropical. Also on the Galapagos Islands.

3. *Cyperus difformis* L.
Tufts, 20–50 cm high. Stems few. Leaves 2–5 mm wide. Inflorescence composed of globular heads; involucral leaves exceeding the length of the inflorescence; heads 10–40, 7–18 mm wide, subglobose; peduncles 0–3 cm; spikelets 50–100, 2–5 mm long, 1 mm wide, elliptic. Collections: 63119, 63210.
Common on moist ground. — Pantropical.

4. *Cyperus esculentus* L.

Stems single, 30–50 cm high. Leaves 4–8 mm wide. Inflorescence digitate; involucral leaves exceeding the inflorescence; spikes 4–6, to 10 cm long; spikelets 10–20, 10–18 mm long, 2 mm wide, inserted over a zone 1–2 cm long. Collections: 63040, 63421.

Occasional in disturbed places. — Subcosmopolitan, including the Galapagos Islands.

Vernacular name: cochito.

5. *Cyperus haspan* L.

Stems several together, 20–60 cm high. Leaves 2–3 mm wide. Inflorescence digitate, rather large and diffuse; involucral bracts 1–2 times as long as the length of the inflorescence; rays 4–8, 3–12 cm long; spikelets 3–10 per spike, 4–10 mm long, 1–1.5 mm wide. Collection: 63206.

Border of swamps. — Pantropical.

6. *Cyperus iria* L.

Small tufts, 20–60 cm high. Leaves 2–4 mm wide. Inflorescence a digitate cluster; involucral leaves to twice as long as the inflorescence; rays 4–10, the rachis to 6 cm long. Spikelets 10–20 per ray, 5–20 mm long, 1.5–2 mm wide, inserted over a zone 1–4 cm long, more or less appressed longitudinally. Collections: 63087, 63102, 63126.

Common in moist grassland. — Cosmopolitan.

7. *Cyperus ligularis* L.

Robust perennial, 50–80 cm high. Stem solitary. Leaves crowded at base of plant, 7–11 mm wide. Inflorescence 8–12 cm long, composed of densely crowded elongated heads; involucral leaves several times as long as the inflorescence; heads cylindrical, 0.5–2 cm long, 8 mm wide. Spikelets sessile, 4–5 mm long, lance-oblong. Collections: 63463, 63959.

Sandy hills along beach. — Tropics of America and Africa. Also on the Galapagos Islands.

8. *Cyperus luzulae* (L.) ROTTB. ex RETZ.

Loose tufts, 20–60 cm high. Leaves 4–10 mm wide. Inflorescence composed of a cluster of elongated heads; involucral leaves several times as long as the inflorescence; heads 1–1.5 cm long, 8–10 mm wide; peduncles 0–2 cm long. Spikelets 50–100 per head, 2–5 mm long, sessile. Collection: 64128.

Uncommon, forming patches at water holes. — Widespread in tropical America.

9. *Cyperus odoratus* L.

Solitary or in tufts, 30–100 cm high. Leaves 4–10 mm wide. Inflorescence digitately branched; involucral leaves largely exceeding the inflorescence; rays 5–10, the rachis to 15 cm long. Spikes 1–4, to 4 cm long; spikelets sessile, 8–20 mm long, barely 1 mm wide. Collections: 63028, 63081, 63150, 63212, 63448, 63502.

Very common at water ponds. — Pantropical.

10. *Cyperus oxylepis* NEES ex STEUD.

Tufts, 30–60 cm high. Leaves 3–4 mm wide. Inflorescence digitately branched, involucral leaves much longer than the inflorescence; rays 5–8; spikelets 4–30 per spike, 14–20 mm long, 3 mm wide, golden brown, inserted over a zone 2–5 mm long. Collections: 63148, 63209, ANDERSSON *s.n.* (S, cited in Areschoug 1869).

Occasional in moist places. — West Indies to Argentina.

11. *Eleocharis elegans* (KUNTH) ROEM. & SCHULT.

Fairly stout, erect, 80–100 cm high, reproducing from a horizontal rootstock. Stems terete, 3–6 mm wide, conspicuously septate; sheaths reddish brown, truncate. Spikelets solitary per culm, cylindrical, 1.5 cm long; scales acute. Collection: 63190.

Rare in shallow waters. — Tropical America.

12. *Eleocharis geniculata* (L.) ROEM. & SCHULT.

Densely tufted, 20–35 cm high. Stems barely 1 mm wide, sheathed at base. Spikelets solitary, 3–5 mm long, ovoid; scales ovate. Collections: 63143, 64025.

Occasional in sandy soils along seasonal streams. — Pantropical.

13. *Eleocharis interstincta* (VAHL) ROEM. & SCHULT.

Erect, 50–70 cm high. Stems terete, 3–5 mm wide, becoming septate with age; sheath membranous, pointed at apex. Spikelets solitary, cylindrical, 2–4 cm long (longest when in fruit); scales ovate. Collection: 63146.

Occasional aquatic. — Florida to South America.

14. *Fimbristylis annua* (ALL.) ROEM. & SCHULT.

Annual tufts, 30–50 cm high. Stem less than 1 mm wide; leaves to 2 mm wide. Inflorescence 5 cm long; involucral bracts 1–3 cm long. Spikelets 3–6 mm long, ovoid. Collections: 63027.

Common in disturbed moist places. — Widespread in tropical and temperate regions. Also on the Galapagos Islands.

15. *Fimbristylis miliacea* (L.) VAHL

Annual tufts, 15–60 cm high, widely spreading. Stem barely 1.5 mm wide; leaves 2–4 mm wide at base. Inflorescence 5–8 cm long; involucral bracts 1–3 cm long, leaf-like. Spikelets 2–3 mm long, ovoid; pedicels 0–1 cm long.

Collections: 63026, 63115, 63124, 63173, 63181, 63213.

Very common in open moist ground in April. — Cosmopolitan.

16. *Fimbristylis spadicea* (L.) VAHL

Large tussocks, 70–100 cm high. Stem 2–3 mm wide, rigid, scabrous. Inflorescence of 15–40 spikelets; involucral bract longer than the inflorescence. Spikelets 8–10 mm long, lance-ovate, black. Collections: 63466, 63974.

Occasional bordering salt marshes. — Pantropical.

17. *Pycreus macrostachyos* (LAM.) J. RAYNAL

Annual, 30–50 cm high. Leaves 3–5 mm wide. Inflorescence digitate; involucral leaves several times as long as the inflorescence; rays 3–7, to 10 cm long; spikelets 6–8 mm long, 1–1.5 mm wide, inserted over a zone 1–2 cm long. Collection: 63144.

Probably a rare aquatic. — Pantropical.

18. *Pycreus pelophilus* (RIDL.) C. B. CLARKE

Small tufts, 10–30 cm long. Leaves 1–2 mm wide. Inflorescence digitate; involucral leaves longer than inflorescence; rays 4–8, to 8 cm long. Spikelets 7–13 mm long, 1.5 mm wide, inserted over a zone 1–1.5 cm wide. Collection: 63039.

Only a single collection. — Pantropical.

19. *Rhynchospora contracta* (NEES) J. RAYNAL

Loosely tufted annual sedge, 20–50 cm high. Stems leafly at base; leaves 1–3 mm wide. Inflorescence lax, much branched, leafy. Spikelets borne in clusters, only 1–1.5 mm long; pedicels 1–15 mm long. Collections: 63043, 63123, 63183, 63352.

Common in moist grassland. — Mexico to Brazil.

20. *Scleria reticularis* MICHX.

Loosely branched ascending sedge, 30–50 cm high. Leaves 2–4 mm wide scabrous at margin. Inflorescence 2–4 cm long, composed of a limited number of unisexual spikelets; staminate ones 3 mm long; pistillate ones 6 mm long. Achene 3 mm long, oblong, white. Collection: 63204.

Rare. — South America to United States.

EBENACEAE (EBONY FAMILY)

Shrubs or trees. Leaves usually alternate, simple, entire; stipules lacking. Flowers mostly unisexual, 3–7-merous; stamens two to four times the number of the corolla lobes. Fruit a berry; calyx often persistent. A tropical family with 500 species.

1. *Diospyros inconstans* JACQ.
Treelet, to 4 m high. Twigs pubescent. Leaves glabrous above, with simple hairs beneath; blade 7–11 cm long, oblong-elliptic, acute to obtuse at base and apex; petiole 0.5 cm long. Flowers not seen. Fruit red, 3 cm wide, red; calyx persistent. Collections: 64149, 75487A.
Occasional understory treelet in the dry forest. — Widespread in South America.

ELATINACEAE (WATERWORT FAMILY)
Subshrubs or herbs. Leaves opposite or verticillate, simple; stipules minute, interpetiolar. Flowers bisexual, regular, 2–5-merous; stamens in two series. Fruit a capsule. A small tropical family of 30 species in aquatic environments.

1. *Bergia capensis* L.
Herb, 10–40 cm high, with ascending erect branches, rooting at nodes. Stem reddish, succulent, glabrous. Leaves decussate; blade 1–5 cm long, narrowly elliptic, serrulate, obtuse, attenuate at base; petiole 1–5 mm long. Inflorescence axillary, 10–15-flowered. Flowers white; pedicels to 3 mm long. Capsule 3 mm long. Collections: 63149, 63304.
Aquatic plant of swampy areas. — Pantropical.

ERYTHROXYLACEAE (COCA FAMILY)
Trees or shrubs. Leaves alternate, glabrous, simple, entire; stipules present. Flowers small, fasciculate; calyx persistent; corolla 5-lobed, the lobes with an appendage inside; stamens 10. Fruit a one-seeded drupe. A pantropical family with 200 species.

1. *Erythroxylum glaucum* O. E. SCHULZ
Deciduous tree, to 15 m high. Branchlets with numerous short shoots at nearly right angle to axis. Leaves glabrous; blade 4–6 cm long, obovate, rounded to retuse, cuneate at base, venation finely reticulate; petiole 3 mm long. Flowers in axils of year-old short shoots, 3–6 per node; pedicels 1.5–3 mm long. Drupe red, 1 cm long, ellipsoid. Collections: 63995, 85302.
Occasional in the dry forests. — Endemic to arid regions of Ecuador and adjacent Peru.
Uses: The wood is used for stakes in the field, furniture and for construction. It is also used to make charcoal.
Vernacular name: coquito.

Euphorbiaceae (Spurge Family)

Trees, shrubs, herbs, or vines. Leaves alternate or opposite, simple or palmately compound; stipules mostly present. Flowers usually minute and unisexual, borne in cymules or cyathia which resemble flowers. Fruit 3-lobed, capsular or drupaceous. A family with 7000 species of world wide distribution, most abundant in the tropics. — Many of the 15 species on Puná Island are weeds.

Key to the Species

1a. Stem succulent, trigonous, spiny; ornamental   13. *Euphorbia lactea*
1b. Stem not as above
  2a. Vines   11. *Dalechampia scandens*
  2b. Herbs or shrubs
    3a. Herbs
      4a. Leaves alternate
        5a. Leaves palmately and deeply 3-lobed   9. *Croton lobatus*
        5b. Leaves not deeply lobed
          6a. Leaves less than 1 cm long   15. *Phyllanthus amarus*
          6b. Leaves more than 1 cm long
            7a. Stems glabrescent   12. *Euphorbia graminea*
            7b. Stems variously hairy
              8a. Inflorescence racemose, the flowers separate; leaves narrow   4. *Caperonia palustris*
              8b. Inflorescence spicate, the flowers crowded; leaves broad
                9a. Female inflorescence 1–1.5 cm wide   1. *Acalypha alopecuroides*
                9b. Female inflorescence 2 mm wide   3. *Acalypha setosa*
      4b. Leaves opposite
        10a. Inflorescence subsessile; leaves to 5 mm wide   8. *Chamaesyce thymifolia*
        10b. Inflorescence pedunculate; most leaves wider than 5 mm
          11a. Stem tomentose distally   7. *Chamaesyce ophthalmica*
          11b. Stem glabrescent throughout
            12. Ovary glabrous   5. *Chamaesyce hypericifolia*
            12. Ovary pubescent   6. *Chamaesyce hyssopifolia*
    3b. Shrubs
      13a. Leaves palmately lobed; cultivated
        14a. Leaf-margin entire; capsule not echinate   14. *Manihot esculenta*
        14b. Leaf-margin serrate; capsule echinate   17. *Ricinus communis*
      13b. Leaves simple; native or naturalised
        15a. Inflorescence an axilllary cluster; leaves less than 3 cm long   16. *Phyllanthus graveolens*
        15b. Inflorescence spicate; leaves more than 3 cm long
          16a. Spikes to 3 cm long; flowers minute; leaves not biglandular at base   2. *Acalypha cuspidata*
          16b. Spikes generally longer than 3 cm; flowers 0.5 cm wide; leaves biglandular at base   10. *Croton rivinifolius*

1. *Acalypha alopecuroides* JACQ.
Herb, to 50 cm high. Stem pilose-glandular. Stipules lanceolate, minute. Leaves alternate, simple; blade 3–6 cm long, subovate, serrate, acuminate, rounded or subcordate at base; petiole 1–5 cm long. Male inflorescence axillary. Female inflorescence terminal, to 5 cm long, 1–1.5 cm wide, covered with trichomes; peduncle 0–2 cm long. Female bracts with long setaceous tips. Capsule 2 mm long, glabrate. Collection: 63554.
Occasional weed on cultivated grounds. — Mexico and the West Indies to Peru.

2. *Acalypha cuspidata* JACQ.
Shrub, to 2 m high. Stem puberulent. Leaves alternate, simple; blade 5–12 cm long, ovate, crenate, acuminate, subcordate at base; petiole 2–5 cm long. Male inflorescence axillary, 2–4 cm long, 2 mm wide, spicate. Collections: 63938, 63998.
Understory shrub in the deciduous dry forest. — Probably American.
Note: The plant is eaten by deer.
Vernacular name: canilla de venado.

3. *Acalypha setosa* A. RICH.
Herb, 50 cm high. Stem sparsely hirsute. Leaves alternate, simple; blade 3–6 cm long, ovate, serrate, more or less ciliate, acuminate, subcordate at base; petiole 1–5 cm long. Male inflorescence axillary, 1 cm long. Female inflorescence terminal, to 4 cm long and 1.5 cm wide, silky-hirsute. Capsule 2 mm wide. Collection: 63051, ANDERSSON *s.n.* (S, cited in Areschoug 1869).
Uncommon in waste places. — Mexico to northwestern South America.

4. *Caperonia palustris* (L.) A. ST.-HIL.
Herb, 0.5–1 m high. Stem stiff-hairy. Leaves alternate, simple; blade 5–11 cm long, narrowly lanceolate to lance-ovate, serrate, acute, obtuse at base; petiole 0.5–3 cm long. Inflorescence 5–10 cm long, racemose, lower flowers female. Flowers white, 4 mm wide, subsessile. Capsule 6–8 mm wide, 3-lobed. Seeds 2 mm long, ovoid. Collections: 63279, 63574.
Uncommon in swamps. — Mexico to Argentina.

5. *Chamaesyce hypericifolia* (L.) MILLSP.
Creeping or erect herb, to 1 m high. Stem glabrescent. Leaves simple, opposite; blade 6–20 mm long, serrate to subentire, subobtuse, oblique at base; petiole 1–3 mm long. Cyathia in congested, terminal or axillary cymes, white. Capsule 2 mm long. Ovary glabrous. Collections: 63335, 63380.
Common in waste places and cultivated fields. — Widespread in South America to Mexico.

6. *Chamaesyce hyssopifolia* (L.) SMALL
Resembles *Chamaesyce hypericifolia* in most characters but the ovary is pubescent. Collection: 63669.
Weed on cultivated grounds. — Subcosmopolitan.

7. *Chamaesyce ophthalmica* (PERS.) D. G. BURCH
Decumbent herb, to 20 cm high. Stem sparsely to densely tomentose distally, otherwise glabrescent. Leaves simple, opposite; blade 1.5–3.5 cm long, rhombic-ovate, obscurely serrate, subobtuse, oblique at base; petiole 1–3 mm long. Cyathia numerous together in congested, terminal or axillary cymes. Collections: 63269, 63386.
Weedy plant. — Widespread in tropical America. Also on the Galapagos Islands.

8. *Chamaesyce thymifolia* (L.) MILLSP.
Prostrate herb, forming small mats. Stem sparsely puberulent. Leaves simple, opposite, reddish; blade 6–9 mm long, narrowly oblong, oblique at base, serrulate in upper half; petiole 1 mm long. Inflorescence axillary at each leaf-pair, composed of 2–several subsessile cyathia. Capsule 1 mm long. Collection: 63184.
Weedy along trails. — Pantropical.

9. *Croton lobatus* L.
Monoecious herb, to 50 cm high. Leaves alternate, palmately and deeply 3-lobed, inconspicuously and stellately hispidulous; blade to 11 cm wide; lobes serrate, acuminate; petiole to 8 cm long. Inflorescence 10 cm long, elongated, many-flowered. Flowers minute; males short-pedicellate; females subsessile. Capsule 8 mm long. Seeds 4 mm long. Collection: 63347.
Uncommon weed in swampy areas. — Tropical America.

10. *Croton rivinifolius* KUNTH
Dioecious shrub, 1–3 m high. Leaves alternate, simple, stellately pubescent; blade 3–10(–21) cm long, ovate, obscurely serrulate, subacuminate, more or less rounded and biglandular at base; petiole 0.5–6 cm long. Inflorescence 3–11 cm long, spicate. Flowers 5 mm wide; males pedicellate; females sessile. Fruit 3-merous, 6–8 mm wide. Collections: 63166, 63310, 63484, 63635, 64004, 64091B, 85327, ANDERSSON *s.n.* (S, cited in Areschoug 1869).
Very common in thorn scrub. — Endemic to arid zones of western Ecuador and adjacent Peru.
Uses: The species is used to treat tooth ache and as firewood. It is believed to be poisonous to the cattle.
Vernacular names: chala, palosangre.

11. *Dalechampia scandens* L.
Monoecious vine. Stem more or less fulvous-hirsute. Leaves alternate; blade
3–11 cm long, broader than long, deeply 3-lobed, acuminate, cordate at base;
lobes serrulate to entire, petiole to 6 cm long. Inflorescence enclosed by two
foliaceous bracts, axillary; penduncle to 7 cm long. Fruiting calyx-lobes with
conspicuously gland-tipped cilia. Capsule brown, to 1 cm wide, 3-parted. Seeds
4 mm wide. Collections: 63326, 63412.
Occasional, climbing over shrubs. — West Indies to tropical South America.
Phenology: Flowers at any time.

12. *Euphorbia graminea* JACQ.
Slender herb, to 1 m high. Stem glabrescent. Leaves alternate, simple; blade to 8
cm long, ovate, distal blades smaller and elliptic-lanceolate. Inflorescence of a
few, white cyathia; peduncle filiform. Capsule 3 mm wide, 3-lobed. Collection:
63252.
Occasional in disturbed places. — Mexico to Peru.

13. *Euphorbia lactea* HAW. [cult.]
An occasional succulent in gardens (Collection: 63765). — Native to East Indies.
Uses: Ornamental.

14. *Manihot esculenta* CRANTZ [cult.]
The cassava (Collection: 63677) is an important locally consumed crop. — Of
American origin but not known in a wild state.
Uses: The starchy tubers are used in soups and other traditional dishes.
Vernacular name: yuca.

15. *Phyllanthus amarus* SCHUMACH.
Erect herb, 20 cm high; branches horizontal. Stem glabrous. Leaves alternate,
simple, subsessile; blade 4–8 mm long, oblong, rounded at base and apex,
entire. Flowers in fascicles of 1–3 per axil, minute, green. Fruit 2 mm wide,
depressed globose, 3-lobed. Collection: 63340.
Uncommon weed. — Pantropical.
Vernacular name: cavansillo

16. *Phyllanthus graveolens* KUNTH
Shrub, 1.5–4 m high. Stem puberulent. Leaves alternate, simple; blade 8–18 mm
long, nearly orbicular, entire, mucronate to emarginate; petiole 1–2 mm long.
Flowers 3–11 together, in axillary clusters, green, white or brown, 2 mm wide;
pedicels 2–10 mm long. Fruit 4 mm wide, 3-parted. Collections: 63522, 63847,
63993.
Common in disturbed, dry forest. — Endemic to Ecuador and adjacent Peru.

17. *Ricinus communis* L. [cult.]

The castor-oil plant is occasionally cultivated or it grows as a spontaneous weed around homesites. — Native to India.

Vernacular name: higuerilla.

FABACEAE (PEA FAMILY)

Trees, shrubs, vines, or herbs. Leaves usually compound and alternate, often with tendrils; stipules mostly present. Inflorescence racemose. Flowers bisexual, zygomorphic (papillionaceous), 5-parted; petals distinctly heteromorphic, the upper (adaxial) forms the standard, the two lateral the wings, and the lower two the keel; stamens 10 or sometimes fewer, the filaments mostly united. Fruit a pod or rarely a nut.

A large family with 12000 species distributed throughout the World. The family is represented on Puná Island by more species than any other family.

Key to the Species

(beans, *Phaseolus* spp., peanuts, and pigeon peas are not included in the key)

1a. Trees and treelets (dbh > 10 cm when full grown)
    2a. Leaves 3-foliolate   17. *Erythrina velutina*
    2b. Leaves pinnately 5–many-foliolate
        3a. Pod 1–2-seeded, to 8 cm long
            4a. Pod 1.5 cm thick, drupaceous; flowers yellow   19. *Geoffroea spinosa*
            4b. Pod less than 1 cm thick, samaroid or flat; flowers violet or white
                5a. Leaves elliptic, acuminate   22. *Lonchocarpus atropurpureus*
                5b. Leaves oblong, subemarginate   23. *Machaerium millei*
        3b. Pod many-seeded, longer than 10 cm   20. *Gliricidia brenningii*
1b. Shrubs, herbs and vines
    6a. Leaves 2–3-foliolate
        7a. Leaflets to 7 mm wide; herbs with lanceolate leaflets
            8a. Leaves 2-foliolate; bracts paired, foliacous   38. *Zornia reticulata*
            8b. Leaves 3-foliolate; bracts not as above   32. *Stylosanthes sympodialis*
        7b. Leaflets wider than 8 mm; otherwise different
            9a. Pods 1–seeded when mature, winged   13. *Desmodium glabrum*
            9b. Pods 2–many seeded
                10a. Terminal leaflets (the larger) more than 8 cm wide; pods at least 1 cm wide and 12 cm long
                    11a. Leaflets rounded; pod 2–2.5 cm wide   9. *Canavalia rosea*
                    11b. Leaflets rhombic; pod 1–1.5 cm wide   10. *Centrosema plumieri*
                10b. Terminal leaflets less than 8 cm wide; pods less than 1 cm wide or less than 12 cm long
                    12a. Leaflets elliptic-ovate to subrotund
                        13a. Pods 1.5 mm wide, constricted   15. *Desmodium scorpiurus*
                        13b. Pods 6-8 mm wide, not constricted   18. *Galactia striata*
                    12b. Leaflets rhombic to variously elongated, if elongated then

distinctly widest at the base
14a. Pedicels mostly 5–12 mm long; pods constricted
    15a. Stipules filiform; annuals   14. *Desmodium procumbens*
    15b. Stipules wider than 1 mm at base, sometimes auriculate;
        perennials   16. *Desmodium tortuosum*
14b. Pedicels 0–3 mm long; pods barely constricted
    16a. Leaflets densely black-dotted beneath; pod less than
        3 cm long   30. *Rhynchosia minima*
    16b. Leaflets not dotted beneath; pods longer than 3 cm
        17a. Pods 8–10 mm wide   34. *Vigna adenantha*
        17b. Pods less than 8 mm wide
            18a. Flowers yellow   35. *Vigna luteola*
            18b. Flowers not yellow
                19a. Pods 4–5 mm wide
                    20a. Terminal leaflets very broadly ovate; pod
                        flat   36. *Vigna peduncularis*
                    20b. Terminal leaflets more or less rhombic;
                        pods almost as thick as wide   37. *Vigna* sp.
                19b. Pods 2–3 mm wide
                    20a. Leaves linear-ovate to lanceolate, sparsely
                        pubescent beneath
                        24. *Macroptilium lathyroides*
                    20b. Leaves ovate-deltoid, more or less
                      tomentose beneath
                        25. *Macroptilium longepedunculatum*
6b. Leaves 4–many-foliolate
  21a. Leaves 4–9-foliolate
    22a. Leaves paripinnate; pod 1–4-seeded, rugose over the seeds
        29. *Poiretia punctata*
    22b. Leaves imparipinnate; pod not as above
        23a. Pod one-seeded, winged in distal half   26. *Nissolia fruticosa*
        23b. Pod many-seeded, not winged   11. *Coursetia caribaea*
  21b. Leaves 10–many-foliolate
    24a. Inflorescence a compact densely hirsute spike,
        3–6 cm long, 1 cm wide   12. *Dalea cliffortiana*
    24b. Inflorescence not as above
        25a. Pod 1(–3)-seeded, strongly winged   6. *Aeschynomene tumbezensis*
        25b. Pod many-seeded
            26a. Pods conspiously sickle-shaped, strongly bent, 1–2 cm long
                21. *Indigofera suffruticosa*
        26b. Pods not as above
            27a. Pods longer than 15 cm; plants generally higher than 1.5 m
                31. *Sesbania emerus*
            27b. Pods less than 8 cm long; plants less than 1.5 m tall
                28a. Largest leaflets wider than 7 mm
                    29a. Leaflets oblong   11. *Coursetia caribaea* var. *ochroleuca*
                    29b. Leaflets obovate   33. *Tephrosia cinerea*
                28b. Leaflets less than 6 mm wide
                  30a. Plants essentially glabrous

31a. Leaflets 1 mm wide; pods with rotund intervals
    between the constrictions   3. *Aeschynomene filosa*
31b. Leaflets 2–5 mm wide; pods with rectangular
    intervals between the constrictions
                 4. *Aeschynomene pluriarticulata*
30b. Plants variously hairy, at least on well developed
    stems
    32a. Pods with rectangular intervals between the
        constrictions   2. *Aeschynomene ciliata*
    32b. Pod with with rotund intervals between the
        constrictions
        33a. Bracts numerous and conspicuously ciliate
                 1. *Aeschynomene americana*
        33b. Bracts often few and not ciliate
                 5. *Aeschynomene sensitiva*

1. *Aeschynomene americana* L. var. *glandulosa* (POIR.) RUDD
Herb or subshrub, 0.5–1 m high. Stem stiff-hirsute; hairs bulbous at base. Leaves pinnate; leaflets 10–25 pairs, 5–14 mm long, 1–2 mm wide, linear, 2–several-costate. Inflorescence axillary, few flowered; bracts ciliate. Flowers brown, to 1.5 cm long. Pod 1–4 cm long, 3–4 mm wide, curved, puberulent; constrictions 2–9, the intervals rotund. Collections: 63014, 63320, 63383, 63436, ANDERSSON *s.n.* (S, cited in Areschoug 1869).
Common in disturbed places. — Widespread in America.

2. *Aeschynomene ciliata* VOGEL
Herb or shrub, to 1 m high. Stem hirsute. Leaves pinnate; leaflets 15–25 pairs, 7–15 mm long, linear, ciliate. Inflorescence terminal, many-flowered. Flowers orange to orange-brown, 1 cm long. Pod 5 cm long, 5 mm wide, flat, hirsute; constrictions 8–10, the intervals rectangular. Collection: 63125.
Rare on disturbed beach. — Mexico to Brazil.

3. *Aeschynomene filosa* C. MARTIUS ex BENTH
Erect herb, to 1 m high. Stem essentially glabrous. Leaves pinnate; leaflets typically 50 pairs, 3–4 mm long, linear. Inflorescence many-flowered. Flowers orange-brown, 4–6 mm long. Pod to 1.5 cm long, 2–3 mm wide; constrictions 1–4, the intervals rotund. Collections: 63219, 63732.
Common in seasonally flooded areas of the savanna. — Cuba and South America.

4. *Aeschynomene pluriarticulata* G. DON
Herb, 0.5 m high, woody at base. Stem essentially glabrous. Leaves pinnate; leaflets 10–20 pairs, 1–1.5 cm long, linear, mucronate. Inflorescence of a few flowers. Flowers brown, 1 cm long. Pods 4 cm long, 3–4 mm wide; constrictions

10–15, the intervals rectangular. Collection: 63289.
Rare in seasonally inundated swamps. — Endemic to southwestern Ecuador
and adjacent Peru.

5. *Aeschynomene sensitiva* Sw.
Herbaceous shrub, to 1 m high. Stem sparsely hirsute. Leaves pinnate; leaflets
15–25 pairs, commonly 6–10 mm long. Inflorescence axillary; racemes 3–4-
flowered. Flowers yellow with brown stripes, 7 mm long. Pod 4–6 cm long, 5–6
mm wide, slightly curved; constrictions 5–10, the intervals rotund. Collection:
63726.
Rare on the beach. — Native to America, becoming pantropical.

6. *Aeschynomene tumbezensis* J. F. Macbr.
Shrub, to 3 m high. Stem sparsely hirsute when young. Leaves pinnate; leaflets
12–18 pairs, 1–2 cm long, linear, mucronate. Inflorescence axillary, few-
flowered. Flowers yellow-brown, 8 mm long. Pod to 1 cm long, 8 mm wide,
prominently winged; constrictions 1–3, the interval rotund. Collections: 63211,
63483, 63586, 63730, 63813.
Disturbed beach. — Endemic to the arid zones of southwestern Ecuador and
adjacent Peru.

7. *Arachis hypogaea* L. [cult.]
The peanut (no specimen) is occasionally grown on the island. — Probably
native to Bolivia and northern Argentina and now widely cultivated
throughout the World.
Vernacular name: maní.

8. *Cajanus cajan* (L.) Millsp. [cult.]
The pigeon pea (Collections: 63676) is common in cultivation on the island. —
Probably native to Africa.
Uses: Edible as beans in vegetable soups.
Vernacular name: fréjol de palo.

9. *Canavalia rosea* (Sw.) DC.
Climbing vine, several meters long. Stem sparsely pubescent. Leaves 3-foliolate;
leaflets to 16 cm long, oblong to subrotund, entire, more or less short-attenuate,
truncate or rounded at base. Inflorescence to 30 cm long, racemose, the flowers
crowded distally. Flowers violet or pink, 3.5 cm long. Pod 15–20 cm long, 2.5
cm wide, nearly straight, slightly pubescent, beaked. Collections: 63275, 63409,
63577, 63806, 63907, 64035.
Very common in closed forest. — Widespread along tropical and subtropical
seacoasts of the world. Also on the Galapagos Islands.

10. *Centrosema plumieri* (TURPIN ex PERS.) BENTH.
Vigorous but comparatively slender vine. Stems lightly hirsutulous. Leaves 3-foliolate; terminal leaflet to 16 cm long, rhombic, attenuate. Inflorescence to 5 cm long, few-flowered. Flowers white or yellow with violet or brown center, 5 cm long. Pod 10–20 cm long, 1–1.5 cm wide, prominently beaked. Collections: 63515, 63599, 63715, 63755.
Common in closed forest. — Widespread in tropical America.

11. *Coursetia caribaea* (JACQ.) LAVIN
Herb or shrub, 20–80 cm high, extremely variable. Stem puberulous. Leaves imparipinnate, gradually larger distally; pairs of leaflets 7–8, to 1.5–2.5 cm long, oblong, rounded at both ends. Inflorescence many-flowered. Flowers green–white, 1 cm long. Pod 5–8 cm long, transversely constricted, the intervals rectangular, pubescent. Collections: 63576 (species); 63670, 63857, 64028 (variety).
A weedy plant, often along trails. — America. The variety var. *ochroleuca* (JACQ.) LAVIN has only 2–3 pairs of elliptic-ovate leaflets to 4–6 cm long, yellow-brown flowers, and glabrous pods. It is probably endemic to southwestern Ecuador and Peru.

12. *Dalea cliffortiana* WILLD.
Herb, 40 cm high. Stem glabrous. Leaves imparipinnate; leaflets 13–17, mostly 5–8 mm long, the ultimate leaflet to 15 mm long; all leaflets linear to linear-elliptic, punctate beneath. Inflorescence 3–6 cm long, 1 cm wide, spicate, cylindrical, conspicuously hirsute. Flowers violet; bracts 6 mm long, narrowly ovate, punctate, ciliate. Collection: 63273, ANDERSSON *s.n.* (S, cited in Areschoug 1869).
Uncommon along trails. — Pantropical.

13. *Desmodium glabrum* (MILL.) DC.
Erect herb, to 1 m high. Stem pubescent. Leaves 3-foliolate; terminal leaflets to 10 cm long, rhombic-ovate, acute. Inflorescence terminal, simple or branched; flowers in fascicles of up to 6 at each node. Flowers white and purple, 6 mm long; calyx 2.5–3 mm long, the lobes lanceolate. Pod to 1 cm long, flat; ultimate fertile segment elliptic-discoid, 1-seeded. Seed 3 mm long. Collections: 63389, 63759.
Common weed. — Widespread in tropical and subtropical America. Known from the Galapagos Islands.

14. *Desmodium procumbens* (MILL.) HITCHC.
Small herb with procumbent branches. Stem striate, pubescent. Leaves 3-foliolate; terminal leaflets to 5 cm long, rhombic-ovate, attenuate. Stipules filiform. Inflorescence composed of numerous paired flowers. Flowers cream or

white; calyx 1.5 mm long; lobes triangular; pedicels 5–12 mm long. Pod many-articulate; segments 3–4 mm long, strongly involute and revolute. Collections: 63121, 63385, 63437, 63578, ANDERSSON 177 (S, cited by Capdevila 1994).
Common in forest clearings and along trails. — Probably native to America, now pantropical. Also on the Galapagos Islands.

15. *Desmodium scorpiurus* (Sw.) DESV.
Creeping herb. Stem slender and delicate, 1 mm wide, sparsely pubescent. Stipules auriculate. Leaves 3-foliolate; terminal leaflet to 3.5 cm long, subelliptic, rounded at base. Inflorescence opposed to a leaf or axillary, the flowers inserted in pairs or groups of three. Flowers pink-violet; calyx to 3 mm long; lobes lanceolate. Pod 2–4 cm long, 1.5 mm wide, cylindrical, pubescent; constricted segments 4 mm long. Collections: 63716, 63762, 63823, 63904.
Common weed in waste places. — Tropical America, becoming pantropical.

16. *Desmodium tortuosum* (Sw.) DC.
Suberect herb, to 2 m high, with distinct main-stem. Stem terete, hirsute. Leaves 3-foliolate or occasionally uni-foliolate; terminal leaflet to 10 cm long, narrowly rhombic-deltoid, rounded at base and apex. Stipules wider than 1 mm at base, sometimes auriculate. Inflorescence terminal and axillary, lax, much branched, the flowers paired or in groups of three. Flowers green or violet; calyx 2–3.5 mm long; pedicels 5–12 mm long. Pod to 2.5 cm long; segments 6–7, to 4 mm wide, disc-shaped. Collections: 63737, 63771.
Occasional weedy plant. — Mexico to South America and introduced in Asia and Africa.

17. *Erythrina velutina* WILLD.
Tree, 4–12 m high. Trunk red-brown, with stout subulate spines. Leaves 3-foliolate; leaflets to 17 cm long, broadly rhombic, stellately pubescent beneath. Inflorescence to 20 cm long, the flowers crowded distally. Flowers orange-red, the standard to 5 cm long and 4 cm wide. Pod to 17 cm long, 1.5 cm wide. Seeds red, 1.5 cm long. Collections: 63659, 64017, 64130.
Common on the west coast, rare elsewhere. — West Indies and northern South America. Reported from the Galapagos Islands.
Note: It is eaten by cattle and goats.
Vernacular names: capué, porotillo.

18. *Galactia striata* (JACQ.) URB.
Tomentose vine. Leaves 3-foliolate; leaflets 3–5 cm long, elliptic, entire, obtuse and mucronulate, rounded at base. Inflorescence 5–10 cm long, many-flowered. Flowers violet or pink. Pod 3–5 cm long, 6–8 mm wide, flat, softly pilose. Collections: 63375, 63671, 63746 (tentative).
Common along trails. — West Indies, South America, and the Galapagos Islands.

19. *Geoffroea spinosa* JACQ.

Tree, 6–15 m high. Trunk gnarled. Leaves pinnate; leaflets 6–8 pairs, 2–3.5 cm long, oblong, rounded. Flowers yellow. Pod 1-seeded, 3 cm long, 2.5 cm wide, 1.5 cm thick, drupaceous. Collections: 63127, 63734, 85313.

Very common in thorn forest. — Colombia to Argentina. Also on the Galapagos Islands.

Phenology: Flowering in March.

Uses: The wood is used for boards, houses, boats, and charcoal. Previously the wood was used to make spindles for looms in the cotton textile manufacture. It is eaten by cattle and donkeys.

Vernacular names: madera seca, seca.

20. *Gliricidia brenningii* (HARMS) LAVIN

Shrub or tree, 4–12 m high. Bark whitish. Leaves deciduous, pinnate; leaflets 10 pairs, commonly 3–4 cm long, oblong, more or less rounded at both ends. Inflorescence racemose, many-flowered. Flowers white and yellow, 2.5 cm long. Pod 12–20 cm long, 2 cm wide, twisted when dehiscing. Seeds 1 cm long, flat. Collections: 63059, 64110, 64122, 85333, 85356.

Common in forest margins and along trails. — Western Ecuador and adjacent Peru.

Uses: Used as a rat poison.

Vernacular name: yuca de ratón.

21. *Indigofera suffruticosa* MILL.

Shrub, to 2 m high. Stem angled, strigose. Leaves pinnate, 17–21 foliolate; leaflets to 3 cm long, elliptic to obovate, mucronate; petiolules 1–2 mm long. Inflorescence 3–5 cm long, racemose, the flowers crowded. Flowers red-brown or white, 5 mm long. Pods 1–2 cm long, 2 mm wide, sickle-shaped, reflexed. Collections: 63338, 63339, 63646, 64136.

Common around homesites. — United States to Argentina, becoming pantropical.

22. *Lonchocarpus atropurpureus* BENTH.

Slender tree, 4–10 m high. Leaves pinnate, 7–9-foliolate; leaflets 3–7 cm long, elliptic, short-acuminate, cuneate at base; rachis angled. Inflorescence of several racemose branches, to 10 cm long. Flowers violet, 1 cm long; pedicels 5 mm long. Pod 4–8 cm long, 8–10 mm wide, flat, 1–2-seeded. Collection: 63719.

Uncommon in the dry forest. — Widespread in America.

Uses: The wood is used for stakes, boards, shores, stanchions, floors, furniture, boats, houses, firewood, and charcoal.

Vernacular name: bálsamo.

23. *Machaerium millei* STANDL.
Tree, 4–10 m high. Bark deeply grooved. Leaves pinnate, (9–)13(–18)-foliolate; leaflets 3–5 cm long, oblong, rounded and subemarginate, rounded at base. Inflorescence to 10 cm long. Flowers green, 1 cm long. Pod 6 cm long, 1 cm wide, 1-seeded and winged in distal two thirds. Collections: 63837, 64095.
Uncommon in thorn forest. — Endemic to southwestern Ecuador and adjacent Peru.
Uses: The wood is used for boards, hatchets, handles, floor boards in houses, and charcoal.
Vernacular name: cabo de hacha.

24. *Macroptilium lathyroides* (L.) URB.
Vine. Stem sparsely hirsute. Stipules 6 mm long, subulate. Leaves 3-foliolate; leaflets to 6 cm long, linear-ovate to lanceolate with broad base, sparsely pubescent beneath. Inflorescence 20–40 cm long, erect, the brown flowers crowded in distal one third. Pod 6–8 cm long, 2 mm wide, inserted several together in a distal cluster, twisting when dehiscing. Seeds black. Collections: 63242, 63285.
Common at borders of swamps. — Native to tropical America, including the Galapagos Islands.

25. *Macroptilium longepedunculatum* (C. MART. ex BENTH.) URB.
Slender vine, white-pubescent in young parts. Stem terete. Stipules filiform. Leaves 3-foliolate, petiolate for 2–5 cm, tomentose beneath; leaflets 2–6 cm long, ovate-deltoid, subacute and mucronulate, rounded to truncate at base, the lateral leaflets subsessile. Inflorescence 20–35 cm long. Flowers 2 cm long, red-brown. Pod 4–8 cm long, 2–3 mm wide, brown. Seeds 3 mm long, brown. Collections: 63276, 63533, 63590, 63729.
Common in dry thickets. — America.
A further specimens (63915) may also belong here, but it has subulate stipules and white flowers with purple wings.

26. *Nissolia fruticosa* JACQ.
Scrambler or liana, 3 m long. Stem with scattered, broad-based hairs. Leaves pinnately 5-foliolate, glabrous above, puberulent beneath; leaflets to 7 cm long, elliptic or oval, acute, rounded to cuneate at base. Inflorescence racemose, dense, axillary, short-pedunculate. Flowers yellow to brown, 1 cm long. Pod 3–4 cm long, 1 cm wide at winged distal half, 1-seeded. Collections: 63606, 63715.
Uncommon. — Central America to Patagonia.

27. *Phaseolus vulgaris* L. [cult.]
The common bean (Collection: 63675) is important in local consumption. — Native to the New World.
Uses: It is used as a vegetable in salads, vegetable soups, or combined with rice dishes.
Vernacular name: verdura.

28. *Phaseolus cf. lunatus* L. [cult.]
Another species of bean is grown on the island (Collection: 63552), which resembles the lima bean.
Uses: Used in vegetable soups or combined with rice dishes.
Vernacular name: haba, haba payar.

29. *Poiretia punctata* (WILLD.) DESV.
Vine. Stem glabrous. Leaves 4-foliolate; leaflets obovate to subrotund, to 3 cm long and 2.5 cm wide, punctate. Inflorescence to 4 cm long. Flowers yellow, 6 mm long. Pod 1–4-seeded, 8–25 mm long, 3 mm wide, rugose over the seeds. Collections: 63491, 63738.
Uncommon. — Mexico to Peru.

30. *Rhynchosia minima* (L.) DC.
Slender, sparsely pubescent vine. Leaves 3-foliolate; leaflets to 5 cm long, broadly rhombic-ovate, densely dotted beneath with black glands. Inflorescence to 12 cm long, racemose. Flowers yellow-brown, 8 mm long; pedicels very short. Pod 2 cm long, 4 mm wide; seeds 1 per pod, 3 mm long. Collection: 63789.
Rare. — Pantropical and subtropical. Reported from the Galapagos Islands.

31. *Sesbania emerus* (AUBL.) URB.
Erect herb, 1–4 m high. Stem glabrous, terete. Leaves pinnate; leaflets 30–50 pairs, to 2.5 cm long, linear, mucronate. Inflorescence axillary, few-flowered. Flowers yellow, 1.5 cm long. Pod pendulous on horizontal branches, to 20 cm long, 3 mm wide, linear. Collections: 63235, 63731.
Common in seasonally flooded parts of the savanna. — Central America to Ecuador.
Note: It is eaten by goats.
Vernacular name: mostaza, mostaza de monte.

32. *Stylosanthes sympodialis* TAUB.
Creeping herb, sometimes to 50 cm high. Stem hirsute. Leaves 3-foliolate, short petiolate; leaflets 1–2.5 cm long, lanceolate. Inflorescence terminal, often 1–few-flowered. Flowers orange-brown, 6–7 mm long. Pod 1 cm long, 2 mm wide, 2-articulate. Collections: 63176, 63214, 63662, 63801.

Common along paths. — Restricted to the arid zone of southwestern Ecuador, including the Galapagos Islands, and adjacent Peru.

33. *Tephrosia cinerea* (L.) PERS.
Herbaceous vine, to 60 cm long. Stem strigose. Leaves pinnately 9–15-foliolate; leaflets commonly 3 cm long, narrowly obovate, rounded. Inflorescence few-flowered. Flowers pink-violet, 1.5 cm long. Pod 4 cm long, 3 mm wide. Seeds 2 mm long. Collections: 63588, 63751.
Common in disturbed sites. — Widespread in tropical America, also on the Galapagos Islands.

34. *Vigna adenantha* (G. MEY.) MARÉCHAL, MASCHERPA & STAINIER
Large vine. Stem sparsely hirsute. Leaves 3-foliolate, petiolate for 4–6 cm; terminal leaflets rhombic-ovate, 6–11 cm long, with prominent nerves beneath. Inflorescence 15–25 cm long. Flowers 3 cm long, white with purple spots. Pod 8–11 cm long, 9 mm wide, rather flat, curved, slightly scabrous. Seeds 5 mm long, 3 mm wide and thick, green-brown. Collections: 63925, 64148.
Uncommon in the dry forest. — Tropical and subtropical America.

35. *Vigna luteola* (JACQ.) BENTH.
More or less hirsute vine, twining over the ground. Leaves 3-foliolate; leaflets of variable size, to 6–10 cm long, narrowly to broadly ovate. Inflorescence to 20 cm long, the flowers crowded distally. Flowers yellow, 1.5 cm long; pedicels 2–3 mm long. Pod 4–7 cm long, 6 mm wide, linear, densely hirsute. Collections: 63529, 63944.
Common on sandy beaches. — The tropics and subtropics of the world. Also on the Galapagos Islands.

36. *Vigna peduncularis* (KUNTH) FAWC. & RENDLE
Sparsely pubescent vine. Stem twiny, more or less grooved. Leaves 3-foliolate, petiolate for 5–12 cm; terminal leaflets 5–9 cm long, very broadly ovate, acuminate, rounded to subtruncate at base; lateral leaflets oblique. Inflorescence 20–35 cm long. Flowers 3 cm long, violet. Pod 9–12 cm long, 5 mm wide, flat, curved at apex, mucronate. Seeds 4 mm long, 2 mm wide, flat. Collections: 63493, 63569A, 63602, 63625, 63810.
Common in dry forest. — Widespread in warm America.

37. *Vigna* sp.
Vine. Stem nearly glabrous. Leaves 3-foliolate, petiolate for 2–4 cm; terminal leaflets 4–7 cm long, more or less rhombic, sometimes narrowly so, usually rounded at base; lateral leaflets oblique. Inflorescence 15–25 cm long, the flowers crowded distally. Flowers white, cream or violet, 2–3 cm long. Pod 8 cm long, 4 mm wide, almost as thick as wide, beaked, moderately pubescent.

Collections: 63439, 63492, 63569B, 63774, 63822.

Common in disturbed places in the thorn forest.

The material may comprise two species.

38. *Zornia reticulata* SM.

Herb, to 40 cm high. Stem glabrous. Leaves 2-foliolate; leaflets 2–3.5 cm long, lanceolate, acute; petiole 1–2 cm long; petiolules 2 mm long. Inflorescence to 20 cm long, unbranched; bracts conspicuous, paired, 1 cm long, foliaceous, elliptic, ciliate. Flowers yellow. Collections: 63277, 63744.

Uncommon along trails. — Widespread in America.

The genus *Zornia* needs taxonomical revision in the New World and the species name is tentative.

FLACOURTIACEAE (FLACOURTIA FAMILY)

Trees or shrubs. Leaves alternate, simple; stipules minute and caducous or lacking. Flowers actinomorphic, bisexual, 4–5-merous; stamens numerous; disc often present. Fruit a berry, capsule or drupe. A tropical family with 1300 species.

Key to the Species

1a. Leaves subglabrous beneath; shrub   1. *Casearia mariquitensis*
1b. Leaves stellately pubescent beneath; tree   2. *Muntingia calabura*

1. *Casearia mariquitensis* KUNTH

Shrub, to 4 m high. Leaves glabrous above, subglabrous beneath; blade 7–12 cm long, elliptic, serrate, attenuate, cuneate to obtuse at base; petiole 2–6 mm long. Inflorescence a fascicle of some 10–15 flowers, often on naked stems. Flowers white, fragrant; stamens about 10; pedicels 3–7 mm long. Fruit 1.5–2 cm long, globose, apiculate. Collections: 63842, 63916, 63930, 63990, 63997.

Common in dry understory vegetation. — Widespread in warm South America.

Phenology: The flowering season begins in August.

Vernacular name: palito blanco.

2. *Muntingia calabura* L.

Slender tree, to 10 m high. Branchlets hirsute. Leaves stellate-tomentose beneath; blade 5–13 cm long, oblong-lanceolate, coarsely and unequally serrate, acute, oblique at base; petiole 3–8 cm long. Flowers white, 2 cm wide; pedicels 2–3 cm long. Fruit 1 cm long, red, globose, fleshy. Collections: 63313, 63532, 85339.

Locally abundant in disturbed, dry forest and on slopes along the beach. — The

Jamaica cherry is widely distributed in forests throughout tropical America.
Uses: The wood is used for shores, deck strakes, frame timbers, stanchions, and
houses. Although the fruits of this species are nutritious (Morton 1987) they are
only eaten by birds according to our local informants.
Vernacular name: niguito.

GENTIANACEAE (GENTIAN FAMILY)

Mainly herbs. Leaves glabrous, opposite, simple and entire; stipules lacking.
Flowers in dichotomously branched inflorescences, twisted in bud,
actinomorphic, 4–5-merous; corolla united and tubular. Fruit usually a capsule.
A family with 1000 species, mainly in temperate and mountain regions.

Key to the Species

1a. Flowers blue, 1 cm long   1. *Centaurium quitense*
1b. Flowers brown, 3 cm long   2. *Schultesia guianensis*

1. *Centaurium quitense* (KUNTH) B. L. ROB.
Erect herb, to 40 cm high, without basal rosette. Leaves sessile; blade 1–2 cm
long, narrowly elliptic. Inflorescence large and slender, diffuse, 100-flowered.
Flowers light blue, 1 cm long, salver-shaped, mostly 4-merous; sepals 7 mm
long, linear; pedicels 2–4 cm long, filiform. Collection: 63174.
Uncommon and restricted to the savanna. — Mexico to Peru and the West
Indies.
Phenology: Flowers in April and May.
Uses: Used medicinally to cure malaria.
Vernacular name: canchalagua.

2. *Schultesia guianensis* (AUBL.) MALME
Erect herb, to 40 cm high. Stem angled. Leaves sessile; blade to 5 cm long,
ovate-lanceolate, acute, rounded and decurrent at base. Flowers solitary,
brown, 3 cm long; calyx 2 cm long, extended. Collections: 63132, 63201.
Common in swampy areas. — Widespread in tropical America.
Phenology: Flowers in April.

GOODENIACEAE (GOODENIA FAMILY)

Herbs or shrubs. Leaves mostly alternate and simple; stipules lacking. Flowers
bisexual, 5-merous; stamens alternate; style 1. Fruits a drupe, nut, or capsule. A
family with 300 species, primarily in Australia and on tropical shores.

1. *Scaevola plumieri* (L.) VAHL
Shrub, to 1.5 m high. Stem glabrous except in leaf axils. Leaves crowded distally, fleshy; blade 2.5–8 cm long, obovate-oblong, entire, obtuse or slightly emarginate, decurrent at base; petiole 0.5–1 cm long, winged. Inflorescence 1–3-flowered; peduncle to 5 cm long. Flowers white or pink, 2 cm long. Drupe 1–2 cm long, subglobose, black or dark purple. Collection: MILLE *s.n.* (US, cited in Fl. Ec.).
Evidently rare on beaches. — Sandy shores of the tropics, also on the Galapagos Islands.

HYDROCHARITACEAE (TAPE-GRASS FAMILY)
Aquatic herbs with fibrous roots. Leaves of various kinds and arrangements. Inflorescence one-flowered or cymose, subtended by a spathe. Flowers uni- or bisexual, 3-merous, variously reduced. Fruit baccate. A family with 100 species of brackish- or fresh waters in warm regions of the world.

1. *Limnobium laevigatum* (HUMB. & BONPL. ex WILLD.) HEINE
Aquatic rosette, propagating by stolons, monoecious. Leaves dimorphic, 2 membranous at base of each rosette and foliaceous ones floating. Blade of foliaceous leaves 2.5–6 cm long, elliptic, decurrent into the 2–10 cm long petiole. Flowers unisexual, white; pedicels to 5 cm long. Collection: 63722.
Rare in ponds. — Widespread from Mexico to Argentina.

HYDROPHYLLACEAE (WATERLEAF FAMILY)
Herbs. Leaves alternate or in basal rosette, simple; stipules lacking. Inflorescence terminal or axillary, more or less paniculate. Flowers small, bisexual, 5-merous; stamens usually 5. Fruit a capsule.
A small family of almost worldwide distribution with 270 species.

1. *Hydrolea elatior* SCHOTT
Erect herb, 20–50 cm high, much branched. Stem sparsely pubescent. Leaves alternate; blade 4–11 cm long, elliptic, entire, acute at base and apex; petiole to 1 cm long. Inflorescence composed of terminal, leafy panicles. Flowers light blue, 1 cm wide, short-pedicellate. Capsule to 5 mm wide, globose. Collections: 63447, 63739, SCHIMPFF 1202 (MO, cited by Jørgensen and León-Yánez, 1999).
Occasional weed in moist areas along trails. — Widespread in South America with disjunct populations in Mexico and Honduras.

LAMIACEAE (MINT FAMILY)

Aromatic herbs or shrubs; stems often 4-angled. Leaves opposite, simple; stipules lacking. Flowers variously clustered, bisexual; calyx regular or 2-lipped, persistent; corolla more or less bilabiate; stamens 4 or 2. Fruit of 4 nutlets. A family with 3500 species of world wide distribution. Several species are grown as condiments and medicinal plants in gardens on Puná Island, such as *Menta piperita* (hierba buena) and *Ocimum basilicum* (albahaca de comer).

Key to the Species

1a. Inflorescence head-like
    2a. Plant nearly glabrous; flowers white   2. *Hyptis savannarum*
    2b. Plant sparsely to moderately hirsute; flowers light blue   4. *Hyptis* sp.
1b. Inflorescence not head-like
    3a. Flowers red-brown; shrubs   1. *Hyptis pectinata*
    3b. Flowers white, blue or violet; herbs
        4a. Flowers clustered in 2–6 flowered whorls   5. *Salvia occidentalis*
        4b. Flowers clustered in 5–20 flowered whorls   3. *Hyptis suaveolens*

1. *Hyptis pectinata* (L.) POIT.

Erect shrub, to 3 m high. Stem pubescent. Leaves to 6 cm long, ovate, serrate; petiole to 2 cm long. Inflorescence terminal, to 50 cm long, the numerous, small flowers clustered on elongate, lateral branches. Flowers reddish brown. Collection: 63743.

Rare at stream banks. — Pantropical.

Vernacular name: monte de torre.

2. *Hyptis savannarum* BRIQ.

Herb, 1 m high. Stem essentially glabrous. Leaf-blade 4–12 cm long, narrowly ovate, serrate–crenate; petiole to 3 cm long. Inflorescence axillary the flowers clustered in a 2 cm wide head; involucral bracts to 3–4 mm wide; peduncle to 5 cm long. Flowers white. Collection: 63749.

Uncommon weed. — America.

3. *Hyptis suaveolens* (L.) POIT.

Herb, to 2 m high. Stem 4-angled, hirsute. Leaf-blade 4–7 cm long, ovate, serrate, acute, rounded at base; petiole to 3 cm long. Inflorescence axillary, distally becoming leafless, composed of 5–20-flowered corymbose whorls. Flowers white ot violet, rather large; calyx 8 mm long; lobes spine-like. Collections: 63535, 63643, ANDERSSON *s.n.* (S, cited in Areschoug 1869).

Common along paths. — Pantropical.

Vernacular name: cuatrofilo.

4. *Hyptis* sp.
Scrambling herb, to 0.5 m high. Stem sparsely to moderately hirsute. Leaf-blade to 4 cm long, ovate, serrate, acute, short-attenuate to rounded at base; petiole 0.5–2 cm long. Inflorescence axillary, the flowers clustered in a 2 cm wide head; involucral bracts 1–2 mm wide, ciliate; peduncle 1–4 cm long. Flowers light blue. Collections: 63120, 63223, 63281, 63300.
Very common in dry scrub.

5. *Salvia occidentalis* Sw.
Herb, 0.5 m high. Stem sparsely pubescent. Leaf-blade to 6 cm long, ovate-rhombic, serrate. Inflorescence terminal, to 20 cm long, the flowers clustered in 2–6 flowered whorls, these 1–2 cm apart. Flowers blue or white, small. Collections: 63709, 63924.
Uncommon along trails. — America, including the Galapagos Islands.

LEMNACEAE (DUCKWEED FAMILY)
Minute, thalloid floating plants. Roots unbranched or lacking. Flowers unisexual, reduced: two staminate flowers and one pistillate flower form the inflorescence which is subtended by a spathe. A nearly cosmopolitan family with 25 aquatic species.

1. *Lemna aequinoctialis* WELW.
Description as the family.
Collections: 63302, 63608, 64044.
Common in water holes and swamps. — America.
Vernacular name: mondongillo.

LENTIBULARIACEAE (BLADDERWORT FAMILY)
Insectivorous herbs. Leaves variable, often replaced by leaf-like stems. Flowers bisexual, zygomorphic; calyx 2–5-parted; stamens 2. Fruit a capsule. A nearly cosmopolitan family of 350 aquatic or subaquatic species of fresh waters.

1. *Utricularia gibba* L.
Aquatic herb, to 20 cm long, submersed, slender, mat-forming. Stem filiform; secondary braches dichotomously branched; insect-traps numerous 1–1.5 mm long, bladder-like. Inflorescence 1–4-flowered; peduncle to 5 cm long. Flowers yellow, small, calyx 2-lobed. Collections: 64127.
Occasional in ponds. — Widespread from Mexico to Argentina and tropical Africa.

LIMNOCHARITACEAE (WATER-POPPY FAMILY)

Semiaquatic herbs with fibrous roots. Leaves basal or alternate, petiolate, parallel-veined, with a sheating base. Flowers 3-merous with sepaloids and petaloids; stamens 6 to many. Fruit a follicle. A tropical family with 12 species in fresh water habitats.

1. *Limnocharis laforestii* DUCHASS. ex GRISEB.

Aquatic herb, to 50 cm high; rhizhome small. Leaves in a basal rosette; blade mostly 8–12 cm long, oblong-elliptical, mucronate, attenuate to rounded at base; petiole to 15 cm long. Inflorescence 1–7-flowered; peduncle commonly 5 cm long, shorter than the petiole. Flowers yellow, 1 cm long. Fruit 1 cm long, flat. Collection: 63303.

Rare in shallow pools. — Widespread from Mexico to Argentina.

LOASACEAE (LOASA FAMILY)

Herbs, shrubs or vines, often with stinging hairs. Leaves opposite or alternate, simple or divided; stipules lacking. Flowers bisexual, 4–5-merous; stamens numerous. Fruit a capsule. A chiefly American family with 250 species.

Key to the Species

1a. Vines; inflorescense many-flowered	1. *Gronovia scandens*
1b. Herbs; inflorescense one-flowered	2. *Mentzelia aspera*

1. *Gronovia scandens* L.

Climbing vine, tendrils lacking. Stem densely pubescent, also bearing glochidiate hairs. Leaves alternate; blade 5–7 cm long, almost orbicular, deeply 5–7-lobate, cordate at base, lobes with 0–3 teeths; petiole 3–5 cm long. Inflorescence cymose, 10–15-flowered; peduncle to 5 cm long. Flowers yellow, 1 cm long, sessile. Collections: 63018, 63099, 63402, ANDERSSON *s.n.* (S, cited in Areschoug 1869).

Common in open scrub. — Mexico to Peru.

2. *Mentzelia aspera* L.

Herb, 20–40 cm high. Stem pubescent, with long glochidiate hairs. Leaves alternate; blade 3–6 cm long, ovate to trilobed; petiole 0.5–3 cm long. Flowers solitary, yellow, 1 cm wide, sessile. Capsule 2 cm long, 3 mm wide, cylindrical. Collections: 63672, 63761, ANDERSSON *s.n.* (S type of *Mentzelia propinqua* F. ARESCH., cited in Fl. Ec.).

Occasional weed. — Widespread in America. Reported from the Galapagos Islands.

Vernacular name: pegapega.

LOGANIACEAE (LOGANIA FAMILY)

Herbs, shrubs, or trees. Leaves opposite, simple; stipules lacking or present. Flowers bisexual, 4–5-merous. Fruit a capsule, berry, or drupe.

A tropical and subtropical family with 500 species.

1. *Spigelia anthelmia* L.

Herb, to 50 cm high. Stem glabrous. Leaves in a distal whorl of 4 (2 decussate pairs), subsessile; blade 4–8 cm long, narrowly ovate, entire, acute, narrowed at base. Inflorescence terminal; branches 1–5, 5–12 cm long, spicate. Flowers white with red stripes inside, 1 cm long, aggregated distally at anthesis, separated by 5–10 mm in fruit. Capsule 5 mm wide, muricate. Collections: 63369, 63667. Common weed in cultivated fields. — Mexico to Peru and Brazil, naturalized in the tropics of the Old World.

LORANTHACEAE (SHOWY MISTLETOE FAMILY)

Semiparasitic shrubs on woody hosts. Leaves opposite, entire, usually well-developed and green. Flowers mostly showy and bird pollinated; tepals 3–6; stamens equalling the tepals. Fruit a berry or a drupe.

A mainly tropical family with 850 species.

Key to the Species

1a. Leaves petiolate, to 14 cm long; flowers whitish yellow to pink   2. *Phthirusa stelis*
1b. Leaves sessile, 2.5–6 cm long; flowers red   1. *Psittacanthus chanduyensis*

1. *Phthirusa stelis* (L.) KUIJT

Large, scandent, dioecious parasite. Leaf-blade to 14 cm long, broadly ovate, usually attenuate; petiole 1 cm long. Inflorescence to 15 cm long, usually branched and with the flowers borne in triads. Flowers whitish yellow to pink, small. Fruit brick red, 1 cm long, ellipsoid. Collections: ANDERSSON *s.n.* (S, cited in Fl. Ec.).

Expected on *Rhizophora mangle*. — Fairly widespread in America.

2. *Psittacanthus chanduyensis* EICHLER

Shrubby parasite on shrubs and trees. Leaves sessile; blade 2.5–6 cm long, oblong, entire, rounded at base and apex. Inflorescence terminal, umbellate, many-flowered. Flowers red, 3.5 cm long, 6-merous. Fruit green, small. Collections: 63130, 63226, 63283, 63382, 63633, 63634, ANDERSSON *s.n.* (MO, S, US; cited in Fl. Ec.), ASPLUND 10121 (S, cited in Fl. Ec.), EGGERS 14760 (US, cited in Fl. Ec.).

Abundant in the savanna and thorn forest and found on a variety of hosts. — Endemic to south western Ecuador and adjacent Peru.

Phenology: Flowers throughout the dry season.

Uses: It is used as a medical plant to cure swellings and colds, remove thorns and acne, and to heal wounds. It is eaten by birds, cattle, and goats.

Vernacular names: chichihua, hierba de pajarito.

LYTHRACEAE (LOOSESTRIFE FAMILY)

Herbs or less commonly woody plants. Leaves opposite or whorled, simple, entire; stipules minute or caducuous. Flowers bisexual, 4–6–8-merous; stamens twice as many as petals. Fruit a capsule. A family of worldwide distribution, but with the majority of its 500 species in the tropics.

Key to the Species

1a. Shrubs
    2a. Leaves petiolate; inflorescence headlike   1. *Adenaria floribunda*
    2b. Leaves subsessile; inflorescence paniculate   4. *Lawsonia inermis*
1b. Herbs
    3a. Flowers sessile, solitary   5. *Rotala ramosior*
    3b. Flowers pedicellate, 2–several
        4a. Capsule 1.5–3.5 mm wide, distinctly longer than calyx
                                  2. *Ammannia auriculata*
        4b. Capsule 3.5–5 mm wide, equalling or slightly longer than calyx
                                  3. *Ammannia coccinea*

1. *Adenaria floribunda* KUNTH

Shrub, 2–4 m high. Twigs tetragonous, pubescent. Leaves opposite; blade 5–10 cm long, elliptic to lanceolate, subacute, cuneate at base; petiole 2–5 mm long. Inflorescence a many-flowered axillary head, 2 cm wide. Flowers white, small, 4–6-merous; pedicels 5 mm long. Capsule 4–5 mm wide. Collections: 63525, 63547, 64092, BARCLAY 479 (F, US; cited in Fl. Ec.).

Common on stream banks in the dry forest. — Mexico to Brazil and Argentina.

Vernacular name: palo asador.

2. *Ammannia auriculata* WILLD.

Annual herb, 20–80 cm high, branched. Stem glabrous. Leaves opposite, sessile; blade 2.5–6 cm long, linear-lanceolate, with prominent mid-nerve, acute, cordate to auriculate at base. Inflorescence axillary, few-flowered; peduncle to 1 cm long. Flowers blue or red, small, 4-merous; pedicels 0.5–9 mm long. Capsule 1.5–3.5 mm wide, distinctly longer than calyx. Collections: 63045, 63141, 63309, 63410.

Margins of wet places on exposed mud. — Pantropical.

Phenology: Flowers in April and May.

3. *Ammannia coccinea* Rottb.
Annual herb, to 1 m high, branched. Stem glabrous. Leaves opposite, sessile; blade 2–8 cm long, linear-lanceolate, acute, cordate to auriculate at base. Inflorescence 2–several-flowered; peduncle 0–9 mm long. Flowers red, 4-merous; pedicels 0.5–2 mm long. Capsule 3.5–5 mm wide, equalling or slightly longer than calyx. Collections: 63169, 63882.
On salt flats. — Nearly cosmopolitan.

4. *Lawsonia inermis* L.
Semi-evergreen shrub, to 5 m high. Branches glabrous, more or less 4-angled, often spinescent. Leaves opposite, subsessile; blade 1.5–5 cm long, elliptic, mucronate, decurrent at base. Inflorescence many-flowered, paniculate, to 40 cm long. Flowers cream, 5 mm wide, 4-merous, fragrant; pedicels 3 mm long. Capsule red-brown, 7 mm wide, depressed globose. Collection: 63418.
Occasional in dry thickets. — Introduced in Venezuela and the Caribbean, and disjunct in coastal Ecuador. Native to the Old World tropics.
Uses: It is used medicinally to treat cough and aches. The wood is used for charcoal. It is also occasionally grown as an ornamental for its odour.
Vernacular name: reseda.

5. *Rotala ramosior* (L.) Koehne
Erect or procumbent herb, to 50 cm high. Stem glabrous. Leaves opposite; blade 2–4.5 cm long, linear or oblanceolate, obtuse. Flowers solitary, axillary, pink, 4-merous, sessile. Capsule 3–4 mm long, ovoid or globose. Collections: 63046, 63308.
Uncommon in moist places. — Pantropical.

Malpighiaceae (Barbados cherry Family)
Trees, shrubs, and lianas. Leaves usually opposite, simple; stipules present. Flowers 5-merous, usually actinomorphic; petals clawed and sometimes fringed; stamens usually 10. Fruit winged, drupaceous. A tropical family with 800 species.

Key to the Species

1a. Flowers yellow; lianescent shrubs
    2a. Fruit fleshy, not winged   1. *Bunchosia plowmanii*
    2b. Fruit dry , winged   3. *Tetrapterys jamesonii*
1b. Flowers pink; shrub or small tree   2. *Malpighia emarginata*

1. *Bunchosia plowmanii* W. R. Anderson
Shrubby liana, several meters long. Stem soon becoming glabrescent. Leaves opposite, short-petiolate; blade 7–13 cm long, elliptic, short-acuminate, entire,

cuneate at base. Inflorescence 3–7 cm long, racemose, the flowers decussate. Flowers light yellow, 6 mm wide; petals clawed; pedicels 4–8 mm long. Drupe orange-red, 8 mm long, subglobose, 2–5-seeded. Collection: 85858.

Rare in disturbed dry forest. — Endemic to southwestern Ecuador and adjacent Peru.

2. *Malpighia emarginata* DC.

Shrub or small tree, 2–5 m high. Twigs appressed hirsute. Leaves densely crowded distally on short shoots; blade 2–5 cm long, elliptic-obovate, entire, emarginate; midvein prominent; petiole to 3 mm long. Flowers solitary or a few together, pink, 1.5–2 cm wide; pedicels to 1 cm long. Fruit green-red, 1–2 cm wide, subglobose, fleshy. Collections: 63400, 63538, 63846, 85315, 85363, ANDERSSON *s.n.* (S, cited in Areschoug 1869), SINCLAIR *s.n.* (K, cited in Flora of Panama).

Common and perhaps native. — From Lesser Antilles to northern South America. The species is known as West Indian cherry and is semi-cultivated throughout the tropics.

Uses: The fruit is edible. The wood is used for charcoal.

Vernacular name: cereza.

3. *Tetrapterys jamesonii* TURCZ.

Shrubby liana, to 4 m long. Stem pubescent. Leaves persistently pubescent beneath; blade 3–6(–11) cm long, ovate, obtuse or mucronate, entire, rounded at base; petiole 0.5–1 cm long. Inflorescence terminal, many-flowered, subpaniculate. Flowers yellow, 10–13 mm wide; pedicels 3–5 mm long. Fruit a nut with 2 cm long wings. Collections: 63029, 63433, 63563B, 63796, 63932, 64118.

Common in forest clearings. — Colombia to Peru.

Uses: The stems are used as lashing for rafts, fences, and corrals. The wood is used to make cups and vessels.

Vernacular names: bejuco ahorca tora, bejuco canelo.

MALVACEAE (MALLOW FAMILY)

Herbs and shrubs, variously and often stellately pubescent. Leaves alternate, simple; stipules present. Flowers bisexual, 5-merous; stamens numerous, with the filaments fused into a tube surrounding the style. Fruit a capsule or a schizocarp.

A cosmopolitan family with 2000 species. Twenty-two species are recorded from Puná Island.

Key to the Species

1a. Inflorescence paniculate or spicate, many-flowered, terminal
    2a. Inflorescence spicate; pedicels 1–5 mm long   3. *Briquetia spicata*
    2b. Inflorescence paniculate; pedicels longer than 8 mm
        3a. Leaves dentate; petals reflexed   21. *Sidastrum paniculatum*
        3b. Leaves subentire; petals straight
            4a. Mericarps 3–4 mm long, 1-seeded   22. *Wissadula divergens*
            4b. Mericarps 6–7 mm long, 2–3-seeded   23. *Wissadula excelsior*
1b. Inflorescence headlike, clustered, or simple, 1–many-flowered, terminal and/or axillary
    5a. Flowers more than 3 cm long or more than 3 cm wide
        6a. Petals reflexed
            7a. Petals usually dissected; cultivated   10. *Hibiscus rosa-sinensis*
            7b. Petals entire; native   1. *Abutilon reflexum*
        6b. Petals not reflexed
            8a. Calyx 3–6 cm long; seeds conspicuously embedded in wool
                9a. Flowers yellow; native   6. *Gossypium barbadense*
                9b. Flowers white; cultivated   7. *Gossypium hirsutum*
            8b. Calyx less than 3 cm long; seeds not embedded in wool
                10a. Leaf-margin entire (the leaves often lobate); flowers white with a purple spot at center   5. *Cienfuegosia tripartita*
                10b. Leaf-margin crenate or crenate-serrate; flowers pink, lavender or rarely white and then throughout
                    11a. Leaves 3–5-lobed   4. *Cienfuegosia hitchcockii*
                    11b. Leaves entire   9. *Hibiscus escobariae*
    5b. Flowers less than 3 cm long and wide
        14a. Inflorescence densely congested and headlike
            15a. Flowers white   12. *Malachra fasciata*
            15b. Flowers yellow
                16a. Fruits 5-merous; stem hispid, the hairs not appressed
                     11. *Malachra alceifolia*
                16b. Fruits c. 10-merous; stem stellately pubescent, the hairs appressed
                     14. *Malvastrum tomentosum*
        14b. Inflorescence simple or composed by a pair or a cluster of flowers
            17a. Flowers sessile, red-brown   16. *Sida ciliaris*
            17b. Flowers pedicellate, not red-brown
                18a. Styles and mericarps 5
                    19a. Leaves typically 5–10 cm long; fruits 8–10 mm wide
                         2. *Bastardia bivalvis*
                    19b. Leaves typically 2–4 cm long; fruits 4–5 mm wide
                         20. *Sida spinosa*
                18b. Styles and mericarps 7 or more
                    20a. Stem stellately 4-armed, the arms oriented longitudinally along the stem axis   13. *Malvastrum coromandelianum*
                    20b. Stem with different pubescens
                        21a. Flowers white
                            22a. Fruits 0.5 cm wide; styles and mericarps 5–8

19. *Sida salviifolia*
22b. Fruits 1.5–2 cm wide; styles and mericarps 10–12
8. *Herissantia crispa*
21b. Flowers not white
24a. Plant prostrate   17. *Sida repens*
24b. Plant erect or ascending
25a. Leaves distichous; pedicels to 1 cm long   15. *Sida acuta*
25b. Leaves not distichous; pedicels to 3 cm long
18. *Sida rhombifolia*

1. *Abutilon reflexum* (LAM.) SWEET
Shrub, to 2 m high. Stem stellately pubescent. Leaf-blade 1–7 cm long, broadly
ovate-cordate, palmately 5–9-nerved, acuminate, crenate-serrate. Flowers
solitary, pale red, 5 cm long, long-pedicellate; petals strongly reflexed, entire;
involucral bracts 1.5 cm long, ovate. Schizocarp 1.5 cm wide, coarsely hirsute
and spiny. Collections: 63407, 63593, 63619, BARCLAY 431 (BM, cited in Fl. Ec.).
Common in dry scrub. — Endemic to the arid zone of coastal Ecuador and
Peru.
Note: The plant is eaten by cattle.
Vernacular name: chupaflor.

2. *Bastardia bivalvis* (CAV.) KUNTH
Shrub, 2 m high. Stem stellately pubescent to hirsute. Leaf-blade 2–7 cm long,
cordate, acute at apex, irregularly crenate, long-petiolate. Flowers few together,
yellow, pedicellate for less than 5 mm; petals 7–8 mm long. Fruits 8–10 mm
wide, 5-loculed. Collections: 63364, 63663.
Occasional in open places on the west coast. — Mexico to Argentina.

3. *Briquetia spicata* (KUNTH) FRYXELL
Annual herb or shrub, 1 m high, usually unbranched except at the inflorecence.
Stem stellately pubescent when young. Leaves long-petiolate at base of plant to
subsessile and clasping immediately below the inflorescence; blade to 15 cm
long, broadly ovate, acuminate, obscurely serrate, cordate at base. Inflorescence
terminal, 30–50 cm long, spicate. Flowers yellow; petals 5 mm long; pedicels
1–5 mm long. Fruits 7–9 mm wide, strigose. Collections: 63112, 63232, 63278B.
Common in disturbed places. — Mexico to Bolivia.

4. *Cienfuegosia hitchcockii* (ULBR.) O. J. BLANCH.
Shrub, to 2 m high. Stem stellately pubescent. Leaf-blade 6–11 cm long, broadly
ovate, 3–5-lobed, irregularly crenate, subtruncate at base; petiole 3–5 cm long.
Flowers solitary, pink, 10 cm wide, long-pedicellate; involucral bracts 1 cm
long, ovate. Capsule 2 cm long. Collections: 63658, 63803.
Common on the west coast. — Endemic to the dry coastal zone of Ecuador and
adjacent Peru.

5. *Cienfuegosia tripartita* (KUNTH) GÜRKE

Herb or subshrub, 40–80 cm high, often unbranched. Stem nearly glabrous with only a few stellate hairs. Leaf-blade 3–7 cm long, lanceolate to ovate, simple to 3–5-lobed, subacute, entire, subobtuse at base; petiole to 1 cm long. Flowers solitary, white with a purple spot at center, 6 cm wide, long-pedicellate; sepals 1.5–2 cm long, linear-ovate. Capsule 1 cm wide. Collections: 63117, 63240, 64008, ANDERSSON 135 (S, cited in Fl. Ec.), EGGERS 14767 (M, cited in Fl. Ec.). Common in the savanna. — Endemic to coastal Ecuador and adjacent Peru.

Phenology: Appears in April and May.

Vernacular name: mosqueta.

6. *Gossypium barbadense* L. (Plate 12)

Shrub, 1–4 m high, much branched. Stem stellately pubescent. Leaf-blade commonly 6–15 cm long, deeply 3–7-lobate; petiole to 8 cm long. Flowers solitary, yellow with a purple spot at center, 10 cm wide, pedicellate; bracts 3–5 cm long, ovate, coarsely serrate-toothed. Capsule 3–6 cm long, 3-celled. Seeds embedded in white to creamy white cotton. Collections: 63192, 63600, 63657, 63814, 63966.

Common in thorn scrub. — Native to South America. Now widely cultivated. Also reported for the Galapagos Islands.

Uses: Used for textiles in ancient times.

Vernacular name: algodón de monte.

7. *Gossypium hirsutum* L. [cult.]

This is the cotton (Collections: 63666, 63869) grown on Puná Island today. — This species from Meso-America is now the World's leading cotton crop.

Uses: Cotton for textiles.

Vernacular names: algodón cocre, algodón criollo, algodón pardo. One or several of these names could belong to another species of *Gossypium*.

8. *Herissantia crispa* (L.) BRIZICKY

Trailing herb, to 1 m high. Stem slender, hirsutely and stellately pubescent. Leaves petiolate for up to 4 cm at base of plant, higher up subsessile; blade 2–6 cm long, ovate, acute, crenate, cordate at base. Flowers solitary, white, 1 cm wide; pedicels to 5 cm long. Schizocarp to 2 cm wide, 10–12-merous, inflated. Collection: 63423.

Occasional weedy plant. — Widespread in warm parts of the World. Also on the Galapagos Islands.

9. *Hibiscus escobariae* FRYXELL

Shrub, 0.5–2 m high. Stem coarsely stellate-pubescent. Leaf-blade 4–10 cm long, ovate, palmately 5-nerved, acute, crenate-serrate, cordate-truncate at base; petiole to 5 cm long. Flowers solitary, lavender to pink or rarely white, 5 cm

long, funnel-shaped; involucral bracts filiform; pedicel to 6 cm long; bracts 8–12 mm long. Capsule 1 cm wide, 5-merous. Collections: 63627, 63900, 64018. Common on dry slopes. — Endemic to coastal Ecuador.
Phenology: Flowers from May to October.
Vernacular name: amapolo.

10. *Hibiscus rosa-sinensis* L. [cult.]
The hibiscus (Collection: 63567) is a well known ornamental in gardens. — Pantropical of uncertain origin.
Vernacular name: peregrina.

11. *Malachra alceifolia* JACQ.
Herb or subshrub, 0.5–1 m high. Stem stellately hispid. Leaf-blade 3–8 cm long, broadly ovate to orbicular, acute or obtuse, serrate-dentate, rounded at base; petiole to 5 cm long. Inflorescence axillary, few-flowered, head-like; peduncle 0–3 cm long. Flowers yellow, 2 cm wide; calyx hispid; involucral bracts 1 cm long, 2 cm wide. Schizocarp 3 mm long, 5-merous. Collections: 63233, 63589.
Margin of salt marshes and in disturbed places. — Mexico to Peru and the Galapagos Islands, and naturalized in the Old World.
Uses: It is used medicinally to cure colds, bone aches, and to clean the stomach.
Vernacular names: malva, malva amarilla.

12. *Malachra fasciata* JACQ.
Herb or subshrub, 50 cm high. Stem stellately hispid. Leaf-blade 3–12 cm long, ovate, shallowly to deeply and irregularly 3–5-lobed, acute, crenate-serrate, truncate at base; petiole 1–6 cm long. Inflorescence short-pedunculate, axillary, few-flowered and head-like, conspicuously hispid. Flowers white; petals 6–8 mm long; involucral bracts filiform, conspicuously ciliate. Schizocarp 3 mm long, 5-merous. Collections: 63013, 63065, 63442.
Common around homesites. — Widespread from Mexico to Bolivia.
Vernacular name: malva blanca.

13. *Malvastrum coromandelianum* (L.) GARCKE
Subshrub. Stem bearing stellately 4-armed hairs, the arms oriented longitudinally along the stem axis. Leaf-blade 3–8 cm long, ovate or lanceolate, dentate; petiole to 4 cm long. Flowers usually solitary, axillary, yellow, pedicels 2–10 mm long. Schizocarp 6 mm long, 10–12-merous. Collections: ANDERSSON 133 = 134 (S, cited in Fl. Ec.).
A single record only. — Almost pantropical. Also on the Galapagos Islands.

14. *Malvastrum tomentosum* (L.) S.R. HILL subsp. *tomentosum*
Herb or shrub, 1–2 m high. Stem stellately pubescent, the hairs appressed. Leaf-blade 2–8 cm long, ovate or ovate-triangular, acute, dentate, subcordate and

entire at base; petiole to 4 cm long. Inflorescence forming axillary and terminal, sessile and long-pedunculate heads. Flowers yellow; petals 6–8 mm long; pedicels 0–2 mm long. Schizocarp 5 mm wide, approximately 10-merous. Collections: 63366, 63664, 63723 and the following which were all cited in Fl. Ec.: ANDERSSON 134 = 135 (S); BARCLAY 352 (BM, US), 456 (BM), 2434 (BM, US); SINCLAIR *s.n.* (GH, K).
Probably common. — Venezuela to Brazil.
Vernacular name: zapán colorado.

15. *Sida acuta* BURM. F.
Herb or subshrub, 50 cm high. Stem sparsely and stellately hirsute. Leaves distichously arranged; blade 4–10 cm long, lanceolate to ovate, acute, serrate, rounded at base; petiole to 1 cm long. Flowers solitary or paired, yellow or white, 1.5 cm wide, short-pedicellate. Schizocarp 8–10-merous. Collections: 63246, 63248.
In disturbed places. — A nearly pantropical weed. Reported from the Galapagos Islands.

16. *Sida ciliaris* L.
Decumbent to suberect herb, 10–50 cm high. Stem stellately pubescent, the hairs appressed and usually 4-armed. Leaves more densely crowded distally; blade 1–2.5 cm long, narrowly elliptic, toothed at apex, ciliate, cuneate at base; petiole 2–8 mm long. Flowers red-brown, 0.5 cm wide, sessile. Schizocarp conical, 5–8-merous. Collections: 63104, 63161, 63336, 63372, ANDERSSON 141=142 (S, cited in Fl. Ec.).
Common along trails. — Southern United States to Argentina.

17. *Sida repens* DOMBEY ex CAV.
Prostrate herb, 20 cm high. Stem sparsely stellate-hirsute. Leaf-blade 3–6 cm long, ovate-cordate to orbicular, short-acuminate, crenate-dentate; petiole 1–3 cm long. Flowers solitary, yellow, 1 cm wide; pedicels 3–7 cm long. Schizocarp 5-merous. Collections: 63430, 63618.
Common along trails. — Pantropical. Also on the Galapagos Islands.
Vernacular name: bejuquito de flor amarillo.

18. *Sida rhombifolia* L.
Herb or subshrub, 0.5–1 m high. Stem sparsely and stellately puberulent. Leaf-blade mostly 3–7 cm long, lanceolate to rhombic, acute to obtuse, serrate, cuneate at base; petiole 2–8 cm long. Flowers solitary, yellow or yellow-orange; pedicels 1–4 cm long. Schizocarp 10–14-merous. Collections: 63272, 63496.
Disturbed sites. — Subcosmopolitan. Known from the Galapagos Islands.
Uses: The stems are used for brooms.
Vernacular names: escoba, escoba de puerco.

19. *Sida salviifolia* C. PRESL

Herb or subshrub, to 80 cm high. Stem stellately and whitish tomentose. Leaf-blade 2–6 cm long, lanceolate, acute, serrate, rounded at base; petiole 5–15 mm long. Flowers white to yellow-orange with red-brown center, congested few together distally on plants; pedicels 2–7 mm long. Schizocarp 5 mm wide, 5–8-merous. Collections: 63348, 63504.

Along trails. — Mexico to Argentina. Also on the Galapagos Islands.

20. *Sida spinosa* L.

Herb or subshrub, 0.5–1 m high. Stem stellately puberulent. Leaf-blade 2–4 cm long, ovate, subacute, serrate and sometimes reddish at margin, subcordate at base; petiole 0.5–2 cm long. Flowers solitary or a few together in leaf axils, white, yellow, or yellow-brown; petals oblique; pedicels 5–10 mm long. Schizocarp 4–5 mm wide, 5-merous. Collections: 63010, 63234, 63735.

Common weedy plant. — Widespread in warm and temperate regions of the world. Reported for the Galapagos Islands.

Uses: The stems are used for brooms. It is eaten by birds.

Vernacular names: escoba, escoba de montaña, escoba silvestre.

21. *Sidastrum paniculatum* (L.) FRYXELL

Herb or shrub, 1–2 m high. Stem stellately pubescent. Leaf-blade 4–11 cm long, lanceolate to ovate, acute, dentate, truncate or subcordate at base; petiole 1–4 cm long. Inflorescence terminal, many-flowered, paniculate, lax. Flowers red-brown; petals 3 mm long, reflexed; pedicels 2–6 cm long, filiform. Schizocarp 5 mm wide, 5-merous. Collections: 63031, 63088.

Weed in open places. — Southern Texas to Bolivia, Hawaii, and the Galapagos Islands.

22. *Wissadula divergens* (BENTH.) BENTH. & HOOK. F.

Subshrub, 1–2 m high. Stem stellately pubescent. Leaf-blade 6–14 cm long, broadly ovate, acuminate, entire, cordate at base; petiole to 8 cm long. Inflorescence terminal, paniculate, many-flowered. Flowers white, 1 cm wide; pedicels 1–2 cm long. Schizocarp 5 mm wide, 4–6-merous; mericarps 3–4 mm long, 1-seeded. Collections: 63494, 63603.

Probably uncommon. — Endemic to the arid zone of southwestern Ecuador.

23. *Wissadula excelsior* (CAV.) C. PRESL

Herb or shrub, 1–2 m high. Stem stellately puberulent. Leaf-blade to 9 cm long, ovate, acuminate, entire, cordate at base; petiole to 3 cm long. Inflorescence terminal, paniculate, many-flowered. Flowers yellow, orange, or white; pedicels 1–3 cm long. Schizocarp 1 cm wide, star-shaped, 5-merous; mericarp 6–7 mm long, 2–3-seeded. Collections: 63239, 63497.

Disturbed places. — America.

MARANTACEAE (PRAYER-PLANT FAMILY)

Herbs with rhizome. Leaves basal, with petiole and an open sheath. Inflorescence conspicuously bracteate. Flowers bisexual, actinomorphic, 3-merous, with 2–4 petal-like staminodes. Fruit fleshy or dry. A pantropical family with 350 species in moist habitats.

1. *Thalia pavonii* KöRN.

Emergent herb, to 1 m high. Leaves inserted at base of plant; blade 10–25 cm long, narrowly ovate, entire, subacuminate; petiole longer than blade. Inflorescence 50 cm long, spicate; lateral branches 2–9, 3–6 cm long, many flowered. Flowers violet, delicate, subtended by fairly conspicuous 1.5 cm long spathes. Fruit nutlike, 1 cm long. Collections: 63152, 63186, ANDERSSON *s.n.* (S, cited in Fl. Ec.), EGGERS 14788 (LE, US; cited in Fl. Ec.).

Common in fresh water swamps in the savanna. — Endemic to the Guayas province.

MENISPERMACEAE (MOONSEED FAMILY)

Shrubs or usually vines without tendrils. Leaves alternate, simple; stipules lacking. Flowers unisexual, minute, often 3-merous. Fruit a drupe. A pantropical family with about 400 species.

1. *Cissampelos pareira* L.

Twining vine, several meters long. Stem grooved, villous. Leaves peltate; blade 1.5–6 cm long, very broadly ovate, palmately nerved, entire and densely hairy at margin, emarginate; petiole 2–7 cm long. Inflorescence axillary, secondary branches subtended by foliaceous bracts, the staminate and pistillate inflorescences easily distinguishable. Flowers white, minute; staminate ones 4-merous; pistillate ones reduced. Drupe 5 mm long. Collection: 85860.

Occasional in fences. — Pantropical. Also on the Galapagos Islands.

MIMOSACEAE (MIMOSA FAMILY)

Trees, shrubs, or occasionally herbs, often armed. Leaves pinnate or usually bipinnate; stipules present. Flowers in spikes or heads, actinomorphic, 4–6-merous; stamens conspicuous, 4–numerous. Fruit a pod. A family with 2800 species in the tropics and subtropics. Sixteen native or naturalised species on Puná Island.

Key to the Species

1a. Floating aquatic with spongy tissue around the stems; herb   12. *Neptunia oleracea*
1b. Terrestrial; shrubs or trees
    2a. Inflorescence spicate

3a. Flowers yellow; pod less than 2 mm thick   13. *Piptadenia flava*
3b. Flowers white; pod 5 mm thick   15. *Prosopis juliflora*
2b. Inflorescence globose or fasciculate, sometimes on elongate branches
    4a. Inflorescence fasciculate
        5a. Stipular spines present; leaflets 4–8   14. *Pithecellobium excelsum*
        5b. Stipular spines absent; leaflets usually more than 8
            6a. Most leaflets shorter than 2 cm long; calyx 3 mm long;
                trees to 12 m tall; wild   6. *Albizia multiflora*
            6b. Most leaflets longer than 2 cm; calyx longer than 5 mm; trees to 25 m
                tall; planted and semi-naturalised
                7a. Trunk with 2 cm thick corky bark; the larger
                    leaflets to 10 cm long   18. *Samanea tubulosa*
                7b. Trunk not as above; leaflets mostly less than 6 cm long
                    8a. Pods pubescent, 2 mm thick   16. *Pseudosamanea guachapele*
                    8b. Pods glabrous, 6–8 mm thick   17. *Samanea saman*
    4b. Inflorescence globose
        9a. Leaflets less than 10, 1.5–5 cm long
            10a. Filaments white; pod 6–12 cm long   8. *Leucaena trichodes*
            10b. Filaments pink or violet; pod 1–1.5 cm long   10. *Mimosa debilis*
        9b. Leaflets more than 10, to 1.5 cm long
            11a. Twigs not spiny
                12a. Filaments white   7. *Desmanthus virgatus*
                12b. Filaments red in distal half   19. *Zapoteca caracasana*
            11b. Twigs spiny
                13a. Spines distinctly recurved
                    14a. Pod 2.5–4 cm wide; shrubby liana   4. *Acacia tenuifolia*
                    14b. Pod 1 cm wide; scandent shrub   11. *Mimosa pigra*
                13b. Spines not distinctly recurved
                    15a. Filaments blue-white to purple; pods spiny at margin
                         9. *Mimosa acantholoba*
                  15b. Filaments yellow, orange, or brown
                    16a. Leaflets usually 5–9 mm long
                      17a. Pinnae 4–9; leaflets 14–21 pairs; pod to 6.5 cm long
                         2. *Acacia farnesiana*
                      17b. Pinnae 2–4; leaflets 5–13 pairs; pod 8–17 cm long
                         5. *Acacia tortuosa*
                  16b. Leaflets usually 1.5–3.5 mm long
                    18a. Pod 3–6 mm wide; pinnae 0.8–2 cm long
                         1. *Acacia aroma*
                    18b. Pod 20–25 mm wide; pinnae 1.5–6 cm long
                         3. *Acacia macracantha*

1. *Acacia aroma* Gillies ex Hook. & Arn.
Broad shrub, 1–3 m high, often forming patches; stipular spines 3–6 cm long. Leaves bipinnate; pinnae 7–24 pairs, 0.8–2 cm long; leaflets 20–34 pairs, 1.5–2 mm long. Inflorescence 1 cm wide, globose; filaments yellow. Pods 6–10 cm long, 3–6 mm wide, constricted between the seeds. Collections: 63639, 63875, 84388, 84389.

Margin of salt flats and beaches on western Puná Island. — Peru to Argentina.
Uses: The wood is used for charcoal and fire wood.
Vernacular name: aroma.

2. *Acacia farnesiana* (L.) WILLD.
Broad tree, to 5 m high; stipular spines to 2 cm long. Leaves bipinnate; pinnae
4–9 pairs, 2–4.5 cm long; leaflets 14–21 pairs, 5–8 mm long. Inflorescence 1 cm
wide, globose; peduncle to 5 cm long. Flowers fragrant; filaments yellow to
orange-brown. Pods to 6.5 cm long, 1.3 cm wide, thick. Collection: 64123.
Uncommon in thorn scrub. — Widely distributed in the tropics and subtropics.
Uses: The wood is used for house construction, charcoal and fire wood.
Vernacular name: aroma.

3. *Acacia macracantha* HUMB. & BONPL. ex WILLD.
Tree, to 10 m high; stipular spines on trunk and twigs 0.2–10 cm long. Leaves
bipinnate; pinnae 9–47 pairs, 1.5–6 cm long; leaflets 20–35 pairs, 2–3.5 mm long.
Inflorescence 8 mm wide, globose; peduncle 2 cm long. Pods 7–9 cm long, 2–2.5
cm wide, broadly linear. Collections: 63763, 63960, 64150, 84385, 84390.
Common in thorn forest. — Mexico to Argentina. Also on the Galapagos
Islands.
Uses: The wood is used for stakes, wedges, houses, and charcoal.
Vernacular name: guarango.

4. *Acacia tenuifolia* (L.) WILLD.
Shrubby liana, to 10 m high, to 10 cm thick at base; stipular spines on twigs
caducous, recurved; bark yellow-brown. Leaves bipinnate; pinnae 13–30 pairs,
1.5–7 cm long; leaflets 22–75 pairs, 3–4 mm long. Inflorescence 1 cm wide,
globose; filaments white or yellow. Pods 9–20 cm long, 2.5–4 cm wide, flat.
Collections: 63939, 64090, 84391.
Common in mature forest. — Mexico to Bolivia.
Uses: The wood is used for firewood and charcoal.
 Vernacular name: uña de gato.

5. *Acacia tortuosa* (L.) WILLD.
Tree, to 6 m high; stipular spines 0.5–3 cm long. Leaves bipinnate; pinnae 2–4
pairs, 2.5–5 cm long; leaflets 5–13 pairs, 5–9 mm long. Inflorescence 1 cm wide,
globose; peduncle to 4 cm long; filaments orange-yellow. Pods 8–17 cm long,
4–9 mm wide, 3–6 mm thick, more or less curved and constricted between the
seeds. Collections: 63488, 63820, 84386, 84387.
Common in disturbed thorn forest. — Florida to Peru.
Uses: The wood is used for house construction, fire wood, and charcoal.
Vernacular name: aroma.

6. *Albizia multiflora* (KUNTH) BARNEBY & J. W. GRIMES var. *multiflora*
Tree, to 12 m high; stipular spines wanting; latex white. Leaves bipinnate; pinnae 3–7, 10–13 cm long; leaflets 7–10 pairs, 1.5–3 cm long. Inflorescence large and elongate, the flowers in fascicles. Flowers fragrant; filaments white. Pods 10–14 cm long, 2 cm wide, 5 mm thick. Collections: 63329, 63527, 63913, 63948, 75484, 85329.
Common in the thorn forest and dry forest. — Probably limited to America.
Uses: The wood is used for firewood and charcoal. The plant is eaten by cattle.
Vernacular name: compoño.

7. *Desmanthus virgatus* (L.) WILLD.
Scandent shrub, to 60 cm high. Stem glabrescent. Leaves bipinnate; pinnae 3–7 pairs, 2–4 cm long; leaflets 15–25 pairs, 3–6 mm long. Inflorescence 0.5 cm wide, headlike; filaments white. Pods few–15 per cluster, 4–6 cm long, 3 mm wide. Collections: 63317, 63420, 63650.
Common weedy plant. — Tropical America. Reported from the Galapagos Islands.

8. *Leucaena trichodes* (JACQ.) BENTH.
Shrub or tree, to 5 m high. Twigs spineless. Leaves pinnately 6–8-foliolate; leaflets 2–5 cm long, elliptic, gradually larger distally, rounded or obtuse at apex. Inflorescence elongated; heads 1.5 cm wide, several per node; filaments white. Pods 10–18 cm long, 1.5–2 cm wide, flat. Collections: 63139, 63179, 63443, 63531, 63626, 63821, 85311, ANDERSSON *s.n.* (S, cited in Areschoug 1869).
Abundant in thorn scrub. — Central America to Peru.
Uses: The wood is used for stakes, fences, ribs of ship's frames, boats, field huts, props for trees or vines, and for charcoal and firewood.
Vernacular names: aguia, pelacaballo.

9. *Mimosa acantholoba* (HUMB. & BONPL. ex WILLD.) POIR.
Small tree, to 5 m high. Spines on twigs short and thorn-like. Leaves deciduos, bipinnate; pinnae 9–10 pairs, 1–2 cm long; leaflets 20–30 pairs, 1–3 mm long. Inflorescence 1 cm wide, globose; filaments blue-white to purple. Pods 4–7 cm long, 2.5 cm wide, flat, long-mucronate; edge armed with subulate spines. Collections: 63001, 63189, 85320.
Common in thorn scrub. — Ecuador, including the Galapagos Islands, and Peru. Also known from Nicaragua.
Uses: The wood is used for charcoal.
Vernacular names: espina de sabana, uña de gato.

10. *Mimosa debilis* HUMB. & BONPL. ex WILLD. var. *aequatoriana* (RUDD) BARNEBY
Shrub or small tree, 1–4 m high. Spines on twigs short and thorn-like. Leaves bipinnately 4–6-foliolate; leaflets 3–7 cm long, ovate-hemispherical.

Inflorescence 2 cm wide, globose; filaments pink or violet. Pods in clusters of 5–12, 1–1.5 cm long, 5 mm wide, flat, conspicuously hirsute. Collections: 63071, 63403, 63621, 63768.

Abundant in the thorn scrub. — Endemic to coastal Ecuador and the Galapagos Islands.

Uses: The wood is used for charcoal. It is eaten by donkeys.

Vernacular names: tapatapa, uña de gato.

11. *Mimosa pigra* L.

Stout shrub, to 1 m high. Stems setose. Spines on twigs recurved and thorn-like. Leaves bipinnate; pinnae 9–12 pairs, 3–4 cm long; leaflets 40–50 pairs, 2–3 mm long. Inflorescence globose; filaments white or pink. Pods 6–8 cm long, 1 cm wide, 4 mm thick, curved, transversely constricted, setose-hispid. Collection: 63943.

Uncommon on sandy beaches. — Tropical America and Africa. Also on the Galapagos Islands.

12. *Neptunia oleracea* LOUR.

Floating herb, to several meters long, bearing large tufts of fibrous roots. Stem thick and spongy. Leaves bipinnate; pinnae 4–6 pairs, 3–4 cm long; leaflets 10–15 pairs, 6–10 mm long. Inflorescence globose, long-pedunculate; petals yellow; filaments white. Pods 2 cm long, 8–10 mm wide, curved, mucronate, in a distal cluster; stalk in fruit to 25 cm long. Collections: 63830, 64129, ANDERSSON *s.n.* (S, cited in Areschoug 1869).

Common in ponds. — Pantropical.

13. *Piptadenia flava* (SPRENG. ex DC.) BENTH.

Tree, 2–4 m high. Spines on twigs and rachis 1–3 mm long, recurved. Leaves bipinnate; pinnae 8–12 pairs, 3–5 cm long; leaflets 20–30 pairs, 4–8 mm long, linear, mucronate, sessile. Inflorescence spicate, 5–7 cm long; filaments yellow. Pods 10–13 cm long, 2 cm wide, flat, irregularly constricted around the seeds. Collections: 63147, 63171, 63294.

Common in thorn scrub. — Peru to Trinidad.

Uses: The wood is used for charcoal.

Vernacular names: espina de sabana, uña de gato.

14. *Pithecellobium excelsum* (KUNTH) MART.

Tree or shrub, commonly multi-stemmed, to 6 m high; stipular spines on trunk and twigs persistent. Leaves 4–8-foliolate; leaflets to 2.5 cm long, elliptic to obovate, rounded. Inflorescence many-flowered, fasciculate, long-pedunculate. Flowers 3 cm long; filaments white. Pods 6–8 cm long, 8 mm wide, strongly curved. Seeds black, aril red or white, conspicuous. Collections: 63030, 63225, 63415, 63807, 85330.

Common in the savanna, thorn scrub, and thorn forest. — Endemic to arid zones of Ecuador and adjacent Peru.
Uses: The wood is used for stakes and charcoal. It is eaten by birds.
Vernacular name: quiriquinche.

15. *Prosopis juliflora* (Sw.) DC.
Shrub or tree, to 8(–15) m high. Trunk gnarled. Brachlets armed with 1–4 cm long spines. Leaves bipinnate; pinnae 3–5 pairs, 6–8 cm long; leaflets 15–20 pairs, 8–10 mm long. Inflorescence to 10 cm long, spicate; filaments white. Pods 10–24 cm long, 8–15 mm wide, 5 mm thick. Collections: 63401, 63733, 64120, 85325.
Dominant tree in the savanna and thorn forest. — Mexico to Peru. Also on the Galapagos Islands.
Uses: This is the mesquite tree, its wood is used in construction of houses and boats, and for stakes, firewood, and charcoal.
Vernacular name: algarrobo.

16. *Pseudosamanea guachapele* (KUNTH) HARMS [cult.]
The rain tree (Collections: 63914, 63927) is occasionally planted and semi-naturalized on Puná Island. — Widely grown in the tropics of the world.
Uses: The pods give fodder for the cattle. The wood is used to construct boats, furniture, boards, and to make charcoal.
Vernacular name: guachapelí prieto.

17. *Samanea saman* (JACQ.) MERR. [cult.]
The golden rain tree (Collections: 63928, 64115, 85365) is occasionally found semi-cultivated on the island. — Native to the Caribbean and northern South America.
Note: It is eaten by donkeys.
Vernacular name: samán.

18. *Samanea tubulosa* (BENTH.) BARNEBY & J. W. GRIMES [cult.]
Rarely planted tree (Collection: 63956) characterised by its thick and corky bark. Occasional in the dry forest. — Ecuador to Bolivia. Perhaps native to western Ecuador according to Barneby and Grimes (1996).
Uses: The wood is used for houses, boards, boats, furniture, and charcoal.
Vernacular name: guachapelí blanco.

19. *Zapoteca caracasana* (JACQ.) H. M. HERN. subsp. *weberbaueri* (HARMS) H. M. HERN.
Scandent shrub, 1 m high. Leaves bipinnate; pinnae 3 pairs, 4–6 cm long; leaflets 12–17 pairs, 4–15 mm long. Inflorescence composed of many-flowered heads. Filaments 2.5 cm long, red in distal half. Pods 6–10 cm long, 7 mm wide,

flat, pubescent. Collection: 86016.

Rare in thickets. — Venezuela to Peru and Hispaniola.

MOLLUGINACEAE (CARPET-WEED FAMILY)

Mostly herbs. Leaves opposite to alternate or whorled, simple, entire. Flowers small and inconspicuous, usually perfect, actinomorphic, 5-merous; stamens mostly 5–10. Fruit a capsule. A small family with 100 species in the tropcics and subtropics.

Key to the Species

1a. Flowers green; leaves obovate   *1. Glinus radiatus*
1b. Flowers white; leaves linear   *2. Mollugo verticillata*

1. *Glinus radiatus* (RUIZ & PAV.) ROHRB.
Annual, prostrate herb, dichotomously branched. Stem red, whitish stellate-tomentose. Leaves in whorls of 3–5, of unequal size; blade 12–25 mm long, obovate; petiole 1–3 mm long. Flowers 2–5 per node, sessile, green, small, barely expanding. Capsule 3 mm long. Collections: 63779, 63979.
Common at dried-up water holes. — Texas to Argentina.

2. *Mollugo verticillata* L.
Annual, slender, dichotomously branched herb. Stem glabrous. Leaves in whorls of 5–6 per node, unequal, sessile; blade 10–22 mm long, linear. Flowers several per node; tepals white, 2 mm long; pedicels 8–12 mm long. Capsule 3 mm long, ovoid. Seeds numerous, minute. Collection: 63342.
Occasional in cultivated land. — Cosmopolitan weed of temperate and tropical regions.

MORACEAE (MULBERRY FAMILY)

Trees, shrubs, or rarely herbs, many are stranglers. Leaves alternate, simple, entire or rarely incised; stipules small, sometimes leaving a circular scar. Flowers actinomorphic, unisexual. Fruit a drupe or a nut, often including the whole infructescence (the fig). A family with 1500 species in tropical regions of the world.
The breadfruit [*Artocarpus altilis* (PARKINSON) FOSBERG] is rare in cultivation on Puná Island where it, as elsewhere, is known as fruta de pan. It is eaten by pigs.

1. *Ficus citrifolia* MILL.
Tree, to 10 m high, when young a liana strangling on other trees. Leaves evergreen, glabrous; blade 9–20 cm long, elliptic-oblong, attenuate; petiole 1–2 cm long. Infructescence (a fig) 1 cm wide, globose, short-pedunculate.

Collections: 63961, 63964, 85336.

Scattered throughout the dry forest. — Florida to South America.

Uses: It is used medicinally to cure problems with the kidneys and the colon, aches, and pains, and to remove the umbilical cord of newborn infants. It is eaten by goats.

Vernacular name: matapalo.

MYRTACEAE (MYRTLE FAMILY)

Trees or shrubs. Leaves opposite or rarely alternate; stipules lacking. Flowers bisexual, 4–5-merous; stamens numerous. Fruit a loculicidal capsule, a berry, or a drupe. A tropical family with 3000 species.

Key to the Species

1a. Fruits 2 cm wide; native	1. *Psidium densicomum*
1b. Fruits 2–4 cm wide; cultivated	2. *Psidium guajava*

1. *Psidium densicomum* DC.

Tree, to 8 m high; bark caducous. Stem glabrous, 4-angled when young. Leaves opposite; blade 5–10 cm long, elliptic to oblong, acute and mucronate, rounded and short-cuneate at base; petiole 0.5–1 cm long. Flowers 1–3 together, white, 3 cm wide; stamens exserted; pedicels 1.5–2.5 cm long. Fruit yellow, 2 cm wide, globose. Collection: 63748.

Uncommon understory treelet. — Known from Brazil, Colombia, and Peru. This species is not listed in the *Catalogue of the Vascular Plants of Ecuador* (Jørgensen and León-Yánez 1999), but included here based on the identification of our specimen by Landrum (ASU) in 1992.

Uses: Used to frame timber, lashing posts for rigging, houses, and to make charcoal. It is eaten by cattle and deer.

Vernacular name: guayaba de monte.

2. *Psidium guajava* L. [cult.]

The guava (no specimen) is cultivated around homesites. — Native to warm America and becoming pantropical.

Uses: Grown for its edible fruit. The wood is used as fuel and for making charcoal.

Vernacular names: guayaba de castilla, guayaba de comer.

NAJADACEAE (WATER-NYMPH FAMILY)

Aquatic, submerged plants with slender stems, rooting at the nodes. Leaves opposite to whorled, narrow. Flowers unisexual, variously reduced. Fruit a 1-seeded nutlet. A pantropical family with 50 species of brackish and fresh waters.

1. *Najas podostemon* MAGNUS

Submersed monoecious herb. Stem profusely branched, internodes to 5 cm long. Leaves 0.7–3 cm long, 1 mm wide, linear, conspicuously serrulate; sheaths wider than the lamina. Unisexual flowers 1–2 per axil, to 2 mm long. Seeds 2 mm long. Collection: 63596.

Rare aquatic plant in fresh waters. — Widely distributed in South America.

NYCTAGINACEAE (FOUR-O'CLOCK FAMILY)

Trees, shrubs, or herbs. Leaves opposite or alternate, simple, entire; stipules lacking. Flowers bi- or uni-sexual, sometimes subtended by bracts; perianth of 5 tepals that persist in fruit; stamens 1–many. Fruit an achene which is sometimes surrounded by the persistent perianth (anthocarp). A family with 400 species mainly in tropical America.

Key to the Species

1a. Herbs
    2a. Flowers surrounded by leaf-like bracts
        3a. Perianth 5 cm long; ornamental   *7. Mirabilis jalapa*
        3b. Perianth less than 1 cm long; weed   *8. Mirabilis cf. violacea*
    2b. Flowers not surrounded by leaf-like bracts
        4a. Fruit 5-merous; pedicels to 5 mm long
            5a. Inflorescence terminal, much branched, leafless; capitula 1–4 flowered
                6a. Anthocarp puberulent   *2. Boerhavia diffusa*
                6b. Anthocarp glabrous   *3. Boerhavia erecta*
            5b. Inflorescence axillary and terminal, weakly branched,
            leaf bearing; capitula 4–12-flowered   *1. Boerhavia coccinea*
        4b. Fruit 10-merous; pedicels 8–12 mm long   *5. Commicarpus tuberosus*
1b. Shrubs, trees or lianas
    7a. Inflorescence bearing colored bracts; cultivated   *4. Bougainvillea spectabilis*
    7a. Inflorescence without colored bracts; native
        8a. Leaf-base subacuminate; fruits 1–1.5 cm long
            9a. Twigs black, smooth; fruit with 4–5 rows of black trichomes
                                  9. Pisonia aculeata
            9b. Twigs grey, rough; fruit with about 10 rows of black trichomes
                              10. Pisonia floribunda
        8b. Leaf-base cordate; fruits 1 mm long   *6. Cryptocarpus pyriformis*

1. *Boerhavia coccinea* MILL.

Herb, to 80 cm high; roots fleshy. Stem puberulent or villous. Leaves opposite, pale beneath; blade 2–6 cm long, ovate, ciliate, rounded to acute, rounded or subtruncate at base; petiole 1–3 cm long. Inflorescence axillary and terminal, commonly to 4 cm long, capitula 3–10 flowered; peduncle to 3 cm long. Flowers purple to violet, subsessile. Anthocarp 3–4 mm long, 5-sulcate, pubescent.

Collections: 63256, 63377, 63798.
Common weed along trails. — Pantropical. Also on the Galapagos Islands.

2. *Boerhavia diffusa* L.
Herb, 0.5 m high. Stem sparsely pubescent to glabrous. Leaves opposite; blade 2–6 cm long, ovate to suborbicular, ciliate, truncate or rounded at base; petiole 1–4 cm long. Inflorescence terminal, to 30 cm long, slender, lax, leafless, the flowers few together. Flowers purple, subsessile. Anthocarp 3–4 mm long, 5-merous, puberulent. Collection: 63864.
Common weed. — Pantropical.
Note: The plant is eaten by donkeys.
Vernacular name: pegajoso.

3. *Boerhavia erecta* L.
Herb, to 1 m high. Stem essentially glabrous. Leaves opposite, pale beneath; blade 2–6 cm long, narrowly to broadly ovate, obtuse to acute, subtruncate at base; petiole 1–5 cm long. Inflorescence terminal, to 30 cm long, slender, lax, leafless, the flowers few together. Flowers white or occasionally pink; pedicels 0–2 mm long. Anthocarp 3–4 mm long, 5-angled, essentially glabrous.
Collections: 63263, 63558, ANDERSSON *s.n.* (S, cited in Areschoug 1869).
Annual weed of cultivated gounds. — Pantropical. Also on the Galapagos Islands.
Note: The plant is eaten by donkeys.
Vernacular name: pegajoso.

4. *Bougainvillea spectabilis* WILLD. [cult.]
The bougainvillea (Collection: 63764) is used as hedge around gardens for its colorful bracts. — Native to Brazil. It is eaten by cattle.
Vernacular name: flor de verano.

5. *Commicarpus tuberosus* (LAM.) STANDL.
Herb, 50 cm high. Stem glabrous. Leaves opposite; blade 2–6 cm long, broadly ovate, short-acuminate, cordate at base; petiole to 1 cm long. Inflorescence terminal, 20–30 cm long, much branched, composed of numerous 4–7-flowered umbels. Flowers purple, 1 cm long; anthers long-exserted; pedicels 8–12 mm long, slender. Anthocarp 8–10 mm long, 10-merous, clavate. Collection: 63910.
Uncommon weed. — Ecuador, including the Galapagos Islands, and Peru.

6. *Cryptocarpus pyriformis* KUNTH
Shrub, 1–3 m tall. Stem viscid-puberulent. Leaves alternate; blade 3–9 cm long, broadly ovate, rounded or emarginate, cordate at base; petiole 0.5–3 cm long. Inflorescence terminal, raceme-like, many-flowered. Flowers white, 2 mm long, short-pedicellate. Fruit 1 mm long, globose, black. Collections: 63641, 63828,

63862, 63893, ANDERSSON *s.n.* (S, cited in Areschoug 1869).

Very common in semi-moist places, also in salt marshes. — Endemic to Peru and Ecuador, including the Galapagos Islands.

Uses: Used medicinally to treat tooth aches, colds, aches, and pains. It is eaten by cattle.

Vernacular names: manglillo salado, palo salado.

7. *Mirabilis jalapa* L. [cult.]

The four-o'clock (no specimen) is grown in gardens. It is native to America.

Uses: An ornamental and magical plant associated with the cures for the evil eye.

Vernacular name: buenas tardes.

8. *Mirabilis cf. violacea* (L.) HEIMERL

Sprawling herb, to 30 cm high. Leaves opposite; blade 3–7 cm long, cordate, acute, cordate or rounded at base; petiole 1–3 cm long. Inflorescence subterminal, to 5 cm long, few-flowered; bracts 5–8 mm long, foliaceous, pubescent, longer than perianth-tube. Flowers purple, 1 cm long; anthers exserted. Collections: 63073, 63571.

Occasional weed along trails. — America.

9. *Pisonia aculeata* L.

Dioecious shrub or treelet, to 5 m high. Twigs black with light spots, smooth; short shoots often terminating into a spine. Leaves fascicled; blade 2–7 cm long, elliptic-obovate, short-attenuate or mucronate, long-cuneate at base; petiole 0.5–2 cm long. Inflorescence in axillary heads, enlarging when in fruit; peduncle 1–4 cm long. Flowers green, 3 mm long, pedicellate; staminate ones campanulate; pistillate ones tubular. Fruit 1.5 cm long, oblong, bearing 4–5 rows of black trichomes. Collections: 63835, 63955, 63957.

Common understory treelet in the dry forest. — Pantropical.

Our specimens are without the stout, recurving spines so often seen in this species.

Phenology: Flowers in October and November.

Uses: The wood is used for making corral gates, firewood, charcoal, and as a dye.

Vernacular name: pegapega.

10. *Pisonia floribunda* HOOK. F.

Dioecious tree, to 10 m high. Twigs grey, rough and irregular. Leaves subopposite, puberulent beneath; blade 6–15 cm long, elliptic, acuminate to rounded, short-acuminate at base. Inflorescence in head-like clusters, enlarging to 15 cm wide in fruit; peduncle 1–4 cm long. Flowers to 5 mm long; staminate ones campanulate; pistillate ones tubular. Fruit ca. 1 cm long, ribbed, with 10 rows of black trichomes. Collections: 64039, 64094, 64107, 85306, 85309, 85312. Common, along trails in closed forest. — Endemic to southwestern Ecuador, including the Galapagos Islands. Previously thought to be endemic to the Galapagos Island.

Phenology: Flowers in October and November.

Uses: The wood is used to make charcoal.

Vernacular name: pegapega.

NYMPHAEACEAE (WATER LILY FAMILY)

Aquatic plants with floating leaves and a rhizome. Leaves alternate, long-petiolate, simple. Flowers bisexual, large and showy; sepals 4–5; petals many; stamens numerous, some staminodial in gradual transition to petals. Fruit a berry. A nearly cosmopolitan family with 65 species of fresh water plants.

1. *Nymphaea ampla* (SALISB.) DC. (Plate 4)

Large deeply rooted herb with floating leaves. Leaves glabrous; blade 20–40 cm long, broadly elliptic, dentate; petiole to 1.5 m long. Flowers white, 10 cm wide, long-pedunculate. Berry large, spongy. Collections: 63595, 63831.

Common in deep ponds. — Widespread in America.

Note: It is eaten by cattle.

Vernacular name: maravilla.

ONAGRACEAE (EVENING PRIMROSE FAMILY)

Herbs or shrubs. Leaves alternate or opposite, simple; stipules none or caducous. Flowers bisexual, usually actinomorphic, 4–5-merous; stamens 4–10. Fruit a capsule or a berry. A chiefly temperate to subtropical family with 650 species.

Key to the Species

1a. Flowers and fruits 4-merous	1. *Ludwigia erecta*
1b. Flowers and fruits 5-merous	2. *Ludwigia leptocarpa*

1. *Ludwigia erecta* (L.) H. HARA

Erect herb, 0.5–3 m high, freely branched. Stem glabrous, angled. Leaves alternate; blade 4–10 cm long, lanceolate, entire, subacuminate, narrowed at base; petiole 2–5 mm long. Flowers solitary, yellow, 1 cm wide, sessile, 4-merous. Capsule 1–2 cm long, 2–4 mm wide, 4-angled. Collections: 63044, 63111, 63167, 63368, ANDERSSON *s.n.* (S, cited in Fl. Ec.).

Very common in the savanna at the end of the rainy season. — Widespread in America, becoming pantropical. Reported from the Galapagos Islands.

2. *Ludwigia leptocarpa* (Nutt.) H. Hara

Ascending herb, to 80 cm high. Stem and leaves sericeous. Leaves alternate, indistinctly petiolate; blade 4–9 cm long, more or less lanceolate, obtuse to acute, attenuate at base. Flowers solitary in leaf-axils, yellow, 1.5 cm wide, 5-merous; pedicels to 3 cm long. Capsule 3–4 cm long, cylindrical, 10–12-nerved, hairy. Collections: 63479, 63498.

Occasional on sandy beaches. — Pantropical. Also on the Galapagos Islands.

Opiliaceae (Opilia Family)

Trees or shrubs. Leaves alternate, simple, entire; stipules lacking. Flowers usually bisexual, 4–5-merous; stamens opposite the petals. Fruit drupaceous. A small pantropical family with 32 species, rare in Ecuador.

1. *Agonandra excelsa* Griseb.

Tree, to 8 m high. Twigs glabrous. Leaves alternate; blade 3–7 cm long, elliptic, entire, acute, cuneate at base; petiole 1–5 mm long; axils lanate. Inflorescences 5 cm long, spicate, simple, 1–5 per axil, cone-like when immature. Flowers green, 4 mm wide, 4-merous, pedicellate; petals reflexed. Drupe green, 1.5 cm long, globose. Collections: 63986, 64049, 64108, 85349, 86014.

Occasional in the dry forest. — South America.

Uses: The wood is used in constructions. It is eaten by cattle and deer.

Vernacular name: limoncillo de monte.

Orchidaceae (Orchid Family)

Herbs, often epiphytic and with swollen stem-base. Leaves alternate, simple, entire, with a closed sheath at the base. Inflorescence often long-pedunculate. Flowers showy or inconspicuous, bisexual, zygomorphic, 3-parted; stamen and pistil joined to form a column. Fruit a capsule. A very large cosmopolitan family with 17000 species.

Key to the Species

1a. Leaves 1 cm wide; pseudobulb onion-shaped   1. *Encyclia angustiloba*
1b. Leaves to 4 cm wide; pseudobulb elongated   2. *Epidendrum bracteolatum*

1. *Encyclia angustiloba* Schltr.

Epiphytic. Leaves paired, to 30 cm long, linear. Inflorescence 0.5 m long, the many flowers borne several together on lateral branchlets. Flowers dark red-brown, 1 cm wide. Collection: 64144.

Uncommon in dry forest. — Endemic to western Ecuador. Mentioned as critically endangered in *Libro Rojo de las Plantas Endémicas del Ecuador 2000* (Valencia *et al.* 2000).

Phenology: Flowers in December.
Vernacular name: flor de navidad.

2. *Epidendrum bracteolatum* C. PRESL
Epiphyte with bulb, forming small clumps. Pseudobulbs elongated, composed
of several nodes. Leaves paired or tripled, 10–17 cm long, to 4 cm wide, linear.
Inflorescence to 50 cm long, erect, the many flowers borne in distal one third.
Flowers white with yellow center, 2 cm wide. Collections: 64030, 64088, 64141.
Very common in the thorn forest and dry forest. — Probably endemic to
western Ecuador.
Phenology: Flowers from October to November.
Uses: Used medicinally to treat swellings, wounds, and fractures.
Vernacular name: suelda con suelda.

OXALIDACEAE (WOOD-SORREL FAMILY)
Herbs, shrubs or trees, sometimes with rhizome. Leaves alternate, palmately or
pinnately compound; stipules lacking. Flowers bisexual, actinomorphic, 5-
merous; stamens usually 10, the filaments united at base. Fruit a somewhat
fleshy capsule. A mainly south hemispherical family with 950 species.

Key to the Species

1a. Leaflets to 2.5 cm long; flowers 1 cm wide	1. *Oxalis dombeyi*
1b. Leaflets to 12 cm long; flowers 2 cm wide	2. *Oxalis jasminifolia*

1. *Oxalis dombeyi* A. ST.-HIL.
Herb, 50 cm high. Stem sparsely pubescent. Leaves 3-foliolate; leaflets 1–2.5 cm
long, obovate to suborbicular. Inflorescence many-flowered, composed of a pair
of 4–6 cm long racemes; peduncle 6–10 cm long. Flowers orange–yellow, 1 cm
wide; pedicels short, to 8 mm long in fruit. Capsule 1 cm long. Collections:
63374, EGGERS 14795 (L, LE, S, US; cited in Lourteig 1994).
Weedy plant of open soils. — Panama to Peru. Also on the Galapagos Islands.

2. *Oxalis jasminifolia* NORLIND
Shrub, 1 m high. Stems densely pubescent. Leaves 3-foliolate; leaflets 5–12 cm
long, elliptic, attenuate, obtuse at base. Inflorescence a distal, many-flowered,
corymbose cluster; peduncle to 10 cm long. Flowers yellow, 2 cm wide.
Collections: 63899, 63908.
Uncommon in disturbed places on southern Puná Island. — Probably endemic
to southwestern Ecuador and adjacent Peru.

PASSIFLORACEAE (PASSION-FLOWER FAMILY)
Shrubs or vines, with tendrils. Leaves alternate, simple or compound; stipules leaf-like. Flowers showy, bisexual, 5-merous, an annular corona of numerous filaments is borne between the corolla and the androecium; stamens 5 or more. Fruit a berry or a capsule. A pantropical and subtropical family with about 600 species.

Key to the Species

1a. Flowers more than 7 cm wide; cultivated
    2a. Flowers white; fruits to 12 cm long   1. *Passiflora edulis*
    2b. Flowers red; fruits 20-30 cm long   4. *Passiflora quadrangularis*
1b. Flowers less than 7 cm wide; native
    3a. Floral bracts 1–3 times pinnatisect; stipules rounded   2. *Passiflora foetida*
    3b. Floral bracts not pinnatisect; stipules linear or filiform
        4a. Flowers 3–4.5 cm wide   3. *Passiflora punctata*
        4b. Flowers 1.5 cm wide   5. *Passiflora tenella*

1. *Passiflora edulis* SIMS [cult.] (Plate 10)
The passion fruit (Collections: 63720A, 63720B) is grown as a hedgeplant for its juicy fruits. — Presumably native to southern Brazil.
Uses: Refreshments are made from the fruit.
Vernacular name: maracuyá.

2. *Passiflora foetida* L.
Hirsute vine, with spreading branches. Stem striate. Stipules 2 mm long, rounded. Leaf-blade 3–7 cm long, 3-lobed, acute; petiole 3–8 cm long. Flowers white, 4 cm wide; bracts 1–3 times pinnatisect; peduncle to 5 cm long. Fruit greenish orange, 3 cm long, ovoid. Collections: 63661, 63867, 63917, 64003, SINCLAIR *s.n.* (K, cited in Fl. Ec.).
Common in low vegetation. — Widespread in America. Also on the Galapagos Islands.
Phenology: Flowers in the dry season. The fruits ripens before the onset of the rainy season. They are eaten by birds.
Vernacular name: bedoca.

3. *Passiflora punctata* L.
Glabrous vine, high climbing. Stem striate. Stipules 2–5 mm long, linear. Leaf-blade 4–6 cm long, much broader than long, 3-lobed, middle lobe reduced or lacking, 3 nerved; petiole to 9 cm long. Flowers white, 3–4.5 cm wide; peduncle to 8 cm long. Fruits globose to ellipsoid, black. Collections: 63947, 63989.
Occasional in dense forest. — Colombia and Peru, along the coast.

4. *Passiflora quadrangularis* L. [cult.]

The giant granadilla was not observed in cultivation on Puná Island, but it is known from an old collection (SCHIMPFF 1181; G, M, MO; cited in Fl. Ec.). — Pantropical crop of uncertain origin.

Vernacular name: badea.

5. *Passiflora tenella* KILLIP

Annual, pubescent or glabrate vine, small and slender, with spreading branches. Stipules 3 mm long, filiform. Leaf-blade 1–2.5 cm long, much broader than long, 3-lobed, middle lobe reduced to a tooth, 3-nerved; petiole to 4 cm long. Flowers greenish white, 1.5 cm wide; peduncle 1–3 cm long. Fruit 1.5–2.5 cm long, fusiform. Collection: 63868.

Occasional weed on open soils. — Endemic to arid coaststal zone of Ecuador and adjacent Peru.

PEDALIACEAE (SESAME FAMILY)

Herbs or shrubs. Leaves opposite or alternate, simple. Flowers bisexual, zygomorphic, 5-lobed, bilabiate; stamens 4. Fruit a capsule. A family with 50 species in Africa, Indomalaysia, and Australia.

1. *Sesamum orientale* L. [cult.]

The sesame (Collection: 63665) is commonly cultivated. — Native to tropical Africa.

Uses: Oil is extracted from the seeds and used in beverages, bread, snacks, or toasted and then eaten.

Vernacular name: ajonjolí.

PHYTOLACCACEAE (POKEWEED FAMILY)

Herbs, shrubs, or trees. Leaves alternate, entire; stipules absent or inconspicuous. Flowers bisexual; sepals 4–5, sometimes petaloid; petals none; stamens few to many. Fruit a berry, drupe, or a nut. A pantropical family with 120 species.

1. *Petiveria alliacea* L.

Herb, to 1 m high. Stem glabrous, with garlic odour. Leaf-blade 4–16 cm long, narrowly elliptic to ovate, entire, acuminate, cuneate at base; petiole 0.5–2 cm long. Inflorescence 10–30 cm long, spicate, the flowers borne 5–15 mm apart. Flowers subsessile, white. Achene to 1 cm long, appressed, with retrorse spines. Collections: 63034, 63250, BARCLAY 483 (US, cited in Fl. Ec.).

Common in disturbed places. — United States to Argentina. Native to Congo and New Guinea (Nueva Guinea) according to Barriga (1992).

Uses: Remedy used to treat jaundice and hepatitis.

Vernacular name: zorrila.

PIPERACEAE (PEPPER FAMILY)

Herbs, shrubs, or trees, often slightly succulent. Leaves mostly alternate, simple. Flowers borne on fleshy spikes, minute, uni- or bisexual; sepals and petals lacking. Fruit drupaceous. A pantropical family with approximately 1500 species.

Key to the Species

1a. Stem villose; leaves obovate	1. *Peperomia glanduligera*
1b. Stem glabrous; leaves cordate-deltoid	2. *Peperomia pellucida*

1. *Peperomia glanduligera* YUNCKER

Epiphytic or terrestrial dwarf herb, slightly succulent. Stem villose, glandular dottet. Leaves 1.5–3 cm long, obovate, ciliate, rounded, palmately 3–5-nerved. Inflorescence spicate, simple, to 10 cm long, 2 mm wide. Collection: 64029.

Occasional at summit of Zambapala hills. — Endemic to Ecuador and Peru. This species is not listed in the *Catalogue of the Vascular Plants of Ecuador* (Jørgensen and León-Yánez 1999), but included here based on the identification of our specimen by Callejas (HUA).

2. *Peperomia pellucida* (L.) KUNTH

Annual herb, to 30 cm high. Stem glabrous, slender and vine-like. Leaves petiolate; blade 1–2.5 cm long, cordate-deltoid, acute, subtruncate at base, pamately 5-nerved. Inflorescence spicate, 1–5 cm long, slender, barely 1 mm thick. Fruit orange, minute. Collection: 63037.

Rare in deep shadow. — Pantropical.

PLUMBAGINACEAE (LEADWORT FAMILY)

Herbs or shrubs. Leaves alternate, simple; stipules lacking. Flowers in panicles, spikes, or heads, bisexual, actinomorphic, 5-merous, bracteate; calyx often persistent in fruit; corolla sympetalous. Fruit a capsule or a nut. A subcosmopolitan family with about 300 species.

1. *Plumbago scandens* L.

Scandent herb or shrub, to 5 m long. Stem glabrous. Leaf-blade 6–12 cm long, lanceolate-elliptic or ovate, entire, acute to acuminate, nearly cuneate at base; petiole 0.5–1 cm long, clasping. Inflorescence spicate, with numerous flowers; bracts 6–7 mm long. Flowers white, 2.5 cm long, salver-shaped, sessile; calyx covered with stipitate glands. Capsule 7 mm long. Collections: 63082, 63322, 63611.

Very common in waste places. — Widespread in the tropics and subtropics from Florida to Chile. Also on the Galapagos Islands.

Uses: Used for corral gates. It is eaten by deer.

Vernacular names: pegapega, pegajoso.

POACEAE (GRASS FAMILY)

Herbs. Culms terete, usually hollow; nodes swollen, solid. Leaves narrow, with a sheath enveloping the culm. Inflorescence variously congested. Flowers solitary or few together in spikelets, minute, variously reduced, often with awns, stamens usually 3, stigmas 2. A large family with about 9000 species and 650 genera distributed throughout the World. Many grasses are of economic importance. Many of the 34 wild species here recorded are weedy.

Key to the Species

(corn, lemon grass, and sugar cane are not included in the key)

1a. Leaves lanceolate to ovate or very narrowly trigonous, *i.e.*, gradually tapering
     from a subtruncate base, usually less than 4 times as long as broad
     2a. Leaves 3–5 cm broad; spikelets subglobose   19. *Lasiacis sorghoidea*
     2b. Leaves generally less than 2.5 cm wide; spikelets much longer than wide
         3a. Spikelets 0.5–1 mm long; pedicels 3–30 mm long; awns absent
                                                                       26. *Panicum trichoides*
         3b. Spikelets longer than 2 mm; pedicels barely discernible; awns present
             4a. Leaves broadest at the base, awns to 2 mm long   17. *Eriochloa pacifica*
             4b. Leaves broadest at the middle; the largest awns longer than 3 mm
                 5a. Inflorescence white-villose; awns finely hispid
                                                                       22. *Oplismenus burmannii*
                 5b. Inflorescence puberulent (barely visible); awns glabrous, shining
                                                                       23. *Oplismenus hirtellus*
1b. Leaves linear or nearly so, generally more than 4 times as long as broad
     6a. Awns 2–4 cm long, scabrous; stout plants with 1–4 cm wide leaves
                                                                       24. *Oryza latifolia*
     6b. Awns not as above; plants variable
         7a. Plants aquatic, emerging or floating
             8a. Racemes to 3 cm long, erect   27. *Paspalidium geminatum*
             8b. Racemes 4–8 cm long, spreading   30. *Paspalum repens*
         7b. Plants terrestrial, but often on mud
             9a. Awns present, conspicuously geniculate   18. *Ischaemum rugosum*
             9b. Awns present and not geniculate or wanting
                 10a. Inflorescence simple, unbranched
                     11a. Awns or bristles either wanting or less than 5 mm lon g;
                          spikelets not inserted distichously on raceme-rachis
                     12a. Inflorescence 5 mm wide, without barbed bristles
                                                                       1. *Anthephora hermaphrodita*
                     12b. Inflorescence 1 cm wide, bearing 2–4 mm long barbed

bristles 4. *Cenchrus brownii*
11b. Awns present, longer than 5 mm; spikelets distichously
    inserted on raceme-rachis 3. *Bouteloua disticha*
10b. Inflorescence branched
  13a. Inflorescence in a distal (sub)digitate cluster or in a panicle
    of racemes, one or several racemes often displaced
    downwards
    14a. Awns present, at least 1 mm long, sometimes caducous
      15a. Awns 1–1.5 mm long 8. *Dactyloctenium aegyptium*
      15b. Awns longer than 2 mm
        16a. Racemes 5–8 cm long 5. *Chloris radiata*
        16b. Racemes 3–4 cm long 6. *Chloris virgata*
    14b. Awns wanting
      17a. Leaves 1–3 mm wide; racemes 2(–3), 1–3 cm long
          31. *Paspalum vaginatum*
      17b. Leaves wider than 3 mm or racemes longer than 3 cm
        18a. Raceme clusters subtended by a leaf
          13. *Enteropogon mollis*
        18b. Raceme clusters naked, not subtended by a leaf
          19a. Spikelets broadly ovate to subrotund
            28. *Paspalum conjugatum*
          19b. Spikelets elongated
            20a. Racemes less than 2 mm wide
              21a. Leaves 12–18 mm wide; sheaths
              densely hirsute 9. *Digitaria aequatoriensis*
              21b. Leaves 4–9 mm wide; sheaths sparsely
              pubescent 10. *Digitaria horizontalis*
            20b. Racemes more than 3 mm wide
              12. *Eleusine indica*
  13b. Inflorescense with lateral branches repeatedly branched, each
    branch terminating in a spikelet
    22a. Leaves 1.5–2.5 cm wide
      23a. Spikelets not supported by bristles
        25. *Panicum maximum*
      23b. Spikelets supported by 1–2 cm long bristles
        33. *Setaria grisebachii*
    22b. Leaves to 1.2 cm wide
      24a. Inflorescence 20–40 cm long, 10–15 cm wide, lax;
        racemes spicate 20. *Leptochloa mucronata*
      24b. Inflorescence not as above
        25a. Awns 1–3 cm long, 3-forked 2. *Aristida adscensionis*
        25b. Awns wanting or minute, simple
          26a. Inflorescence to 1 cm wide (sub)cylindric
            27a. Plants perennial, with long rhizomes;
              spikelets 1-flowered
              35. *Sporobolus virginicus*
            27b. Plants annual, without rhizomes; spikelets
              many-flowered 15. *Eragrostis ciliaris*

26b. Inflorescence wider than 1 cm, not frondosely
    spicate
  28a. Inflorescence composed of 3–15 remote
    racemes; spikelets in rows
    29a. Spikelets glabrous
      30a. Spikelets elongate, 2-sided along
        rachis   37. *Urochloa mutica*
      30b. Spikelets subrotund, in two rows
        one-sided along rachis
                29. *Paspalum convexum*
    29b. Spikelets pubescent
      31a. Spikelets 1.5–2.5 mm long
                11. *Echinochloa colona*
      31b. Spikelets 3.5–4 mm long
                36. *Urochloa mollis*
  28b. Inflorescense a dense to lax panicle;
    spikelets not in rows
    32a. Spikelets 1-flowered
               34. *Sporobolus pyramidatus*
    32b. Spikelets several-flowered
      33a. Leaves not viscose, except at ciliate
        ligules   14. *Eragrostis amabilis*
      33a. Leaves sparsely viscose
              16. *Eragrostis* cf. *viscosa*

1. *Anthephora hermaphrodita* (L.) KUNTZE
Annual bunch grass, 20–40 cm high. Leaves 4–8 mm wide, sparsely hirsute; ligule 3 mm long, membranous, curved. Inflorescence 4–5 cm long, spicate; rachis strongly zigzag; spikelets fused into 4–6 mm long burs each containing 4 spikelets; awns absent. Collections: 63067, 63230, 63318.
Common weed of open grounds. — Tropical America. Also on the Galapagos Islands.

2. *Aristida adscensionis* L.
Annual grass, 20–50 cm high, moderately branched from base. Culms striate. Leaves 1–2 mm wide; ligules ciliate. Panicles 12–20 cm long, fairly lax. Spikelets proper 7–9 mm long; awns 3-forked, 1–3 cm long. Collections: 63224, 63394, ANDERSSON 17 (S, cited in F. Ec.).
Common in disturbed open grounds. — Widespread in warm parts of America and the Old World.

3. *Bouteloua disticha* (KUNTH) BENTH.
Annual grass, to 60 cm high, sparsely branched, ascending and self-supporting. Leaves 3–7 mm wide, sparsely pilose, slightly scabrous. Inflorescence terminal, simple, 8–15 cm long; spikelets in distichously arranged clusters, separated by several mm, 5–8 mm long, subsessile; awns 8–15 mm long. Collections: 63266,

63391, 63539, 63673, ANDERSSON *s.n.* (S, cited in Areschoug 1869).
Common, scrambler along trails. — From Mexico to Peru. Also on the Galapagos Islands.

4. *Cenchrus brownii* ROEM. & SCHULT.
Annual, decumbent grass, to 60 cm high, often rooting at lower nodes. Leaves 5–12 mm wide. Inflorescence to 12 cm long, 1 cm wide, spicate, composed of 5 mm wide burs, each containing 2–3 indistinct spikelets and bearing 2–4 mm long retrosely barbed bristles; awns wanting. Collection: 63264.
Occasional in disturbed places where the adhering fruits are dispersed by livestock. — American, but becoming pantropical.

5. *Chloris radiata* (L.) SW.
Annual, tufted and short-stoloniferous grass; culms arching, to 60 cm high. Leaves 3–6 mm wide; sheaths sparsely pilose at margin. Inflorescence a terminal, digitate cluster; racemes 7–15, 5–8 cm long spicate; spikelets appressed one-sided along rachis; awns 1 cm long. Collections: 63054, 63182, 63205, ANDERSSON *s.n.* (S, cited in Areschoug 1869).
Common weed of waste places. — Mexico to Argentina. Also on the Galapagos Islands.

6. *Chloris virgata* SW.
Annual, loosely tufted grass, to 40 cm high. Leaves 2–4 mm wide, essentially glabrous. Inflorescence a terminal, digitate cluster; racemes 4–6, 3–4 cm long, flexuous; spikelets 3 mm long, sessile, one-sided along rachis; awns 4–7 mm long. Collection: 63110.
Rare on dry grounds. — Pantropical.

7. *Cymbopogon citratus* (DC) STAPF [cult.]
A perennial tussock of lemon grass (Collections: 63425) is found at every farm house. It rarely flowers. — Native to Asia, but not known in a wild state.
Uses: The leaves are used for an aromatic beverage. It is eaten by cattle and donkeys.
Vernacular name: hierba luisa.

8. *Dactyloctenium aegyptium* (L.) WILLD.
Annual, small-tufted grass, 20–40 cm high, rooting at nodes. Leaves mostly inserted near base of plant, 2–6 mm wide, pilose. Inflorescence a stout digitate cluster; racemes 2–4, 2–5 cm long, 5 mm wide; spikelets inserted in two rows one-sided along rachis; awns 1–1.5 mm long. Collections: 63060, 63097, 63202, ANDERSSON *s.n.* (S, cited in Areschoug 1869).
Common weed in disturbed places and on cultivated grounds. — Pantropical and introduced to America. Known from the Galapagos Islands.

9. *Digitaria aequatoriensis* (HITCHC.) HENRARD

Perennial, climbing grass, to 1 m tall, sparsely branched. Leaves 12–20 mm wide; ligules ciliate; sheaths distinctly hirsute. Inflorescence broom-shaped; racemes 15–25, 8–12 cm long, lower ones separate, upper ones clustered; spikelets 2.5 mm long, pubescent, spirally arranged, appressed, awnless. Collections: 63516, 63770.

Weed in cultivated fields. — Ecuador and Brazil. Described from Guayaquil and perhaps occuring disjunct in northeastern Brazil.

10. *Digitaria horizontalis* WILLD.

Annual, decumbent grass, to 60 cm high. Leaves 4–9 mm wide. Inflorescence a distal digitate cluster, often with a few racemes irregularly displaced below the cluster; racemes 2–5(–10), 6–8 cm long, slender; spikelets 2 mm long, spirally arranged, appressed; florets ciliate, caducous; awns absent. Collections: 63068, 63098, 63819.

Common weed of open places. — Pantropical. Also on the Galapagos Islands.

11. *Echinochloa colona* (L.) LINK

Annual grass, 20–70 cm high, sparsely branched; culm glabrous except at nodes. Leaves 3–8 mm wide; ligule absent. Inflorescense 5–12 cm long, more or less pyramidal, composed of 5–12 branches; racemes one-sided, 1–2 cm long; spikelets 1.5–2.5 mm long, sessile, pubescent; awns absent. Collections: 63090, 63199, 63231, 63480, 63518, 85867.

Very common on beaches and disturbed open grounds. — Pantropical and native to the Old World. Known from the Galapagos Islands.

12. *Eleusine indica* (L.) GAERTN.

Short-lived perennial, sprawling grass, to 60 cm high. Leaves 1–5 mm wide, often slightly scabrous. Inflorescense subdigitate, with one to several racemes displaced 1–5 cm below; racemes (1–)3–10, 3–12 cm long; spikelets 5 mm long, sessile; rachis visible; awns absent. Collections: 63056, 63108, 63134, 63217, 63258, ANDERSSON *s.n.* (S, cited in Areschoug 1869).

Common weed on waste land. — A nearly cosmopolitan species of tropical and warm temperate regions, introduced to the New World. Reported from the Galapagos Islands.

13. *Enteropogon mollis* (NEES) CLAYTON

Annual, cespitose grass, to 60 cm high. Leaves 6–9 mm wide; ligules ciliate. Inflorescence a subdigitate panicle, to 12 cm long; racemes 7–12, 5–10 cm long. Spikelets 3–5 mm long, imbricate; awns caducous. Collections: 63393, ANDERSSON *s.n.* (S, cited in Areschoug 1869).

A single record from cultivated fields. — Tropical America.

14. *Eragrostis amabilis* (L.) WIGHT & ARN. ex NEES
Annual, tufted grass, 15–30 cm high, slender. Leaves 2—5 mm wide, glabrous; ligules ciliate. Inflorescence 6–15 cm long, cylindrical, lax, the branches diverging; spikelets 1–2 mm long, 5–7-flowered, pedicellate; florets bearing cilia; awns absent.
Collections: 63006, 63089, 63156.
Locally abundant weed. — Pantropical, native to the Old World.

15. *Eragrostis ciliaris* (L.) R. BR.
Annual, tufted grass, 10–50 cm high. Leaves 1–4 mm wide. Inflorescense 2–12 cm long, barely 1 cm wide, frondosely spike-like; branches 5–25 mm long, ascending and more or less appressed. Spikelets 2–3 mm long, many-flowered; florets bearing cilia. Collections: 63267, 63392, 64020, ANDERSSON *s.n.* (S, cited in Areschoug 1869).
Waste places often on sandy soils. — Pantropical weed, also on the Galapagos Islands.

16. *Eragrostis cf. viscosa* (RETZ.) TRIN.
Annual grass, loosely cespitose; culms to 70 cm high, decumbent to erect. Leaves 3–6 mm wide, sparsely covered with viscoid hairs; ligula ciliate. Inflorescence 15–20 cm long, ovoid-cylindrical, lax, the branches diverging. Spikelets 2–4 mm long, 6–10-flowered, pedicellate; florets bearing cilia; awns absent. Collections: 63195, 63236, 63286.
Common weed. — Pantropical.

17. *Eriochloa pacifica* MEZ
Perennial, loosely tufted and stoloniferous grass, 20–40 cm high. Leaves 4–10 mm wide, very narrowly trigonous, tapering from a subtruncate base. Inflorescence 3–6 cm long, narrow; racemes 3–8, 1–2 cm long, ascending and appresed to rachis; spikelets 3–4 mm long, pubescent; awns 2 mm long. Collections: 63063, 63131, 63172; EGGERS 14772 (US, MO; types; cited in Jørgensen and León-Yánez 1999).
Common on sandy grounds. — Endemic to coastal Ecuador, including the Galapagos Islands, and adjacent Peru.

18. *Ischaemum rugosum* SALISB.
Annual, tufted and stoloniferous grass, to 70 cm high; culms hollow. Leaves 5–10 mm wide, sparsely hirsute; ligules conspicuously ciliate. Inflorescences few per plant, at first seemingly simple but at anthesis 2-digitate; racemes 5–8 cm long, spicate; spikelets 5 mm long, superficially resembling a crustacean shell; awns conspicuously geniculate, stout in lower 5–7 mm, loosely twisted and slender in distal 8–15 mm. Collection: 63503.
A single observation on the beach. — Pantropical weed originating in Asia.

19. *Lasiacis sorghoidea* (DESV.) HITCHC. & CHASE
Perennial, robust grass, 1 m high or more, with arching to scandent branches. Leaves elliptic, 3–5 cm wide, acuminate. Inflorescence lax, pyramidal, 11–15 cm long; lower branches remote; spikelets 3 mm long, subglobular, pedicellate; awns absent. Collection: 63431.
Uncommon in forest edges. — Mexico to Argentina.

20. *Leptochloa mucronata* (MICHX.) KUNTH
Annual, sparsely branched, erect grass, to 80 cm high. Leaves 3–7 mm wide, sparsely hispid. Inflorescence 20–40 cm long, lax, paniculate; racemes numerous, remote, often paired below, 2–10 cm long; spikelets 1–2 mm long; awnless. Collections: 63265, 63424.
Common in open, disturbed places. — Widespread in warm America and becoming pantropical. Also on the Galapagos Islands.

21. *Leptochloa uninervia* (J. PRESL) HITCHC. & CHASE
Perennial erect grass, to 80 cm high, sparsely branched. Leaves 2–6 mm wide, glabrous. Inflorescence 20–40 cm long, paniculate; racemes numerous, 4–9 cm long, remote; rachis scabrous. Spikes 4–8 mm long, ascending, more or less appressed to axis. Spikelets 2 mm long, 1-nerved. Collection: ANDERSSON *s.n.* (S, cited by Jørgensen and León-Yánez, 1999).
Only recorded from the above collection but could be common. — Pantropical.

22. *Oplismenus burmannii* (RETZ.) P. BEAUV.
Annual, creeping and slender grass, forming 20 cm high, loose mats, rooting at nodes. Leaves fairly short, narrowly ovate, 8–20 mm wide, clasping at base. Inflorescence narrowly paniculate, soft; racemes 4–12, 1–2 cm long, ascending and appressed to axis; spikelets 2 mm long, sessile; awns dimorphic, finely hispid, to 12 mm long, white. Collections: 63432, 63449.
An occasional weed. — Pantropical.

23. *Oplismenus hirtellus* (L.) P. BEAUV.
Perennial, sprawling grass, to 80 cm long, sparsely branched, rooting at nodes. Leaves lanceolate-ovate, 1–2 cm wide, sessile, clasping at base. Inflorescense 8–15 cm long, narrowly pyramidal; racemes 4–7, 1–2.5 cm long, diverging. Spikelets 3–4 mm long, paired; awns dimorphic, glabrous, shining, the largest 5–9 mm long. Collections: 63453, 63769.
Uncommon along stream beds. — Pantropical.

24. *Oryza latifolia* DESV.
Perennial, robust grass, to 2 m high, branched at base. Leaves 1–4 cm wide, scabrous. Inflorescence a terminal, lax panicle, to 30 cm long; branches borne in fascicles. Spikelets 5–6 mm long; pedicels 0–3 mm long, scabrous; awns 2–4 cm

long. Collections: 63193, 63280, 63545, ANDERSSON *s.n.* (S, cited in Areschoug 1869). Common in swamps. — Central America and West Indies to Ecuador and Brazil. This wild rice was once cultivated in Brazil.

25. *Panicum maximum* JACQ. [cult.]
The perennial Guinea grass (Collections: 63678) is native to Africa. — Recent in cultivation, now naturalised throughout tropical America, including the Galapagos Islands.
Uses: Grown for forage. It is eaten by donkeys.
Vernacular name: paja de cebolla.

26. *Panicum trichoides* SW.
Annual, slender and decumbent grass, forming 40 cm high, tangled mats. Leaves ovate-lanceolate, 8–18 mm wide, more or less clasping at base. Inflorescence a terminal, diffuse panicle, 8–20 cm long; branches ascending, partly re-branching in whorls. Spikelets to 1 mm long; pedicels to several cm long, filiform; awns absent. Collections: 63019, 63075, 63221, 63450, ANDERSSON *s.n.* (S, cited in Areschoug 1869).
Common at margins of dried-up streams. — Pantropical weed.

27. *Paspalidium geminatum* (FORSSK.) STAPF
Perennial, long-creeping, aquatic grass, rooting at nodes. Leaves 5–10 mm wide. Inflorescence to 20 cm long, below patially included by uppermost sheaths; racemes 5–15, 1.5–3 cm long, erect. Spikelets 2 mm long, inserted in two rows, one-sided along rachis; awns absent. Collections: 63896.
Halfway submerged in pond. — Pantropical. Also on the Galapagos Islands.

28. *Paspalum conjugatum* BERGIUS
Short-lived perennial, creeping and stoloniferous grass, rooting at nodes; culms to 50 cm high, erect. Leaves 8–12 mm wide, glabrous; ligules ciliate. Inflorescence 2(–3)-digitate; racemes 8–12 cm long, diverging. Spikelets 1.5 mm long, broadly ovate to subrotund, inserted in two rows, one-sided along rachis, subsessile; awns absent. Collection: 63583.
Uncommon at margin of seasonal stream. — Pantropical weed, also on the Galapagos Islands.

29. *Paspalum convexum* HUMB. & BONPL. ex FLÜGGÉ
Annual, tufted, stoloniferous grass, to 50 cm high. Leaves 4–10 mm wide, glabrous; ligules membranous. Inflorescence 5–12 cm long; racemes 2–6, 1–4 cm long, ascending; spikelets 2 mm long, glabrous, inserted in two rows, one-sided along rachis; pedicels 0.5–1 mm long; awns absent. Collections: 63228, 63291.
Common in seasonal swamps. — United States to Brazil.

30. *Paspalum repens* Bergius
Perennial, creeping or floating aquatic grass, to 60 cm high. Leaves 5–10 mm wide, glabrous, with finely branched roots at nodes. Inflorescence terminal, to 15 cm long, bearing numerous solitary and whorled racemes on a scabrous axis; racemes 4–8 cm long, progressively shorter distally; spikelets 2 mm long, appressed, short-pedicellate, born one-sided along the raceme; rachis broader than rows of spikelets; awns absent. Collection: 63597.
Rare in pond. — Widespread in America.

31. *Paspalum vaginatum* Sw.
Perennial, stoloniferous or rhizomatous grass, rooting at nodes; culms to at least 20 cm high, erect. Leaves disticuous, 1–3 mm wide. Inflorescence short and distal; racemes 2(–3), 1–3 cm long; spikelets 3 mm long, inserted in two rows, one-sided on rachis; awns absent. Collections: 63660, 63728.
Forming colonies on salty flats. — Along sea-coasts of the tropics and subtropics, including the Galapagos Islands.

32. *Saccharum officinarum* L. [cult.]
Sugar cane (Collection: 63674) is grown only for local consumption. — Native to the Old World.
Uses: To prepare sugar, molasses, and liqueur.
Vernacular names: caña de azúcar, caña dulce.

33. *Setaria grisebachii* E. Fourn.
Annual stout, erect grass, to 80 cm high. Leaves 1–2.5 cm wide; sheaths and ligula ciliate. Inflorescence a spicate panicle, to 30 cm long, 5 cm wide; spikelets or clusters of spikelets subtended by conspicuous, 1–2 cm long, solitary bristles; spikelets 2 mm long; awns absent. Collections: 63462.
Uncommon in waste places. — Warm America.

34. *Sporobolus pyramidatus* (Lam.) Hitchc.
Annual, slender and cespitose grass; culms 20–40 cm high, erect. Leaves 2–4 mm wide, glabrous; ligules ciliate. Inflorescence to 9 cm long, pyramidal; branches 1–2 cm long, inserted in fascicles of 2–6. Spikelets 1–1.5 mm long, 1-flowered; awns absent. Collections: 63145, 63168.
Common on sandy soils. — From United States to Argentina. Reported from the Galapagos Islands.

35. *Sporobolus virginicus* (L.) Kunth
Perennial, stoloniferous grass; rhizome long-creeping, rooting at nodes, 2 mm wide, straw-coloured; culms 15–30 cm high. Leaves distichous, 1–3 mm wide. Inflorescence 3–8 cm long, 1 cm wide, compact, densely flowered; branches to 2 cm long, ascending and more or less appressed. Spikelets 2 mm long, 1-

flowered; awns absent. Collection: 63653, ANDERSSON *s.n.* (S, cited in Areschoug 1869).

Occasional in salt marshes. — Sandy sea-coasts of the tropics, including the Galapagos Islands.

36. *Urochloa mollis* (SW.) MORRONE & ZULOAGA

Annual tufted grass, to 60 cm high, loosely branched with erect stems, rooting at nodes. Leaves 5–10 mm wide. Inflorescence to 10 cm long; racemes 5–10, 1–4 cm long; rachis ridged but not flattened, pilose. Spikelets 3.5–4 mm long, solitary, pubescent; awns absent. Collection: 63390.

On sandy soils. — Mexico to Argentina.

37. *Urochloa mutica* (FORSSK.) T. Q. NGUYEN

Perennial, decumbent grass, to 2 m long, rooting at nodes. Leaves 6–10 mm wide. Inflorescence to 15 cm long; racemes 10–numerous, 2–6 cm long; rachis flat, undulate. Spikelets 3 mm long, solitary or grouped, inserted 2-sided along rachis, glabrous; awns absent. Collection: 63465.

Occasional in marshes. — Widespread in the tropics, native to Africa.

38. *Zea mays* L. [cult.]

Maize (Collection: 63555) is a crop of major importance in local consumption. — It is an ancient American crop.

Uses: Used for flour, roasted cornmeal, beverages, refreshments, toasted maize, and for popcorn. It is eaten by pigs and birds.

Vernacular names: maíz, maíz blanco, maíz canguil, maíz cocre, maíz colorado, maíz corriente, maíz dos quince, maíz sesenta días.

POLYGALACEAE (MILKWORT FAMILY)

Herbs, shrubs, trees, or vines. Leaves alternate or opposite; stipules usually absent. Flowers zygomorphic, 5-merous; stamens 4–10. Fruit a capsule, nut, or a drupe. A family with 800 species in tropical to temperate regions.

Key to the Species

1a. Herbs
    2a. Leaves linear, 2 mm wide — 1. *Polygala leptocaulis*
    2b. Leaves ovate, more than 5 mm wide — 2. *Polygala violacea*
1b. Shrubs or lianas — 3. *Securidaca diversifolia*

1. *Polygala leptocaulis* TORR. & A. GRAY

Herb, to 50 cm high. Stem glabrous. Leaves alternate; blade 1–2 cm long, 2 mm wide, linear. Inflorescence racemose, the flowers crowded in distal 4 cm. Flowers light blue, short-pedicellate. Capsule 2 mm long. Collections: 63177, 63203.

Common in moist grassy savanna. — Southern United States to South America.
Phenology: Flowers in April and May.

2. *Polygala violacea* AUBL.

Herb, to 50 cm high. Stem sparsely hirsute. Leaves alternate; blade 2–4 cm long,
narrowly ovate, acute, entire; petiole 2 mm long. Inflorescence 6 cm long,
spicate. Flowers violet to purple, 5 mm long. Collections: 63180, 63278A.
Common in the savanna. — Central and South America.
Phenology: Flowering in April and May.

3. *Securidaca diversifolia* (L.) S. F. BLAKE

Scandent shrub or liana, to 5 m long. Stem terete. Leaves alternate; blade 4–9
cm long, oblong-ovate, obtuse or acute, entire, rounded to cuneate at base;
petiole 4–6 mm long. Racemes 5–10 cm long, simple or branched, many-
flowered. Flowers purple, 1 cm long; pedicels 3–7 mm long. Capsule (samara) 4
cm long, winged, 1-seeded. Collections: 64112, 85368.
Uncommon in living fences. — Mexico to Peru and the Lesser Antilles. This
showy species is easily mistaken for a Fabaceae.

POLYGONACEAE (BUCKWHEAT FAMILY)

Herbs, shrubs, or trees, often swollen at the nodes. Leaves simple; stipules
forming a membraneous sheath (ocrea) or lacking. Flowers minute, uni- or
bisexual, 3–5-merous; stamens 2–9. Fruit a one-seeded nutlet (achene). A family
with 800 chiefly north temperate species.
Apart from the species mentioned below, *Triplaris cumingiana* FISCH. & C.A.
MEY. *ex* C.A. MEY. — known as 'fernán sánchez' — may occur on Puná Island.

1. *Coccoloba ruiziana* LINDAU

Shrub or small tree, mostly 2–6 m high, dioecious. Ocrea 5–8 mm long,
caducous. Leaves alternate, glabrous; blade 3–8 cm long, orbicular-obovate,
entire, obtuse to rounded, shallowly cordate at base; petiole 5 mm long.
Inflorescence 8–17 cm long, spicate. Unisexual flowers white, 3 mm wide. Fruit
5 mm wide, globose, somewhat juicy. Collections: 63191, 63208, 63282, 63414,
63906, 63965, 85322, ANDERSSON *s.n.* (cited in Fl. Ec.), ASPLUND 10119, 10120 (S,
cited in Fl. Ec.).
Very common in periodically flooded areas. — Endemic to arid zones of
Ecuador and adjacent Peru.
Uses: The wood is used for stakes, net weaving needles, net frames, wooden
pins, looms, shovels, to cover charcoal ovens, and charcoal. It is eaten by birds.
Vernacular name: licuanco.

PONTEDERIACEAE (WATER-HYACINTH FAMILY)

Aquatic or semiaquatic plants. Leaves simple, with petiole and blade, sheathed at base. Flowers 3-parted; stamens 1–6. Fruit a capsule or a nut. A family with 30 species in fresh waters in warm regions.

Key to the Species

1a. Flowers blue
    2a. Inflorescences 1–2-flowered; leaves 2–4 cm wide   3. *Heteranthera rotundifolia*
    2b. Inflorescences many-flowered; leaves more than 6 cm wide
        3a. Plant floating   1. *Eichhornia crassipes*
        3b. Plant rooted   2. *Eichhornia paniculata*
1b. Flowers white   4. *Heteranthera spicata*

1. *Eichhornia crassipes* (MART.) SOLMS

Floating; roots fibrous. Leaves in basal rosette; blade 3–10 cm long, round. Inflorescence 5–13 cm long, spicate, 4–15-flowered. Flowers blue. Collection: ASPLUND 5235 (CAS, US; cited in Fl. Ec.).

Huge masses of this aquatic weed float down the Guayas river at the end of the rainy season. It surely occurs on the island as well. — Pantropical pest in rivers and estuaries. Native to Brazil.

Vernacular name: lechuga de agua.

2. *Eichhornia paniculata* (SPRENG.) SOLMS

Semiaquatic, rooted. Leaves in basal rosette; blade of petiolate leaves 6–10 cm wide, cordate, acuminate to acute; petiole to 30 cm long. Inflorescence paniculate, 20–100-flowered; spathe 2–6 cm long. Flowers blue; stamens 6. Collections: 63151, 63185, ANDERSSON *s.n.* (S, cited in Areschoug 1869), EGGERS 14799 (US, cited in Fl. Ec.).

Common in seasonal swamps. — Disjunct in northeastern Brazil and Nicaragua.

3. *Heteranthera rotundifolia* (KUNTH) GRISEB.

Semi-aquatic, procumbent herb. Leaf-blade of petiolate leaves 2–4 cm wide, round to ovate, obtuse, cordate at base. Inflorescence 1–2-flowered; spathe 2–3 cm long. Flowers blue. Collections: 63024, 63128, 63229, 63306, 85868, ANDERSSON *s.n.* (S, cited in Areschoug 1869).

Abundant in seasonal water holes. — Widespread in America, also in Europe.

4. *Heteranthera spicata* C. PRESL

Semi-aquatic herb. Leaves in basal rosette on a short stem; blade of petiolate leaves 3–6 cm long, cordate, acuminate to acute; petiole to 15 cm long. Inflorescence 8–17 cm long, spicate, 5–20-flowered. Flowers white. Collections: 63023, 63135, 63305.

Abundant in seasonal water holes. — Central America to northwestern Brazil. In Ecuador only known from the Guayas province.

PORTULACACEAE (PURSLANE FAMILY)

Herbs or shrubs, often succulent. Leaves alternate or opposite, simple; stipules present or lacking. Flowers solitary or clustered, bisexual; sepals 2; petals 4 or 5; stamens 4 to numerous. Fruit a circumscissile capsule. A subcosmopolitan family with about 600 species.

Key to the Species

1a. Leaves broad; stem-nodes not conspicuously hirsute
    2a. Plants erect
        3a. Flowers 2 cm wide   3. *Talinum fruticosum*
        3b. Flowers less than 1 cm wide   4. *Talinum paniculatum*
    2b. Plants prostrate to ascending   1. *Portulaca oleracea*
1b. Leaves linear; stem-nodes conspicuously hirsute   2. *Portulaca rubricaulis*

1. *Portulaca oleracea* L.

Prostrate to ascending annual herb, dichotomously branched. Stem glabrous. Leaves alternate (though apparently opposite), short-petiolate; blade 0.5–3 cm long, narrowly obovate, rounded, cuneate at base. Inflorescence axillary, 1–5-flowered within involucre. Flowers sessile, yellow, 5 mm wide, 4–5-parted. Capsule 6–9 mm long, ovoid. Collections: 63354, 63615, 63833.

Common weed on trampled soils. — Nearly cosmopolitan. Also on the Galapagos Islands.

Uses: Cooked as vegetable in soup. It is eaten by donkeys and birds.

Vernacular names: achocha, verdolaga.

2. *Portulaca rubricaulis* KUNTH

Succulent herb, to 30 cm wide, rather freely branched; roots fleshy. Stem prominently white-hirsute at nodes. Leaves alternate, sessile, 1–3.5 cm long, 3–4 mm wide, linear, acute. Inflorescence terminal, the flowers borne 2–5 together in head-like clusters, subtended by an involucre of leaves and copious, white hairs. Flowers yellow, 2 cm wide, sessile. Fruit 5–7 mm wide, obconical. Collections: 63175, 85869.

Occasional in saline marshes and disturbed savanna. — Bahamas and Florida to Ecuador.

Vernacular name: trébol.

3. *Talinum fruticosum* (L.) A. JUSS.

Erect herb, 20–50 cm high. Stem glabrous. Leaves alternate, subsessile; blade 3–6 cm long, obovate, retuse, decurrent at base. Inflorescence racemose, many-flowered. Flowers white or pink, 2 cm wide; pedicel 1 cm long. Capsule yellow-brown, 5 mm wide. Collections: 63015, 63016, 63253, 63255, 63378, MILLE 795 (US, cited in Fl. Ec.).

Common weed on disturbed soils. — Native of tropical South America and introduced to West Africa.

4. *Talinum paniculatum* (JACQ.) GAERTN.

Erect herb, to 80 cm high; roots thick and fleshy. Stem glabrous. Leaves alternate; blade 3.5–8 cm long, elliptic to obovoid, acute, cuneate or attenuate at base; petiole 1–3 mm long. Inflorescence terminal, 10–40 cm long, lax, multi-flowered. Flowers pink, 5 mm wide; pedicels 1–2.5 cm long. Capsule 3 mm wide. Collection: 63512.

Uncommon along trails. — Pantropical weed native of America. Also on the Galapagos Islands.

POTAMOGETONACEAE (PONDWEED FAMILY)

Aquatic herbs, with fibrous roots and slender stems. Leaves narrow. Inflorescence a spike or a panicle of spikes. Flowers bisexual, 2–4-merous. Fruit a drupe. A cosmopolitan family with some 100 species.

1. *Ruppia maritima* L.

Aquatic herb. Stem much branched, slender. Leaves 4–7 cm long, 0.5–1 mm wide, linear, minutely serrulate below apex; stipular sheaths 7 mm long. Inflorescence few-flowered. Fruit 2 mm long, beaked; gynophore 1–2 cm long. Collection: 64009.

Our collection is from northern Puná Island. — Cosmopolitan species of brackish waters, even in Europe. Reported from the Galapagos Islands.

RHAMNACEAE (BUCKTHORN FAMILY)

Shrubs, trees or vines, sometimes armed with spines. Leaves alternate (here), simple, usually 3–5-nerved. Flowers small, bisexual, actinomorphic, 4–5-merous; stamens opposite petals. Fruit a drupe, capsule, or a berry. A family with 900 species distributed in most parts of the world.

Key to the Species

1a. Trees or shrubs; fruit not winged
    2a. Twigs angular; leaves to 2.5 cm wide; fruit 5 mm long   *2. Scutia spicata*
    2b. Twigs terete; leaves wider than 3 cm; fruit 10–20 mm long
        3a. Fruit orange; leaves entire   *4. Ziziphus* sp.
        3b. Fruit yellow-green to yellow-brown; leaves crenate   *3. Ziziphus thyrsiflora*
1b. Lianas or climbing shrubs; fruit 3-winged   *1. Gouania mollis*

1. *Gouania mollis* REISSEK

High climbing shrub or liana, to 10 meters long. Stem tomentose. Leaves alternate; blade 6–14 cm long, ovate to elliptic, serrate or entire, acute, rounded at base; petiole 0.5–1 cm long. Inflorescence terminal, large, multi-flowered; lateral spikes numerous, to 15 cm long, racemose. Flowers white, minute. Fruit 1 cm wide, 3-winged, dry. Collections: 63526, 63542, 63543, 63757.

Common in open, disturbed forest. — Widespread in South America.

2. *Scutia spicata* (HUMB. & BONPL. ex WILLD.) WEBERB.

Scandent shrub, 1–3 m high. Twigs glabrous, angled, green; spines 4–6 cm long, stout. Leaves alternate, short-petiolate; blade 1–4 cm long, ovate to oblong, entire, obtuse with a fine notch, rounded at base. Flowers green, 3 mm wide, in small fascicles on lateral twigs. Berry red at maturity, 5 mm long, ellipsoid. Collections: 63873, 63884.

Common on salt flats. — Endemic to arid coastal regions of Ecuador, including the Galapagos Islands, to southern Peru.

Uses: The wood is used for charcoal.

Vernacular names: pechiche, pechiche silvestre.

3. *Ziziphus thyrsiflora* BENTH.

Tree, 5–15(–20) m high, young trunks and branches spiny. Leaves alternate, glabrous, 3-nerved; blade 4–7 cm long, ovate to subrotund, shallowly to distinctly crenate, obtuse to emarginate, rounded at base; petiole 1–1.5 cm long. Inflorescence 5–20-flowered, short or elongated; flowers green, 5 mm wide. Fruit yellow-green to yellow-brown, 1–2 cm long, globose; stalk 0.5 cm long. Collections: 63055, 63461, 75482, 85307, 85328, 86013.

Common in the dry forest. — Probably endemic to Ecuador.

Phenology: Flowers in May and June.

Uses: The wood is used for boards, houses, furniture, stakes in the fields, and charcoal. It is eaten by cattle, goats, donkeys, and deer.

Vernacular name: ébano.

4. *Ziziphus* sp.

Tree, to 10 m high. Spines on stems and twigs to 2 cm long, stout. Leaves alternate, glabrous; blade 5–8 cm long, attenuate, entire, rounded at base. Fruit orange, 1 cm long, globose, stalked. Collection: 63714.

Occasional in mature forest.

Vernacular name: modroño.

RHIZOPHORACEAE (RED MANGROVE FAMILY)

Trees or shrubs, often viviparous. Leaves usually opposite and leathery; stipules deciduous, leaving an interpetiolar scar. Flowers rather small, bisexual;

stamens twice the number of petals. Fruit a 1-seeded berry. The mangrove family includes 120 species.

Key to the Species

1a. Inflorescence 5–50-flowered 1. *Rhizophora harrisonii*
1b. Inflorescence 2(–4)-flowered 2. *Rhizophora mangle*

1. *Rhizophora harrisonii* LEECHM.
In habit and vegetative characters seemingly identical to the *R. mangle*, except for its many-flowered inflorescence and various minor differences in fertile parts.
Grows sympatrically with *R. mangle* in the estuaries but is fairly rare. — Mangroves of Africa and America.
The species was seen on Puná Island but not considered a separate species. We include it here following its recognition by Prance (in Jørgensen and León-Yánez 1999). Interestingly, *R. harrisonii* represents the sole tree species on the island, which was distinguished by the botanists but not considered worth recognition in the local vernacular classification system. This is particularly surprising inasmuch as at least two varieties of *R. mangle* were recognized by local informants on the basis of the quality of the wood, the climbing form 'gateado' being of inferior value.

2. *Rhizophora mangle* L. (Plates 3, 8)
Tree, 5–20(–30) m high; trunk becoming erect and straight with age, often creeping-ascending and entangled while juvenile or small-sized. Leaves opposite, glabrous; blade 9–14 cm long, elliptic, decurrent into the 1–2 cm long petiole, entire, leathery, midnerve prominent. Inflorescence 2(–4)-flowered; peduncle 2–3 cm long. Petals white, 1 cm long; pedicels 0.5–1 cm long. Fruit viviparous, 15–30 cm long, 1.5 cm wide, terete, pendulous. Collections: 63332, 63640, 63872, 104083, 104084, ANDERSSON *s.n.* (S, cited in Areschoug 1869).
This is the red mangrove, by far the dominant tree in the mangrove. — Widespread in America, West Africa, Oceania, and New Caledonia, including the Galapagos Islands.
Uses: The timber is used for house construction, boards, ribs of ship's frames, to produce dye, and for charcoal.
Vernacular names: gateado, mangle blanco, mangle colorado.

RUBIACEAE (MADDER FAMILY)
Trees, shrubs, or herbs. Leaves opposite or whorled, simple, and usually entire; stipules leaving an interpetiolar scar. Flowers mostly bisexual and actinomorphic, 4–5-merous, epigynous; corolla tubular. Fruit a capsule or a berry. A cosmopolitan family with 6000 species.

Key to the Species

1a. Shrubs, sometimes lianescent
    2a. Branches spiny   5. *Randia* sp.
    2b. Branches spineless
        3a. Inflorescence an axillary, few-flowered cluster; cultivated   2. *Coffea arabica*
        3b. Inflorescence terminal, 10–20-flowered; native   4. *Psychotria microdon*
1b. Herbs
    4a. Largest leaves 2–4 mm wide; inflorescence a 2–4-flowered umbel; flowers
        pedicellate   3. *Oldenlandia corymbosa*
    4b. Largest leaves more than 5 mm wide; inflorescence a condensed head;
      flowers subsessile
        5a. Stem pubescent, variously puberulent to hirsute
            6a. Flowers 3 mm long; inflorescence axillary   1. *Borreria scabiosoides*
            6b. Flowers 10 mm long; inflorescence subterminal   6. *Richardia scabra*
        5b. Stem essentially glabrous
            7a. Capsule 2 mm long; leaves opposite to subverticillate
                                              7. *Spermacoce confusa*
            7b. Capsule 4–5 mm long; leaves verticillate   8. *Spermacoce tenuior*

1. *Borreria scabiosoides* CHAM. & SCHLTDL.
Perennial herb, 20–50 cm high. Stems 4-angled, puberulent to pubescent, more densely so along angles; interpetiolar sheaths bordered by 20–30, 1–2 mm long, hyaline teeth. Leaves opposite, sessile; blade 3–7 cm long, narrowly ovate, acute, attenuate at base. Inflorescence an axillary subglobose head, 1–1.5 cm wide. Flowers numerous, 3 mm long, white, subtended by linear, ciliate bracts. Collections: 63220, 63346, 63766.
Common weed on disturbed soil. — America.
The identity of this taxon remains uncertain because of the lack of capsules and herbarium material for comparison. Our specimen could possibly belong to *Diodia incana* F. ARESCH. (ANDERSSON *s.n.*; S, type; cited in Areschoug 1869) from Isla Puná, which may actually be the same as the widespread *Diodia teres* Walter according to Taylor (in Jørgensen and León-Yánez 1999).

2. *Coffea arabica* L. [cult.]
The coffee (Collection: 63839) is found cultivated and spontaneous around homes and farms. — Native to the highlands of Ethiopia.
Uses: The roasted fruits are used to make coffee for local consumption only.
Vernacular name: café.

3. *Oldenlandia corymbosa* L.
Sprawling herb, 10–20 cm high. Stem essentially glabrous; interpetiolar sheaths with about 10 hyaline teeths at margin. Leaves subsessile, green above, beneath whitish and bearing short, appresed hairs; blade 1.5–3 cm long, 2–4 mm wide, linear-lanceolate, gradually tapering towards both ends. Inflorescence an axillary, 2–4-flowered umbel; peduncle 1–2 cm long. Flowers white, 2 mm

wide, 4-merous; pedicels 4–7 mm long. Capsule 2 mm long. Collection: 63341.
Uncommon in disturbed places. — Pantropical weed.

4. *Psychotria microdon* (DC.) URB.
Lianescent shrub, 1–2 m high; stem to 3 cm wide at base. Interpetiolar stipules
broadly ovate. Leaves glabrous; blade 4–10 cm long, obovate, entire, attenuate
at base and apex, petiole to 3 cm long. Inflorescence terminal, often borne on
lateral twigs, to 15 cm long, with 10–20 flowers borne distally. Flowers white,
1.5 cm long, funnel-shaped, short-pedicellate. Fruit red, 1 cm long. Collection:
63456.
Common understory shrub in the dry forest. — Mexico to northern South
America.

5. *Randia* sp.
Shrub, 2–4 m high. Branches black when young; short-shoots terminating with
a cluster of 3–4, 5–12 mm long, stout spines; interpetiolar stipules early
caducous, broadly ovate, mucronate. Leaves glabrous; blade 4–9 cm long,
elliptic, entire, short-attenuate at base and apex; petiole 5–10 mm long. Flowers
solitary or few together on the short-shoots, white, 5-merous. Fruit grey-brown,
1.5–2.5 cm long, woody, stalked. Collections: 63717, 63783, 63898, 85301, 85350.
Common in thorn scrub.
Uses: The wood is used to make charcoal.
Vernacular names: crucita, jazmín de cruz.

6. *Richardia scabra* L.
Creeping herb, to 40 cm high. Stems terete, hirsute, the hairs subulate. Leaves
2–5 cm long, narrowly ovate, ciliate, acute, decurrent at base; petiole poorly
defined, 0–5 mm long. Inflorescence in terminal heads, subtended by foliaceous
bracts, pedunculate. Flowers white, 1 cm long, subsessile. Capsule 2 mm long,
dehiscing into 3 cocci. Collections: 63301.
Uncommon in disturbed places. — Pantropical.

7. *Spermacoce confusa* RENDLE ex GILLIS
Scrambling herb, to 50 cm high. Stem glabrous; interpetiolar sheaths of 10–15,
2–3 mm long filiform teeths and often a cluster of trichomes. Leaves opposite to
subverticillate, bearing short subulate hairs; blade 2–6 cm long, lanceolate,
acuminate, cuneate at base; petiole indistinct, 2–10 mm long. Inflorescence an
axillary, many-flowered head, to 7 mm wide in fruit. Flowers white, 2 mm long,
4-merous, subtended by pubescent bracts. Capsule 2 mm long, obovoid, 2-
seeded; seeds 1.5 mm long, oblong. Collections: 63047, 63254, 63360, 63362.
Very common in waste places. — Tropical weed. Also on the Galapagos
Islands.

8. *Spermacoce tenuior* L.

Annual, ascending herb, to 40 cm high. Stem essentially glabrous; interpetiolar sheaths 5 mm deep, at margin bearing about 10, 1–1.5 mm long hyaline teeth. Leaves verticillate, distal ones sessile, lower ones short-petiolate; blade 3–5 cm long, linear-lanceolate, acuminate, narrowed at base. Inflorescence an axillary, headlike clusters, to 12 mm wide in fruit. Flowers white, 3 mm long, 4-merous, subtended by glabrous bracts. Capsule 4–5 mm long, 2-seeded; seeds 3 mm long, linear-oblong. Collections: 63125, 63160, ANDERSSON *s.n.* (S, cited in Areschoug 1869).

Occasional in waste places. — Tropical America.

RUTACEAE (RUE FAMILY)

Trees or shrubs, sometimes armed with spines. Leaves alternate, simple or compound, usually glandular-punctate with aromatic oils. Flowers bisexual, usually actinomorphic, 4–5-merous; stamens same number as or twice the number of the petals. Fruit variable. A family with 1600 species in warm regions, many of which have economically important fruits.

Key to the Species

1a. Leaves simple; cultivated   1. *Citrus aurantifolia*
1b. Leaves compound; native   2. *Zanthoxylum rigidum*

1. *Citrus aurantifolia* (CHRISTM. & PONZER) SWINGLE [cult.]

The lime tree is planted on most farms. — Native to southeast Asia.

Uses: The juice of the fruit is used as a flavour in raw marinated fish and seafood and refreshments, and to cure colds and heal wounds.

Vernacular name: limón.

2. *Zanthoxylum rigidum* HUMB. & BONPL. ex WILLD. subsp. *rigidum*

Shrub or small tree, 2–5 m high. Spines on trunk with broad bulbous base, spines on twigs thornlike, to 5 mm long. Leaves 10–20 cm long, 6–8-foliolate, shiny; leaflets 3–10 cm long, elliptic or oblong, attenuate, suboblique at base, short-petiolate; rachis sometimes spiny. Inflorescence axillary, to 10 cm long, much branched, many-flowered. Flowers white, 5 mm wide, rotate; pedicels 2–4 mm long, slender. Fruit dry, splitting into two valves and exposing the 3 mm wide, black seed. Collections: 63036, 63607, 63849, 63933, 85326.

Common in thorn scrub. — South America.

Phenology: Flowers throughout the year.

Uses: The wood is used for charcoal and firewood.The plant is eaten by goats.

Vernacular name: salsafrán.

SAPINDACEAE (SOAPBERRY FAMILY)

Trees, shrubs, lianas, or vines, sometimes with tendrils. Leaves mostly alternate, simple or pinnately compound; stipules usually lacking. Flowers small, uni- or bisexual, more or less zygomorphic, 3–5-merous; disc often present; stamens mostly 5–10. Fruit variable, dry. A family with 1500 species in the tropics and subtropics.

Key to the Species

1a. Vines or lianescent shrubs
    2a. Tendrils present
        3a. Vines; fruit inflated, membranous, not winged   *2. Cardiospermum corindum*
        3b. Lianescent; fruit not inflated, 3-winged   *4. Serjania brevipes*
    2b. Tendrils absent   *1. Allophylus* sp.
1b. Trees   *3.Sapindus saponaria*

1. *Allophylus* sp.
Liana, without tendrils. Stem pubescent. Leaves 3-foliolate; ultimate leaflet 9–20 cm long, narrowly ovate, more or less attenuate at base, remotely serrulate, acute. Inflorescence spicate, moderately branched. Flowers pedicellate. Fruits indehiscent, 1-seeded, green when unripe. Collection: 85859.
In fences, probably uncommon.
Vernacular name: cabo de lampa.

2. *Cardiospermum corindum* L.
Tendrillate vine, sparsely white-pubescent. Leaves 6–12 cm long, biternate; leaflets 3-segmented, coarsely toothed and lobed. Inflorescence many-flowered; peduncle to 10 cm long. Flowers white, 5 mm wide. Fruits 3 cm long, inflated and membranous. Collections: 63411, 63544, 63656.
Common in thorn scrub. — Pantropical. Also on the Galapagos Islands.
Vernacular name: pajarito.

3. *Sapindus saponaria* L.
Tree, to 15 m high; trunk unbranched; bark whitish and thick with age. Leaves pinnately 5–11-foliolate; leaflets 7–13 cm long, elliptic, subentire, acuminate; rachis winged. Inflorescence to 25 cm long, thyrsoid, multi-flowered. Flowers white, 5 mm wide, unisexual by abortion. Fruit brown, 2–3 cm wide, globose, sticky. Collections: 63750, 64091A, 85348.
Common in disturbed dry forest. — Mexico to Argentina, becoming pantropical. Also on the Galapagos Islands.
Uses: The fruits are used for washing of clothes. The wood is used for firewood and charcoal. It is eaten by donkeys.
Vernacular name: jaboncillo.

4. *Serjania brevipes* BENTH.
Climbing shrub or liana, with tendrils. Stem pubescent. Leaves 3-foliolate; terminal leaflet 4–12 cm long, ovate-oblong, serrate-toothed, mucronate, cuneate at base. Inflorescence spicate, axillary spikes 8–12 cm long, simple, terminal spikes to 30 cm long, much branched. Flowers several together on lateral pedicels, white, 5 mm wide; pedicels 5 mm long. Fruit 2–3 cm long, 3-winged, the seed borne distally. Collections: 63856, 63920, 64021.
Common in mature forest. — Probably endemic to arid regions of coastal Ecuador and adjacent Peru.
Phenology: Flowers late in the dry period.

SAPOTACEAE (SAPODILLA FAMILY)
Trees or shrubs. Leaves usually alternate, simple, entire. Stipules usually wanting. Flowers rather small, perfect, actinomorphic, mostly 5-merous; stamens attached to the petals. Fruit fleshy, dehiscent. A family with nearly 1000 species, mainly in the tropics. In addition to the species mentioned below *Pouteria caimito* (RUIZ & PAV.) RADLK. and *Pouteria sapota* (JACQ.) H.E. MOORE & STEARN

Key to the Species

1a. Fruit wider than 4 cm; leaves wider than 2 cm; cultivated
    2a. Fruit without white latex   1. *Calocarpum mammosum*
    2b. Fruit with white latex   2. *Chrysophyllum obtusifolium*
1b. Fruits 1 cm wide; leaves less than 2 cm wide; native   3. *Sideroxylon obtusifolium*

1. *Calocarpum mammosum* (L.) PIERRE [cult.]
The mamey sapote (Collection: 63922) is an uncommon fruit tree on Puná Island.
Vernacular name: mamey colorado.

2. *Chrysophyllum oliviforme* L. subsp. *oliviforme* [cult.]
The fruit tree known as caimito (no specimen) on Puná Island probably belongs here according to Valverde (1998) (as *Chrysophyllum cainito* L.). Its english equivalent is star apple.
Vernacular name: caimito.

3. *Sideroxylon obtusifolium* (ROEM & SCHULT.) T.D. PENN.
Tree, 4–8 m tall. Short-shoots often teminating into a spine. Leaves alternate, puberulent; blade 2–4 cm long, obtuse or rounded, entire, cuneate at base; petiole 3–5 mm long. Inflorescence several cm long. Flowers not seen. Fruit black, 1–1.5 cm long, ellipsoid, long-mucronate, drupaceous; calyx 4-merous, persistent. Collection: 75481.

Rare in the dry forest on the southern part of the island. Probably the third record of this species in Ecuador. — Widespread in warm America.

SCROPHULARIACEAE (FIGWORT FAMILY)

Herbs, shrubs, or vines. Leaves alternate or opposite, simple, typically serrate; stipules lacking. Flowers bisexual, more or less zygomorphic, mostly 5-merous with fused corolla; stamens 4 or 2; carpels 2. Fruit a capsule or rarely a berry or a drupe. A family of 2800 species distributed throughout the World.

Key to the Species

1a. Leaves opposite or in whorls of 3–4
  2a. Leaves sessile
    3a. Flowers subsessile
      4a. Stem glabrous; flowers white   3. *Bacopa sessiliflora*
      4b. Stem hirsute; flowers blue   7. *Stemodia durantifolia*
    3b. Flowers pedicellate for at least 5 mm
      5a. Plant erect, terrestrial; flowers in 1–3 flowered fascicles   6. *Scoparia dulcis*
      5b. Plant prostrate, aquatic or semi-aquatic; flowers solitary
        6a. Leaves 1(–3)-veined; capsule 5 mm long   1. *Bacopa monniera*
        6b. Leaves 7–9-veined; capsule 3 mm long   2. *Bacopa repens*
  2b. Leaves petiolate   5. *Lindernia crustacea*
1b. Leaves alternate   4. *Capraria peruviana*

1. *Bacopa monniera* (L.) WETTST.
Prostrate semi-aquatic, succulent herb, rooting at nodes. Stem glabrous. Leaves opposite, sessile, 1(–3)-veined; blade 12–18 mm long, oblanceolate, entire, rounded, cuneate at base. Flowers solitary, axillary, light blue or white; pedicel 1.5–2.5 cm long. Capsule 5 mm long, ovoid. Collections: 64022, 64100.
Occasional at streambeds and springs. — Pantropical.
Vernacular name: verdolaga.

2. *Bacopa repens* (Sw.) WETTST.
Prostrate, aquatic succulent herb. Stem glabrous below, pubescent distally. Leaves opposite, sessile, palmately 7–9-veined; blade 1–2(–4.5) cm long, obovate, rounded. Flowers solitary, axillary, blue or white; pedicel to 2 cm long. Capsule 3 mm long, subglobose. Collections: 63140, 63290, 85864.
Submersed in shallow waters. — United States to coastal Ecuador.

3. *Bacopa sessiliflora* (BENTH.) PULLE
Upright herb, to 40 cm high; roots fibrous. Stem glabrous, obscurely 4-angled. Leaves opposite, sessile; blade 2–5 cm long, narrowly oblanceolate, shallowly serrate, acute. Flowers solitary, axillary, white, subsessile. Capsule 3 mm long, ovoid. Collections: 63133, 63159, 63287, 63355.

Common in moist places, often in standing water. — Northern South America to Guatemala.

4. *Capraria peruviana* BENTH.
Erect shrub or herb, to 1.5 m high. Stem glabrous. Leaves alternate, sessile; blade 5–11 cm long, oblanceolate, entire to toothed, acute, cuneately decurrent at base. Inflorescence axillary, in fascicles of 1–3-flowers. Flowers yellow-white, 8 mm wide; pedicels to 1.5 cm long. Capsule 5 mm long. Collections: 63886, 64024, ANDERSSON *s.n.* (S, cited in Areschoug 1869).
Common at stream banks. — Colombia to Peru. Also on the Galapagos Islands.

5. *Lindernia crustacea* (L.) F. MUELL.
Prostrate annual herb, much branched, small. Stem essentially glabrous, 4-angled. Leaves opposite, petiolate; blade 8–14 mm long, broadly ovate, more or less crenate, obtuse to rounded, cuneate to truncate at base. Flowers solitary, axillary, blue and white, 7 mm long; pedicel 1–2.5 cm long. Capsule 3–4 mm long, globose, mucronate. Collections: 63297, 63337.
Common in moist places. — Widespread throughout warm temperate and tropical parts of the world.

6. *Scoparia dulcis* L.
Erect herb, to 1 m high. Stem nearly glabrous, ribbed from decurrent leaf bases. Leaves opposite or in whorls of 3–4, sessile; blade 2–4 cm long, narrowly rhombic-ovate, coarsely serrate, cuneate at base. Inflorescence axillary, 1–3 flowered fascicles. Flowers white, 7 mm wide; corolla 4-lobed; pedicel to 9 mm long. Capsule 3–4 mm long, globose. Collections: 63022, 63050, 63080, 63298, 63396, 63652.
Abundant in disturbed sites. — Pantropical. Also on the Galapagos Islands.
Uses: It is used medicinally to cure swellings and acne, remove thorns, and heal wounds.
Vernacular name: tiatina.

7. *Stemodia durantifolia* (L.) SW.
Erect herb or halfshrub, to 1 m high. Stem hirsute. Leaves opposite or in whorls of 3, sessile; blade 3–7 cm long, narrowly lanceolate to oblanceolate, serrate-dentate, clasping at base. Inflorescence spiciform. Flowers blue, 7 mm long, subsessile. Capsule 4 mm long. Collection: 63397.
Uncommon in wet places. — Widespread in America.

SOLANACEAE (POTATO FAMILY)
Trees, shrubs, or herbs, variously hairy. Leaves alternate, simple or compound; stipules lacking. Flowers bisexual, usually actinomorphic, mostly 5-merous;

stamens 5 or rarely less, inserted on the corolla tube, carpels 2. Fruit a berry or a capsule. A diverse family with 2300 species, particularly in the Neotropics.

Key to the Species

1a. Leaves pinnately compound   10. *Solanum lycopersicum*
1b. Leaves simple
   2a. Fruit surrounded by the persisting, membranous calyx
      3a. Flowers cream or yellow with brown center   8. *Physalis angulata*
      3b. Flowers blue   6. *Nicandra physalodes*
   2b. Fruit not surrounded by a membranous calyx
      4a. Flowers rotate to campanulate
         5a. Calyx truncate, the lobes evident   4. *Lycianthes* sp.
         5b. Calyx deeply 5-lobed
            6a. Herbs; stems subglabrous   9. *Solanum americanum*
            6b. Shrubs or trees; leaves whitish stellate-pubescent   11. *Solanum hazenii*
      4b. Flowers tubular, funnelform or salver-shaped
         7a. Flowers blue
            8a. Leaves wider than 15 mm; fruit a capsule   1. *Browallia americana*
            8b. Leaves to 8 mm wide; fruit a berry   5. *Lycium americanum*
         7b. Flowers not blue
            9a. Flowers longer than 10 cm   3. *Datura inoxia*
            9b. Flowers shorter than 5 cm long; cultivated
               10a. Fruit a berry   2. *Capsicum annuum*
               10b. Fruit a capsule   7. *Nicotiana tabacum*

1. *Browallia americana* L.
Herb, to 1 m high. Stem sparsely puberulent. Leaves simple; blade 4–9 cm long, ovate to broadly ovate, entire, acute, more or less rounded at base; petiole 5–35 mm long. Inflorescence racemose, few to many-flowered, lax, leafy. Flowers blue with yellow center, 2 cm wide, salver-shaped; calyx 8 mm long; pedicels 5 mm long. Capsule 4–5 mm wide, ovoid. Collections: 63316, 63791.
Among the most abundant herbs in clearings and along trails, especially in the thorn forest. — Mexico to Peru. Reported from the Galapagos Islands.
Vernacular name: boca de león.

2. *Capsicum annuum* L. [cult.]
The chili pepper (Collection: 63565) is domesticated in yards and gardens. — The origin lies probably in Bolivia and Brazil. Also *Capsicum frutescens* L. may be found on the island.
Uses: The fruit is much used as condiment.
Vernacular names: ají, ají de gallinazo, ají de mesa, ají grande, ajicito.

3. *Datura inoxia* MILL.
Broad herb, to 50 cm high. Stems and leaves more or less densely whitish powdery. Leaves simple; blade 6–20 cm long, ovate, irregularly and often

coarsely sinuate-dentate, acute, oblique at base; petiole to 5 cm long. Flowers solitary, white, 12 cm long, erect; calyx 10 cm long. Fruit 5 cm long, dry, covered with stiff spine-like tubercles. Seeds ovate-discoid, 5 mm long. Collection: 63795.

Rare on disturbed soils. — Widespread in the tropics.

Uses: It is used to cure 'the evil eye', which is a non-somatic sickness.

Vernacular name: campanita, campanita de castilla.

4. *Lycianthes* sp.

Shrub, 1–2 m high. Stem essentially glabrous, irregularly ridged. Leaves simple; blade 2–7 cm long, narrowly elliptic, entire, attenuate, cuneate to attenuate at base; petiole 5–15 mm long. Inflorescence terminal, 1–10-flowered. Flowers white, 1.5 cm across; calyx 2–3 mm long, truncate, cupular, enlarging in fruit; pedicels 2 cm long. Berry 1 cm wide. Collections: 63622, 86017.

Uncommon in disturbed places.

5. *Lycium americanum* JACQ.

Shrub, to 2 m high. Stem essentially glabrous, irregularly angled. Leaves in subsessile clusters, simple; blade 8–15 mm long, entire, acute, spatulate to narrowly obovate. Flowers solitary and axillary, light blue, 1 cm long; pedicels to 2 cm long. Berry 8 mm wide; stalk 2 cm long. Collections: 63103, 63197, 63467.

Common on beaches and borders of salt marshes. — Antilles to South America.

6. *Nicandra physalodes* (L.) GAERTN.

Herb, to 2 m high. Stem glabrous. Leaves simple; blade 7–18 cm long, ovate, shallowly lobed at edge, acute, abruptly and obliquely decurrent at base; petiole narrowly winged, to 4 cm long. Flowers solitary, blue, 3 cm wide, pedicellate. Berry 1–2 cm wide, persisting membranous calyx to 3 cm long. Collection: 63584, ANDERSSON s.n. (S, cited in Areschoug 1869).

Occasional in waste places. — Subcosmopolitan. Also on the Galapagos Islands.

7. *Nicotiana tabacum* L. [cult.]

The tobacco (Collection: 63860) is cultivated around homes and sometimes has escaped. — Western South America.

Uses: The leaves are used to make cigarettes.

Vernacular name: tabaco.

8. *Physalis angulata* L.

Herb, to 1 m high. Stem essentially glabrous. Leaves simple; blade 3–13 cm long, ovate to narrowly ovate, entire or coarsely sinuate-dentate, acute, oblique at base; petiole 0.5–6 cm long. Flowers cream or yellow with brown center, 1.5 cm wide, solitary; pedicels to 1.5 cm long, slender. Berry 1 cm wide, surrounded by the extended, 3 cm wide membranous calyx. Collections: 63343, 63416, 63519, 63897, ANDERSSON *s.n.* (S, cited in Areschoug 1869).

Common at disturbed seasonally moist places. — Subcosmopolitan. Reported from the Galapagos Islands.

Uses: The fruit is used by children as a toy.

Vernacular names: chapuca, chapuca morada.

9. *Solanum americanum* MILL.

Herb, to 1 m high. Stem usually glabrous. Leaves simple; blade 6–10 cm long, ovate, entire or sinuate-dentate, acute, attenuate at base; petiole to 4 cm long. Inflorescence a few-flowered umbel; peduncle to 5 cm long. Flowers white, 3–5 mm wide with the lobes strongly reflexed; calyx deeply 5-lobed; pedicels 5–10 mm long. Berry black, 5–8 mm wide. Collections: 63299, 63358, 63457, 63647.

Common at disturbed sites. — Cosmopolitan.

Uses: It is used as a condiment and as a medicinal plant to treat swellings, to remove acne or thorns from the skin, to treat kidney problems, and to heal wounds.

Vernacular name: hierba mora.

10. *Solanum hazenii* BRITTON

Shrub or treelet, to 4 m high. Stem and underside of leaves conspicuously and whitish stellate-pubescent. Leaves simple; blade 10–22 cm long, ovate, entire, acute to acuminate, oblique at base. Inflorescence subterminal, to 20 cm long, cymose, long-pedunculate. Flowers white, 1 cm wide; pedicels to 8 mm long. Berry yellow, to 1 cm wide. Collections: 63548, 63718, 64036.

Occurs in disturbed sites. — Mexico to northern South America.

Vernacular name: cojojo.

11. *Solanum lycopersicum* L.

Herbaceous vine, to 50 cm high. Leaves 6–15 cm long, pinnately or bipinnately compound; lobes unequal, ovate. Inflorescences opposite the leaves, to 12 cm long, 5–10-flowered, cymose. Flowers yellow; pedicels to 2 cm long, slender. Berry red, 1 cm wide, globose, juicy. Collections: 63419, 64033.

Common weed in disturbed sites. — Native to Ecuador and Peru.

Uses: Used in jams and to cure 'the evil eye', a non-somatic sickness. The fruit is eaten by birds.

Vernacular names: tomatillo, tomatillo de monte.

STERCULIACEAE (CACAO FAMILY)

Trees, shrubs, vines, or herbs, usually stellately pubescent. Leaves alternate, simple or compound; stipules caducous. Flowers mostly bisexual, actinomorphic or zygomorphic; stamens in two whorls, the outer whorl usually sterile. Fruit a capsule or a schizocarp. A family with about 1000 species, mainly in the tropics.

Key to the Species

1a. Trees	4. *Guazuma ulmifolia*
1b. Herbs or shrubs	
2a. Stem spiny	3. *Byttneria parviflora*
2b. Stem not spiny	
4a. Calyx membranous in fruit	5. *Melochia lupulina*
4b. Calyx not membranous in fruit	
5a. Flowers pedicellate	
6a. Flowers white or violet with yellow center; fruit an angulate capsule	6. *Melochia pyramidata*
6b. Flowers white; fruit not as above	
7a. Leaf-base truncate to rounded; pedicels 0.5–1 cm long	1. *Ayenia magna*
7b. Leaf-base cordate; pedicels 1–2 cm long	2. *Ayenia pusilla*
5b. Flowers sessile	7. *Waltheria ovata*

1. *Ayenia magna* L.
Scrambler, to 1 m high. Stem pubescent. Leaf-blade 3–8 cm long, ovate-cordate, serrate, acuminate, cordate at base; petiole to 3 cm long. Inflorescence axillary, few-flowered, pedunculate. Flowers white, 5 mm wide; androgynophore very short; pedicels 1–2 cm long. Fruit 5 mm wide, globose, echinate. Collection: 63053.
Rare at disturbed sites. — Central and South America.

2. *Ayenia pusilla* L.
Herb, to 60 cm high. Stem bearing short recurved trichomes. Leaf-blade 3–6 cm long, ovate-cordate, coarsely serrate-dentate, acute, truncate or rounded at base; petiole to 2 cm long. Inflorescence axillary, simple or up to 8-flowered. Flowers white, minute; androgynophore 1.5–2 mm long; pedicels 0.5–1 cm long, slender. Fruit 6 mm wide, subglobose, echinate. Collections: 63058, 63106, 63363.
Common in dry scrub. — Often treated as a widespread species but considered endemic to southwestern Ecuador and adjacent Peru by Cristóbal (1960).

3. *Byttneria parviflora* BENTH. (Plate 15)
Shrub, to 4 m high. Stem bearing spines, glabrate with age, marked by coloured ridges. Leaf-blade 4–8 cm long, ovate to narrowly ovate, serrate, acute, rounded at base; petiole to 2 cm long. Inflorescence a many-flowered cluster at the nodes. Flowers white, small. Fruit 1 cm wide, globose, echinate. Collections: 63021, 63072, 63330, 63495A, 64111, 85353, ANDERSSON *s.n.* (S, cited in Areschoug 1869).

Very common in dry scrub. — Endemic to Ecuador and adjacent Peru.

Uses: Previously used to make temple rods in looms in the cotton textile manufacture. It is eaten by goats and pigs.

Vernacular names: barbaimanta, chiquihua.

4. *Guazuma ulmifolia* LAM.

Tree, to 20 m high. Twigs densely stellately pubescent. Leaf-blade 7–13 cm long, oblong to broadly ovate, serrulate, attenuate, obliquely cordate at base; petiole to 2 cm long. Inflorescence a many-flowered axillary cyme. Flowers cream, 5 mm wide, fragrant. Fruit black, 2–4 cm wide, globose, with sharp tubercles. Collections: 63321, 63901, 64132, 85347.

Common in the dry forest. — Mexico to Peru.

Uses: The wood is used for boards and charcoal. Previously the wood was used to make temple rods in looms in the cotton textile manufacture. It is eaten by cattle.

Vernacular name: guasmo.

5. *Melochia lupulina* SW.

Herbaceous to shrubby scrambler, to 3 m high. Stem stellately and softly pubescent. Leaf-blade 4–11 cm long, ovate, serrate, short-acuminate, subcordate at base; petiole to 5 cm long. Inflorescence a many-flowered axillary cluster. Flowers white with yellow center, pedicellate. Fruit 3 mm long, enclosed by membraneous calyx. Collections: 63446, 63562, 63713.

Common along trails. — Peru to Central America and the West Indies.

6. *Melochia pyramidata* L.

Erect herb, to 1 m high. Stem glabrous or sparsely stellate-pubescent. Leaf-blade 3–7 cm long, broadly to narrowly ovate, serrate, acute or obtuse, rounded at base; petiole to 2 cm long. Inflorescence 1–3-flowered and axillary; peduncle 1–2 cm long. Flowers white or violet with yellow center, short-pedicellate. Capsule 8 mm wide, angled. Collections: 63261, 63262, 63371, 63824.

Common weed of open soils. — Warm regions of the New World, naturalized elsewhere.

7. *Waltheria ovata* CAV.

Broad shrub, 0.5–1.5 m high. Stem stellately white-pubescent. Stipules linear. Leaf-blade 3–8 cm long, ovate to broadly ovate, serrate, acute, subcordate at base; petiole 1–2 cm long. Inflorescence axillary; glomerules commonly 2–6-flowered, sessile to short-pedunculate. Flowers yellow, sessile. Capsule 3 mm long. Collections: 63649, 63854, ANDERSSON *s.n.* (S, cited in Areschoug 1869).

Common. — Coastal, arid regions of Ecuador, including the Galapagos Islands, and Peru.

THEOPHRASTACEAE (THEOPHRASTA FAMILY)
Trees, or shrubs. Leaves usually alternate, simple; stipules lacking. Flowers bi- or unisexual, actinomorphic, 4–5-merous; stamens in two whorls, outer whorl sterile and petaloid. Fruit a drupe or a berry. A small family with about 110 species in tropical America and West Indies.

1. *Jacquinia sprucei* MEZ (Plate 13)
Tree, to 8 m high. Trunk white-spotted. Leaves evergreen, more densely crowded distally; blade coriaceous, 2–6 cm long, narrowly obovate to oblanceolate, long-mucronate, entire and revolute, cuneately decurrent at base. Inflorescence 3–10-flowered; flowers orange-brown, 1 cm wide. Fruit orange, 2–4 cm wide, globose, persisting for one year. Collections: 63489, 63587, 64019, 85319, ANDERSSON 77 (S, cited in Fl. Ec.), BARCLAY 357 (BM, cited in Fl. Ec.), HINDS *s.n.* (K, cited in Fl. Ec.), LINDEN *s.n.* (K, cited in Fl. Ec.).
Common in the savanna and thorn forest. — Ecuador and Peru.
Uses: A poison used to kill fry is extracted from this plant. It is also used to make nets, charcoal, and to cure bat bites on farm animals. It is eaten by deer.
Vernacular name: barbasco.

TILIACEAE (LINDEN FAMILY)
Trees, shrubs, or herbs, often stellately hairy. Leaves alternate, simple; stipules deciduous. Flowers bisexual, actinomorphic, 4–5-merous; stamens 10 to numerous. Fruit usually a capsule or a nut, rarely a schizocarp. A cosmopolitan family with 400 species.

Key to the Species

1a. Herbs
    2a. Capsule 2–3 cm long, winged, with 3 horns at beak   1. *Corchorus aestuans*
    2b. Capsule 6 cm long, not winged, narrow at beak   2. *Corchorus orinocensis*
1b. Shrubs   3. *Triumfetta semitriloba*

1. *Corchorus aestuans* L.
Herb, to 1 m high, sometimes scandent, woody at base. Stipules subulate. Stem pubescent. Leaf-blade 4–7 cm long, ovate, serrate-crenate, acute, rounded at base with the two lowest serrations often bristle-tipped; petiole to 2 cm long. Flowers 1–2 together, short-pedicellate, yellow, 0.5–1 cm wide. Capsule 2–3 cm long, winged, the beak with 3 horns. Collections: 63017, 63095, 63331, 63370, 63594.
Common at border of water holes and on beaches. — Pantropical.

2. *Corchorus orinocensis* KUNTH
Herb or half shrub, to 1 m high. Stem puberulent when young. Stipules

filiform. Leaf-blade 5–10 cm long, narrowly elliptic, serrate, acute, rounded at base; petiole to 1 cm long. Flowers 1–2 together, yellow, 0.5–1 cm wide, short-pedicellate. Capsule linear, 4–7 cm long, 2 m wide, narrow at beak. Collections: 63105, 63486, 63506.

Beaches and margin of pools. — Texas to Peru. Also on the Galapagos Islands.

3. *Triumfetta semitriloba* JACQ.

Shrub, to 3 m high. Stem bearing simple and stellate trichomes. Leaf-blade 5–14 cm long, ovate or shallowly 3-lobed, 3-nerved from base, serrate, subcordate at base; petiole to 4 cm long. Inflorescence few-flowered, axillary. Flowers yellow, 8 mm long, short-pedicellate. Fruit globose, 8 mm wide, bearing 3 mm long hispidulous spines. Collections: 63581, 63818.

Locally common along trails in the forests. — Widespread in tropical America.

TROPAEOLACEAE (NASTURTIUM FAMILY)

Vines or herbs, without tendrils. Leaves alternate, mostly simple; stipules lacking. Flowers solitary, axillary, bisexual, zygomorphic, spurred, 5-merous; stamens 8. Fruit a 3-seeded schizocarp. A family with 50 species mostly in montane regions of America.

1. *Tropaeolum harlingii* SPARRE

Glabrous, climbing vine. Leaves simple, peltate; blade subrotund, 1.5–6 cm long, 5–7-sublobulate, the lobes mucronulate; petiole to 7 cm long. Flowers solitary, 5 cm long, orange and red; petals serrate-ciliate; peduncle 7–13 cm long. Collections: 63485, 63572, 63612, ANDERSSON 165 (S, cited in Fl. Ec.).

Common in the thorn forest. — Endemic to coastal Ecuador and adjacent Peru.

Phenology: Flowers in June.

Uses: It is used to cure swellings and ear aches.

Vernacular name: mastuerzo.

TURNERACEAE (TURNERA FAMILY)

Herbs, shrubs, or rarely trees. Leaves alternate, simple, usually serrate; stipules small or wanting. Flowers bisexual, actinomophic, 5-merous; stamens 5. Fruit a capsule. A small family with 100 species in warm regions of both hemispheres.

1. *Turnera pumilea* L.

Herb, to 40 cm high, sparsely branched. Stem white-hirsute. Leaves densely crowded distally on stem; blade 3–5 cm long, narrowly ovate, coarsely serrate, subacute, cuneate at base; petiole 0.5–1 cm long. Inflorescence a distal cluster, nearly sunken in between the leaves. Flowers orange, less than 1 cm long. Capsule 5 mm long, 3-valvate. Collections: 63353, 85866.

Occasional weed along trails. — Widespread from Mexico and throughout South America. This species is not listed in the *Catalogue of the Vascular Plants of Ecuador* (Jørgensen and León-Yánez 1999), but included here based on the identification of our specimens by L. Dorr (US) in 1999.

TYPHACEAE (CAT-TAIL FAMILY)

Erect, grass-like herbs, with rhizome. Leaves linear, parallel-veined. Inflorescence stout and unbranched, below with a section of female flowers, above with a section of male flowers. Flowers small and crowded. Fruit a nutlet. A family with 15 species growing in swamps, chiefly in north temperate regions.

1. *Typha domingensis* PERS.
Erect, to 2 m high. Leaves to 1 m long, 1–1.5 cm wide, linear. Inflorescence long-pedunculate; pistillate section 20–30 cm long, 1.5 cm wide, cylindrical, brown; staminate section 20 cm long. Collection: 64131.
Rare, moist grounds at border of stream. — Pantropical.

ULMACEAE (ELM FAMILY)

Trees or shrubs, often with stiff hairs. Leaves alternate, simple, mostly serrate and oblique at base; stipules caducous. Flowers uni- or bisexual, zygomorphic; sepals 4–9; petals none; stamens usually 4–6, erect. Fruit a drupe or a samara. A family with 150 species, mainly in tropical America and Asia.

1. *Trema micrantha* (L.) BLUME
Tree, to 6 m high. Leaves scabrous; blade 7–11 cm long, broadly lanceolate, serrate, attenuate at apex, rounded at base, 3-nerved; petiole to 1 cm long. Inflorescence axillary, 2 cm long, of ca. 10 flowers. Flowers white, 2 mm wide, imperfect. Drupe orange, 3 mm long, ellipsoid. Collections: 63033, 63155.
Uncommon pioneer in disturbed forest. — Florida to Argentina. Also on the Galapagos Islands.
Uses: The bark is used to tie up sacks and timber for houses. It is eaten by birds.
Vernacular names: sapán, sapán de paloma.

URTICACEAE (NETTLE FAMILY)

Mostly herbs, often with stinging hairs. Leaves alternate or opposite, simple; stipules present. Flowers small, usually unisexual; perianth-segments and stamens in staminate flowers 2–5. Fruit an achene. A cosmopolitan family with 700 species.

1. *Laportea aestuans* (L.) Chew

Herb, 1 m high. Stem glandular hirsute. Leaves alternate; blade 7–12 cm long, ovate, coarsely and sharply serrate, acuminate, subcordate at base; petiole to 8 cm long. Inflorescence to at least 15 cm long, paniculate, the panicles slender-pedunculate. Flowers white, 2 mm wide. Collection: 63092.

Rare plant in deep shadow. — Pantropical, also on the Galapagos Islands.

VERBENACEAE (VERBENA FAMILY)

Herbs, shrubs, trees, or vines. Twigs often tetragonal. Leaves opposite or whorled, simple or palmately compound; stipules lacking. Flowers usually bisexual, more or less zygomorphic, 4–5-merous; stamens usually 4 or 2. Fruit a drupe or a schizocarp. A mainly tropical and subtropical family with 2600 species.

Key to the Species

1a. Leaves palmately 3–5-foliolate	11. *Vitex gigantea*
1b. Leaves simple	
2a. Herbaceous plants	
3a. Inflorescence head-like, 1 cm long	9. *Phyla strigulosa*
3b. Inflorescence racemose, to 15 cm long	10. *Priva lappulacea*
2b. Woody plants	
4a. Trees (dbh > 10 cm) of the mangrove	1. *Avicennia germinans*
4b. Shrubs on dry grounds	
5a. Infloresence not headlike	
6a. Inflorescence racemose	2. *Citharexylum* sp.
6b. Inflorescence umbellate	3. *Clerodendrum molle*
5b. Inflorescense a distal head	
7a. Heads solitary or paired at each node	
8a. Peduncle shorter than 3 cm	7. *Lippia alba*
8b. Peduncle longer than 3 cm	
9a. Involucral bracts broadly ovate; leaves soft-pubescent above	
	6. *Lantana svensonii*
9b. Involucral bracts narrowly ovate; leaves scrabrous above	
10a. Hairs on stems and leaves conspicuously	
broad-based	4. *Lantana camara*
10b. Hairs on stems and upper side of	
leaves not broad-based	5. *Lantana scabiosiflora*
7b. Heads 4–6 per node	8. *Lippia americana*

1. *Avicennia germinans* (L.) L.

Shrub or tree, to 10 m high, producing numerous pneumatophores. Stem glabrous. Leaves opposite; blade 7–12 cm long, ovate-elliptic, entire, rounded at apex, cuneate at base; petiole to 2 cm long. Inflorescence of numerous distal flowers borne on short-peduncles. Flowers white, 8 mm long, sessile. Capsule 1.5 cm long, flat. Collections: 63469, 63636, 63871, 63975, 64097, ANDERSSON *s.n.* (S, cited in Areschoug 1869).

Common in mangrove swamps. — Florida to Brazil. Also on the Galapagos Islands.

Phenology: Flowers appear predominantly from December to March.

Uses: The wood of the white mangrove is used to construct canoes and to make charcoal. The plant is eaten by goats.

Vernacular names: mangle salado, palo salado.

2. *Citharexylum* sp.

Shrub or tree, to 5 m high; trunk grey-white. Twigs 4-angled. Leaves opposite, glabrous above, puberulent beneath; blade 6–19 cm long, elliptic, entire, attenuate at base and apex; petiole 1–2 cm long. Inflorescence racemose. Infructescence formed by two pendulous spikes, many fruited. Fruits red, 8 mm long, ovoid; calyx persistent. Collections: 63836, 85303, 85304, 86015, 104082.

Uncommon understory treelet.

Note: It is eaten by cattle, goats, and birds.

Vernacular names: fruta de gallina silvestre, fruta de pava, pavita.

3. *Clerodendrum molle* KUNTH

Shrub, to 5 m high. Twigs terete, pubescent when young. Leaves opposite or whorled; blade 3–6 cm long, elliptic, acuminate to obtuse, short-attenuate and conspicuously swollen at base; petiole to 2 cm long. Inflorescence terminal, many-flowered, umbellate. Flowers pink with white limb, 2.5 cm long, salver-shaped, fragrant. Fruit 8 mm wide, globose. Collections: 63495B, 63632, 64093, 64114.

Common in thorn scrub. — Panama to Peru. Also on the Galapagos Islands.

Phenology: Observed in flower at the beginning and the end of the dry season.

Note: It is eaten by the cattle.

Vernacular name: cucuñique.

4. *Lantana camara* L.

Shrub, to 2 m high. Stem and upper side of leaves bearing stiff hairs without bulbous bases. Lower side of leaves soft-pubescent. Leaf-blade 4–8 cm long, crenate, acute to acuminate, subtruncate and oblique at base; petiole to 2 cm long. Inflorescence in axillary pairs, headlike; bracts lanceolate; peduncles 4–7 cm long. Flowers yellow or commonly with some orange. Collections: 63035, 63992.

Uncommon in disturbed forest. — Naturalized in the tropics.

Lantana species are difficult to identify and the names provided are provisional.

5. *Lantana scabiosiflora* KUNTH

Shrub, 1–2 m high. Stem and upper side of leaves scabrous, bearing conspicuous bulbous-based hairs. Leaf-blade 3–10 cm long, ovate, crenate, acute, acuminate at base; petiole to 3 cm long. Inflorescence axillary, headlike; bracts lanceolate; penduncle 4–8 cm long. Inner flowers yellow, outer ones white. Collections: 63325, 63598.

Uncommon in waste places. — From Ecuador to Bolivia.

6. *Lantana svensonii* MOLDENKE

Shrub, 1 m high. Stem and leaves puberulent. Leaf-blade 4–7 cm long, ovate, crenate-serrate, acute, acuminate at base; petiole 0.5–1 cm long. Inflorescence headlike, elongated; bracts broadly ovate; peduncle 4–7 cm long. Flowers white, 1 cm long. Collection: 63644.

Rare in dry thickets. — Endemic to southwestern Ecuador.

7. *Lippia alba* (MILL.) N. E. BR. [cult. and wild]

Shrub, to 1 m high. Leaves opposite; blade 2–5 cm long, narrowly ovate, serrulate, acute, attenuate at base; petiole 2–8 mm long. Inflorescence in axillary pairs, elongated, head-like; peduncle 1–2 cm long. Flowers purple with yellow center. Collections: 63727, 63865 (cultivated).

Cutivated and escaped. — Tropical and subtropical America.

Uses: It is a medicinal plant used to treat stomach pains and bone aches, cramps, and colics.

Vernacular name: mastranto

8. *Lippia americana* L.

Shrub, to 4 m high. Stem sparsely hairy to glabrescent. Leaves opposite, scabrous; blade 3–14 cm long, elliptic, serrate, acute, cuneate-attenuate at base. Inflorescence axillary, 2–3 pairs per node; heads 5 mm wide; peduncle 5–15 mm long. Flowers white with yellow base, minute. Collections: 63440, 63508, 63528, 63604, 63623, 63736, 63788, ANDERSSON *s.n.* (S, cited in Areschoug 1869).

Very common understory shrub, particularly at stream banks. — America.

Vernacular name: palito blanco.

9. *Phyla strigulosa* (M. MARTENS & GALEOTTI) MOLDENKE

Procumbent herb, to 20 cm high, rooting at nodes. Stem white-hirsute. Leaves opposite; blade 2–6 cm long, elliptic, cuneate at base, coarsely serrate in upper two thirds; petiole to 1 cm long. Inflorescence in axillary pairs; head 1 cm long, ovoid; peduncle 4–8 cm long. Flowers white, minute. Collections: 63427, 63614.

Common weed. — Widespread from United States to Bolivia. Also on the Galapagos Islands.

Vernacular name: mastranto de monte.

10. *Priva lappulacea* (L.) PERS.
Herb, to 80 cm high. Stem with few scattered hairs. Leaves opposite; blade 6–9 cm long, broadly ovate, serrate, acute-attenuate, subtruncate at base; pedicels to 2 cm long. Inflorescence terminal, racemose, 10–15 cm long, unbranched. Flowers white to blue, petiole 1–2 mm long. Fruit enclosed by a well developed, swollen calyx. Collections: 63048, 63070, 63367.
Common weed along trails. — Nearly cosmopolitan, including the Galapagos Islands.

11. *Vitex gigantea* KUNTH
Tree, to 10 m high. Leaves deciduous, palmately 3–5-foliolate, soft pubescent beneath; terminal leaflets to 16 cm long, elliptic, entire, short-attenuate at apex. Inflorescence few-flowered, pedunculate. Flowers light blue with white throat, 2 cm long. Drupe 2 cm long. Collections: 64121, 64146.
Probably common in the dry forest. — Endemic to western Ecuador and adjacent Peru.
Phenology: The leaves appear in November simultaneously with the flowers and two month before the rainy season starts.
Uses: The wood is used for boats, boards, shores, deck strakes, barrels, tubs, and charcoal. The fruit is used to make jams.
Vernacular name: pechiche.

VITACEAE (GRAPE FAMILY)
Tendrillate vines, rarely shrubs or trees, often swollen at nodes. Leaves alternate, simple or compound; stipules present. Inflorescence opposite a leaf. Flowers small, uni- or bisexual, actinomorphic, 4–5-merous; disc evident; stamens 4–5, opposite petals. Fruit a berry.
A mainly tropical family with 700 species.

Key to the Species

1a. Leaves 3-foliolate; flowers yellow or orange   1. *Cissus microcarpa*
1b. Leaves simple; flowers white   2. *Cissus verticillata*

1. *Cissus microcarpa* VAHL
Vine, climbing, to 10 m long. Stem more or less reddish when fresh, somewhat striate. Leaves 3-foliolate; lateral leaflets oblique; terminal leaflet 7–10 cm long, rhombic, remotely serrate, rachis 4–20 mm long; petiole 3–6 cm long. Inflorescence cymose; peduncle to 2 cm long. Flowers yellow or orange, minute. Berry red, 6–8 mm wide. Collections: 63062, 63078, 63227, 63546, 63624.
Common in the dry forest. — Central America to Bolivia.
Phenology: Flowering in May and June. Note: The fruits are eaten by birds.
Vernacular name: picamano.

2. *Cissus verticillata* (L.) NICOLSON & C. E. JARVIS
Vine or liana, often on the ground. Stem glabrous. Leaves simple; blade 6–10 cm long, ovate, remotely serrate, acuminate, cordate at base, 3–5-nerved; petiole 3–7 cm long. Inflorescence cymose; peduncle 2–3 cm long. Flowers white, 3 mm long; pedicels 4 mm long. Berry black, 8 mm wide, 1-seeded. Collections: 63084, 63408.
Occasional in disturbed dry forest. — Central America to Paraguay. Also on the Galapagos Islands.

ZYGOPHYLLACEAE (CREOSOTE-BUSH FAMILY)
Herbs or shrubs. Leaves usually opposite, simple or even-pinnately compound; interpetiolar stipules present. Flowers bisexual, actinomorphic, usually 5-merous; stamens in two or three whorls of 5. Fruit a capsule or a schizocarp.
A family with 250 species, widespread in dry, subtropical regions.

1. *Kallstroemia pubescens* (G. DON) DANDY
Creeping herb. Stem hirsute, the hairs pointed towards apex of plant. Leaves pinnately 4–6-foliolate; leaflets 9–15 mm long, oblong, entire, mucronate, rounded at base. Flowers solitary, yellow or white, 8 mm wide; pedicels 1 cm long. Schizocarp 10-merous, 3–4 mm wide, stout-beaked. Collections: 63395, 63668.
Uncommon in disturbed sites. — Pantropical weed.

Literature Cited

Acosta-Solís, M. 1959. *Los Manglares del Ecuador*. Quito.

Acosta-Solís, M. 1961. *Los Bosques del Ecuador y sus Productos*. Ed. Ecuador, Quito.

Acosta-Solís, M. 1968. *Divisiones Fitogeográficas y Formaciones Geobotánicas del Ecuador*. Casa de la Cultura, Quito.

Acosta-Solís, M. 1970. *Geografía y Ecología de las Tierras Áridas del Ecuador*. Quito.

Alsedo y Herrera, D. [1741] 1987. *Compendio Histórico de la Provincia de Guayaquil*. Departamento de Publicaciones de la Facultad de Ciencias Económicas de la Universidad de Guayaquil, Guayaquil.

Andersson, N. J. 1853. *En Verldsomsegling skilrad i Bref af N. J. Andersson. Naturforskare under Expeditionen med Fregatten Eugenies åren 1851, 1852 och 1853. Första delen Medeira och Sydamerika*. Samson & Wallin, Stockholm.

Andersson, N. J. 1854. *En Verldsomsegling skilrad i Bref af N. J. Andersson. Naturforskare under Expeditionen med Fregatten Eugenies åren 1851, 1852 och 1853. Andra delen Kalifornien och Oceanien*. Samson & Wallin, Stockholm.

Andersson, N. J. 1857 [reprint 1910]. *Om Galapagos-Öarnas Vegetation. Kongeliga Svenska Fregattan Eugenies Resa omkring Jorden under befäl af C. A. Virgin. Åren 1851–1853. Vetenskapliga Iaktagelser på Konung Oscar den Förstes befalling utgifna af K. Svenska Vetenskaps-akademien. Första delen. Botanik*. Almqvist & Wiksells, Uppsala.

Anonymous, 1980. 'Puná Island' *Encyclopædia Britannica Online* (accessed 27 March 2000).

Anonymous. 1983. *Anuario Meterológico 1981*. **21**. Instituto Nacional de Meteorología, Quito.

Anonymous. 1986. *Anuario Meterológico 1983*. **23**. Instituto Nacional de Meteorología, Quito.

Anonymous. 1989. *Lost Crops of the Incas. Little-Known Plants of the Andes with Promise for Worldwide Cultivation*. Report of an Ad Hoc Panel of the Advisory Committee on Technology Innovation Board on Science and Technology for International Development National Research Council. National Academy Press, Washington.

Areschoug, F. W. C. 1869. *Plantæ novae sub itinere navis bellicæ Eugeniæ anno 1852* a N. J. *Andersson circa Guayaquil collectæ, quas descripsit F. W. C. Areschoug.* Stockholm.

Armesto, J. J., J. D. Mitchell & C. Villagran. 1986. A comparison of spatial patterns of trees in some tropical and temperate forests. *Biotropica* **18**: 1–11.

Balslev, H. 1988. Distribution patterns of Ecuadorian plant species. *Taxon* **37**: 567–577.

Balslev, H., J. L. Luteyn, B. Øllgaard & L. B. Holm-Nielsen. 1987. Composition and structure of adjacent unflooded and floodplain forest in Amazonian Ecuador. *Opera Botanica* **92**: 37–57.

Balslev, H., J. E. Madsen & R. Mix. 1988. *Las Plantas y el Hombre en la Isla de Puná, Ecuador.* Universidad Laica Vicente Rocafuerte, Guayaquil.

Barneby, R. C. & J. W. Grimes. 1996. Silk tree, guanacaste, monkey's earring: A generic system for the synandrous Mimosaceae of the Americas. Part I. *Abarema, Albizia*, and allies. *Memoirs of the New York Botanical Garden* **74**: 1–292.

Beard, J. S. 1953. The savanna vegeation of northern tropical America. *Ecological Monographs* **23**: 149–215.

Béarez, P. 1998. FOCUS: First archaeological indication of fishing by poison in a sea environment by the Engoroy population at Salango (Manabí, Ecuador). *Journal of Archaeological Science* **25**: 943–948.

Belscher, R. N. 1843. *Narratives of a Voyage around the World, performed in Her Majesty's Ship Sulphur, during the Years 1836–1842, including Details of the Naval Operations in China, from Dec, 1840, to Nov. 1841.* Vol. I–II. Henry Colburn, London.

Bentham, G. 1844–1846 [reprint 1968]. *Botany of the Voyage of the Sulphur.* J. Cramer, Lehre.

Best, B. J. (ed.). 1992. *The Threatened Forests of South-west Ecuador.* Biosphere Publications, Leeds.

Bonifáz de Elao, C. 1997. El estado actual de los bosques de la costa. *Herbarium - Publicaciones Herbario GUAY* **2**: 1–7.

Borchsenius, F. 1997. Patterns of plant endemism in Ecuador. *Biodiversity and Conservation* **6**: 379–399.

Brako, L. & J. L. Zarucchi. 1993. Catalogue of the flowering plants and gymnosperms of Peru. *Monographs of Systematic Botany Missouri Botanical Garden* **45**: i–xi, 1–1286.

Brummitt, R. K. & C. F. Powell. 1992. *Authors of Plant Names - A List of Authors of Scientific Names of Plants, with Recommended Standard Forms of their Names, including Abbreviations.* Royal Botanic Gardens, Kew, London.

Camelbeke, K. 1993. Bijdrage tot een revisie van de Cyperaceae van Ecuador. Unpublished PhD thesis, Faculty of Sciences, University of Gent.

Cañadas C., L. 1983. *El Mapa Bioclimático y Ecológico del Ecuador.* MAG - PRONAREG, Quito.

Cañadas C., L. & W. Estrada. 1978. *Ecuador Mapa Ecológico*. PRONAREG-Ecuador, Ministerio de Agricultura y Ganadería.

Capdevila, M. B. 1994. A taxonomic revision of the genus *Desmodium* Desv. (Leguminosae) for Flora of Ecuador and a general study on the genus and its close relatives. Unpublished M.Sc. thesis, Dept. Syst. Botany, University of Aarhus.

Cárdenas, J. G. & K. M. Greiner. 1988. *Walking the Beaches of Ecuador*. Empresa Editora Porvenir, Quito.

Cerón M., C. E. & C. Montalvo A. 1998. Flora de las islas Salango y de La Plata, Parque Nacional Machalilla, Manabí-Ecuador. *Funbotanica* **6**: 10–19.

Cerón, C., W. Palacios, R. Valencia & R. Sierra. 1999. Las formaciones naturales de la costa del Ecuador. Pp. 55–78 in R. Sierra (ed.), *Propuesta Preliminar de un Sistema de Clasificación de Vegetación para el Ecuador Continental*. Proyecto INEFAN/GEF-BIRF y EcoCiencia, Quito.

Chapman, V. J. 1976. *Mangrove Vegetation*. J. Cramer, Vaduz.

Clapperton, C. M. 1993. Nature of environmental changes in South America at the last glacial maximum. *Palaeogeography, Palaeoclimatology, Palaeoecology* **101**: 189–208.

Clayton, L. A. 1978. *Los Astilleros de Guayaquil Colonial*. Archivo Histórico, Guayaquil.

Colinvaux, P. A. 1972. Climate and the Galapagos Islands. *Nature* **240**: 17–20.

Colinvaux, P. A. 1984. The Galapagos climate: present and past. Pp. 55-69 in R. Perry (ed.), *Galapagos*. Pergamon Press, Oxford.

Colinvaux, P. A. & E. K. Schofield. 1976a. Historical ecology in the Galapagos Islands. I. A Holocene pollen record from el Junco Lake, Isla San Cristóbal. *Journal of Ecology* **64**: 989–1012.

Colinvaux, P. A. & E. K. Schofield. 1976b. Historical ecology in the Galapagos Islands. II. A Holocene spore record from el Junco Lake, Isla San Cristóbal. *Journal of Ecology* **64**: 1013–1028.

Costta, C. A. A. 2000. *Diccionario Biográfico Ecuatoriano*. FED and Editorial Raíces, Quito.

Cristóbal, C. L. 1960. Revisión del género *Ayenia* (Sterculiaceae). *Opera Lilloana* **4**: 1–230.

Cronquist, A. 1981. *An Integrated System of Classification of Flowering Plants*. Columbia Univ. Press, New York.

Cruz, L. C. 1983. *El Mapa Bioclimático y Ecológico del Ecuador*. MAG–PRONAREG, Quito.

Curtis, J. T. & R. P. McIntosh. 1951. An upland forest continuum in the prairie-forest border region of Wisconsin. *Ecology* **32**: 476–496.

Cuttler, H. C. & T. W. Whittaker. 1969. A new species of *Cucurbita* from Ecuador. *Annals of the Missouri Botanical Garden* **55**: 392–396.

Dahlgren, R. M. T., H. T. Clifford & P. F. Yeo. 1985. *The Families of the Monocotyledons - Structure, Evolution, and Taxonomy*. Springer Verlag,

Berlin.

Dampier, W. [1697] 1927. A New Voyage Round the World. With an Introduction by Sir Albert Gray. Argonaut Press, London.

Daniel, T. F. & D. C. Wasshausen. 1993. A new *Carlowrightia* (Acanthaceae) from South America. *Nordic Journal of Botany* **13**: 653–656.

Dekker, J. 1997. Weed diversity and weed management. *Weed Science* **45**: 357–363.

Dodson, C. H. & A. H. Gentry. 1978. Flora of the Río Palenque Science Center. *Selbyana* **4**.

Dodson, C. H. & A. H. Gentry. 1991. Biological extinction in western Ecuador. *Annales of the Missouri Botanical Garden* **78**: 273–295.

Dodson, C. H., A. H. Gentry & F. M. Valverde B. 1985. *La Flora de Jauneche*. Banco Central del Ecuador, Quito.

Eggers, H. 1892. Die Manglares in Ecuador. *Botanisches Centralblatt* **52**: 49–52.

Eggers, H. 1894. Das Küstengebiet von Ecuador. *Geographische Gesellschaft Bremen* **17**: 265–289.

Enock, C. R. 1909. *The Great Pacific Coast*. Grant Richards, London.

Erwin, F. 1958. Eine Studie über den Zusammenhang zwischen Bodentyp, Klima und Vegetation in Ecuador. *Plant and Soil* **9**: 215–236.

Estrada, Y. [1957] 1979. Prehistoria de Manabí. *Publicaciones del Museo* **4**. Guayaquil.

Estrada, Y. 1990. El Puerto de Guayaquil: Crónica Portuaria. *Colecciones Monográficas* **2**. Banco Central del Ecuador. Centro de Investigación y Cultura, Guayaquil.

Estrella, E. 1989. Introductio historica et adnotationes. In J. Tafalla, *Flora Huayaquilensis, Sive descriptiones et icones plantarum Huayaquilensium secundum systema Linnaeanum digestae. Horto Regio.* Matritense (C.S.I.C.), Madrid.

Estrella, E. 1995. *La 'Flora Huayaquilensis' de Juan Tafalla. Crónica e Iconografía de una Expedition Silenciada (1799–1808)*, ed. 2. Banco del Progreso - Jardín Botánico de Guayaquil, Guayaquil.

Ferreyra, R. 1957. Contribución al conocimiento de la flora costanera del norte peruano (Departamento de Tumbes). *Boletín de la Sociedad Argentina de la Botánica* **6**: 194–206.

Ferreyra, R. 1983. Los tipos de vegetación de la costa peruana. *Anales Jardin Botánico Madrid* **40**: 241–256.

García Barriga, H. 1992. *Flora Medicinal de Colombia. Botánica Médica. I–III.* ed. 2a. Tercer Mundo, Bogota.

Gentry, A. H. & C. H. Dodson. 1987. Contribution of nontrees to species richness of a tropical rain forest. *Biotropica* **19**: 149–156.

Givnish, T. J. 1978. On the adaptive significance of compound leaves, with particular reference to tropical trees. Pp. 351–380 in B. P. Thomlinson & H. Zimmermann (eds.), *Tropical Trees as Living Systems*. Cambridge

University Press.

Glantz, M. H. 1996. *Currents of Change: El Niño's Impact on Climate and Society.* University Press, Cambridge.

González-Suárez, F. 1904. *Prehistoria Ecuatoriana. Ligeras reflexiones sobre las razas indígenas que poblaban antiguamente el territorio actual de la República del Ecuador.* Quito.

Guppy, H. B. 1906. *Observations of a Naturalist in the Pacific between 1896 and 1899. Volume II. Plant-Dispersal.* MacMillan, London.

Hansen, B. C. S. 1995. A review of lateglacial pollen records from Ecuador and Peru with reference to the Younger Dryas event. *Quaternary Science Review* **14**: 853–865.

Harling, G. & B. Sparre (eds.). 1973–1986. *Flora of Ecuador* **1–24**.

Harling, G. & L. Andersson (eds.). 1986–2000. *Flora of Ecuador* **25–64**.

Heine, J. T. 1993. A reevaluation of the evidence for a Younger Dryas climatic reversal in the tropical Andes. *Quaternary Science Review* **12**: 769–779.

Hernández, C. & C. Josse. 1997. *Plantas Silvestres Comestibles, Parque Nacional Machalilla.* Abya-Yala, Quito.

Holdridge, L. R., W. C. Grenke, W. H. Hatheway, T. Liang & J. A. Tosi. 1971. *Forest Environments in Tropical Life Zones - A Pilot Study.* Pergamon Press, Oxford.

Holmgren, P. K., N. H. Holmgren & L. C. Barnett. 1990. *Index Herbariorum. Part I: The Herbaria of the World. 8th ed.* New York Botanical Garden, Bronx.

Horn, E. F. 1945. Forest resources and forest types of the province of El Oro, Ecuador. *Caribbean Forester* **6**: 210-218.

Humboldt, F. W. H. Al. v. & A. J. A. Bonpland. 1808–1809. *Plantes équinoxiales, recueillies au Mexique, dans l'ile de Cuba, dans les provinces de Caracas, de Cumana et de Barcelone, aux Andes de la Nouvelle-Grenade, de Quito et du Pérou, et eur les bords de Rio-Negro, de l'Orénoque et de la rivière dee Amazones.* Tubingue, Paris.

Humboldt, F. W. H. Al. v., A. J. A. Bonpland & S. Kunth. 1815–1825. *Nova Genera et Species Plantarum.* Lutetiae Parisiorum [Paris].

I.G.M. 1961–1990. Aerial photographs (1:60,000) covering Isla Puná [Oct–1961: 518–525, 606–611, 632–634; May-1962: 1478–1483; Aug-1969: 8607–8613; Jul-1977: 4484–4488; Nov-1977: 6062–6069; Jul-1978: 7162-7169; Sept-1982: 17373–17379; Nov-90: 29947–29959, 29970–29982.

I.G.M. 1967–1982. Geographical maps 1:50,000 [3585-IV, 3585-I, 6685-IV, 3585-III, 3585-II, 3584-IV, 3584-I].

Jørgensen, P. M. 1999. History of collecting. Pp. 25–41 in P. M. Jørgensen & S. Léon-Yánez (eds.), Catalogue of the vascular plants of Ecuador. *Monographs of Systematic Botany of the Missouri Botanical Garden* **75**.

Jørgensen, P. M. & C. U. Ulloa. 1994. Seed plants of the high Andes of Ecuador — a checklist. *AAU Reports* **34**.

Jørgensen, P. M. & S. León-Yánez (eds.). 1999. Catalogue of the vascular plants of Ecuador. *Monographs of Systematic Botany of the Missouri Botanical Garden* **75**: i–viii, 1–1182.

Josse, C. & H. Balslev. 1994. The composition and structure of a dry, semideciduous forest in western Ecuador. *Nordic Journal of Botany* **14**: 425–434.

Juan, J. & A. de Ulloa [1748, 1826] 1982. *Noticias secretas de América I–II.* Ediciones Turner, Madrid and Librimundi, Quito. Facsimile of the edition published by D. Barry in London 1826.

Keil, D. J. & T. F. Stuessy. 1981. Systematics of *Isocarpha* (Compositae: Eupatorieae). *Systematic Botany* **6**: 258–287.

Kessler, M. 1992. The vegetation of south-west Ecuador. Pp. 7–79 in B. J. Best (ed.), *The Threatened Forests of South-west Ecuador.* Biosphere Publications, Leeds.

Koepcke, H.-W. 1961. Synökologische Studien an der Westseite der peruanischen Anden. *Bonner Geographischer Abhandlungen* **29**.

Laviana C., M. L. 1984. *La Descripción de Guayaquil por Francisco Requena 1774.* Escuela de Estudios Hispanoamericanos, Sevilla.

Lawesson, J. E. 1990. Alien plants in the Galapagos Islands, a summary. *Monographs of Systematic Botany of the Missouri Botanical Garden* **32**: 15–20.

Lawesson, J. E., H. Adersen & P. Bentley. 1987. An updated and annotated check list of the vascular plants of the Galapagos Islands. *Reports from the Botanical Institute, University of Aarhus* **16**.

Lodge, D. M. 1993. Biological invasions: Lessons for ecology. *Trends in Evolution and Ecology* **8**: 133–137.

Lourteig, A. 1994. *Oxalis* L. Subgénero *Thamnoxys* (Endl.) Reiche emend. Lourteig. *Bradea* **7**: 1–199.

Macía, M. J. & A. S. Barfod. 2000. Cultivation, management and economic botany of Ovo (*Spondias purpurea* L.) in Ecuador. *Economic Botany* **54**: 449–458.

Madsen, J. E., D. Dione, A. S. Traoré & B. Sambou. 1996. Flora and vegetation of Niokolo-Koba National Park, Senegal. Pp. 214–219 in L. J. G. van der Maesen, X. M. van der Burtg & J. M. van Medenbach de Rooy (eds.), *The Biodiversity of African Plants.* Kluwer, Dordrecht.

McVaugh, R. 1972. Botanical Exploration in Nueva Galicia, Mexico, from 1790 to the present time. *Contribution for the University Michigan Herbarium* **9**: 205–358.

Mori, S., B. M. Boom, A. M. de Carvalino & T. S. dos Santos. 1983. Ecological importance of Myrtaceae in an eastern Brazilian wet forest. *Biotropica* **15**: 68–70.

Morton, J. F. 1987. *Fruits of Warm Climates.* Media, Greensboro.

Naranjo, P. 1985. El Fenómeno El Niño y sus efectos en el clima del Ecuador. Pp. 3–27 in: G. Robinson. & E. M. del Pino (eds.), *El Niño en Las Islas Galápagos: El evento 1985 de 1982–83.* Quito.

Neil, A. 1999. Vegetation types. Pp. 14–25 in P. M. Jørgensen & S. Léon-Yánez (eds.), Catalogue of the vascular plants of Ecuador. *Monographs of Systematic Botany of the Missouri Botanical Garden* **75.**

Norse, E. A. (ed.) 1993. *Global Maritime Biological Diversity: a Strategy for Building Conservation into Decision Making.* Island Press, Washington.

Opler, P. A., G. W. Frankie & H. G. Baker. 1980. Comparative phenological studies of treelet and shrub species in tropical wet and dry forests in the lowlands of Costa Rica. *Journal of Ecology* **68**: 167–188.

Parker, T. A. & J. L. Carr (eds.) 1992. *Status of the Forest Remnants in the Cordillera de la Costa and Adjacent Areas of Southwestern Ecuador. RAP Working Paper* 2. Conservation International Publ., Washington.

Piperno, D. R. & D. M. Pearsall. 1998. *The Origins of Agriculture in the Lowland Neotropics.* Academic Press, San Diego.

Porras G. & I. Pedro. 1974. *El Encanto-La Puná: un Sitio Insular de la Fase Valdivia Asociado a un Conchero Anular.* Luis Piana Bruno, Quito.

Porter, D. M. 1983. Vascular plants of the Galapagos: Origin and dispersal. Pp. 33–54 in R. I. Bowman & A. E. Leviton (eds.), *Patterns of Evolution in Galapagos Organisms.* Pacific Div., San Francisco.

Porter, D. M. 1984. Endemism and evolution in terrestrial plants. Pp. 85–99 in R. Perry (ed.), *Galapagos.* Pergamon Press, Oxford.

Quimi, R. L. & K. E. Stothert. 1994. *El Uso Vernáculo de los Árboles y Plantas en la Península de Santa Elena.* Fundación Pro-Pueblo, Cemento Nacional & Subdirección Programas Culturales Banco Central del Ecuador, Guayaquil.

Rauh, W. 1985. The Peruvian-Chilean deserts. Pp. 239–267. in: M. Evenari, I. Noy-Meir & D. W. Goodall (eds.), *Hot Deserts and Arid Shrublands. Ecosystems of the World* **12A**. Elsevier, Amsterdam.

Raunkiaer, C. 1934 [reprint 1977]. *The Life Forms of Plants and Statistical Plant Geography.* Arno Press, New York.

Rodbell, D., G. O. Seltzer, D. M. Anderson, M. B. Abbot, D. B. Enfield & J. H. Newman. 1999. An ~15,000-year record of El Niño-driven alluviation in southwestern Ecuador. *Science* **283**: 516–520.

Rundel, P. W., M. O. Dillon, B. Palma, H. A. Mooney, S. L. Gulmon & J. R. Ehleringer. 1991. The phytogeography and ecology of the coastal Atacama and Peruvian deserts. *Aliso* **13**: 1–49.

Sauer, W. 1971. *Geologie von Ecuador.* Borntraeger, Berlin.

Saville, M. 1907–1910. *Antiquities of Manabí.* Heye Foundation, New York.

Sheppard, G. 1932. The salt industry in Ecuador. *Geographical Review* **22**: 403–410.

Sheppard, G. 1937. *The Geology of South-western Ecuador.* Thomas Murby, London.

Sierra, R. 1999. *Vegetación Remanente del Ecuador Continental. Circa 1996. 1:100.000.* Proyecto INEFAN/GEF & Wildlife Conservation Society.

Quito, Ecuador.

Sierra, R., C. Cerón, W. Palacios & R. Valencia. 1999a. *Mapa de Vegetación del Ecuador Continental. 1:100.000.* Proyecto INEFAN/GEF-BIRF, Wildlife Conservation Society & Ecociencia. Quito, Ecuador.

Sierra, R., C. Cerón, W. Palacios & R. Valencia. 1999b. Criterios para la clasificación de la vegetación del Ecuador. Pp. 29–54 in R. Sierra (ed.), *Propuesta Preliminar de un Sistema de Clasificación de Vegetación para el Ecuador Continental.* Proyecto INEFAN/GEF-BIRF y EcoCiencia, Quito.

Sørensen, T. 1948. A method of establishing groups of equal amplitude in plant sociology based on similarity of species content. *Det Kongelige Danske Videnskabelige Selskabs Biologiske Skrifter (Copenhagen)* **5**: 1–34.

Stafleu, F. A. & R. S. Cowan. 1976–1988. *Taxonomic Literature: a Selective Guide to Botanical Publications and Collections with Dates, Commentaries and Types. 2. ed.* Bohn, Scheltema & Holkema, Utrecht. *Regnum Vegetabile.*

Stafleu, F. A. & E. A. Mennega. 1992–2000. *Taxonomic literature: a selective guide to botanical publications and collections with dates, commentaries and types. Supplement I–VI.* Koeltz Scientific Books, Königsstein. *Regnum Vegetabile.*

Standley, P. C. & J. A. Steyermark. 1958. Flora of Guatemala. *Fieldiana* **24**(6).

Steele, A. R. 1982. *Flores para el Rey. La Expedición de Ruiz y Pavón y la Flora del Perú (1777–1788).* Serbal, Barcelona.

Svenson H. K. 1946a. Vegetation of the coast of Ecuador and Peru and its relation to the Galapagos Islands. I Geographical relations of the flora *American Journal of Botany* **33**: 394–426.

Svenson H. K. 1946b. Vegetation of the coast of Ecuador and Peru and its relation to the Galapagos Islands. II. Catalogue of plants. *American Journal of Botany* **33**: 427–498.

Szaszdi, A. 1988. *D. Diego Tomala - cacique de la Isla de la Puná. Un caso de aculturación socioeconómica.* Museo Antropológico Banco Central del Ecuador, Guayaquil.

Terchunian, A., V. Klemas, A. Segovia, A. Alvarez, B. Vasconez & L. Guerrero. 1986. Mangrove mapping in Ecuador: the impact of shrimp pond construction. *Environmental Management* **10**: 345–350.

Twilley, R. R., M. Pozo, V. H. García, V. H. Rivera-Monroy, R. Zambrano & A. Bodero. 1997. Litter dynamics in riverine mangrove forests in the Guayas River estuary, Ecuador. *Oecologia* **111**: 109–122.

Urban, I. 1906. Vitae itineraque collectorum botanicum (Anderson, Nils Johan). *Flora Brasiliense* **1**:1.

Valencia, R., H. Balslev, W. Palacios, D. Neil, C. Josse, M. Tirado & F. Skov. 1998. Diversity and family composition of trees in different regions of Ecuador: A sample of 18 one-hectare plots. Pp. 569–584 in F. Dallmeier & J. A. Comiskey (eds.), *Forest Biodiversity in North, Central, and South America, and the Caribbean: Research and Monitoring.* – (Man and the Biosphere, v. 21). Unesco, Paris.

Valencia, R., N. Pitman, S. León-Yánez & P. M. Jørgensen (eds.) 2000. *Libro Rojo de las Plantas Endémicas del Ecuador 2000.* Herbario QCA, Pontificia Universidad Católica del Ecuador, Quito.

Valverde B., F. M. 1998. *Plantas Útiles del Litoral Ecuatoriano.* Ministerio de Medio Ambiente, Guayaquil.

Valverde B., F. M., G. Rodríguez de Tazán & C. García R. 1979. *Cubierta Vegetal de la Península de Santa Elena.* Universidad Guayaquil, Guayaquil.

Valverde B., F. M., G. Rodríguez de Tazán & C. G. Rizzo. 1991. *Estado Actual de la Vegetación Natural de la Cordillera Chongon-Colonche.* Univ. Guayaquil, Guayaquil.

Van der Hammen, T. 1991. Palaeoecological background: Neotropics. *Climatic Change* **19**: 37–47.

Van der Hammen, T. & M. L. Absy. 1994. Amazonia during the last glacial. *Palaeogeography, Palaeoclimatology, Palaeoecology* **109**: 247-261.

Velasco [1789] 1981. *Historia del Reino de Quito* (original title: *Historia del Reino de Quito en la América Meridional*). Ed. Ervantes, Ecuador.

Vitousek, P. M., C. M. D'Antonio, L. L. Loope, M. Rejmánek & R. Westbrooks. 1997. Introduced species: A significant component of human-caused global change. *New Zealand Journal of Ecology* **21**: 1–16.

Walter, H. 1979. *Vegetation of the Earth and Ecological Systems of the Geo-biosphere.* 2. *ed.* Springer, New York.

Webb, L. J. 1959. A physiognomic classification of Australian rain forests. *Journal of Geology* **47**: 551–570.

Weberbauer, A. 1929. Die Pflanzendecke Nordperus im Departamento Tumbez und angrensenden Teilen des Departamento Piura. *Botanische Jahrbücher für Systematische Botanik, Pflanzengeographie* **63**: 29–48, Pl. 1–5.

Weberbauer, A. 1945. *El Mundo Vegetal de los Andes Peruvianos. Estudio Fitogeográfico. Nueva edición, revisada y ampliada, de Die Pflanzenwelt der peruanischen Anden (Wilhelm Engelmann, Leipzig, 1911).* Ministerio de Agricultura, Lima.

Werger, M. J. A. 1983. Tropical grasslands, savannas, woodlands: natural and manmade. Pp. 107–137 in W. Holzner, M. J. A. Werger & I. Ikusima (eds.), *Man´s Impact on Vegetation,* Junk Publishers, The Hague.

Wiggins, I. L. & D. M. Porter. 1971. *Flora of the Galapagos Islands.* Stanford University Press, California.

Wolf, T. 1892. *Geografía y Geología del Ecuador. Publicada por Órden del Supremo Gobierno de la República.* Brockhaus, Leipzig.

Index to Names of Plants

Boldface refers to a description or main entry. *Italics* refers to an illustration or table. An asterix (*) indicates a page reference to a historical name or a name used outside Puná Island. Vernacular names are indicated by (vern.) and English names by (eng.).

Index to Places and Historic Persons

Boldface type refers to a map. *Italics* indicate a page refence with an illustration or a table. Dates to historic persons mainly from Costta (2000).